CRIME, GENDER AND
CONSUMER CULTURE IN
NINETEENTH-CENTURY ENGLAND

Crime, Gender and Consumer Culture in Nineteenth-Century England

TAMMY C. WHITLOCK
University of Kentucky, USA

ASHGATE

Published by
Ashgate Publishing Limited
Gower House
Croft Road
Aldershot
Hampshire GU11 3HR
England

Ashgate Publishing Company
Suite 420
101 Cherry Street
Burlington, VT 05401-4405
USA

Ashgate website: http://www.ashgate.com

British Library Cataloguing in Publication Data
Whitlock, Tammy C.
 Crime, gender and consumer culture in nineteenth-century England. – (The history of retailing and consumption).
 1. Female offenders – England – History – 19th century 2. Women consumers – England – History –19th century 3. Shoplifting – England – History – 19th century 4. Fraud – England – History – 19th century 5. Retail trade – England – History – 19th century 6. Consumerism – England – History – 19th century 7. Kleptomania 8. England – Social life and customs – 19th century
 I. Title
 364.3'74'0942'09034

Library of Congress Cataloging-in-Publication Data
Whitlock, Tammy C., 1967-
Crime, gender, and consumer culture in nineteenth-century England / Tammy C. Whitlock.
    p. cm. – (The history of retailing and consumption)
  Includes bibliographical references and index.
  ISBN 0-7546-5207-6 (alk. paper)
  1. Retail trade – England – History – 19th century. 2. Consumption (Economics) – England – History – 19th century. 3. Women consumers – England – History – 19th century. 4. Consumer behavior – England – Sex differences – History – 19th century. 5. Crime – England – History – 19th century. 6. England – Social life and customs – History – 19th century. I. Title. II. Series.

HF5429.6.G72E69 2005
306.3'0942'09034—dc22

2004016884

ISBN 0 7546 5207 6

Printed and bound in Great Britain by MPG Books Ltd, Bodmin, Cornwall

Contents

The History of Retailing and Consumption
General Editor's Preface

It is increasingly recognised that retail systems and changes in the patterns of consumption play crucial roles in the development and societal structure of economies. Such recognition has led to renewed interest in the changing nature of retail distribution and the rise of consumer society from a wide range of academic disciplines. The aim of this multidisciplinary series is to provide a forum of publications that explore the history of retailing and consumption.

Gareth Shaw

University of Exeter, UK

List of Figures

Acknowledgements

I would like to thank my colleagues and the staff at the University of Kentucky especially Gretchen Starr-LeBeau for providing me with a 'Room of One's Own' to continue this work. Rice University provided both the support I received to travel to archives and libraries in the United Kingdom and a wonderful faculty and staff. To Helena Michie, Daniel Sherman, and Carl Caldwell, thank you for enriching this study with your insightful comments. To Martin Wiener, I owe a great debt for guiding, editing, and discussing this work throughout my years at Rice. Although this work required research at a variety of institutions, I would especially like to thank the staff of Fondren Library, the Yale Center for British Art, and William T. Young Library. Julie Anne Lambert of the John Johnson Collection at the Bodleian deserves special mention for her untiring aid and trans-Atlantic support.

For reading and discussing various parts of this manuscript Ellen Furlough, Anya Jabour, Leslie Allen, Julie Early, and Margot Finn deserve special recognition. To Rebecca Stern, Amy Williams, and Amy Masciola, I am grateful for generously sharing their research. Words cannot express my gratitude to Carolyn White for her commentary and for giving me such an excellent start in British history. And to T. Wayne Beasley, thank you for helping to inspire my love of history in the first place. For comparative comments and especially for tolerating numerous discussions of shoplifting, the staff of the *Journal of Southern History*—Patricia Bixel, Evelyn Nolen, Elizabeth Turner, Patricia Burgess and John Boles—forever have my gratitude. And lest I forget, my parents, Janet and David Hall, who are to blame for instilling an early love of learning.

Thanks to all of those who commented at conferences held by the Berkshire Conference on the History of Women, Northeast Victorian Studies Association, Southern Conference on British Studies, North American Conference on British Studies, and Interdisciplinary Nineteenth-Century Studies Association.

Finally, I would like to thank my husband Michael for his support over the seemingly endless years of graduate work and postgraduate work and my son Miles for providing comic relief. Last, but not least, thanks to Maeve for waiting until I finished the manuscript.

Introduction

Crime, Gender and Consumer Culture in Nineteenth-Century England

A Bit of Lace

In retrospect the nineteenth-century obsession with consumer goods as well as the occasional sensation caused by a woman pilfering a handkerchief or a bit of lace seems trivial. Ribbons of silk or edgings of lace, however, signified much more than one's taste in clothing. In Jane Austen's novel *Northanger Abbey* the silent calculations of material status at the meeting of two old friends in Bath suggests the significance:

> Mrs. Thorpe, however, had one great advantage as a talker over Mrs. Allen, in a family of children; and when she expiated on the talents of her sons, and the beauty of her daughters,—when she related their different situations and views—that John was at Oxford, Edward at Merchant-Taylors', and William at sea,—and all of them more beloved and respected in their different station than any other three beings ever were, Mrs. Allen had no similar information to give, no similar triumphs to press on the unwilling and unbelieving ear of her friend, and was forced to sit and appear to listen to all these maternal effusions, consoling herself, however, with the discovery, which her keen eye soon made, that the lace on Mrs. Thorpe's pelisse was not half so handsome as that on her own.[1]

Around the time that Austen was penning *Northanger Abbey*, her own family was forced to acknowledge the importance of a bit of lace when they became involved in a sensational trial.

In August 1799 Jane Austen's aunt, Jane Perrot,[2] bought some lace in a haberdasher's shop in the town of Bath where Perrot's husband was being treated for gout. This simple purchase led Perrot into an ordeal that lasted until March of the following year. Shortly after buying the lace, a shop woman ran after Perrot accusing her of taking another card of lace with her parcel, and when Perrot handed over the parcel, the extra lace was in it. The discovery led to Perrot's arrest

---

[1] Jane Austen, *Northanger Abbey* (London: Penguin Books, 1995), 29. *Northanger Abbey* was written between 1798 and 1803; during that period Jane Austen spent time with her uncle and aunt in Bath. See Marilyn Butler's introduction, *Ibid.*

[2] Jane Austen's mother's older brother, James, adopted this surname when he became the heir of his great-uncle Thomas Perrot. See W.J.B. Owen, 'De Quincey and Shoplifting,' *The Wordsworth Circle*, 21, no. 2 (Spring 1990), 73.

for shoplifting—a serious offense in 1799. Any thief convicted of stealing items worth over five pounds was liable to hanging. While Perrot waited for her trial in Ilchester gaol, a scandal ensued pitting the lady, Mrs. Perrot, against the shopman, Charles Filby and his employer, Elizabeth Gregory. Although Perrot's lawyers had difficulty casting doubt on the character of the shop owner, Elizabeth Gregory, they managed to disparage the reputation of Filby who had twice gone bankrupt in his haberdashery business before being reduced to becoming an assistant. A bevy of character witnesses, including women who claimed to have found extra goods planted or mistakenly added to their parcels in the same shop, led to an acquittal. The accusation that Filby had mistakenly or purposely wrapped extra items in ladies' parcels particularly weighed in Perrot's favor: "[Miss Blagrave] . . . bought the veil from Filby, she went home, and on opening the parcel, she found two in the said parcel, next day she went to the shop to return the veil . . . ."[3] The questions raised by this case remained an item of debate throughout the nineteenth century.[4]

In this repeating drama of English consumerism, it was often difficult to tell precisely who was cheating whom. Were dishonest shopkeepers preying upon innocent ladies, hoping their husbands would pay dearly to avoid scandal, or were the ladies not to be trusted among the ever-increasing goods on display in English shops?[5] In her trial, Perrot had asked, "Placed in a situation the most affluent with a supply so ample, that I was left rich, . . . what inducement could I have to commit such a crime?"[6] In the decades that followed, various public discussions and trials recorded in newspaper reports, pamphlets, and periodicals reflected this tension over retail crime.[7] In many of the cases, like Perrot's, a respectable lady was shopping alone when an accusation of crime suddenly transformed a normally mundane transaction. If Jane Perrot had been caught shoplifting at the end of the century instead of the beginning, she would probably have been diagnosed as a

---

[3] *Trial of Jane Leigh Perrot, at Taunton Assizes, on Saturday the 29th of March, 1800; Charged with Stealing a Card of Lace, in the Shop of Elizabeth Gregory, Haberdasher & Milliner, of the City of Bath* (Bath: W. Gye, 1800; reprint in *British Trial Series,,* Lincoln's Inn Library; London: Chadwyck-Healey Ltd, 1990), microfiche, 18.

[4] *Ibid.* See Thomas De Quincey, 'The Household Wreck,' *Blackwood's Edinburgh Magazine*, January 1838, 1-32; Owen, 'De Quincey and Shoplifting,' 72-76; and the trial report in the British Trials series complete with diagrams.

[5] In many ways, the kleptomania diagnosis and attitudes toward women as shoplifters has changed little from its inception in the nineteenth century. See Loren E. Edwards, *Shoplifting and Shrinkage Protection for Stores.* (Springfield, Illinois: Charles C. Thomas, 1958); William Stekel, *Peculiarities of Behavior: Wandering Mania, Dipsomania, Cleptomania, Pyromania and Allied Impulsive Acts* (New York: Boni and Liverwright, 1924); and Marcus J. Goldman, 'Kleptomaniac: Making Sense of the Nonsensical,' *American Journal of Psychiatry* 148, 8 (August 1991): 986-997.

[6] *Trial of Jane Leigh Perrot*, 17.

[7] The richest sources for this information remain newspaper accounts, trials, and magazine articles along with related stories in literature. The government debates over regulating consumption are haphazard and seem to be inspired by occasional "panics" especially those over pure food and drugs, but a careful reading also demonstrates a great concern over fraud in general and its prevalence in an urban, anonymous society.

"kleptomaniac," but this option was not available to her or her counsel in 1800. Beginning as a genderless, if not classless, ailment, the kleptomania diagnosis slowly developed throughout the nineteenth century to become the favored explanation for cases of female middle-class shoplifting. The shifts in the perception of shoplifting and other retail crimes occurred as a result of the changing landscape of English consumption in the nineteenth century.

The History of Shopping and Retail Crime in England

As the industrial kingpins of England concentrated on larger factories, better machinery, and cheaper labor to spur the expansion of the British economy, a less noticed transformation occurred in arcades, bazaars, and small shopfronts across England. Sometimes overlooked in the history of English capitalism, the development of a new kind of consumer culture laid the foundations for the later feminine world of materialist fantasy—emphasizing display and consumption— that enchanted *fin de siècle* shoppers. Accused by such luminaries as William Makepeace Thackeray and Anthony Trollope of selling without substance, retailers incorporating new methods, which included bazaar shopping, 'cheap shops,' and large emporiums with open displays, grew in popularity and were the progenitors of the great department stores. Inspired by class aspirations, the women who inhabited this new realm of conspicuous consumption with its ever-expanding array of goods provided the driving force for the new culture, a culture that created a host of anxieties for English society. Unchecked consumerism led to fears of crime and fraud perpetrated by both buyers and sellers. Women's involvement in this seedy business of selling was especially troubling to middle-class, male commentators.

If England was once a nation of shopkeepers, by the 1860s, critics contended that the country had become a nation of frauds and shoplifters with women in the lead of those satisfied with the pursuit of selling without substance. For both buyer and seller, the uninhibited flow of goods in English retail trade encouraged morally dubious as well as respectable profit making.[8] Debates over new selling methods and heightened prosecutions of retail crime during the first three-quarters of the century illustrate the unsettling effect of the already burgeoning consumer culture on gender and class roles before the *grand magasins* opened their doors.

---

[8] See Richard Altick, *The Shows of London* (London: Belknap Press), 1978; Tony Bennett, 'The Exhibitionary Complex,' *New Formations* (Spring 1988): 73-102; Asa Briggs, *Victorian Things* (London: B.T. Batsford), 1988; Leonore Davidoff and Catherine Hall, *Family Fortunes; Men and Women of the English Middle Class, 1780-1850* (Chicago: University of Chicago Press, 1986) for the growth in retail, profusion of goods, and enterprise oriented toward public consumption.

With a rapidly growing economy, English consumption underwent disturbing changes in the early nineteenth century, as a German visitor to London reported home in 1814:

> The uninterrupted range of shops that line both sides of the street, prevents you indeed from looking upwards, for here you discover wealth and magnificence that you would in vain look elsewhere for . . .. Here costly shawls from the East Indies, there brocades and silk-tissues from China, . . . an ocean of rings, watches, chains, bracelets, and aigrettes, ready-dresses, ribbons, lace bonnets, and fruit from all the zones of the habitable world—attract, tempt, astonish, and distract your eyes.[9]

In the nineteenth century smaller, family run shops began to give way to larger, multiple-employee shops. Businesses adopted innovative retail practices such as cash sales and openly marked pricing of goods. Shops used elaborate window dressing and aggressive advertisements to attract customers. These larger scale, ready-money establishments—especially linen drapers' and haberdashers' shops— served as transitional forms in the evolution of the department store and modern consumer culture.

Other innovations in nineteenth-century retail developed in the exotically named bazaars. Beginning just after the Napoleonic wars, charity and commercial shopping bazaars used techniques such as tempting open displays, flower shows, and entertaining dioramas to attract visitors. Innovations credited to the opening of the *grand magasins* developed first in bazaars, markets staffed, patronized and often stocked by women. For upper-class ladies, the charity bazaar or fancy fair afforded opportunities to showcase their artistic talents through the sale of watercolors, embroidery and wax models, while they fulfilled a social welfare function and replaced older methods of charity. Perhaps more importantly, bazaars gave aristocrats and selected members of the middle class an opportunity to exhibit *themselves* and to display their class pretensions on a public stage. For the middle-class and working-class women who worked in commercial bazaars, it was a chance at a livelihood—a slim piece of the nineteenth-century entrepreneurial ideal. Parliamentary petitions, newspaper reports, and trials illustrate the curiously exhibitionist nature of these new open markets and the way they helped to feminize the consumer experience as well as make way for consumer culture on an even grander scale at the end of the nineteenth century.

The success of the new bazaars and drapery emporiums, along with their familiar and innovative approaches to retail, elicited fears that businesses were defrauding customers in their pursuit of profit. Observers ranging from satirical ballad writers to journalists accused the new shops of undermining the character of English retail trade and duping the consumer into buying worthless and

---

[9] *Letters From Albion, Vol. I* (London: Gale, Curtis, and Fenner, 1814), 79-80. See also Simon Jervis, 'Rudolph Ackerman,' in *London: World City, 1800-1840*, ed. Celina Fox (New Haven: Yale Univeristy Press, 1992): 97-110 for a discussion of the profusion of goods in the early nineteenth century.

misrepresented goods. In court cases, letters to the *Times*, and fiction, retailers were charged with blackmailing respectable ladies by planting goods on them and then threatening to prosecute for shoplifting.[10] According to middle-class commentators, the new shops preyed upon the gullible female shopper and destroyed the previously sterling character of English shopkeepers by threatening to turn a nation of shopkeepers into a nation of frauds.

According to critics, the fraudulent atmosphere of English shops corrupted the consumer as well as the retailer. Respectable women were compared to prostitutes in their materialism, and wives were told that if they went out alone and something dreadful happened (like being wrongfully accused of theft), it was their fault.[11] These fears may have arisen partly in connection with the switch from home production to commercial production, but there is also a noted discomfort about women's obvious economic role as new consumers and their power over the family purse.[12] While Victorian men were encouraged to be tigers of capitalism as wage-earners and businessmen, Victorian society was not willing to accept the changes that women's new role as consumers brought. Fearing and warning women against exposure in the public sphere of shops, critics, especially journalists and satirists, also characterized the female consumer as a shopping demon allowing nothing to prevent her enjoyment of opportunities to consume, or by browsing, to leisurely enjoy the shopping culture created for her at the expense of the shopkeeper.[13]

---

[10] This anxiety over consumer culture is clearly evident in literature and newspaper reports of the period. Particularly good examples are short stories by Thomas De Quincey, 'The Household Wreck,' *Blackwood's Edinburgh Magazine*, January 1838, 1-32; Charles Dickens, *Sketches by Boz and Other Early Papers, 1833-1839* (London: J.M. Dent, 1994); a play, Robert Louis Stevenson, 'The Charity Bazaar: An Allegorical Dialogue,' (Edinburgh, 1866); various writings in *The Comic Almanack*; from 1848 William Makepeace Thackeray, *Vanity Fair: A Novel Without a Hero* (New York: Quality Paperback Book Club, 1991). However, John Tallis's *London Street Views* (London: John Tallis, 1838-40) not surprisingly, lauds the changes in London's consumer landscape. John Tallis, *London Street Views*.

[11] See Gary Dyer, 'The 'Vanity Fair' of Nineteenth-Century England: Commerce, Women, and the East in the Ladies' Bazaar,' *Nineteenth-Century Literature* (September 1991): 196-222; and Judith R. Walkowitz, *City of Dreadful Delight; Narratives of Sexual Danger in Late-Victorian London* (Chicago: University of Chicago Press, 1992).

[12] See notes 1 and 7.

[13] Both Elaine Abelson and Judith Walkowitz have looked at the problems created by women's public role as consumers in the late nineteenth century; however, no one has yet explored the tensions caused by the female buyer in this earlier, formative period. Elaine S. Abelson, *When Ladies Go A-Thieving: Middle-Class Shoplifters in the Victorian Department Store* (New York: Oxford University Press, 1989); Walkowitz, *City of Dreadful Delight*. See also Jane H. Hunter, *How Young Ladies Became Girls: The Victorian Origins of American Girlhood* (New Haven: Yale University Press, 2002) for the American perspective on women's increasing forays into the public world of consumption.

Women participated not only as legitimate shoppers in this emerging culture of consumption in the nineteenth century but also as retail criminals who acquired goods without purchasing them. With items so easy to plunder in bazaars and even in shops where customers were frequently shown a number of articles at one time—the customer was often also the thief.[14] For their part, many customers used false names and false credit to acquire merchandise.[15] With few laws and regulations controlling businesses and protecting consumers, English retail trade became a battle between wary shoppers and shopkeepers fearful of losing their stock with the identity of the female consumer hanging in the balance. In response to these depredations, retailers began to form trade protection societies in the late eighteenth century, a movement that quickly expanded from London retailers to national organizations in the nineteenth century. In their confidential circulars, trade protection societies named and described persons who had defrauded them or were believed to be shoplifters.[16] Victorians dealt with retail crime through various methods including trade protection societies, regulatory laws, criminal law changes, and constructing an identity for the problematic middle-class shoplifter.[17]

---

[14] Abelson, *When Ladies Go A-Thieving* explores later nineteenth-century shoplifting, but the concerns over shoplifting existed much earlier—especially in England. For detailed accounts of this earlier growth in consumer culture see Gary Dyer, 'The 'Vanity Fair' of Nineteenth-Century England,' 196-222; Hilary M. Schor, 'Urban Things: The Mystery of the Commodity in Victorian Literature' (paper presented at the Interdisciplinary Nineteenth-Century Studies Conference on The Nineteenth-Century City: Global Contexts, Local Productions, Santa Cruz, California, 7-8 April 1995); and Nicole Tonkovich, 'Foreign Markets in Domestic Locations: Frances Trollope's Cincinnati Bazaar, 1828-1830' (paper presented to the Interdisciplinary Nineteenth-Century Studies Conference, Massachusetts Institute of Technology, 1996).

[15] See especially Margot Finn, 'Fair Trade and Foul: Swindlers, Shopkeepers, and the Use and Abuse of Credit in the Nineteenth Century'(paper presented to the North American Conference on British Studies meeting, October 1995) for her case studies.

[16] James Henry Dixon, *A Statement of Facts In Reference to the City of London Trade Protection Society* (13, Swithin's Lane,) *and the Mode in Which it Discharges it Pecuniary Obligations* (London: Effingham Wilson, Royal exchange,1851): 1-11; *City of London Trade Protection Circular* (London) April 1848-November 1849; 'The Amalgamated Societes,' *City of London Trade Protection Circular* (London) 28 October 1848; 'Metropolitan Institutue for Protection of Trade,' *Trade Protection Record* (London) 25 August 1849; Society for Prosecuting Felons, Forgers, Shoplifters, Domestic Thieves and Persons Giving False Character to Servants; also for Defraying the Expenses of Advertisements, Hand Bills, and Rewards, March 1767, 'Police and Public Security,' Box I, John Johnson Collection, Bodleian, Oxford; Sherbourne Association for the Protections of Property, 1824 'Police and Public Security,' Box I, John Johnson Collection, Bodleian, Oxford; Radwinter Association for the Protection of Property, 1831, 'Police and Public Security,' Box I, John Johnson Collection, Bodleian, Oxford.

[17] There were numerous government attempts to deal with this consumer culture unleashed. See Hugh Cunningham, 'The Metropolitan Fairs: a Case Study in the Social Control of Leisure,' in *Social Control in Nineteenth Century Britain*, ed. A.P. Donajgrodzki (London: Croom Helm, 1977), 163-184; Steve Inwood, 'Policing

In their warnings of known frauds and shoplifters, the trade societies were reacting to the perception of a growing criminal consumption. In one notorious example in 1844, Jane Tyrwhitt supposedly secreted a two-shilling microscope up her sleeve at a popular London bazaar. Her trial prompted an avalanche of arguments and outrage in the media. Tyrwhitt, who had family connections to the aristocracy, claimed that the unscrupulous owners had framed her. The case sparked heated debate and emotional letters in the *Times*, demonstrating fears not only about shoplifters but also about shop owners: businesses were defrauding the customers just as the customers were trying to get away with the goods.

This debate, along with other shoplifting trials and fictional accounts of the era, illustrates the uneasy relationship between women and consumer culture in this period. The role of women as aggressive consumers clashed with their home-centered image, and their role in retail crime complicated class division. Fraught with class tension, images of 'cheap shopkeepers' searching shopping ladies or planting goods on them terrified the middle classes just as lower-class shoplifters posing as ladies alarmed shopkeepers. Middle-class shoplifting was problematic before the department store, and the gendered image of the shoplifter was already developing before the wide acceptance of kleptomania in the later nineteenth century. The Tyrwhitt case and similar trials of this era shows how women's apparently increasing role in consumer culture, and consequently consumer crime, shook their domestic image, blurred the divisions that formed class identities, and laid the groundwork for what became the kleptomania diagnosis. In a less well-publicized case in 1859, the same Jane Tyrwhitt received very different treatment when tried for fraudulently ordering goods under false names. "Lady" thieves like Tyrwhitt were joined by a host of other less famous and more or less respectable women and men committing retail theft and fraud.[18]

Contemporary Scholarship

Once firmly linked to the rise of genteel consumption in the eighteenth century, Linda Levy Peck now asserts that the growth in luxury consumption began in the sixteenth century.[19] Peck's work complicates the dominant explanation of

---

London's Morals: The Metropolitan Police and Popular Culture, 1829-1850,' *London Journal*, 15, no. 2 (1990): 129-146; Markham V. Lester, *Victorian Insolvency: Bankruptcy, Imprisonment for Debt, and Company Winding-up in Nineteenth-Century England* (Oxford: Clarendon Press, 1995); Anthony Ogus, *Regulation: Legal Form and Economic Theory* (Oxford: Clarendon Press, 1994).

[18] See *Times* (London) 1820-1879. I have also found about 50 fraud cases that deal specifically with shoppers (women) defrauding retailers by various methods including false names and addresses, false currency, and building credit with the name of important 'acquaintances' established in the town.

[19] Linda Levy Peck, 'Luxury and War: Reconsidering Luxury Consumption in Seventeenth-Century England' [Presidential Address: The North American Conference on British Studies], *Albion*, 34,1 (Spring 2002): 1-23.

consumer culture as a product of the gentry of the eighteenth century found in John Brewer and Roy Porter's work.[20] Nineteenth-century historians of Europe, England and America see the next great leap in consumption taking place with the invention of the department store.[21] The role of shopper, whether it be manipulated victim or empowered pleasure seeker remains under debate in the works of Victoria De Grazia, Ellen Furlough, Margot Finn and others.[22] This study links the consumption of the early modern period so well detailed by Peck, Brewer and Porter with the commodity culture of the later Victorian era and demonstrates the key role women played in this transition.

The treatment of shoplifting as a crime highlights social discomfort with the public role of women in the English economy and their primary role in consumer culture.[23] Recent scholarship on the phenomenon of the department store by Elaine Abelson, Michael Miller, and Patricia O'Brien emphasizes this tension. However, middle-class shoplifting and other middle-class retail crime did *not* emerge with the advent of the department store, but appeared much earlier.[24] Gareth Shaw and

---

[20] John Brewer and Roy Porter, *Consumption and the World of Goods* (London: Routledge, 1993); Neil McKendrick, John Brewer, and J. H. Plumb. *The Birth of a Consumer Society: The Commercialization of Eighteenth-Century England* (Bloomington: Indiana University Press, 1982); Lorna Weatherhill, *Consumer Behavior and Material Culture in Britain, 1660-1720* (Cambridge, 1988); Carole Shammas, *The Pre-Industrial Consumer in England and America* (Oxford, 1990). See also Sarah Lloyd, 'Pleasing Spectacles and Elegant Dinners: Conviviality, Benevolence, and Charity Anniversaries in Eighteenth-Century London,' *Journal of British Studies*, 41, 1. (Jan., 2002): 23-57.

[21] Erika D. Rappaport, "The Halls of Temptation': Gender, Politics, and the Construction of the Department Store in Late Victorian London,' *Journal of British Studies* 35, 1 (1996): 58-83; William R. Leach, 'Transformations in a Culture of Consumption: Women and Department Stores, 1890-1925,' *The Journal of American History* 71, 2 (1984): 319-42; T. J. Jackson Lears, and Richard Wrightman Fox, eds., *The Culture of Consumption: Critical Essays in American History* (New York: Pantheon Books, 1983); Michael B. Miller, *The Bon Marché: Bourgeois Culture and the Department Store, 1869-1920* (Princeton: Princeton University Press, 1981).

[22] Victoria De Grazia and Ellen Furlough, eds., *The Sex of Things: Gender and Consumption in Historical Perspective* (Berkeley: University of California Press, 1996); Margot Finn, 'Debt and Credit in Bath's Court of Requests, 1829-39,' *Urban History* 21, 2 (1994): 211-36; Lori Anne Loeb, *Consuming Angels: Advertising and Victorian Women* (New York: Oxford University Press, 1994); Leslie Camhi, 'Stealing Femininity: Department Store Kleptomania As Sexual Disorder' *Differences* 5, 2 (1993): 27-50; Rachel Bowlby, *Just Looking: Consumer Culture in Dreiser, Gissing, and Zola* (New York: Methuen, 1985); Rosalind H. Williams, *Dream Worlds: Mass Consumption in Late Nineteenth-Century France* (Berkeley: University of California Press, 1982).

[23] See especially Walkowitz, *City of Dreadful Delight*.

[24] Many authors focus on the post-1850s era as the most expansive in consumer culture. See W. Hamish Fraser, *The Coming of the Mass Market, 1850-1914* (Hamden, Connecticut: Archon Books, 1981); Thomas Richards, *The Commodity Culture of Victorian England: Advertising and Spectacle, 1851-1914* (Stanford: Stanford

John Benson's studies of overall retail growth in the nineteenth century reveal that retail evolution was not one great forward march to the department store, but a complex growth of competing systems of various sizes.[25] Examining the anxiety over retail crime that paralleled the economic growth of the nineteenth century provides important insights not only into the early development of consumer culture, but also into the changing position and characterization of women in this culture and its effects on class identity, medicine, and English law.[26]

Despite England's lead in many aspects of consumer culture in the nineteenth century, most of the historical studies of women and retail crime have concentrated on France and the United States linking consumer crime to late nineteenth-century consumption. Elaine Abelson's study of middle-class shoplifters in the postbellum United States focuses on the connections between consumer culture, the rise of department stores, and an apparently growing incidence of "lady" thieves. Abelson concluded that society avoided the critique of consumer capitalism that middle-class shoplifting should have elicited by blaming the women instead: the problem of shoplifting was feminized and categorized in a way that circumvented a critique of the new consumer society. Leslie Camhi's study of the later development of kleptomania centered on urban, middle-class, female consumers in the late nineteenth and early twentieth centuries in France. For Camhi, there was an intimate connection between kleptomania, consumerism, and feminine identity. Femininity itself became a sort of commodity. Patricia O'Brien found kleptomania connected to department stores in France, and asserts that this diagnosis was one of the cornerstones of the rise of the medical professional in court. This argument also appears in Michael Miller's work.[27]

University Press, 1990); Loeb, *Consuming Angels*. The development of the department store remains the focus as the impetus for change in consumer culture by continental and American scholars. See Leach, 'Transformations in a Culture of Consumption,' 319-342; Miller, *The Bon Marché*; Rappaport, 'The Halls of Temptation', 58-83; Williams, *Dream Worlds*.

[25] John Benson and Gareth Shaw, eds., *The Evolution of Retail Systems, c1800-1914* (Leicester: Leicester University Press, 1992).

[26] Taking a cue from Jean Christophe Agnew, 'Coming up for air: consumer culture in historical perspective,' in *Consumption and the World of Good,*, ed. John Brewer and Roy Porter (London: Routledge, 1993), 19-39 and other more recent scholarship, I depart from the older mostly negative view of the rise of mass consumption as an overall evil that turned consumers (especially women) into passive, manipulated addicts of the new abundance.

[27] See Abelson, *When Ladies Go A-Thieving*; Camhi, 'Stealing Femininity,' 27-50; Miller, *The Bon Marché*. Insanity as a factor in criminal trials has a long history. See John Haslam, *Medical Jurisprudence As It Relates to Insanity, According to the Law of England* (London: 1817); Roger Smith, *Trial By Medicine :Insanity and Responsibility in Victorian Trials* (Edinburgh, Scotland: Edinburgh University Press, 1981). Patricia O'Brien notes the increasingly specific group covered by the diagnosis most frequently made about shoplifters in the nineteenth century in Patricia O'Brien, 'The Kleptomania Diagnosis: Bourgeois Women and Theft in Late Nineteenth-Century

British historians have paid little attention to shoplifting as a crime, shopkeeper fraud, or the diagnosis of kleptomania as a historical development specific to the later nineteenth century. However, Margot Finn's ongoing work on consumer debt is highlighting the important role of women who were usually seen as passive consumers and nominal actors in the Victorian economy.[28] Both Erika Rappaport in *Shopping for Pleasure* and Judith Walkowitz in *City of Dreadful Delight*, explore the aura of danger surrounding the female shopper of the Victorian era.[29] Definitions of femininity, class, medicine, the economy, and the Victorian struggle with public and private all play a part in the anxiety about retail crime. A close examination of these problems also reflects the overall trends in punishment and English law, especially concerning women, in the nineteenth century. These consumer crimes fit into the evolution of English crime and punishment described by Martin Wiener and Lucia Zedner who stress the shift away from harsh physical punishment to imprisonment and the medicalization of women's crime.[30] With the passage of Romilly's bill in 1820, shoplifting ceased to be a hanging offense. However, women still suffered imprisonment and, more rarely, transportation, for shoplifting offenses. Responses to the female, middle-

---

France,'   *Journal of Social History* 17 (1983):   65-67. Those diagnosed as kleptomaniacs were increasingly middle-class women.

[28]   See Finn, 'Debt and credit in Bath's court of requests, 211-236; Finn, 'Fair Trade and Foul'; Margot Finn, 'Victorian Women as Consumer Debtors: Theory and Practice' (presented to the North American Conference on British Studies meeting, Montreal, October 1, 1993). Also women's power as consumers and consumer criminals is related to their position as both married and unmarried women under the law. See Mary Lyndon Shanley, *Feminism, Marriage, and the Law in Victorian England* (Princeton: Princeton University Press, 1989).

[29]   See Erika D. Rappaport, *Shopping for Pleasure: Women in the Making of London's West End* (Princeton, New Jersey: Princeton University Press, 2001); Walkowitz, *City of Dreadful Delight*.

[30]   Overall, women's participation in retail crime seems to highlight general trends in Victorian justice including the decreasing seriousness of punishment for property crimes, especially petty crimes, over the century. See J.M. Beattie, *Crime and the Courts in England, 1660-1800* (Princeton University Press, 1986); V.A.C. Gatrell, *The Hanging Tree: Execution and the English People, 1770-1868* (Oxford University Press, 1994). Secondly, they illustrate the change from moralization to medicalization of crime. See Martin Wiener, *Reconstructing the Criminal: Culture, law, and policy in England, 1830-1914* (New York: Cambridge University Press, 1990); Lucia Zedner, *Women, Crime, and Custody in Victorian England* (Oxford: Clarendon Press, 1991). There may also be a connection to the 'disappearance' of women in the criminal process in the nineteenth century in the sense that shoplifting was a severely under-reported crime. See Malcolm M. Feely and Deborah L. Little, 'The Vanishing Female: The Decline of Women in the Criminal Process, 1687-1912,' *Law & Society Review* 25, no. 4 (1991): 719-757. Lastly, fraud on both sides of the counter is tied to the nineteenth century's relatively unrestrained capitalism. See George Robb, *White-collar Crime in Modern England; Financial Fraud and Business Morality, 1845-1929* (Cambridge: Cambridge University Press, 1992).

class shoplifter, on the other hand, evolved from treating her crimes with denial to medicalizing her crime with the invention of kleptomania.

The solution to consumer fraud remained elusive throughout the nineteenth century. This problem was never successfully dealt with by the criminal justice system, and the message remained—"let the buyer/debtor beware." Retailer fraud was beginning to be controlled by laws regulating the content of food and drugs, although this type of fraud again sparked debate in the Edwardian era when muckraking journalists in the United States and England brought it to public attention. For their part, larger retailers found a separate solution in private police forces along with store detectives and security systems outside the criminal justice system.

Crime, Capitalism and the British Economy

The Nature of Capitalism

Since in theory capitalism is based on the idea of meeting need through better and more efficient means of production, criminal consumption like shoplifting and fraud would seem to be a subversion of Adam Smith's dream. However, especially after initial demands are met in industries like textiles in the 1700s, production in the nineteenth century is more concerned with minor improvements in machinery or methods, producing ever cheaper staples, and creating greater choice. The liberal use of aniline dyes in the 1860s is a good example of adding choice by providing the usual goods in a variety of bold new colors. Even with these less demand-oriented approaches, markets become saturated in the nineteenth century leading to the infamous bust cycles so well catalogued by writers like Elizabeth Gaskell in her novel *North and South*. For the nineteenth century, overproduction is a reality. Overproduction combined with increasing retail competition— especially that provided by urbanization and emporiums—leads to unsold goods. Once simple demand is met, retailers and producers have to either market goods to a new class of shoppers via the cheaper or discount emporiums *or* create more demand with display and marketing. In the end, successful capitalism (in the sense of an exponentially expanding market) is not about adopting a particular method of production or distribution, but about expanding markets by simultaneously creating demand while continually democratizing goods.

Class and Status

In a post-capitalist economy like the one developing in the nineteenth century, the role of status is not the same as in earlier periods of English history. During the era of the famous Elizabethan sumptuary laws prohibiting the wearing of certain luxurious clothing, the problem was not a mass of consumers, but a small class of wealthy merchants brokering for aristocratic power. By the 1800s aristocrats were losing power if not all of their prestige. Likewise, the shift to moveable property made status more difficult to determine and therefore more important for the rising middle classes. Although luxury consumption is important for higher status, it is too narrow a base for the nineteenth century's economies of scale. Further complicating matters is that class and status are constantly shifting socially, culturally, and economically. In spite of criticism by moralists—goods become increasingly important in the recognition of status and class because goods help symbolize outward evidence of moveable property.

The Problem: "Necessaries" vs. Needs

So how does consumer culture work in conjunction with the creation of status to continue to support an ever expanding post-capitalist economy in the nineteenth century and into the twentieth century? The problems are multi-fold: the cost and status enhancing ability of the goods fluctuate because (1) stores must try and convince more and more consumers to make seemingly unnecessary purchases once an original demand is met; (2) the democratization of luxury provided by mass production and cheaper bulk retail constantly threatens the boundaries of both the middle class and the gentry; and (3) when cheaper versions of fashions inevitably fall into working-class hands, the middle class and gentry are forced to "pull the ladder up" and change to something new—as well as implementing social control measures like changing rules for employees like servants and shifting their own class etiquette. Therefore goods make unstable class boundaries because they are in constant flux. As they become cheaper, more or a different type are soon required. Also, to compete and constantly reverify status and hold those boundaries, middle-class women especially recognize that fripperies are really *necessaries* after all. The problem is compounded by the *nouveau riche* who fail to absorb all the fluctuating rules of acquisition that constantly reverify class status, and simply buy new and cheaply made goods without understanding the "rules" of using them. This problem is partially addressed by a rise in etiquette and self-help manuals.

So, the reason that the acquisition of goods is not perfectly equivalent to social status is the constant fluctuation of boundary guardians like changing fashions as a response when cheaper versions are created (based on previously more expensive items); class bound rituals for use that are also being constantly exposed by etiquette manuals, and the changing amount of goods required to hold status—i.e. not just the "right" dress, but the right number in the right colors. Goods do equal status, but in a socially and culturally specific way that provides those striving or guarding status with the appearance of stability on the quicksand foundation of changing social boundaries. The success of consumer capitalism depends on both the ever changing nature of goods-based status and the appearance of the stability of that status at any one point in time. Most importantly, society's main consumers, women, begin to recognize the importance of goods and their definition, especially among middle-class women, expands over the century to include more and more items as necessary. This *need* was not simply a rationalization of the individual shopper; it was real. In an urban, or suburban, post-capitalist society, families and individuals do not function autonomously where they can simply choose to live without the consumer goods of their historical, social and cultural milieu.

Conclusion

This study uses traditional archival sources and sources from popular culture to examine the changing role of the female consumer and of English retail in the nineteenth century. Trial records from the Middlesex Sessions, Old Bailey Sessions, and police-court reports in newspapers reveal not only shifts in the treatment of retail criminals, but also tell us about "normal" shopping practices including the items purchased and the extension of credit. Less traditional sources like the John Johnson Collection of ephemera at Oxford's Bodleian Library show the changing image of the female shopper as well as changes in retail reflected in advertising and handbills of the period. The criticism of the shifts in buying and selling are traced in letters to newspaper editors, songs, and novels like Anthony Trollope's satire of an English drapery emporium, *The Struggles of Brown, Jones, and Robinson.*

The concerns over retail crimes like shoplifting, consumer fraud, and retailer fraud as exhibited by the kleptomania debate, the 'cheap shopkeeper' scare, and other criticisms of women in the marketplace hid an even greater concern in nineteenth-century society—anxiety over the new consumer culture. The strange new world of profuse abundance and display that appeared in nineteenth-century England alarmed critics with its hollow credo of selling for the sake of selling and seemingly buying for the sake of buying. Rather than shying away from this new phenomenon emphasizing cheapness, bargains, variety over quality, and encouraging appearances over realities, women were helping to create and expand this new very public world. Criticized at every turn for their participation in charity bazaars, commercial bazaars, linen and haberdashery emporiums, and shopping as a "sport," women continued to venture into this ever widening public space of consumption with all its attendant dangers, delights, and opportunities. Working-class and lower-middle-class women were entrepreneurs in commercial bazaars—selling and often making their own products. Some could even establish their own commercial empires and fashionable London shops. Or, more appalling to observers, they might pose as wealthier, more respectable women to gain the luxuries and status that this world of consumption provided. Middle-class and upper-class women became vendors of a sort in their own charity bazaars, and they too committed acts of shoplifting and fraud, but not necessarily because of some mental weakness. Their own society was redefining need, and class aspirations made a little bit of lace significant indeed to the middle-class woman who did not possess it. These related movements in consumer culture gave new employment to women not only as small retailers but also as "matrons" and later shopwalkers who policed theft and fraud on the shop floor. Evidence in the records of the debate over this consumer culture and its concomitant anxieties shows a powerful change in the English economy. Women were the key to this transformation.

PART I
DESTROYING THE
'NATION OF SHOPKEEPERS'

Chapter 1

Ready Money Only:
Small Shops and New Retail Methods

What would London be without its shops? How dull to the pedestrian,
on a fine Sunday in June, is the formal, Quaker-like aspect of the
shuttered shops of Fleet Street and the Strand!
                                        —'Shopping in London,' 1844

Retailing Evolution in the Late Eighteenth and Early Nineteenth Centuries

Mrs. Moore, a shopkeeper trading haberdasheries in the fashionable London retail area of Grafton Street[1] in the late eighteenth or early nineteenth century circulated an extensive handbill to advertise her new wares:

BEST ENGLISH Silk Stockings, Worsted Gaiters, & Cambric Muslin Gloves.
Plain, Tambour, and Japanned Muslins,
Cambric, Lace and Piquet Ditto,
. . .
Large Muslin Shawls, Linen ditto, and Veils.
A Fashionable Assortment of Hats and Bonnets.
Mourning Articles of every Description.
Ladies Tunbridge Work and Writing Boxes.

The Superior Quality of the above Goods, she trusts will obtain the Approbation of her Customers, who may rely on purchasing to peculiar Advantage having arranged her Dealings for READY MONEY ONLY.[2]

Moore's handbill illustrates the growing sophistication of English retail. Aggressively touting both the variety and quality of her wares, and her competitive prices, a price structure made possible by a business based on cash transactions,[3]

---

[1] Alison Adburgham, *Shops and Shopping, 1800-1914: Where and in What Manner the Well-Dressed Englishwoman Bought Her Clothes* (London: Barrie and Jenkins, 1964), 4.

[2] Moore, formerly Clarkson & Moore, 'Women's Clothing and Millinery,' John Johnson Collection, Box I. Note: spelling modernized.

[3] See especially Hoh-cheung and Lorna H. Mui, *Shops and Shopkeeping in Eighteenth Century England* (Montreal: McGill-Queen's U. Press,1989), 238-239 who connect this phenomenon to the innovations of linen drapers.

shopkeepers like Moore represent the vanguard of English shops in the later eighteenth and early nineteenth centuries.

All English shopkeepers, however, did not incorporate innovations like advertising, expensive shop fixtures, and cash-only trade in the eighteenth and early nineteenth centuries. Only a small sector of business people in especially competitive trades like retail clothing initiated the new methods that would become the hallmark of nineteenth-century trade.[4] Along with these new developments in retailing methods came new settings for selling such as the arcade—a luxurious enclave protected from inclement weather with a variety of shops for the upper-class shopper. Despite the adoption of new techniques by some traders, in the eighteenth century most shopkeepers, especially in smaller towns and villages, continued to trade in traditional ways with slow turnover, a limited variety of goods, and on a credit basis. Shopping as a leisure activity remained the privilege of the few prior to the nineteenth century. Changes in English shopping in this period served as the basis for nineteenth-century consumer society, but did not affect the bulk of the selling or buying public; these innovative sales techniques were mainly limited to the upper and middling classes. The small but growing section of middling folk with their demand for better and wider varieties of consumer goods eventually propelled English consumption into a new era.[5]

The work of Neil McKendrick, John Brewer and Roy Porter among others gives ample evidence that consumer society was already firmly rooted by the 1700s.[6] The English home market expanded throughout that century. Demand was high and the amount of goods available increasing—fueled in part by England's growing industry. In this boom period, London reigned as England's retail capital. Facing competition from London, provincial shops began to adopt London innovations such as those demonstrated by Moore's advertisement.[7] Market expansion and the concomitant shifts in English retail formed the base of nineteenth-century consumer society in England.

The emphasis on consumption as a driving economic force is a recent one in historical scholarship. Whether influenced by the impact of Britain's recent industrial decline or the legacy of nineteenth-century classical economists,

---

[4] *Ibid.* 71-72, 221-239.

[5] Rosalind Williams finds a similar difference between consumption in nineteenth and pre-nineteenth-century France in Rosalind H.Williams, *Dream Worlds: Mass Consumption in Late Nineteenth-Century France* (Berkeley, University of California Press, 1982), 3.

[6] See Neil McKendrick, John Brewer and J.H. Plumb, *The Birth of a Consumer Society: The Commercialization of Eighteenth-Century England* (Bloomington: Indiana University Press, 1982); John Brewer and Roy Porter, eds., *Consumption and the World of Goods* (London: Routledge, 1993). For a similar study focusing on the American colonies see Cary Carson, Ronald Hoffman, and Peter J. Albert, eds., *Of Consuming Interests: The Style of Life in the Eighteenth Century* (Charlottesville: University Press of Virginia and United States Capital Historical Society, 1994).

[7] Mui and Mui, *Shops and Shopkeeping in Eighteenth Century England*, 7, 71-72.

historians traditionally focused on production as the key to analyzing economic growth.[8] In the past two decades, historians have begun to search for the origins of modern, mass consumer society in the advertisements, shop improvements, and trade developments of the eighteenth and nineteenth centuries. Mass consumption is distinguished by the mass production and sale of similarly styled and packaged goods, and a dissociation of a commodity from its means of production. The spendthrift attitude of consumers is also an integral part of mass consumption.[9] Many historians agree that the engine driving this modern consumption was advertising.

More than just placards posting prices or denoting the uses of objects, advertising in a society of mass consumption emphasizes the image associated with a commodity rather than the utility of the commodity itself.[10] In Britain, many historians have posited that this mass market originated in the mid-nineteenth century. A combination of economic growth providing an increase in living standards for a majority of the population and the impetus of modern advertising marks the era between the 1851 Crystal Palace Exhibition and the First World War as the beginning of English mass consumer culture. According to Hamish Fraser and Thomas Richards, sophisticated sales techniques like advertising dependent on association with desirable images rather than promises of low prices or quality marshaled this growth.[11] Others scholars pinpoint the development of the department store as the onset of the era of consumer culture. The department stores of *fin de siècle* England, France, and America were temples of consumption where the image of the goods exhibited reigned over their more mundane functions in luxurious displays.[12] All of these developments—the Crystal Palace Exhibition,

---

[8] See William Lancaster, *The Department Store* (London: Leicester University Press, 1995), 2; Mui and Mui, *Shops and Shopkeeping in Eighteenth Century England*, 6. The Muis argue that the growth in consumption pre-dates the impetus of production from industrialization. See also pages 44-45.

[9] See especially Williams, *Dream Worlds*, 3.

[10] Colin Campbell argues that such "image" advertising is the key to a successful appeal to the consumer and the creation of modern consumerism. See Colin Campbell, *The Romantic Ethic and the Spirit of Modern Consumerism* (London: Basil Blackwell, 1987), 48. See also T.J. Jackson Lears, *Fables of Abundance: A Cultural History of Advertising in America* (New York: Basic Books, 1994); T.J. Jackson Lears, 'From Salvation to Self-Realization: Advertising and the Therapeutic Roots of Consumer Culture, 1880-1930,' in *The Culture of Consumption: Critical Essays in American History*, ed. T. J. Jackson Lears and Richard Wrightman Fox (New York: Pantheon Books, 1983).

[11] See W. Hamish Fraser, *The Coming of the Mass Market, 1850-1914* (Hamden, Connecticut: Archon Books, 1981); Thomas Richards, *The Commodity Culture of Victorian England: Advertising and Spectacle, 1851-1914* (Stanford: Stanford University Press, 1990).

[12] See Lancaster, *The Department Store*; Michael B. Miller, *The Bon Marché: Bourgeois Culture and the Department Store, 1869-1920* (Princeton: Princeton University Press, 1981); Williams, *Dream Worlds*; William R. Leach, 'Transformations in a Culture of Consumption: Women and Department Stores, 1890-1925,' *The Journal of American*

modern advertising, and department stores—encouraged consumer culture and shopping as an increasingly time-consuming activity, especially for middle-class women.

Modern consumer culture, particularly the connection between image and goods and the participation in shopping as a major pastime, does not begin with either the Crystal Palace or the emergence of department stores, which both had their origins in earlier forms. Consumer culture did not remain stagnant between the consumer revolution of the later eighteenth century and the exhibitions, advertising, and shopping palaces of the later nineteenth century. The vanguard shops of the late eighteenth century prepared the way for the bazaars, emporiums, and finally the department stores of the nineteenth century.

Despite significant changes in eighteenth-century retail, most shop owners operated as petty shopkeepers usually assisted by a spouse and perhaps a single worker from outside the family. The luxurious, fashionable shops of London's retail centers represented the exception to that rule. These relatively small businesses distributed the majority of English goods to consumers in the 1700s. However, the histories of such small shops are difficult to trace.[13] Unlike later department stores, such small businesses often left little record of their existence.[14] Fortunately, advertisements and trade cards, small cards with the shop's name, address, and type of business, provide a glimpse into the world of late eighteenth- and early nineteenth-century retail trade.

Women and Shopkeeping in the Late 1700s and Early 1800s

An example from the eighteenth century is the shop of Mary and Ann Hogarth in London. Their beautifully illustrated trade card by their brother William Hogarth advertised their location and wares:

> from the old Frock-shop the corner of the Longwalk facing the Cloysters, Removed to ye Kings Arms joyning to ye Little Britain-gate, near Long Walk. Sells ye best & most Fashionable Ready Made Frocks, suits of Fustian, Ticken & Holland, striped Dimmity & Flanel Waistcoats, blue and canvas Frocks, . . .white stript Dimmitys . . . by Wholesale or Retail, at Reasonable Rates.[15]

History 71, no. 2 (September 1984): 319-342; Elaine S. Abelson, *When Ladies Go A-Thieving: Middle-Class Shoplifters in the Victorian Department Store* (New York: Oxford University Press, 1989).

[13] Mui and Mui, *Shops and Shopkeeping in Eighteenth Century England*, 219-220. For the family partnerships that often operated these businesses see Leonore Davidoff and Catherine Hall, *Family Fortunes: Men and Women of the English Middle Class, 1780-1850* (Chicago: University of Chicago Press, 1987), 193-315.

[14] Mui and Mui, *Shops and Shopkeeping in Eighteenth Century England*, 6. This dearth of records is also true for smaller shops in the nineteenth century.

[15] Mary and Ann Hogarth, 'Trade Cards,' Box XII, John Johnson Collection, Bodleian, Oxford. See also Mui and Mui, *Shops and Shopkeeping*, 239 who date this card from the 1730s.

In the eighteenth and well into the nineteenth centuries, women not only traded with their husbands, but also owned autonomous shops. Married women operated independently, single women, and widows ran retail businesses. Women also participated in retail as dressmakers. In 1826 Mrs. Tomlinson sent out a handbill to 'the Nobility and Gentry' to invite them to her dressmaking shop in New Bond Street, London. Running a rather large shop at which 'first rate French and English talent is constantly employed under her supervision,' Tomlinson sold everything from ball dresses to hats and corsets.[16] This common occupation in the eighteenth and early nineteenth centuries was to decline in pay and status in the course of the nineteenth.

Women participated in such trade despite the traditional common law principle of coverture transferring a married woman's property to her husband. This trading could be accomplished by separating from the husband and hoping he did not find out about the business. Alternatively, a woman whose husband deserted her could get a protection order allowing her to trade as a *femme sole*. Women could also make legal pre-nuptial and post-nuptial agreements with their spouse that permitted them to carry on independent trade.[17] Most common, however, especially in the eighteenth century, was the family run business with both spouses working in a partnership.

By the nineteenth century, commentators complained that women once content to serve behind the counter seemed more interested in consuming goods than selling them. In 1817 Priscilla Wakefield protested: ' . . . for what tradesman would venture to burden himself with a wife, who, by her mistaken ambition of gentility, would consume all the produce of his industry . . ..'[18] An 1845 book on how to succeed in business warned prospective retailers: 'a gentle considerate helpmate will cheer and assist him; a vulgar, dressy, ostentatious woman will be his ruin.'[19] As gentility and middle-class status became more dependent on de-emphasizing the role of women in the household as producers[20] and accentuating their role as consumers and displayers of goods, English society focused on

---

[16] Mrs. Tomlinson, 'Women's Clothing and Millinery,' September 1826, Box III, John Johnson Collection, Bodleian, Oxford. See also Miss Smart, 'Trade Cards,' Box XII, John Johnson Collection, Bodleian, Oxford, for a similar advertisement. In the nineteenth century the image of the oppressed seamstress worn out by overwork and poor pay overshadowed the earlier status of dressmaking. See The Dressmaker, 'Trades and Professions,' Box 3, John Johnson Collection, Bodleian, Oxford. This illustration is of a young woman worn out by close needlework and poor pay—pictured working by her candle at night. See also Helen E. Roberts, 'Marriage, Redundancy, and Sin' in *Suffer and Be Still: Women in the Victorian Age*, ed. Martha Vicinus (Bloomington: Indiana University Press, 1973), 58-63.

[17] 'Trading By Married Women,' *The Draper* (London) 7 January 1870.

[18] Priscilla Wakefield, *Reflections on the Present Condition of the Female Sex* (London: Barton, Harvey, and Darton, 1817), 113.

[19] C.B.C. Amicus, *How to Rise in Life* (London: Longman, Brown, Green, and Longmans, 1845), 48.

[20] See especially Davidoff and Hall, *Family Fortunes*, 314-315.

women as buyers rather than sellers. In Trollope's 1870 novel *Brown, Jones and Robinson*, George Robinson describes his ideal wife: 'I love to see beauty enjoying itself gracefully. My idea of a woman is incompatible with the hard work of the world. I would fain do that myself, so that she should ever be lovely.'[21] Although women still worked in retail trade, the era dominated by the small family run shop was disappearing.

Another change in consumer culture along with the trend away from the small, family shop was the transformation of the geography of London shopping in the late 1700s and early 1800s. London grew rapidly in the nineteenth century and with it shopping districts were born, thrived, and fell. More traditional shopping areas like Fleet Street, the Strand and Cheapside gave way to the primacy of the West End, at least in the category of upper-class and the best of middle-class shops.[22] Numerous successful retail shops trace their origins to Regent Street and Oxford Street. Peter Robinson, Debenhams, Marshall and Snelgrove, Harrods, Harvey Nichols, and Swan and Edgar are just a few of the shops tracing their beginnings to the early nineteenth-century boom of the West End.[23] Most of these businesses began as drapery or haberdashery shops.

Changing Geographies and Changing Scale

The West End

The West End, including Piccadilly, Oxford Street, Bond Street, and Regent Street, emerged as London's and England's preeminent shopping district by both evolution and architectural planning. Old Bond Street, begun in 1686, long housed the elite shops of the aristocracy. Later, when New Bond Street was added to its length, the old shopkeepers complained about the association with the new retail establishments. Although not possessing the tradition of elite service of Old Bond Street, New Bond Street had its share of fashionable shops in the nineteenth century and benefited from the association between Bond Street and aristocratic shopping. Bond Street, old and new, was also a center for theatres and circulation libraries in the nineteenth century.[24]

The area of Piccadilly in the West End, roughly the area between Coventry Street and Albemarle Street, now best known for the circus connecting the thoroughfares of Regent Street and Piccadilly, also emerged around the same time as a retail center. Throughout the eighteenth century the area of Piccadilly remained a haunt of the aristocracy, a place of fashionable shops and grand houses

---

[21] Anthony Trollope, *The Struggles of Brown, Jones, and Robinson: By One of the Firm* (London: Smith, Elder & Co., 1870), 136.

[22] 'Shopping in London,' *The Living Age* 1, 4 (June 1844), 250.

[23] Thelma H. Benjamin, *London Shops & Shopping* (London: Herbert Joseph Limited, 1934), 159-176.

[24] *Ibid.*, 108-109.

including those of the Earls of Clarendon and Burlington. The famed grocers Fortnum and Mason originated in Piccadilly in 1708 and moved to their present site in Piccadilly in the mid-1800s.[25]

Regent Street, which crosses through Piccadilly Circus, was an intricately planned affair. Intended to connect the Regent's home at Carlton House with the newly dubbed Regent's Park, this brainchild of Regency architect Thomas Nash changed the face of the West End. Between 1818 and 1820 smaller streets and homes were swept away to accommodate this newer, wider street with its fine shops. Nash even built colonnades from Glasshouse and Vigo Streets to Piccadilly to shelter aristocratic shoppers and loungers. Although some complained that the fashionable street provided a rendezvous for the debauched upper classes, others enjoyed the new shopping and entertainment opportunities it afforded.[26]

Along with fashionable loungers, Regent Street hosted many of the finest stores of nineteenth-century London. The men's clothing firm of Messrs. Nicoll and Company settled into the newly built street and became legendary for fine men's clothing including serving among others, the Duke of Wellington. When George Swan's original shop was demolished to make way for Piccadilly circus, Swan reopened his drapery firm at numbers 9 and 10 Regent Street in 1821. Swan and his younger assistant William Edgar made over £80,000 during their first year in operation at the new address. Hodge and Lowman, a successful drapery emporium, soon joined them in Regent Street at numbers 252-254. These shops sold material and accessories for clothing, fans, gloves, hats, umbrellas and even underwear.[27]

Intended as the avenue of the fashionable, Regent Street also became the thoroughfare of fashion in England. John Tallis's *London Street Views* from the late 1830s describes it as a place of 'palace-like shops, in whose broad showy windows are displayed articles of the most splendid description, such as the neighboring world of wealth and fashion are daily in want of.'[28] In Regent Street one could buy almost anything including 'every novelty in fancy manufactures' from 'Paris, Vienna, and Frankfort.'[29] However, Regent Street, like Bond Street, began as the playground and shopping domain of the nobility and gentry. Inevitably, the association of the West End with the best in shopping attracted

---

[25] Arthur Dasent, *Piccadilly in Three Centuries* (London: Macmillan and Co., Limited, 1920); A.M. Broadley, *Piccadilly 1686-1906* (London, 1906), 8 and 16.

[26] Nicolls and Regent Street, 'Women's Clothing and Millinery,' Box I, John Johnson Collection, Bodleian, Oxford; Peter Jackson, *George Scharf's London: Sketches and Watercolours of a Changing City, 1820-50* (London: John Murray, 1987), 129. In 1848 the colonnades were destroyed at the request of shop owners who feared the prostitutes and loungers underneath them discouraged respectable trade.

[27] Nicolls and Regent Street, 'Women's Clothing and Millinery,' Box I, John Johnson Collection, Bodleian, Oxford; Hermione Hobhouse, *A History of Regent Street* (London: Macdonald and Jane's, 1975), 48-50 and 95.

[28] John Tallis, *London Street Views*, No. 4, Regent Street (London: John Tallis, 1838-40) 1.

[29] T.A. Simpson & Co., 'Bazaars and Sales,' Box I, advertisement from unknown source, John Johnson Collection, Bodleian, Oxford.

larger-scale stores with a somewhat wider clientele: the middling folk found their way into the West End.

The wealth of the West End spread north to Oxford Street in the early to mid-nineteenth century. By the late 1830s Oxford Street consisted 'almost exclusively of retail shops.' At no. 61, Messrs. Williams and Sowerby offered 'foreign velvets, satins, and fancy articles of the richest description.' Buying directly from their suppliers, Williams and Sowerby were able to offer the height of fashion at a more reasonable cost. According to John Tallis, this shop was nicknamed "the Grande Centre of Distribution" by manufacturers on the continent.[30] Oxford Street, Regent Street, and Bond Street were the center for elite retail trade, the envy of the rising middling classes, and the location for many retail innovations like emporiums and department stores—two types of retail establishments that placed aristocratic dreams of consumption within the grasp of the non-landed classes.

Along with retail, the West End was an area of fashionable entertainment like the 'picture' shows of dioramas and panoramas including Barker's in Leicester Square. When tired of shopping, people could also visit the small museums such as Sir Ashton Lever's. One of the West End's retail innovations, the Burlington Arcade, an architectural wonder that was part entertainment and part shopping avenue, was founded in the late 1820s.[31]

Arcades

One of the first signs of a shift in traditional retail culture in the early nineteenth century was the emergence of shopping arcades in London and other densely populated cities in England.[32] These arcades combined aspects of the modern mall—the advantage of being weatherproof and providing a variety of proprietors under one roof—with characteristics of elite eighteenth-century shopping. Despite their impressive arches and covered walkways, these arcades still consisted of separate shops with separate entrances and windows. Most notable and perhaps the most successful of shopping arcades, the Burlington Arcade in London represented the arcade ideal with its convenient, clean, rainproof walkway guarded by beadles[33] against the entrance of a non-elite public. The Burlington Arcade, which still operates in its original location today, combined the high society shopping experience of late-eighteenth-century London with an indoor twist including shops with 'bowed fronts looking for all the world like some quaint array of eighteen

---

[30] John Tallis, *London Street Views*, No. 34, Oxford Street—Division II (London: John Tallis, 1838-40), 1-2.

[31] See E. Beresford Chancellor, *The West End Yesterday and Today* (London: The Architectural Press, 1926), 7-13; Erika D. Rappaport, "The Halls of Temptation:' Gender, Politics, and the Construction of the Department Store in Late Victorian London,' *Journal of British Studies* 35, no. 1 (January 1996): 62.

[32] Lancaster, *The Department Store*, 8.

[33] Named after the minor parish officials in English churches who kept order and ushered, the beadles of the Burlington Arcade were a mixture of private policemen and modern doormen.

century opera boxes . . .. And then too the small squares of glass, such a relief from the great pompous expanses of plate glass [which] give a scale to the goods that they shield.'[34] This haven for the wealthy shopper opened in 1819.

Built between Burlington House and Bond Street in 1819 by Lord George Cavendish and designed by Samuel Mare, the Burlington Arcade quickly became the shopping haunt of fashionable London specializing in luxury goods and services.[35] The Arcade housed a variety of traders including the famous P. Truefitt, who advertised:

Ladies & Gentlemen's
Fashionable Hair Cutter's
'Dyer'
Manufacturer of
ORNAMENTAL HAIR
and Dealer in English and Foreign Perfumery.[36]

Truefitt suffered along with other Burlington Arcade shopkeepers in an 1836 fire. The fire report reveals that in 1836 there were around sixty people trading in the arcade including a boot-maker, a bookseller, two hosiers, a milliner, a jeweler, and another hairdresser in addition to Truefitt. At least two of the shops were reported as being owned by unmarried women, 'Miss Stamford,' a hosier, and Louisa Asser, proprietor of the child-bed linen warehouse.[37]

The wide variety of retailers in the arcade may seem similar to that of modern covered shopping malls; however, the public nature of the arcade was tempered by its exclusivity. The arcade emphasized fashion and genteel display under its arches. Customers and would-be customers were aware of this emphasis. In Charles Dance's 1839 play, *The Burlington Arcade*, a character explained the importance of fashionable appearance in the Arcade: 'I havn't watched the Burlington Arcade so long without learning the principal ingredients in the formation of a dandy. I'll buy a pair of straw-coloured kid gloves—and a new hat—and a shirt front—and a satin stock—and after that, if I've money enough left, I'll buy a coat, and a pair of never-whisper-ems.'[38] The upper-class atmosphere of the Arcade was further assured by a patrolling beadle in full livery who made sure that only the well-dressed and respectable were allowed entrance.

---

[34] H.J.B., *Burlington Arcade: Being a Discourse on Shopping for the Elite* (London: Favil Press, 1925), 18-19.

[35] *Ibid.*, 3, 13. See also Benjamin, *London Shops & Shopping*, 113-114.

[36] P. Truefitt, 'Trade Cards,' Box XII, John Johnson Collection, Bodleian, Oxford. Satirized as a 'Mr. Wigton' in Charles Dance's 1839 Burletta *The Burlington Arcade*, Truefitt represented the high service, luxury product, fashion-oriented purveyors for which the arcade was known. See Charles Dance, *The Burlington Arcade; A Burletta, In Theatre*.

[37] *Times*, (London) 28 March 1836. Note: all following references to the *Times* are to the *London Times*.

[38] Dance, *The Burlington Arcade*, 11.

In the play, Dance's beadle character complained: 'Now, I should be glad to be told what can be better known all over the whole world, than that people is not to wear pattens and spread umbrellas through the Burlington Arcade; and yet half of my precious time is taken up in repeating on it.' When he was not shouting at customers acting or dressing inappropriately, Dance's satirized beadle spent most of his time shouting at 'dirty little boys' to keep them out of the shelter of the Arcade.[39]

Although innovative in its architecture and the number of vendors it housed, the Burlington Arcade thrived on its reputation for exclusivity and luxury items— the heart of eighteenth-century aristocratic retail. It remained popular for decades.[40] George Augustus Sala, however, writing in 1858, mocked the outdated attention to aristocratic luxury goods and service in the Arcade:

> I don't think there is a shop in its enceinte where they sell anything that we could not do without. Boots and shoes are sold there, to be sure, but what boots and shoes—varnished and embroidered and be-ribboned figments . . .. Paintings and lithographs for gilded boudoirs, collars for puppy dogs, and silver-mounted whips for spaniels, pocket handkerchiefs, in which an islet of cambric is surrounded by an ocean of lace, embroidered garters and braces, fillagree boudices, firework-looking bonnets, scent bottles, sword-knobs, brocaded sashes, worked dressing-gowns, inlaid snuff-boxes, and kibalas of all descriptions . . ..[41]

Although Sala lampooned the non-utilitarian frippery of the Arcade's wares, such status-announcing 'useless' goods, once associated only with the genteel classes, formed the foundation of middle-class consumer culture in the nineteenth century. Shopping arcades brought the older, aristocratic individualized shopping for luxury goods into an innovative nineteenth-century form.

Its imitators reflect the success of the Burlington Arcade in the early nineteenth-century. Named in honor of Lord Lowther, Commissioner of Woods and Forests, the similarly styled Lowther Arcade opened in the Strand in 1830.[42] However, no imitator surpassed the Burlington Arcade, that temple to the consumer culture of the wealthy just after the Napoleonic Wars. With high quality goods and individualized service, the Burlington Arcade remained as it was designed: ' . . . essentially intimate . . . Here is none of the vast impersonality that characterises the mighty emporia of our vast cities; individual attention, and individual courtesy, and individual goods appeal to those for whom shopping is still a lingering delight, a delectable pastime . . ..'[43]

---

[39] *Ibid.*, 12-13.

[40] Leigh Hunt, *A Saunter Through the West End* (London: Hurst and Blackett, 1861), 24.

[41] George Augustus Sala, *Twice Round the Clock: Or The Hours of the Day and Night in London* (New York: Humanities Press, 1971 [1858]), 185.

[42] 'The Lowther Arcade,' *The Mirror of Literature, Amusement, and Instruction*, XIX, 541 (7 April 1832), 210; Chancellor, *The West End Yesterday and Today*, 69.

[43] H.J. B., *Burlington Arcade*, 21-23.

The Innovations of Haberdashers and Linen Drapers

If the Burlington Arcade was the last great achievement of eighteenth-century aristocratic shopping, then we must look beyond its covered architecture for the beginnings of mass consumer culture in the nineteenth century to the firms that eventually transformed themselves into grand emporia and department stores. The shops that most commonly gave birth to these larger stores were already in the vanguard of retail early in the century. Haberdashers and drapers, particularly linen-drapers, experienced a healthy but increasingly competitive trade in the late eighteenth and early nineteenth centuries. Their response to competition varied from increasing the volume and variety of products, to aggressive advertising, uniform open ticket pricing, ready-money sales, and new display techniques like window-dressing.

Originally, haberdashers were small dealers who sold the odds and ends of clothing retail like trimmings, collars, threads, and the decorations associated with women's dress. In the City of London the Haberdasher's Company was first incorporated in the mid-1400s. Beginning as a subset of mercers dealing only in small items, their stalls were in Cheapside.[44] By the early 1800s Haberdashers had their own shops like drapers and the larger shops employed assistants. William Ablett, a draper and haberdasher, served as an assistant in one of these shops in early nineteenth-century London. As a boy he worked until ten o'clock five days a week and until midnight on Saturdays. He described his workplace:

> [P]eople used to chagger and haggle about the price when they wanted to buy anything, and this healthy system of sticking to one price was just coming into vogue, and was the means of saving much time, ours being a pushing and ticketing shop; window dressing also was just then beginning to be made a great point of, and long alleys, and vistas of goods were upon occasions arranged half down that side of the shop where the shelves which contained the goods kept in wrappers, and which were least likely to be wanted or disturbed were kept.[45]

Although using new techniques like fixed, marked prices and using the shop's small windows to display goods, this shop was in many ways still like an eighteenth-century establishment with many goods wrapped in parcels and difficult to reach.

Haberdashers' shops similar to that of Ablett's employer and Mrs. Moore in Grafton Street carried a variety of goods early in the century—a variety and volume that only increased as the century progressed.[46] These early nineteenth-century haberdashers did not sell big-ticket items, but had to be familiar with many

---

[44] 'The Haberdasher's Company,' *The Draper* (London) 28 October 1870.

[45] William Ablett, 'Reminiscences of An Old Draper,' *Warehousemen and Draper's Trade Journal* (London) 15 April 1872; William Ablett, *Reminiscences of An Old Draper* (Sampson, Low, Marston, Seale and Rivington, 1876), 108.

[46] See Moore, formerly Clarkson & Moore, 'Women's Clothing and Millinery,' Box I, John Johnson Collection, Bodleian, Oxford.

different types of goods. *The Haberdasher's Guide* printed in 1826 lists a number of these goods including stay tape, bobbins, cottons, colored sewing cottons, pins, hair pins, needles, bodkins, thimbles, coat binding, carpet binding, venetian binding, and stay laces.[47] These small necessities were the staple business of haberdashers; however, haberdashers increasingly expanded into new and different kinds of goods. E.E. Perkins, writing a *Lady's Shopping Manual* in 1834, claimed that haberdashers often also sold items as varied as 'Reticules and Baskets, Lucifer Boxes, Imitation Cigars, Snap Bracelets, Neck-chains, Watch-guards, Tooth-picks, Tweezers, Thermometers,' and even 'foreign clocks.'[48] Along with traditional haberdashery goods like sewing threads, needles, and yarn and fancy goods like decorative jewelry, haberdashers also began to expand into the territory of the larger fabric dealers, the drapers. Haberdashers soon added linens, calicoes, and printed muslin to their lists of available goods.[49]

Just as haberdashers expanded into drapery fabrics, drapers sometimes added haberdashery departments to their shops for profit and customer convenience. The author of a retail guide in 1826 claimed: [H]aberdashery being now so generally connected with MERCERY and DRAPERY, renders it a business of some importance . . . both in the buying and selling departments.'[50] In London, large, wholesale haberdashery shops kept these mixed shops supplied with accessory goods. In this early period of expansion, advice manuals urged shopkeepers to pay more attention to the small goods of haberdashery departments and not to leave the sale of haberdashery (as was traditionally done) to the youngest and most inexperienced employees. A knowledgeable staff and high turnover rate of these small items could produce hefty profits for haberdashers and those who combined drapery and haberdashery in larger stores.[51]

If haberdashers were the crown princes of early nineteenth-century English clothing retail, drapers were the kings of the trade. They sold the larger, more expensive pieces of fabric varying from everyday linen to velvets and brocades in the fancier shops. Drapery was one of the most remunerative retail trades in the

---

[47] *The Haberdasher's Guide: A Complete Key to All the Intricacies of the Haberdashery Business* (London: R.P. Moore, 1826), 7-35. See also E.E. Perkins, *Haberdashery, Hosiery, and General Drapery; Including the Manchester, Scotch, Silk, Linen, and Woollen Departments, Foreign and Domestic* (London: William Tegg, 1830).

[48] E.E. Perkins, *The Lady's Shopping Manual and Mercery Album; Wherein the Textures, Comparitive Strengths, Lengths, Widths, and Numbers, of every description of Mercery, Hosiery, Haberdashery, Woollen and Linen Drapery, are pointed out for Domestic Economy, and which will be found of great advantage to the Heads of Families and Charitable Institutions for Clothing the Poor* (65, St. Paul's Churchyard, London: T. Hurst, 1834, 103-107. See also Perkins, *Haberdashery, Hosiery, and General Drapery.*

[49] See Perkins, *Haberdashery, Hosiery, and General Drapery.*

[50] *The Haberdasher's Guide*, 3.

[51] Perkins, *Haberdashery, Hosiery, and General Drapery*, vii.

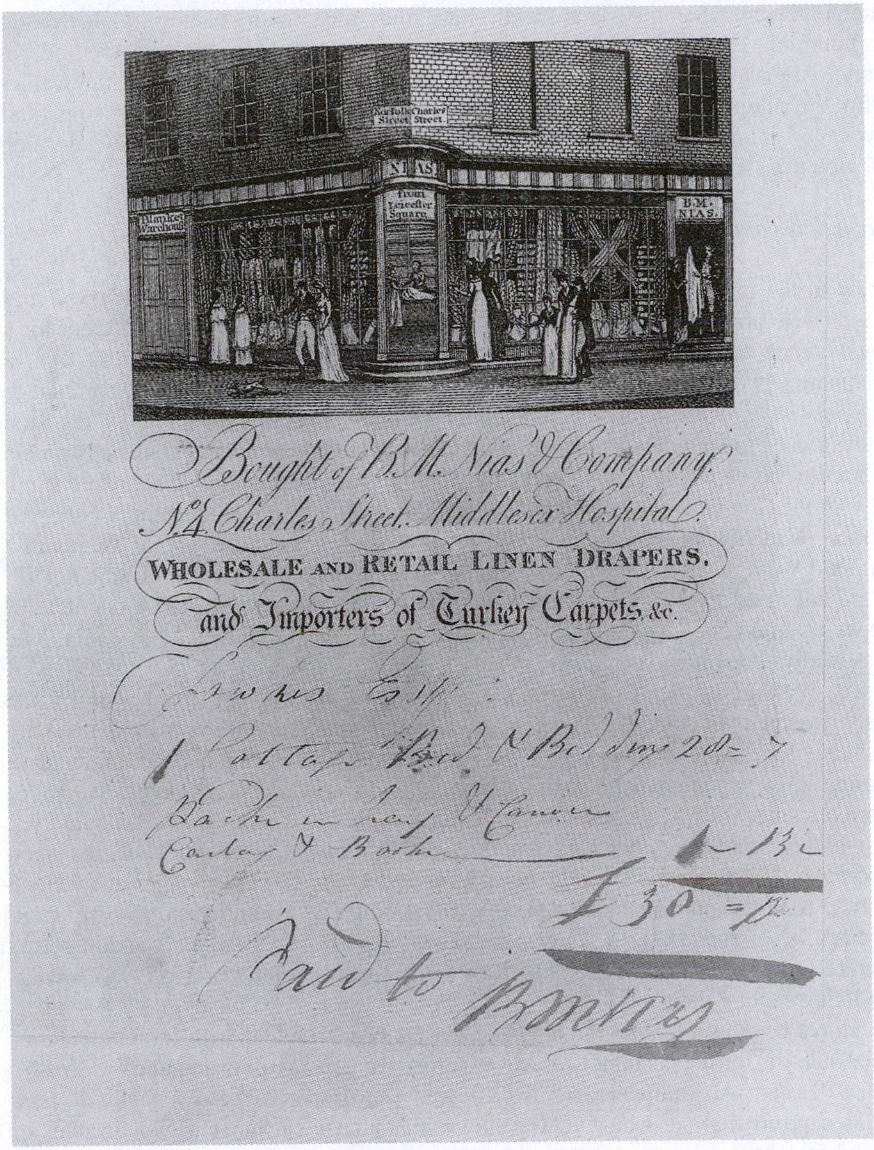

Figure 1.1 This elaborate bill heading from Nias and Company clearly illustrates ladies both 'window shopping' and counter shopping in the large retail establishment. Nias and Co. Wholesale and Retail Linen Drapers, 1825. Bodleian Library, University of Oxford: John Johnson Collection; Bill Headings 22 (71).

late eighteenth century and well into the nineteenth century.[52] Increased competition, especially in London, encouraged drapers to adopt new methods in trade. Arguably, drapers may have been the first and most successful innovators with the adoption of set prices, ready-money sale, aggressive advertising, and expanded shops as early as the later 1700s. London witnessed a popular adoption of such practices in the first few decades of the nineteenth century.

Cash Sales and Open Ticket Pricing

Prior to the nineteenth century, in most retail shops prices were not marked and prices were arrived at through a process of haggling. Prices might be different for a loyal versus an occasional customer; or if the shop owner's rent was due, a fortunate customer might luck upon a 'bargain' sale. This haphazard approach to pricing fell into disuse in the nineteenth century. Drapers were one of the first retail groups to insist on set-prices clearly marked. They convinced their customers to accept the new method by promising that the lowest possible prices were used. One of the first firms known for this technique in London was the drapery shop of Robert Waitham on the corner of Fleet Street. A former employee of Waitham's named Everington soon spread the practice in his competing shop on Ludgate Hill. Waitham's and Everington's were not shops for the masses, but had a clientele of upper middle-class women and specialized in expensive shawls from India. The reasons for the shift to set-prices are varied.[53]

At Waitham's and Everington's the new pricing system saved women the embarrassment of price haggling. Marked prices made shopping a more friendly exercise for ladies by making it easier to browse and purchase items with a minimum of argument with shopkeepers or shop assistants. However, set-prices were also useful for stores catering to lower middle-class customers who could tell at a glance whether or not they could afford an item. The adoption of this open pricing system in the nineteenth century catered to the female shopper and helped democratize the purchasing process by alleviating the intimidation of 'mystery' pricing. Also, according to Ablett, the sheer volume of the larger London stores required marked prices for the benefit of the assistants selling the goods as well as the ladies buying them.[54]

Stores began promising the absolute lowest price marked with 'no abatement.' The trade-off for the customer for lower set-prices was the new demand for 'ready-money' sales. An immediate return allowed the draper to have a faster if less-inflated profit than he would under the credit system. In the first few decades of the nineteenth century the term 'ready money' became more and more frequent in the advertisements of drapery shops. A business advice writer credits Mr. Flint of London's Grafton House as one of the first large-scale drapery shops established

---

[52] See especially Mui and Mui, *Shops and Shopkeeping*, 234-236.

[53] William Ablett, *Reminiscences of An Old Draper*, 60-61.

[54] See *Ibid.*, 61. By the 1860s this practice had become the norm. See *A Handy Guide for the Draper and Haberdasher* (20 Paternoster Row, London: F. Pitman, 1864), 16.

on the principle of ready-money payment. Flint's Grafton House was a favorite shopping haunt of the Austen family where Jane Austen bought gowns for her sister and mother in the earliest years of the nineteenth century.[55] Like Flint, Andrew Kelly, an Oakham linen and woolen draper who also dabbled in hats, hosiery, and haberdashery, promised low prices 'FOR READY MONEY ONLY' in his October 1829 list of goods.[56] E. Reeve, a draper and tailor with a shop in the Lowther Arcade in his advertisement described 'Ready Cash' as the 'only Terms, on which E.R. can do Business.'[57] By 1864 *A Handy Guide for the Draper and Haberdasher* described ready money as the only way for drapers and haberdashers to succeed in business: 'If possible sell for ready money only. The difference between that and book-debts is much greater than people generally suppose. Twelve months' credit is equal . . . to eight per cent. . . . No cash, no goods.'[58] Ready money did not completely replace credit sales; however, it was a sign of the new retail trade.

Set-pricing and cash sales were typically used in conjunction with other new retail methods like more aggressive advertising. Trade cards had been in use throughout the 1700s; however, by the end of the century trade cards began to take on a more modern appearance. A linen draper named Cowlam on Leicester Square advertised on his card that he possessed 'the largest assortment of Plain and Worked Muslins, of any House in England.'[59] Andrew Kelly, the draper who was so insistent on ready-money sales, also produced a large, single-page advertisement in October 1829:

His ready-made cloaks, are remarkably low
of Ladies' Pelisse Cloths, he has for inspection,
An excellent stock, well worth their attention.
Of blankets he's taken particular care
To lay a good stock in, before they get dear;
To those who would purchase he offers a chance
For as Winter approaches, they'll surely advance.
As the times are so bad, and the wages so small,
He will use well those servants, that give him a call.[60]

---

[55] Amicus, *How to Rise in Life*, 44-47; Adburgham, *Shops and Shopping*, 4.

[56] Andrew Kelly, 19 October 1829, 'Women's Clothing and Millinery,' Box 1, John Johnson Collection, Bodleian, Oxford.

[57] E. Reeve, 'Women's Clothing and Millinery,' Box I, John Johnson Collection, Bodleian, Oxford. See also an 1834 advertisement for Hodge and Lowman who also insist on 'Ready Money.' Hodge & Lowman, 1834, 'Bill Headings,' Box 16, John Johnson Collection, Bodleian, Oxford.

[58] *A Handy Guide for the Draper and Haberdasher*, 31.

[59] Cowlam, 'Trade Cards,' Box XXI, John Johnson Collection, Bodleian, Oxford. See also for another example Isaac Newton, 'Trade Cards,' Box XXI, John Johnson Collection, Bodleian, Oxford.

[60] Andrew Kelly, 'Women's Clothing and Millinery,' John Johnson Collection. This 'draper's list' was probably used as an advertising handbill and distributed to customers and possible customers near the shop.

Although Kelly's advertisement seems unsophisticated to modern eyes, it illustrates an important shift from the simple trade card to the handbills and newspaper advertisements of the nineteenth century.

Larger Premises

Differing in technique from their predecessors, many of the new shops also differed in scale. The small-fronted, intimate sized-shop of the 1700s gave way to more extensive premises. Some of these were purposely built as large shops; others were successful small shops that expanded into ever-grander stores with multiple addresses. The February 1819 letter advertisement of another larger-scale shop, the new shop of White and Greenwell in Oxford Street, indicates that this drapery shop had all of the ingredients of the new retail:

> [T]he above Establishment, . . . has since undergone considerable alterations, rendering it very commodious, and adapting it for a most extensive Trade; . . . with a very choice, elegant, and fashionable assortment of every description of Goods, usually kept by LINEN DRAPERS, MERCERS, HOSIERS, HABERDASHERS, and LACEMEN. . . . Goods of a SUPERIOR QUALITY, but at Prices UNUSUALLY LOW; and we assure you, that it is our determination to offer every Article EXTREMELY CHEAP; and we wish much, to impress on those Ladies who may be pleased to honor us with their Article, as all our Goods will invariably be offered at WHOLESALE PRICES,—our ONLY TERMS being Prompt Payment.[61]

In 1819 White and Greenwell were already promising the goods of different retail specialists like hosiers under one 'commodious' roof along with exceptional selection, cheap prices, and all for cash only payment. Vendors like White and Greenwell were the heralds of the new consumer culture.

The new pattern of retail was drawn from traditional drapers' and haberdashers' shops. Its most successful pioneers became nineteenth-century household names. One of these was James Shoolbred who opened up a small store in Tottenham Court Road in 1817 when the area was becoming fashionable as a suburb. Under the patronage of the gentry, the store quickly grew from a typical draper's shop to a large store and eventually a department store.[62] At Tottenham House Shoolbred offered a variety of goods including 'Tapestry and Brussels Carpets of superior quality . . . the finest makes in Velvet Carpets, in seamless

---

61 White and Greenwell, Commerce House, 61, Oxford Street, London, 16 February 1819, 'Trade Cards,' Box XII, John Johnson Collection, Bodleian, Oxford. See also a bill from the shop of Nias & Company, wholesale and retail linen drapers on Leicester Square in the West End in 1825. The bill has a detailed illustration of this large, well-stocked shop with its windows stuffed with displayed goods. Nias & Co., 'Bill Headings,' Box 22, no. 71, John Johnson Collection, Bodleian, Oxford.

62 Ablett, 'Reminiscences of An Old Draper'; See Adburgham, *Shops and Shopping*, 13; William Ferry, *A History of the Department Store* (New York: Macmillan, 1960), 11.

squares and by the yard . . . offered for sale at exceptional low prices . . ..'[63] From a large-scale drapery establishment Shoolbred's blossomed into an emporium and finally a department store in the second half of the nineteenth century. It remained at the Tottenham Road location until 1930.[64]

Another draper's shop that grew along similar lines was that of John Howell, founder of Howell and James. Born in North Wraxall, Wiltshire in 1776, he worked a variety of jobs including errand boy for a book dealer in Bath. Finally, he gained a position in Harding's linen drapery in Pall Mall where he eventually became a lace buyer and partner. Soon after Nash's Regent Street was completed in the early 1820s, Howell established his own separate shop there.[65] Like Shoolbred's, Howell and James's shop went far beyond simple drapery. An 1847 bill from the shop lists silk mercery, drapery, haberdashery, furriery, and lace vending as part of the shop's operation. By 1847, they also sold millinery with 'Court and Ball Dresses' and had separate rooms for jewelry and perfumes. Preferring ready money, for which they allowed a five-percent discount, Howell and James also gave discounts for a three-month short-term credit and had special arrangements for Christmas.[66] Both Shoolbred and Howell are examples of shopkeepers who began with eighteenth-century style businesses and built them into nineteenth-century 'emporiums' by the end of their lifetimes.

Emporiums

Eventually, many of these larger shops turned into 'emporiums,' trading every type of retail clothing and putting out of business speciality shops like shawl shops, hosiers, and lace vendors whose trade they took up.[67] William Lancaster has argued that the 1830s and 40s in England witnessed the first emporium-style shops; large-scale enterprises with fixed, marked prices and accepting cash payment. However, Lancaster identifies the northern retail stores in northern industrial cities as the first true emporiums.[68] However, these northern stores were merely combining methods that had long been employed by London retail shops. One of the founders of the first of these retail emporiums in the North was Emerson Muschamp Bainbridge. Bainbridge learned his trade at the large London silk and shawl warehouse of Lewis and Allenby in Regent Street, and then returned to Newcastle to begin his own drapery establishment. He implemented new methods, most importantly among them ready-money payment. Speedier

---

[63] James Shoolbred & Co., 'Bazaars & Sales,' Box I, John Johnson Collection, Bodleian, Oxford.

[64] Ferry, *A History of the Department Store*, 11.

[65] 'The Late Mr. John Howell Linendraper,' *The Draper* (London) 5 April 1872.

[66] See Howell & James, 14 July 1847, 'Bill Headings,' Box 18, John Johnson Collection, Bodleian, Oxford.

[67] For examples of these various vendors see 'Shopping in London,' *The Living Age*, 1, 4 (June 1844), 253; Perkins, *The Lady's Shopping Manual and Mercery Album*, 81; Ward, Lace Man, 'Trade Cards,' Box XXI, John Johnson Collection, Bodleian, Oxford.

[68] Lancaster, *The Department Store*, 3-4, 1-14.

realization of profit allowed him to offer quality goods at lower prices. By 1849 his store had twenty-three separate departments.[69] By the 1870s, Bainbridge was a figure of not only local but also national importance in English retail.[70]

Stores like Bainbridge's and his Manchester competitors, Kendal, Milne and Faulkner,[71] mark the era of English stores too large to simply be called shops, stores that had their origins in the innovations of late eighteenth-century retail and the increasing competition of London retail trade. Lancaster differentiates these Northern stores from their London rivals, in part by emphasizing the lower middle- and upper working-class origins of the Northern shops' clientele.[72] After all, the palatial London stores still relied heavily on the patronage of the gentry for their success, and even shops like Howell and James, which preferred ready money, did not give up credit entirely. However, London emporiums welcomed the trade of at least the middle classes, and there is strong evidence that the innovative methods utilized by these shops began much earlier.

By the 1840s and 50s, the term and the concept of retail 'emporiums' became an established part of popular culture. More than just larger in scale, for the critics, who ranged from traditional retailers to satirists, the new stores had unseemly associations with dubious sales methods and an emphasis on display. Profit in the new stores depended on volume sales. Some found the pushy sales methods used to achieve this volume distasteful. In 1859 a writer in *Chamber's Edinburgh Journal* described such a shop:

> [A] large new shop—no 'emporium,' for so the handbills with a splendid vignette at the top, displaying bales of Irish linen, and rolls of silk, bound together with wreaths of roses, designated it—was opened hard by. . . . It was 'a shop on the new plan;' and the old-fashioned people of this locality, accustomed to quieter doings, were 'put out' with the wide shop, and its two counters, and the staff of assistants, male and female, who bustled about, and asked if you wanted 'anything more', before they had served you with what you came to purchase, and teased you with 'wonderful bargains' of gloves and flowers, when you were inquiring the price of flannel.[73]

Large expanses of counters, advertising, bright window displays, and a staff of aggressive assistants went along with the marked prices and ready-money payment of the new shops.

The new emporiums, however, also had their supporters. London shoppers voted with their pocketbooks. In an 1834 shopping guide, E. Perkins particularly recommended shopping at Donovan's Irish Linen Company in Bloomsbury Square

---

[69] *Ibid.*, 8-10; Adburgham, *Shops and Shopping*, 43.
[70] William Ablett dedicated his memoirs in part to the successful Newcastle draper. See Ablett, *Reminiscences of An Old Draper*, v-vi.
[71] For the concurrent rise of Kendal, Milne and Faulkner see Lancaster, *The Department Store*, 9-13.
[72] *Ibid.*, 13.
[73] 'Old London Shops and Shopkeepers,' *Chamber's Edinburgh Journal*, 31 (1859), 372.

because of the 'greater assortment of linen goods at this establishment than is generally kept by the drapers and mercers.' This large drapery establishment first opened in 1800 and expanded to a massive trade.[74] Even mourning drapers adopted the new plan of emporium shops. W.C. Jay was the largest and most famous warehouse for mourning cloth and accessories in mid-nineteenth century London. The shop was so large that it occupied both numbers 247 and 249 in Regent Street. Jay's lavishly illustrated trade card touted: 'Established for the Sale of every Article Requisite for Court, Family or Complimentary Mourning.' The fashionable mourning accessories were housed in a multiple story shop with plate-glass windows.[75] By the mid-1870s there were emporium-sized drapery and haberdashery establishments in many different parts of London, especially in the West End.[76]

Emporiums changed both the scale of selling and method of consumption. In the process they heralded the eventual decline of the small operator as was noted in 1853: 'We have, in fact, now . . . examples of retail-trades carried on, so to speak, by wholesale. The snug shop under the control of its single proprietor . . . is transformed into a monster establishment, which has disembowelled a dozen houses to make room for its stock—which . . . does away with middlemen of every class—buys it raw . . ..'[77] Such shops, argued critics, would not only force the 'small trader . . . to retire from the field,' but would also do away with the need for wholesale houses, because high-volume retailers bought goods directly. Actually, many of the emporium shops sold both to individual customers and to smaller dealers, making both retail and wholesale profits. This change, however, could translate into lower cost for the individual buyer who could buy more goods without paying for the multiple profits of 'middlemen.'[78]

By 1855 the Bon Marché, the first French department store, had opened in Paris, and retail emporiums had graced London and some of England's larger city centers since the late 1830s. Separating the emerging department stores from the older emporiums, Lancaster cites the class differences between the 'mature bourgeoisie' eager to exploit their new status in the new department stores like the Bon Marché and the lower-middle class who demanded quality goods cheaply at English emporiums.[79] However, emporiums also sold items less expensive but still redolent of luxury and fashion like silk ribbons, lace, and gloves. The lower middle classes seemed as interested in these 'luxuries' as their upper middle-class

---

[74] Perkins, *The Lady's Shopping Manual and Mercery Album*, 66.

[75] See W.C. Jay, 'Trade Cards,' Box XII, John Johnson Collection, trade card, Box XII, Bodleian, Oxford. See also Adburgham, *Shops and Shopping*, 65.

[76] Stores like Howell and James, Swan and Edgar, and Shoolbred's in the West End were joined by shops like Messrs. Venables and Company of Whitechapel and Allan and Company of St. Paul's Churchyard in the business of large-scale retail. See William Ablett, *Reminiscences of An Old Draper* (London: Sampson Low, Marston, Searle, and Rivington, 1876,) 188.

[77] 'London Shops, Old and New,' *Chamber's Edinburgh Journal*, 20 (1853), 251.

[78] See 'London Shops, Old and New,' *Chamber's Edinburgh Journal*, 20 (1853), 252.

[79] Lancaster, *The Department Store*, 16-18.

counterparts. Although not yet on the scale of full-sized department stores, the massive emporiums of mid-nineteenth-century retail, like the earlier large drapery and haberdashery shops of the late 1700s and early 1800s, signaled the beginning of a new era of retail.[80]

The Birth of More Modern Retail Innovations, 1800-1850

Drapers and haberdashers themselves were amazed at the modernizing leaps in retail and warned business owners to take heed of the changes. In 1875 J.W. Hayes warned haberdashers and drapers not to use the old methods of giving 'good measure'—a little more than the yard, foot, or inch requested—to their customers. He also warned against the money-losing practice of giving away small amounts of sewing cotton and pins instead of returning a customer's small change.[81] There was no room for these friendly practices in modern drapery establishments. Ablett, a draper who began his career very early in the nineteenth century, was dazzled by the array of ready-made articles in later nineteenth-century drapery houses. When he began his career most clothing items came from cloth bought from the bolt although some shops sold pieces already cut for sewing. By contrast in the 1870s: '[T]here are departments exclusively for women's petticoats, mantles, &c.; . . . there are wholesale houses which keep nothing else but gentleman's made-up neckties . . ..' The drapers were the first to begin this trend by providing women's cloaks and capes for sale ready-made.[82] Drapers and haberdashers were also some of the first establishments to promote the sales of their goods through ornate window displays.

Chamber's Edinburgh Journal compared those first eighteenth-century attempts by haberdashers and mercers at window display to the mid-nineteenth-century method of plate-glass display: 'How dull must the scarlets and orange

---

[80] For a good illustration of the scale of these larger shops see the trade card etching of Lillington's Hosiery, Glove, and London Hat Warehouse, 'Trade Cards,' Box XII, John Johnson Collection, Bodleian, Oxford. According to the illustration, Lillington's had floor to ceiling windows stuffed with displays and a large, open shop with well-stocked shelves also stretching from floor to ceiling. See also Figure 1.1, the detailed illustrations of the extensive drapery establishment of Nias & Co. Nias & Co., 1825, 'Bill Headings,' John Johnson Collection. Nias seemed even larger in scale with windowed facades on both Norfolk Street and Charles Street. A similar illustration of an even larger mid-century shop is that of Smith, Son & Wethered of Pimlico. Their elaborate trade card shows a roomy interior, long counters, multiple-employees, and a circular staircase leading to an upstairs 'linen department.' See Smith, Son & Wethered, Drapers, Hosiers & Haberdashers, 'Trade Cards,' Box XII, John Johnson Collection, Bodleian, Oxford. A more famous shop was W.C. Jay's General Mourning Warehouse which occupied two addresses, nos. 247 and 249 Regent Street and had a full façade of plate-glass windows. See W.C. Jay, 'Trade Cards,' John Johnson Collection.

[81] Hayes, *Hints on Haberdashery and Drapery*, 22-23.

[82] Ablett, *Reminiscences of An Old Draper*, 54-55. See also Andrew Kelly, 'Women's Clothing and Millinery,' John Johnson Collection.

colours have looked, how faded the lilacs behind those thick dingy, green glass panes, enclosed in their clumsy wooden frames.'[83] Ablett also commented that Everington's, considered one of the finest of early nineteenth-century shops, 'would be considered but a poor, shabby sort of affair now' when compared with even 'second rate draper's shops.'[84] This emphasis on display allowed customers not only to compare prices through shop windows, but also to let them fantasize about ownership, according to Colin Campbell, a hallmark of modern consumer culture.[85]

Although the new emporiums seemed to suffer no lack of customers, many critics found the new improvements unfriendly with their high-volume, large-scale, and impersonal methods. Contemporaries began to romanticize the older-style eighteenth-century family shop just as drapers and haberdashers were celebrating the new modernization of methods. 'Those little low-browed shops—what a contrast to the lofty plate-glass windowed 'establishments' towering four and five stories high!' bemoaned the writer of 'Old London Shops and Shopkeepers' in *Chamber's* in 1859.[86] An article six years earlier decried the disappearance of the simple-fronted, stall-like, one-person shop that still permeated London around 1800.[87] To such critics, the difference between the eighteenth and nineteenth centuries was one of time and quality: 'the buyer bought and the seller sold, with due deliberation, there was time for the low bow, or the courtsey, and the quiet remark about the weather . . . while a modern white-neckclothed assistant, in some 'Crystal Palace Emporium,' would have sold half-a-dozen 'desperate bargains.'[88] Consumption's sheer scale had become overwhelming to those who remembered earlier forms of shopkeeping.

Others were not only upset by the effect on consumption, which by the mid nineteenth century often took place at high-speed in vast emporiums, but also condemned the effect of the new retail on the shopkeeping classes. The author of 'Shopping in London' in the 1840s complained that older methods of

---

[83] 'Old London Shops and Shopkeepers,' *Chamber's Edinburgh Journal*, 31 (1859), 371. See also *Ibid.* for a discussion of the vast displays of a new-style drapery shop.

[84] Ablett, *Reminiscences of An Old Draper*, 89.

[85] See Campbell, *The Romantic Ethic and the Spirit of Modern Consumerism*, 92.

[86] See 'Old London Shops and Shopkeepers,' 369 and see Nancy Cox, *The Complete Tradesman: A Study of Retailing, 1550-1820* (Aldershot: Ashgate, 2000).

[87] See 'London Shops, Old and New,' 251. See also 'Old London Shops and Shopkeepers,' 369. For a good illustration of these simpler eighteenth-century style shops see James Pollard, *The Fruitmarket (The Greengrocer)*, watercolor, 1819, Yale Center for British Art; James Pollard, *Poultry Market*, watercolor, 1819, Yale Center for British Art; James Pollard, *The Meat Market*, watercolor, 1819, Yale Center for British Art.

[88] 'Old London Shops and Shopkeepers,' 371. See also a similar romanticizing of earlier shops written 21 years later by Anthony Trollope. Anthony Trollope, *London Tradesmen* (London: Elkin Mathews & Marrot Ltd., 1927), 93. 'The eleven sketches which compose this volume appeared at intervals in the Pall Mall Gazette from July 10th to September 7th, 1880.'

entrepreneurism allowed individual shopkeepers to become self-made men and rise from the lowest beginnings through their own hard work to 'a valuable magistrate . . . and a public-spirited citizen; in Oxford-street a saddle-maker, in Park Crescent a gentleman of fortune, at the Mansion House a man of law and authority.'[89] Such citizens did not spring from the shop assistants of large linen drapery emporiums. Also, the same writer complained that formerly respectable shopkeepers fell victim to these new methods. Once thriving businesses now inhabited a retail nether-realm: 'These seem to be surviving shops of the last century, which, having fallen into reduced circumstances, have retired from the prosperous thoroughfares to these dusky regions, where presides over their commerce a venerable lady in white hair, and silver spectacles, or a superannuated gentleman, as old as themselves . . ..'[90]

Were the shops of London a 'means of education, and amusement . . ., repositories of taste and virtue, libraries of industry, science, [and] intellect,'[91] or did advertising, ready money, and large-scale emporiums turn them into a circus of greed and consumption? Historians as well as nineteenth-century commentators have succumbed to the temptation of oversimplifying and romanticizing eighteenth-century shops and shopping. The description of eighteenth-century English shops as friendly, family-run businesses with tiny bowed windows and local flavor is only partly accurate. In London and larger cities and towns, these more traditional businesses were already being challenged by new competition and new methods of sale in the second half of the eighteenth century. More modern advertising began in the 1700s with the trade card, handbill, and, later, newspaper advertisements. Drapers and Haberdashers distributing England's production of factory-made cloth goods began to adopt larger volume, lower profit, cash-only sales methods in the late eighteenth century. The West End was also already established as an area for fashion and the fashionable in Georgian England.[92]

The nineteenth century brought a wider use of these relatively new techniques, and the building of Regent Street created a new haven for London retail. Older businesses moved in and formed fresh businesses on a new scale. Likewise, the craze in arcade building occurring in the same time period added a new dimension to English retail, the multiple vendor establishment under one roof. Yet, even the new Burlington Arcade retained the divided characteristics of eighteenth-century street shopping with each shop in its own little enclave. Old Bond Street held onto

---

[89] ' Shopping in London,' *The Living Age*, 1, 4 (June 1844), 251.

[90] *Ibid.*, 254.

[91] *Ibid.*, 250.

[92] For a more detailed discussion of these innovative changes in retail see Mui and Mui, *Shops and Shopkeeping in Eighteenth Century England*, 225-248. Mui and Mui also point to the book trade as helping introduce the ready-money concept and patent medicine makers for spreading the use of advertising. See also Nancy Cox, The *Complete Tradesman: A Study of Retailing, 1550-1820* (Aldershot: Ashgate, 2000) for her discussion of the innovations of early modern English retail.

its origins as aristocratic purveyors. Of all the innovations of the later eighteenth century and first half of the nineteenth century, the most important in the evolution of modern mass consumerism was the spread of the 'monster-shop,' the emporiums derived from larger haberdashery and linen drapers' shops. Shops like Hodge and Lowman's in Regent Street used methods of direct supplies from the manufacturer, aggressive advertising, ready-money sale, window displays and large premises to make the privilege of fashion more affordable. These emporiums of the 1830s, 40s, and 50s were directed not at the masses of working-class people, but at the middling classes. In the space of fifty years London's middling classes learned new shopping habits and the convenience of the better prices and variety of emporium shopping.

There was also a second forerunner of the department store in England, using similar methods of ready-money sale and offering a wide variety of goods. Like the Burlington Arcade, it provided shoppers with multiple vendors under one roof, but unlike an arcade there was no attempt to recreate the intimate setting of the individual eighteenth-century shops within this new retail establishment. Nineteenth-century shopping bazaars presented instead hundreds of feet of open counters contained in an enormous space—even by comparison to the so-called 'monster-shops' of the linen drapers and haberdashers. The shopping bazaar as another forerunner of the department store in England had some of the earliest and most wide-ranging effects on consumer culture.

Chapter 2

Vanity Fairs:
The Growth of Bazaars and Fancy Fairs

A fringed parasol, or a toad-in-the-hole,
A box of japan to hold backy;
Here's a relief for a widow in grief—
A quartern of Hodge's jacky.
—*'The Soho Bazaar'* [1]

Bazaars for Profit, Charity and the 'Reasonable Inclincations' of Ladies

In July of 1838 in Newport a domestic dispute so extraordinary occurred that it found its way into the *Times*. The subject of this argument was a bazaar:

> A woman, by the name of Phillips, wished to attend a fashionable bazaar, . . but her husband objected, . . . upon which she declared if he did not allow her to go she would immediately chop off her finger. . . . strange to say she carried her intention into effect, and no sooner was one off than a second shared the same fate; when with the most extraordinary perseverance, she exclaimed, 'Here's to go at the hand.' The hatchet . . . immediately fell just below the wrist, and severed the whole of the tendons . . . She declared, . . . she would do the samething again rather than any restraint should be put upon her 'reasonable'inclinations.[2]

This woman from Newport was making a statement, be it an extreme one, about the importance of a growing consumer culture, a culture her husband did not accept as a necessary part of existence. A celebration of consumption, the ladies' bazaar, reached its pinnacle of popularity shortly after its invention in the early nineteenth-century. Only a few decades before the Newport incident there would have been no bazaars for Mrs. Phillips to attend.

Bazaars were novelties first proposed just after the Napoleonic wars. In the spring of 1816 established shopkeepers presented Parliament with 'a petition, signed by 1,600 housekeepers and tradesmen, against the new markets opened

---

[1] 'The Soho Bazaar,' n.d. in Hindley, *The Life and Times of James Catnatch*, 194. This text is taken verbatim.

[2] The *Bristol Mirror* quoted in the *Times*, 2 August 1838. Note: all following references to the *Times* are to the *Times* of London.

called Bazaars.'[3] Despite their critics, the commercial shopping bazaars and later charity bazaars became fixtures of early nineteenth-century culture and provided women with a public space for consumption and display. Innovations like open displays recently credited to the *grand magasins* evolved first in bazaars. Luxuriously decorated, bazaars served as markets catering to women where buyers, sellers, and producers were female. In charity bazaars, upper-class women exhibited and sold their own artworks and craft products while buying similar goods produced by other women. For the middle-class and working-class women employed in commercial bazaars, it was a chance at a semi-independent existence as traders. The women of shopping bazaars, customers and stall keepers, bought and sold status-oriented products designed for a female market. Parliamentary petitions, newspaper reports and trials for shoplifting reveal the curiously exhibitionist nature of these new open markets, and the way they helped to feminize the consumer experience as well as prepare England for consumer culture on an even larger scale at the end of the nineteenth century.

In the early nineteenth century, England emerged from the Napoleonic wars as one of the most powerful countries in Europe. Despite the rapidly growing industrial north, London was still the economic center of England, while emerging as the world's financial center as well. At the beginning of the century, London was the world's only city with a population of over one million and it continued to grow throughout the 1800s as London's higher wage rates attracted workers from all over England. Serving as the world's banking center and a magnet for the surrounding populace, London was also the great retail shop of England.[4]

London had long been the center for fashionable goods in England. In the nineteenth century the middle classes followed the earlier examples of the gentry in their thirst for London goods. England's factories kept London retailers well-stocked. The wars with France further encouraged production of stylish English goods when French supplies dwindled during the war.[5] The Napoleonic wars, along with England's other imperial adventures, also acquainted the English better with

---

[3] *Times*, 14 May 1816; Joseph Nightingale, *The Bazaar, Its Origin, Nature, and Objects Explained, and Recommended as an Important Branch of Political Economy; In a Letter to the Rt. Hon. George Rose, M.P.* (London: Davies Michael and Hudson, 1816), 54; Gary Dyer, 'The Vanity Fair of Nineteenth-Century England: Commerce, Women, and the East in the Ladies' Bazaar,' *Nineteenth-Century Literature* 46, no. 2 (September 1991): 204.

[4] See Celina Fox, 'Introduction,' and Martin Daunton, 'London and the World' in *London: World City 1800-1840*, ed. Celina Fox (New Haven: Yale University Press, 1992): 11-20, 21-38; Roy Porter, *A Social History of London* (London: Hamish Hamilton, 1994), 185-204; Asa Briggs, *A Social History of England* (London: Weidenfeld and Nicolson, 1994), 203-217.

[5] For a discussion of the eighteenth century see John Brewer and Roy Porter, eds., *Consumption and the World of Goods* (London: Routledge, 1993). See also, Porter, *A Social History of London*, 199-201, for growth of London shops and Alison Adburgham, *Shops and Shopping: 1800-1914* (London: Barrie and Jenkins, 1964), 1-41.

Near Eastern products and places. Indian cottons especially influenced fabrics and fashion both as imported goods and as fabrics to be imitated by English mills. English retailers in the nineteenth century quickly exploited their access to cheaper products at home and more 'exotic' wares like paisley shawls from India. England's interest in empire extended far beyond the acquisition of colonies or political influence; this growing world power hungered for all things 'exotic'—the material wealth of empire, that vast profusion and richness England perceived as 'the East.'[6]

Commercial Bazaars

'Diddling all London': The Soho Bazaar

The choice of an Eastern appellation for a nineteenth-century English retail innovation is thus not surprising. The first bazaar in England was an amalgam of two types later becoming separate forms—the commercial and the charity bazaar. The Soho Bazaar opened by John Trotter in 1815 was the first English marketplace to style itself a 'bazaar,' and was followed by a quick succession of imitators. A profiteer of the Napoleonic wars, Trotter found a use for his enormous Soho warehouse by founding this 'benevolent' marketplace. Named after the famous eastern markets,[7] the purpose of Trotter's emporium was to give small vendors a chance to sell their wares at a fair profit—from millinery to fancy articles. He claimed he was providing the families of fallen soldiers a means of support. Trotter rented his counter space to vendors for three pence per foot per day.[8] The 300 by 150 foot building housing the bazaar extended from Soho Square to Dean Street and Oxford street. Under one roof it provided counter space for around 160 vendors.[9] Here the 'united stock must form an attractive display of great variety and would allow reduced tradesman to recover their credit and connexions; beginners to form friends and habits before they venture upon more extensive speculations; and artists, artisans, and whole families . . . to vend the produce of

---

[6] Adburgham, *Shops and Shopping*, 11, 54 and 99. See also Dyer, 'Vanity Fair.'

[7] 'The Bazaar,' *The Gentleman's Magazine* 86 (March 1816): 272. See also Dyer, 'Vanity Fair,' 196.

[8] 'The Bazaar,' *Gentleman's Magazine*, 272; *A Visit to The Bazaar*, 5; Joseph Nightingale, *The Bazaar, Its Origin, Nature, and Objects Explained, and Recommended as an Important Branch of Political Economy; In a Letter to the Rt. Hon. George Rose, M.P.* (London: Davies Michael and Hudson, 1816), 7. See also Dyer, 'Vanity Fair,' 196.

[9] Charles Hindley, *The Life and Times of James Catnatch, (Late of the Seven Dials), Ballad Monger* (London: Reeves and Turner, 1878), 193. More conservative estimates of the building's size are quoted by Nightingale in 1816— '270 feet, and on the western side into Dean Street, upwards of 130 feet.' Hindley's figures may be rounded. See Nightingale, *The Bazaar*, 6.

their labour . . ..'[10] Trotter's leviathan retail outlet overshadowed the traditional scale of English shopkeeping. Most London shops were still quite small in footage and in the variety of goods offered. Through this ostensibly benevolent institution, Trotter increased his substantial wealth, created an innovation that frightened British shopkeepers, and became the vanguard of retail in the early to mid-nineteenth century.

The opening of the bazaar brought both praise and criticism. The praise mainly came from supporters of Trotter like Joseph Nightingale who envisioned bazaars as the perfect mixture of capitalism and charity working in unison.[11] However, critics of the bazaar were suspicious of this new development that strayed from traditional modes of retail trade. A ballad, *The Soho Bazaar*, printed by James Catnatch illustrates the critics' position that the bazaar was a sinful place emphasizing display over quality and honesty in trade:

> Ladies in furs, and genmen in spurs,
> Who lollop and lounge about all day:
> The Bazaar in Soho is completely the go—
>   Walk into the shop of Grimaldi!
>   . . .
> Here's a cock'd hat, for an opera flat—
>   Here's a broad brim for a Quaker;
> Here's a white wig for a Chancery prig,
>   And here's a light weight for a baker.
>   Soho Bazaar, &c.[12]

Bazaars seemed to many to serve not as a functional area of trade, but more as a pleasure ground for a dissipated and leisured upper class, emphasizing the shopping experience over the actual goods purchased. Furthermore, the odd variety and mixture of goods contrasted with the more specialized trade of smaller shops and more traditional retailers. Finally, critics accused bazaars of existing as opportunities for fraud and dubious trade: a place where a baker could buy short weights to cheat his customers, where widows could purchase intoxicating liquor. This picture of the bazaar drawn by its detractors contrasted markedly with the image depicted by its supporters who held it up as a great hope for charity and respectable female employment.

Perhaps the suspicions of the new bazaar came partly from its location. Soho had once been the fashionable haunt of nobility, but had experienced some decline since its heyday around 1700. Once the home of the Duke of Monmouth, it was known as 'the place of palaces.' The Duke's house was built by Christopher Wren

---

[10] 'The Bazaar,' *Gentleman's Magazine*, 272.
[11] Nightingale, *The Bazaar*. In this open letter published by Nightingale he defends Trotter's bazaar to gain politicians' support.
[12] 'The Soho Bazaar,' in Hindley, *The Life and Times of James Catnatch*, 194. This text is taken verbatim.

and survived until 1773. Like Monmouth House, Soho experienced its own rise and fall, and although still prestigious in the Georgian era, it suffered along with other areas of London in the nineteenth century when the nobility began to flee London altogether as a site for their main residences. The building of the bazaar was yet another evolution of the once fashionable Soho—this time as a shopping district.[13]

Not all observers saw the new bazaar in Soho as a representation of the area's further decline. Trotter himself feverishly promoted it along with others who believed bazaars would be a successful blend of profit and charity. *A Visit to The Bazaar*, a pro-bazaar children's book and thinly veiled advertisement sold at the Soho Bazaar, sang the praises of the new institution. The heroine of the story, Mrs. Dumford, explains to her children how the Bazaar had enabled a gentlewoman whose family had fallen on hard times to support 'her aged mother and her two helpless brothers. The one you know is a cripple, and the other was born blind.'[14] Yet, the commercial side of the bazaar, in the story as well as in life, quickly overshadowed its 'charitable' purpose. Most of *A Visit to The Bazaar* is dedicated to the sumptuous display and wide variety of goods that entertain and await patrons of the bazaar. The book describes the walls of the bazaar as draped in red cloth with reflective mirrors at each end of the building.[15] The bazaar also boasted a huge dining hall and kitchen with 'dining tables fifty feet in length' where tea and lunches were served.[16] According to *A Visit to The Bazaar*, the Soho establishment contained various retailers including a toymaker, artificial flower maker, seller of English china, hair merchant, shoe maker, gun smith,[17] and a green house that sold exotic plants: "How lovely is the Illicium Floridanum with its large red flower! . . . I must purchase one on purpose that I may enjoy the scent. It comes from Florida."[18] The bazaar also contained a milliner, chemist, print seller, grocer, furrier, dressmaker, brush maker, bookseller and hosier among many others.[19] All of these retailers were available under one roof, and unlike the Palais Royale in Paris, a large, arcaded building subdivided into individual shops, the Soho Bazaar presented a sea of open stalls and counter space.[20]

The Success of Imitators

Immediately prosperous, the Soho Bazaar spawned a quick succession of imitators. By 1816 there were at least sixteen other imitators in London alone.[21] The quick succession of imitators remains the most convincing testimony of the appeal of the

---

[13] *The Story of Old Soho* (London: T. Pettitt & Co.,1893), 6 & 23.
[14] *A Visit to The Bazaar*, 2.
[15] *Ibid.*, 11-12.
[16] Nightingale, *The Bazaar*, 59.
[17] *A Visit to The Bazaar*, 27-55.
[18] *Ibid.*, 55.
[19] *Ibid*, 56-88.
[20] Nightingale, *The Bazaar*, 43.
[21] *Ibid.*, 67-68.

new bazaar to English shoppers. Within months of the Soho Bazaar's grand opening, bazaars appeared in Leicester Square, Newman Street, Bond Street, St. James's Street, and the Strand.[22] Despite complaints that as a profession, trade was unstable enough without added competition, bazaars increased in popularity.[23] Yet, despite resistance to bazaars by the 1840s bazaars were an accepted part of the retail scene.[24] According to *Punch*, bazaar shopping required new strategies:

> In bazaar-shopping, beat each stall separately. Many patterns, colours, novelties, conveniences, and other articles will thus strike your eye, which you would otherwise have never wanted or dreamt of. . . . Whatever you think very cheap, that buy, without reference to your need of it; it is a bargain.[25]

Commercial bazaars still flourished in the 1840s, and their 'useless' articles found numerous buyers. Of course, not every establishment was as grand as the Soho or Pantheon Bazaar. The Lowther Bazaar opened opposite to the Lowther Arcade, itself an imitation of the Burlington Arcade. The Opera Colonnade tried to become a successful bazaar, but by 1843 was already 'a spiritless affair.'[26] Others, however, like the Oxford Street Bazaar became a popular shopping haunt for years along with a series of bazaars near the Panorama in Leicester Square.[27] Although these

---

[22] Dyer, 'Vanity Fair,' 197.

[23] Drapers were one of the most commonly bankrupt of all occupations in the nineteenth century. Lester V. Markham, *Victorian Insolvency: Bankruptcy, Imprisonment for Debt, and Company Winding-up in Nineteenth-Century England* (Oxford: Clarendon), 250-251. Dickens describes just such a bankruptcy in his 'Sketches by Boz.' 'Street Sketches No. 2,' *Morning Chronicle* (London) 10 October 1834: 62-63. Dickens also made references to the profusion of goods available in London in *Nicholas Nickelby*. See Hilary M. Schor, 'Urban Things: The Mystery of the Commodity in Victorian Literature' (paper presented to the Interdisciplinary Nineteenth-Century Studies Conference, Santa Cruz, California 7-8 April 1995), 5.

[24] Works ranging from critical poetry to the original petition against Trotter's bazaar demonstrate the resistance of traditional retailers; however, there was no effective movement or organization launched against them by retailers. Christopher Hosgood asserts this political impotence was due to a lack of trade organization in the early part of the century. Christopher Hosgood, 'A 'Brave and Daring Folk'? Shopkeepers and Trade Associational Life in Victorian and Edwardian England,' *Journal of Social History* (Winter 1992): 290.

[25] *Times*, 26 September 1844 reprinted from *Punch*.

[26] Charles Knight, ed., *London*, vol. 5 (London: Charles Knight, 1843), 397. The idea of the   commercial bazaar was also imported to America by Francis Trollope. Trollope ventured to bring the English commercial bazaar to America and constructed the Cincinnati Bazaar in 1829. See Nicole Tonkovich, University of California, San Diego, 'Foreign Markets in Domestic Locations: Frances Trollops's Cincinnati Bazaar, 1828-1830' (paper presented to the Interdisciplinary Nineteenth-Century Studies, Yale Center for British Art, 1996), 4-6.

[27] Nightingale, *The Bazaar*, 67-68.

bazaars were more directly commercial in their intent, they kept their theme and method of operations similar to Trotter's. These bazaars were controlled versions of the 'exotic' bazaars of the East—sanitized and anglicized for the enjoyment of urban English men and women.

Like an amusement ride in twentieth-century Disneyland, bazaars promised the variety and thrills of the Eastern experience without the dangers. In their description of the Soho warehouse, *The Gentleman's Magazine* lauded the premises as 'large, dry, commodious, well lighted, warmed, ventilated and properly watched . . ..'[28] The vendors and shoppers themselves were also 'properly watched.' Especially in the first few decades of the bazaar, one had to meet certain standards of dress and respectability to enter.[29] The stall keepers, mainly women, had to possess 'an irreproachable character.'[30] Partially these rules sought to ensure that the bazaar experience remained safe enough to attract the shoppers of the wealthier classes, but as Tony Bennett notes of Mechanics' Institute exhibitions, such rules also existed to ensure that the spectacle of the bazaar was not spoiled by the ugliness of poverty or the suggestion of sin.[31]

Over time, the emphasis on spectacle and display increased. Temples to consumption, bazaars utilized the newest visual and mechanical innovations along with the most fashionable methods of entertainment, live music for example, to draw shoppers. By the 1830s the bazaar had established itself as a staple of London shopping and entertainment. In 1831 another larger bazaar called the Pantechnicon opened on the northwest corner of Belgrave Square. This impressive building was 500 feet long with four floors for exhibiting a variety of goods. The Pantechnicon specialized in the sale of carriages, but also sold furniture, had special iron chests for deeds, and served as a 'place of public resort' for gentlemen to conduct business.[32] he exact number of bazaar patrons is difficult to judge. Nightingale claimed in 1816 that 12,000 people passed through the Soho Bazaar in one week.[33] In the 1830s the Queen's Bazaar in Oxford Street contained 1,100 feet of counters alone and had its own separate furniture department. In April of 1836 the Queen's Bazaar took in over £382 in rent from its counters in one month and £27 from the diorama.[34] By the 1830s, the bazaar had become more than an innovation in consumption—it ranked as a new form of entertainment. In 1831 the New Royal Bazaar at Leicester Square advertised a:

---

[28] 'The Bazaar,' *Gentleman's Magazine*, 272; Nightingale, *The Bazaar*, 10. See also Dyer, 'Vanity Fair,' 200.

[29] Dyer, 'Vanity Fair,' 204.

[30] 'The Bazaar,' *Gentleman's Magazine*, 272. Women had to be recommended by respectable references and were supervised by the bazaar's staff.

[31] Tony Bennett, 'The Exhibitionary Complex,' *New Formations* 4 (Spring 1988): 85.

[32] Pantechnicon, August 1831, 'Bazaars and Sales,' Box I, John Johnson Collection, Bodleian, Oxford.

[33] Nightingale, *The Bazaar*, 32.

[34] Queen's Bazaar, 13 April 1836, 'London Play Places,' Box I, John Johnson Collection, Bodleian, Oxford.

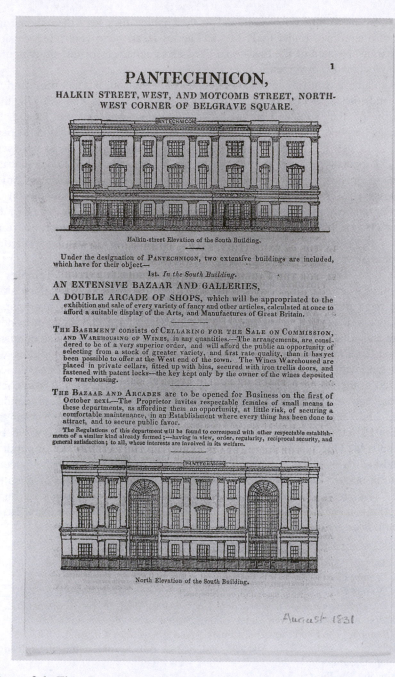

Figure 2.1 The Pantechnicon, Halkin Street, London. Bodleian Library, University of Oxford: John Johnson Collection; Bazaars and Sales.

VARIETY of DAY and EVENING EXHIBITIONS, . . .; comprising the Mechanical and Musical Automats, which were made expressly for the Emperor of China, . . . and cost upwards of 30,000*l.*; Grand Udoramic and Cosmoramic Views.. . . The Evening Exhibition commences at Seven o'clock, with the Automats, followed by an Experiment in Chemistry, called the Laughing Gas; after which . . . Magnificent Evanescent Views and Optical Illusions, and the celebrated Dance of Witches.[35]

Front row seats for these extravaganzas cost only 1 s. 6 d.[36] The goods for sale at the bazaar were not even mentioned in the advertisement.

Like the later department stores, bazaars had the advantage of a large selection of various goods under one roof with competitive prices. One Edwardian author writing on mid-Victorian London noted that: 'In the days before . . . huge emporiums for the sale of everything had come into existence, it was 'bazaars' that supplied the maximum of selection with the minimum of locomotion, such as today is to be found in the huge *caravanseri yclept* 'Stores', and in Tottenham Court Road and Westbourne Grove in particular.'[37] Later department stores were also similar to bazaars in their mixture of consumption, entertainment, and display. The Baker Street Bazaar was the first site of Madame Tussaud's Waxworks, which to this day resides in Baker Street.[38]

The New Female Industry

The attraction of the bazaar was as much the display of goods and the display of pleasurable entertainments as it was the purchase of the fancy goods and fripperies usually sold there. Some critics argued that the attractions of bazaars lay also in the display of the young women employed there.[39] Although Trotter's and other bazaars were founded in part to support needy families, in practice this translated into employing women.[40] The bazaar at Leicester Square in 1830 boasted that its bazaar at Saville House allowed 'widows, orphans, and others' to sell their

---

[35] New Royal Bazaar, October 1831, 'London Play Places,' Box I, John Johnson Collection, Bodleian, Oxford.

[36] For non-British readers— s.=shillings and d. =pence.

[37] Donald Shaw, *London in the Sixties* (London: Everett & Co., 1908), 229.

[38] *Ibid.*, 231; E. Beresford Chancellor, *The West End Yesterday and Today* (London: The Architectural Press, 1926), 26.

[39] See Dyer, 'Vanity Fair.' Although Dyer thoroughly discusses the moral threat of the bazaar as an arena for female prostitution and display, he neglects the economic innovation they attempted in women's employment.

[40] The original idea was to support families who had lost a wage earner. See Nightingale, *The Bazaar*, 26; 'The Bazaar,' *The Gentleman's Magazine*, 86 (March 1816), 272.

artwork.[41] As styled by its supporters, the bazaar provided safe haven for middle-class families that had fallen into financial difficulty, and more important, provided a place for the daughters of those families to earn a living safely and respectably: '[T]he daughters of persons in trade, with large families and contracted fortunes, how are the anxious parents to provide for their beloved offspring? . . . they are above the class of servants; governesses are now more numerous than pupils; and they have not wherewithal to embark them in business . . .'[42] These aims were at least in part realized: 'I went over about five weeks ago with Lady Bellenden, who has placed two very amiable young women there, both of whom are the orphan daughters of a country curate, one of them has a counter for all sorts of painted ornaments, the other for fine needle work . . ..'[43]

Nightingale proposed to create a whole new outlet for female industry, especially for the daughters of the genteel who had fallen on hard times, or who worried that their unmarried daughters would be left without support: '. . . keep your oldest girl in the Bazaar. Try her there; . . . Your younger daughter may execute something at home to be disposed of at this place . . ..'[44] Nightingale observed that of 200 people working at Trotter's bazaar in 1816, only two were men, and they were working with their wives.[45] The purpose of the bazaar to encourage 'female domestic industry' proved a success, but it went far beyond only supporting genteel women who had lost a male wage earner.[46] In 1878 the Soho bazaar had offices for hiring servants and governesses.[47] As early as 1816, the Soho bazaar provided an employment outlet for 'persons educated by benevolent institutions' like the young girls trained in charity schools.[48]

One of the most noticeable parts of the successful bazaar formula copied by so many was the employment of women to serve the mainly lady shoppers. Although they were under the watchful eye of bazaar management, these women were, in a sense, self-employed — renting their counters individually. It was a miniaturized version of the nineteenth-century entrepreneurial ideal. Davidoff and Hall found retail the largest occupation of middle-class women in the period from 1780-1850.[49] Yet, there was a dubious status attached to working behind the counter and

---

[41] New Bazaar, 10 January 1830, 'London Play Places,' Box I, John Johnson Collection, Bodleian, Oxford.

[42] Nightingale, *The Bazaar*, 30.

[43] *A Visit to The Bazaar*, 6-7. See also page 9 for the description of 'Susan Boscawen, who was a daughter of a deceased tradesman, long a resident in this village, and for whom they all entertained a sincere regard . . ..'

[44] Nightingale, *The Bazaar*, 30.

[45] *Ibid.*, 42.

[46] 'The Bazaar,' *The Gentleman's Magazine*, 86 (March 1816), 272.

[47] Hindley, *The Life and Times of James Catnatch*, 193.

[48] Nightingale, *The Bazaar*, 31.

[49] Leonore Davidoff and Catherine Hall, *Family Fortunes: Men and Women of the English Middle-Class, 1780-1850* (Chicago: University of Chicago Press, 1986), 301-302. However, the large draper's shops, generally agreed as the immediate progenitors

being 'sullied' by trade. For working-class women shop employment represented success; however, middle-class women were not supposed to participate in the business of trade.[50] Although the shoppers at the Soho Bazaar may have gladly served at a 'fancy fair,' they did not want to exchange places with the women behind the counters who may have been respectable, but were fallen in circumstances.

In 1829 a fire in the Oxford Street bazaar has left a record that gives us something of an idea of the economic value of these working women's trade and their stocks. The losses incurred by the women stall keepers were over £2,341 of uninsured goods, and the men lost £3,592 worth of merchandise. At a meeting held to discuss the damage, a Mr. Cottam even suggested that 'the funds which may be raised should first be apportioned to the female sufferers, and afterwards the male sufferers.'[51] This idea was seconded by others at the meeting who saw the women's distress as more severe than the men's because the bazaar was their only means of support. On the day of the fire they found at least 75 cases of women whose livelihood was destroyed by the fire.[52] The bazaar also served as a career for other women employed at the bazaar. The bazaar matrons, who watched the vendors and the customers, helped keep the appearance of the bazaar respectable. A Mrs. Harker had been working as a matron of the Soho Bazaar for seventeen years.[53] Bazaars gave women a place in the English economy in ways they were designed to and some in which they were not.

To protect the respectability of the bazaars, both traders and customers were policed by watchful eyes. After all, the Soho Bazaar was founded on the principle of preserving the honor of respectable women who had experienced a financial setback. Following strict rules of dress, and opening their stalls only in daylight hours, the women in the Soho Bazaar had to keep up respectable appearances. Supervising matrons ensured that the women greeted their customers in proper attire.[54] The bazaar rules insisted dress be 'clean, plain, neat, without feathers or flowers . . ..'[55] Of course, this also served the purpose of clearly delineating the stall girls from the shoppers, thus protecting *their* status. Employees of bazaars were at the same time watching the patrons to make sure they were respectable and

---

of the department store, started employing large numbers of female assistants only after the mid-nineteenth century. See Dorothy Davis, *A History of Shopping* (London: Routledge & Kegan Paul Ltd., 1966), 260.

[50] Davidoff and Hall, *Family Fortunes*, 303-304.

[51] *Times*, 5 June 1829.

[52] *Ibid.*

[53] *The Annual Register: Or a View of the History and Politics of the Year 1844* (London: F.& J. Rivington, 1845), 368; W.C. Harker, 32, Upper Seymour Street, Friday evening, to the Editor, 24 December 1844, *Times*, 25 December 1844.

[54] Knight, *London*, vol. 5, 396. See also Dyer, 'Vanity Fair,' 199.

[55] Nightingale, *The Bazaar*, 10.

were not stealing merchandise or dressed improperly for the spectacle.[56] In June of 1832, a 'respectable' man was shocked to find himself denied entrance to the Pantheon of the Oxford Street Bazaar: 'Now, if it is required of those lieges who may be in want of toothpicks, or, needle-cases, to go to this new place of attraction in full court-dress, the managers of it ought surely to condescend to intimate that much to the public—I beg their pardon, to the 'nobility and gentry.'' He further asserted that it was he, a member of the middle class, who provided the real profit for the bazaar, because the upper classes only went to the bazaar to exhibit themselves and not to purchase.[57] Yet, if this anonymous man, or even someone below him on the class scale, had been dressed properly, he probably would have made his way into the bazaar. While trying to preserve such class divisions, the bazaars also encouraged class pretensions, and the charity bazaars especially attracted those, like the fictional Becky Sharp and Dickens's ambitious 'young ladies,' who desired a higher station and the luxuries concomitant to it.[58] The opportunities created for women by charity and commercial bazaars both challenged the divisions between classes by exposing all to the same public view and supported class boundaries with strict rules of dress and decorum.

Novelty Goods and Novel Selling Methods

The concentration on female employment was one facet of what made bazaars a unique retail development. That 'fancy articles' were the center and not the periphery of their sale goods also made bazaars different from other types of retail trade. Bazaars specialized in delicately made, but inexpensive, formerly 'luxury' goods such as highly decorated gilt-paper flower cases, card racks, perfumes, decorative boxes, and toys.[59] Such non-utilitarian products filled the rooms and emptied the purses of the middling classes as they marked their status with gilded paper and lace. Critics who supported more traditional shopkeeping criticized the emphasis of the new marts on such 'useless' novelties.

Novelty, however, had its pitfalls. The crowds of London quickly became jaded and would-be bazaar moguls risked the fickleness of the marketplace when opening these large-scale enterprises. The case of the Royal Victoria Bazaar in Holborn illustrates these dangers. It opened in February of 1834 and failed a few months later. The bankrupt owner, Joseph Briggs, was left with over 1,000 packages of Windsor soap, 360 silver thimbles, twenty gross of Dutch toys, and hundreds of

---

[56] *Annual Register*, 368; W.C. Harker, 32, Upper Seymour Street, Friday evening, to the Editor, 24 December 1844, *Times*, 25 December 1844.

[57] A., to the Editor, *Times*, 12 June 1832.

[58] For an excellent discussion of Victorian problems with character, class, and respectability and the ease of feigning all of these, see Rebecca F. Stern, 'Historicizing Performativity: Constructing Identities in Victorian England,' (Ph.D. diss., Rice University, 1996).

[59] *A Visit to The Bazaar*, 67; Royal Victoria Bazaar, February 1834, 'London Play Places,' Box I, John Johnson Collection, Bodleian, Oxford.

other unsold items.[60] Bazaars, nevertheless, especially the larger among them, remained popular despite the criticisms of their emphasis on display and showy items of minimal usefulness.

The derogatory attitude of more traditional tradesmen and other middle-class critics of bazaars may have been spawned as much by the success of their innovations as by the relative uselessness of their goods. The female traders who rented out stalls in bazaars cut the wholesale dealer out of the chain of sale. Prior to bazaars, vendors who did not have their own premises had to sell their goods to wholesale dealers who would then sell them to other dealers before they made their way to the public.[61] Bazaars left a higher profit margin for the women trading there. Clearly marking items with their prices and not deviating from those prices also separated bazaars from more traditional types of trade where some haggling still held as the rule, and connected them to the new-style linen drapery and haberdashery shops.[62] Most disturbing of all to their competitors, bazaar keepers avoided one of the most dangerous aspects of Victorian trade—giving credit. Giving credit to customers cost many a nineteenth-century business owner their livelihood, but not bazaar keepers:

'Put it down to the bill,' is the fountain of ill;
  This has the shopkeepers undone;
Bazaars never trust—so down with your dust,
  And help us to diddle all London.
            Soho Bazaar, &c.[63]

The benefits of this all cash system are obvious. The women of the bazaars did not give credit to customers and with a daily rent, the owners of the bazaars were not forced to give credit to stall keepers.[64]

The success of the bazaars and their 'female traders' sparked a variety of criticisms, especially from those who supported more traditional forms of trade. John Agg, alias Humphrey Hedgehog, lampooned the new markets in his 1816 poem, 'The London Bazzaar, or, Where to Get Cheap Things.' Agg criticized the new marts throughout the poem for the types of goods they sell—cheap and impractical. Agg also implied that, despite the many safeguards of respectability,

---

[60] Royal Victoria Bazaar, February 1834, 'London Play Places,' Box I, John Johnson Collection, Bodleian, Oxford; Royal Victoria Bazaar, 26 March 1834, 'London Play Places,' Box I, John Johnson Collection, Bodleian, Oxford; Victoria Bazaar, May 1834, 'London Play Places,' Box I, John Johnson Collection, Bodleian, Oxford.

[61] Nightingale, *The Bazaar*, 19.

[62] *Ibid.*, 15.

[63] 'The Soho Bazaar,' in Hindley, *The Life and Times of James Catnatch*, 194. See also Humphrey Hedgehog [John Agg], 'The London Bazzaar, or, Where to Get Cheap Things' (19, Little Queen Street, Lincoln's Inn Fields, London: J. Duncombe, 1816), 7.

[64] See Nightingale, *The Bazaar*, 40.

the women were selling themselves along with their fancy goods. He contrasted this den of women, sin and shoddy goods with the 'honest man' in trade:

> Assure you, that no Honest man
> Would contribute the smallest aid,
> To them—while we in legal Trade!
> Turn Bankrupts—and tho' more deserve,
> Are daily seen almost to starve . . .
> Must their longstanding shops be clos'd;
> Must Legal Trade be thus opposed?[65]

The most virulent criticisms of bazaars emerged when they first opened after the Napoleonic wars, but the protests neither led to their closure nor harmed their popularity. Retail trade did not experience the predicted destruction, and bazaars became an accepted part of nineteenth-century shopping culture. Their emphasis on display and shopping as entertainment grew as the century progressed and even spread into some unlikely places. Shopping bazaars evolved into a new way of giving alms. Organizers of urban charity bazaars were especially adept at using sumptuous decor and a grand thematic display to create temptations for the eye to entice buyers and increase the coffers of their charitable societies.

Dramatic Displays: Fancy Fairs, Commercial Bazaars and Entertainment

The nineteenth century was an epoch of charitable societies and associations. Around mid-century there was an enormous expansion of hospitals in London alone, and all of these institutions required financial support.[66] Increasingly, these societies drew on the technique of the bazaar to raise money for their charities. Open for only a few days, charity bazaars mastered the techniques of showmanship of the commercial bazaar while giving it an elegant, upper-class twist. The bazaar held in 1846 for the hospital for the cure of consumption and diseases of the chest boasted stalls highlighted by a system of hanging marquees that 'formed wings to an enormous circular tent.'[67] Five years earlier, for a bazaar held to pay for a new church at Sunderland, 'the large hall of the Athenaeum was . . . tastefully decorated with white muslin drapery, chastely relieved with pink rosettes, which had a most enlivening effect.'[68] Whether occupying gardens, parade grounds, or majestic hall, the men and women of the charity bazaar prided themselves on their elaborate if ephemeral displays.

---

[65] Hedgehog [John Agg], 'The London Bazzaar,' 16.

[66] Frank Prochaska, *Philanthropy and the Hospitals of London; The King's Fund, 897-1990* (Oxford: Clarendon Press, 1992), 1-5.

[67] *Times*, 19 June 1846.

[68] *Times*, 24 September 1841. Six years later a bazaar for the Distressed Irish was similarly decorated. *Times*, 27 May 1847.

Only using the term and technique of 'bazaar' from the 1820s,[69] these charitable 'fancy fairs' developed into magnificent productions in a short period. In 1832 a bazaar was held for the British Orphan Asylum at the Egyptian Hall. The Hall, opened by William Bullock only a few years before the opening of Trotter's Bazaar, served as a museum exhibiting everything from Napoleon's carriage to antiquities. All or part of the hall was available for rent for various types of exhibitions and shows.[70] In October of 1832, the Duchess of Kent, Lady Mayoress, and other aristocratic women presided over a bazaar at the Egyptian Hall: 'In the centre of the hall a stand is erected and tastefully hung with crimson cloth for the accommodation of Wiepert's band . . ..'[71] No element was neglected from displaying some of the orphans themselves to employing a band to entertain those browsing the goods on display.

In Regent's Park in 1830, at the bazaar for the Royal Dispensary, bands of music were merely 'in attendance.'[72] However, in 1832 at the now annual bazaar for the Royal Dispensary for Diseases of the Ear, 'the scene was enlivened by many pieces of vocal music, performed by the chorus singers of the German company, and by Mr. Fisher, the Bohemian singer' as well as a military band.[73] At the bazaar for the Distressed Irish in 1847, not one, but three military bands played;[74] however, such stirring aural accompaniment was not restricted to charity bazaars. Although the ladies keeping stalls at charitable societies may have been of nobler rank, they learned many marketing lessons from the already flourishing commercial bazaars. The short-lived 1834 Royal Victoria Bazaar in Holborn attempted to attract customers with a 'beautiful self-performing Euterpeon, four barrels playing 24 tunes . . ..'[75] Whether at charitable bazaars lasting only a few days or more permanent commercial bazaars, such displays were expensive. An 1859 bazaar raising funds for a church spent over £23 on the 'expenses of bands' and £165 to rent the premises. Yet, the popularity of these bazaars led to a total intake of over £1,200 for the few days of the bazaar.[76]

In 1845, the fancy bazaar was even adopted for political purposes by that middle-class group, the Anti-Corn Law League. The National Anti-Corn Law League Free Trade Bazaar at the Covent-Garden Theatre mimicked the luxurious

---

[69] Dyer, 'Vanity Fair,' 208.

[70] Richard Altick, *The Shows of London* (London: Belknap Press, 1978): 235-252.

[71] *Times*, 23 October 1832.

[72] *Times*, 20 July 1830.

[73] *Times*, 14 June 1832.

[74] *Times*, 27 May 1847. Refusing to be outdone by the Irish, the Scottish Highland Emigration Fund bazaar entertained its 1853 attendees with a band from the Caledonian Asylum Schools led by the Queen's piper. *Times*, 28 May 1853.

[75] Victoria Bazaar, May 1834, 'London Play Places,' Box I, John Johnson Collection, Bodleian, Oxford. The Euterpeon was apparently a sort of mechanical, self-playing organ. See also for a similar story on the Baker Street Bazaar, *Times*, 13 June 1840.

[76] George Rooper, Nascott, Watford, to the Editor of the *Times*, 19 October 1859, *Times*, 20 October 1859.

display of the charity bazaar with its Gothic theme. Decorated with stained-glass, lanterns, and material to form vaulted arches, the organizers transformed the entire theater into a 'Gothic Hall.' Upon entering the hall, visitors heard a variety of tunes played by a traditional band and a new musical instrument called the Rock Harmonicon.[77] Its organizers also took the idea of a sliding scale of admission from charity bazaars: '10s. 6d. the first day, 5s. the second, and so on until it reaches the lowest limit of 1s.'[78] Shoppers could buy the same fancy items as at other bazaars—snuff boxes, thimble cases, and pearl stands for example, but there were also more substantial items like baby clothes, nightgowns, boots, shoes, and furniture.[79] One of the most popular items at the bazaar was a new book by Harriet Martineau entitled *Dawn Island*: 'This was written expressly for the Bazaar . . . The scene of the story is laid in Polynesia, and the design is to illustrate the beneficial influence of commerce on a savage people . . ..'[80] Martineau's hero of the novel, a British sea captain, concludes the story: ' . . . it warmed my heart and filled my head to see how these children of nature were clearly destined to be carried on some way toward becoming men and Christians by my bringing commerce to their shores.'[81] Throngs of shoppers visited the Anti-Corn Law Bazaar.[82]

Whether political or charity oriented, by the 1840s and 1850s fancy bazaars were expected to have a certain scale of grandeur and spectacle. In 1850, the *Times* criticized the Quakers for their lackluster bazaar held to benefit the peace movement: 'Each stall has its own nationality to maintain on very inadequate resources. Scotland, for instance, is represented by one or two pieces of tartan, and the other countries of the earth are typified in a similarly meager fashion. . . . . The whole exhibition is very far inferior to that which our metropolitan charities have strength enough to get up at this season of the year.'[83] Throwing a proper bazaar took more than dedication to one's cause and sufficient Christian spirit. The

---

[77] *Times*, 9 May 1845; Anti-Corn Law League, 'Leading Article,' *National Anti-Corn Law League Bazaar Gazette*, no. 11 (1845), 5.

[78] *Ibid.* This example and others demonstrate that the idea of an increasingly lower price of admission developed before the Crystal Palace. See Bennett, 'Exhibitionary Complex,' 85.

[79] Anti-Corn Law League, 'Leading Article,' *National Anti-Corn-Law League Bazaar Gazette*, no. 14 (1845), 3; Anti-Corn Law League, 'Leading Article', *Anti-Corn Law League Bazaar Gazette*, no. 10 (1845), 2; Anti-Corn Law League, 'Leading Article,' *Anti-Corn-Law League Bazaar*, no. 2 (1845), 1-2.

[80] Anti-Corn Law League, 'Leading Article,' *National Anti-Corn Law League Bazaar Gazette*, no. 12 (1845), 6.

[81] Harriet Martineau, *Dawn Island* (Manchester: J. Gadsby, 1845), 93-94.

[82] However, this group did not include John Holland who called the bazaar 'monstrous' and criticized the 'Quaker men and women' who helped to launch the bazaar. Holland, *The Bazaar*, 8.

[83] *Times*, 1 June 1850.

Society of Friends may not have possessed the prerequisite knowledge of fashion that was common to upper-class ladies.

Perhaps their brevity added to the attraction of charity bazaars. Some were annual, but even those lasted less than a week. Commercial bazaars also attracted shoppers with the appeal of temporary displays and special exhibits. At the 1840 Baker Street flower show, 'rare specimens of Cacti, Orchidaceae, [and] Camellias' were exhibited and later sold at auction. They were also arranged for optimum display with 'a respect to their several genera and species . . ..'[84] On a much grander scale was a later exhibition and plant sale at the Crystal Palace in the 1850s which claimed an attendance of 6,000 on the first day.[85] As impressive as the original 1851 and subsequent exhibitions of the Crystal Palace seem to both contemporary and modern eyes, it was, in many ways, the culmination of a much longer tradition of such shows. Also held in the Baker Street bazaar, an exhibition of a 'Colossal Vase of Cut Glass' in 1831 amazed the public. Manufactured by Gunby and Co.: 'Its height is 14 feet, it is 12 feet in diameter at the top, and is capable, according to the statement of the bills, of containing eight pipes, or 5,400 bottles of wine.'[86] Of course the Gunby vase and even the hundreds of exotic flowers and plants served a dual purpose. These attractions, shown for a limited time, enticed buyers to the bazaars, and served as advertisements for their particular companies.

Many of the exhibitions and displays at commercial bazaars were, like the crystal vase, more directly associated with the process of selling goods, but many others were simply entertainments to attract crowds to their establishments. A Mr. Falck put on a 'natural magic' show for the Queen's Bazaar in which he performed many feats including causing a flower to grow from a cup of mold. 'Natural' magicians were illusionists, claiming no supernatural abilities, and often used elaborate machinery to perform their feats.[87] In 1840 at Tulley's Bazaar in Gravesend, another magician named Johnson and styling himself the Wizard of the North[88] performed a famous gun trick still performed by magicians today. After a member of the audience fired a bullet from a real gun, the magician 'caught' the bullet in his teeth. The Wizard made news when an audience member misfired the gun and hit a violinist with the discharge from it (there was, of course, no bullet in the gun). The violinist survived.[89]

Although some of the entertainments providing the attraction and spectacle in bazaars were circus-like in atmosphere, other displays at bazaars aspired to greater cultural achievements. These artworks, like the magic shows and music, served to

---

[84] *Times*, 13 June 1840.

[85] *Times*, 16 April 1858.

[86] *Times*, 21 June 1831. See also Bennett, 'Exhibitionary Complex,' 74.

[87] *Times*, 5 November 1835; Altick, *Shows of London*, 76.

[88] Altick, *Shows of London*, 2. Altick mentions a 'Wizard of the North' in his book, but lists his name as Anderson. Perhaps Johnson was an imitator.

[89] *Times*, 28 September 1840; A version of this trick is in the act of Penn and Teller.

attract patrons to the bazaars. The works on view in commercial bazaars were often slightly less elevated versions of the art available in English high culture of the time. In many of these exhibits, the focus was on progress and a celebration of English national achievement.[90] A perfect example is the 'Padorama' shown at the Baker Street bazaar in 1834 that amazed its viewers with a representation of the most important technological wonder of the nineteenth century— railroads. With mechanical drums, 10,000 square feet of painted canvas, and a separate movable foreground, Bazaar goers were treated to the illusion of traveling on a train from Manchester to Liverpool.[91] However, these giant moving canvases were only one example of the visual illusions available at bazaars, and other examples emphasized art as much as artifice.

Appearing at the beginning of the century as a form of exhibition, the panorama was at its simplest a huge landscape painted on the interior of an enormous cylinder. Viewing the picture from the center produced the illusion of a seamless whole. Baker's, later known as Burford's, panorama in Leicester Square was the first and one of the most famous.[92] Dioramas created their illusions differently. First introduced in Britain in 1824, diorama pictures were rectangular and viewed through a darkened hallway with the only source of light focused on the painting. By changing the colors and intensity of light, operators produced the illusion of change and motion. The popularity of dioramas and panoramas produced a sort of 'orama'-mania in England. Bazaars were major sites for presenting these innovations.[93]

Landscapes, famous monuments, and paintings of recent events were the most popular themes for both forms of exhibition. In 1832 the Queen's Bazaar in Oxford street had a show that included 'King's College Chapel, Cambridge, the ruins of Melrose Abbey, the coronation of their Majesties in Westminster Abbey, and Bristol on fire during the riots.' In his admiration for the Melrose Abbey painting, the *Times* reviewer quoted Sir Walter Scott.[94] Not long into the life of the diorama, however, the painters began imitating higher forms of art. The grand scale of the works of John Martin was especially suited for dioramic displays. In June of 1833 a painter named Sebron exhibited his copy of Martin's *Belshazzar's Feast* in the diorama: 'In this copy that appearance of a vast extent of space, the peculiar feature in all Mr. Martin's paintings, is well preserved, and perhaps rendered more

---

[90] In his list of institutions in the 'exhibitionary complex' Bennett includes the dioramas and panoramas frequently shown in bazaars with the emerging museums. Bennett, 'Exhibitionary Complex,' 80. See also *Ibid.*, 73.

[91] *Times*, 12 May 1834.

[92] Shaw, *London in the Sixties*, 48-49; E. Beresford Chancellor, *The West End Yesterday and Today* (London: The Architectural Press, 1926),7-13.

[93] Beresford, *The West End Yesterday and Today*, 7-13; Altick, *Shows of London*, 129-210; William Feaver, *The Art of John Martin* (Oxford: Clarendon Press, 1975), 68.

[94] *Times*, 19 April 1832.

imposing from the enlarged scale on which the diorama is executed.'[95] Soon
original dioramic works were produced in the manner of Martin. E. Lambert a
professional dioramist replaced the Belshazzar copy with his own 2,000 foot
canvas of the *Destruction of Jerusalem* in May of 1834. It led the *Times* critic to
declare: 'This picture has also the merit of originality, which its predecessor,
confessedly a copy from Mr. Martin's picture, had not.'[96] His next painting in
December of that year was a contemporary history painting of Parliament's
October fire. However, one wonders if it too was not in the style of Martin.[97]

There were dangers as well as delights in being in the forefront of consumer
culture and this use of this new technology. The Royal Bazaar in Oxford Street
burned to the ground in 1829: 'The fire originated, it is supposed, from some spirits
of turpentine communicating to a beautiful transparency in the Diorama
representing 'The Destruction of York Minster by Fire.''[98] In their efforts at
realistic effects, the operators eschewed the older skylight method of lighting their
diorama for a more volatile innovation. However, the bazaar rose like a phoenix
and rebuilt its premises, diorama and all. Renamed the Queen's Bazaar, it went on
to show other works, like the *Destruction of Jerusalem*, in the same dangerous
manner.[99]

Later in the century, dioramas and panoramas would be replaced by newer
innovations in commercial shows. By the late 1830s, the work of Martin had fallen
out of favor, cheapened, according to Feaver, by the mass produced imitations and
dioramic copies. With the 'orama' artworks that complemented bazaars 'profits
came from admission fees, programme sales, and souvenir prints.'[100] Reaching
above cheap broadsides and comic prints, yet below the Academy, it was art for the
masses and art for consumption. Used in part to bring consumers to the
commodities for sale in the Bazaars, the dioramas and panoramas were
commodities in themselves— 'selling' art and a vision of English culture to an ever
larger multitude.

The displays of the bazaars, the paintings, flower shows, bands, and lavish
décor, were designed as temptations for the eye. Whether directly or indirectly
related to the commodities shown, these enormous displays attracted the buyer to
the place of purchase. The buyers themselves, however, the customers of the

---

[95] *Times*, 25 June 1833;   John Martin, *Belshazzar's Feast*, Oil on Canvas, 1820, Yale
Center for British Art. Sebron was a student of Louis Daguerre, the Frenchmen who
first patented the painting method of the diorama. See Feaver, *Art of John Martin*, 68.

[96] *Times*, 17 May 1834.

[97] *Times*, 25 December 1834.   This connection brought problems for John Martin and the
serious acceptance of his work. See Feaver, *Art of John Martin*, 112; Altick, *Shows of
London*, 414-415.

[98] *Times*, 28 May 1829; Queen's Bazaar, 13 April 1836, 'London Play Places,' John
Johnson Collection. See also Altick, *Shows of London*, 176. See also Queen's Bazaar,
13 April 1836, 'London Play Places,' John Johnson Collection for continuing exhibits.

[99] Altick, *Shows of London*, 176.

[100]Feaver, *Art of John Martin*, 69-70. See also *Ibid.*, 112.

bazaar, were part of the pageantry along with the stall keepers, who were almost exclusively female. In charity bazaars especially, contemporary critics denounced not the temptations of the eye in the display of goods, but the temptations of the flesh in the display of the women who kept and frequented the establishments.

Ladies' Benefit or for the Benefit of the Ladies?

The Victorian association of prostitution with women selling goods is well known. Writers protesting the new bazaars in the early part of the century referred openly to these dangers.[101] In Agg's 'The London Bazaar' he defines the 'female trade' taking place in bazaars:

> What bargains there are sold and bought—
> But, 'faith, I mean of female sort.
> For, you must know, th'industrious fair
> There getting a living by their ware
> . . .
> For there are lots of 'beauteous ware'
> For anybody's cash, I'll swear.
> Though coy they seem, touch but your fob,
> And I'll be bound you do the job!
> For well 'tis known Bazaars are made
> To Encourage (only) female Trade—[102]

The connection between women selling merchandise and selling themselves was already an old one in the nineteenth century. In eighteenth-century Paris successful female shopkeepers elicited fears that such sexualized commerce would lure all the male customers to the women's shops.[103] With their multitude of young, female stall keepers, bazaars evoked similar anxieties. Even the charity bazaars held by

---

[101]Gary Dyer explicitly traces this connection in his article on Thackeray, *Vanity Fair*, and the Soho Bazaar. He asserts that Thackeray and his contemporaries combined the new fears of this retail innovation with older 'misogynistic notions of feminine corruption and duplicity.' Dyer, 'Vanity Fair,' 197. See also Judith Walkowitz, *City of Dreadful Delight; Narratives of Sexual Danger in Late-Victorian London* (Chicago: University of Chicago Press, 1992), 46; Schor, 'Urban Things,' 12. According to Schor, 'Thackeray stands as the most visibly commodity-happy novelist of this period, and his connection between the purchasing of goods, the purchasing of women, and the purchasing of happiness needs little expansiveness.' Schor, 'Urban Things,' 4.

[102]Hedgehog [John Agg], 'The London Bazzaar,' 3-7.

[103]Jennifer Jones, '*Coquettes* and *Grisettes*: Women Buying and Selling in Ancien Régime Paris,' in *The Sex of Things: Gender and Consumption in Historical Perspective*, ed. Victoria de Grazia and Ellen Furlough (Berkeley: University of California Press, 1996), 31-32.

genteel women were viewed as sites of marriage market commerce if not direct sexual commerce.

The bazaars held by charitable societies in the nineteenth century were originally called 'fancy fairs,' and occasionally retained that appellation even after the opening of commercial bazaars. Reminiscent of older traditional fairs, charity bazaars were annual and seasonal, and, like the older fairs, they did not escape the critical moral eye of nineteenth-century commentators.[104] Held for a variety of objectives from 'Diseases of the Ear' to the building of churches, the fancy fair was a favorite institution of the upper classes from the 1820s to the later Victorian era.[105] Although the fairs were lucrative and provided funds for churches and hospitals, their lush display and mixing of the sexes brought criticism from strict Christian commentators[106] as well as some not so Christian ones.

Reverend J.A. James of Birmingham gave a description of a charity bazaar that makes it seem akin to a Roman orgy: "Recall, the scene itself, the gay dress, the music, and the rabble, —flattery and compliment instead of truth. . . . Skill excercised in making that which is worthless pass for much. . .. Then follows ennui after excitement; the gaze on the heap of trifles left to be disposed of, or that will do for other Bazaars . . .."'[107] John Holland, writing some time in the 1850s, likewise lambasted what he saw as the false piety of charity bazaars, many for religious objects, that stressed materialism, display, and salesmanship over Christian charity. It especially bothered Holland that participation in these bazaars had become the measure of one's devotion to the church.[108]

Although critics like James and Holland found many unchristian facets of charity bazaars, one of the most bothersome was the nature of items sold at bazaars— 'making that which is worthless pass for much.' As their alternative name, fancy fairs, suggest, charity bazaars like commercial bazaars concentrated their sales in a variety of fancy articles. Upon entering a bazaar, tables upon tables heaped with pleasant, decorative, and impractical items greeted the viewer's eye; items detractors described as 'frivolous' and 'trumpery.'[109] Whether raising money for a church or a hospital charity, these fancy fairs sold the same kind of fancy

---

[104]See Steve Inwood, 'Policing London's Morals: The Metropolitan Police Force and Popular Culture, 1829-1850,' *London Journal* 15, no. 2 (1990): 144; Hugh Cunningham, 'The Metropolitan Fairs: A Case Study in the Social Control of Leisure,' *Social Control in Nineteenth-Century Britain*, ed. A.P. Donajgrodski (London: Croom Helm, 1977): 164-168.

[105]*Times*, 20 July 1830, 2 May 1837, 23 September 1839, 22 June 1840, 30 July 1851, 25 April 1856, 23 July 1860.

[106]Dyer, 'Vanity Fair,' 210.

[107]Quoted in John Holland, *The Bazaar; or Money and the Church* (Sheffield: Pawson and Brailsford, 1850s, 27.

[108]Holland, *The Bazaar*, 28. Note: the British Library catalog lists the date as sometime in the 1830s, but it is actually later, sometime in the 1850s as it refers to both the Anti-Corn Law League Bazaar 1845 and the Crystal Palace.

[109]Holland, *The Bazaar*, 15. See also Dyer, 'Vanity Fair.'

items found in the commercial bazaars of London. A book from an 1846 charity
bazaar details some of the objects for sale at one particular ladies' booth that
included cosmetics and perfumes. The book contains colored sketches along with
descriptions of the cosmetics and toiletries for sale such as 'Parfum D'Elyse' and
'Rouge Superior.' The description for 'Genuine Court Plaster' would have upset
any Christian critic:

> Flattery is 'Truth,' adorn'd and dressed,
> Painted and Patched, and made to look her best,
> 'Neath this disguise her plainness all she covers—
> Princes admire, and Kings become her lovers![110]

Along with ladies' perfumes, bazaars sold books and poems privately printed for
their benefit.

Dependent on the novelty-loving female consumer, the growth of commercial
and charity bazaars was a threat to the ordinary shop merchants. In Stevenson's
1866 allegory of the Charity bazaar he explains: 'And all this is not to be sold by
your common Shopkeepers, intent on small and legitimate profits, but by Ladies
and Gentlemen, who would as soon think of picking your pocket . . ., as of selling a
single one of these many interesting, beautiful, rare, quaint, comical, and necessary
articles at less than twice its market value.'[111] One ornate example of such a book
from an 1839 bazaar at Leeds features poetry and original sketches by juvenile
artists.[112] Another book was itself a promotional advertisement for the charity
bazaar. *The Bazaar; or Fragments of Mind. In Prose and Verse* began with a story
of a little girl whose father is explaining the purpose of a charity bazaar in
Lancaster. The father tells his daughter of the people who benefit from the bazaars
and asserts that such bazaars compete with 'the most extensive fancy dealer the
Metropolis could furnish' in their selection, and variety.[113]

Critics, like Holland, viewed this not as a benefit, but as a dilemma. Similar to
John Agg's 1816 declaration that commercial bazaars were threats to legal trade,[114]
Holland accused charity bazaars of stealing business from legitimate traders and
threatening traditional merchants. Even more threatening, the ladies of bazaars
were not replacing legitimate trade with useful goods, but mainly with 'decorative
nuisance[es].'[115] At the age of sixteen, in 1866, Robert Louis Stevenson wrote an

---

[110]*The Ladies' Hand-book, Being Coloured sketches for sale at a bazaar, with descriptive
lines in verse* (London: Privately printed,1846).

[111]Robert Louis Stevenson, 'The Charity Bazaar : An Allegorical Dialogue' (Edinburgh:
1866), 1.

[112]*Original Sketches and Ryhmes, Contributed by a Few Friends, for the Bazaar at Leeds*,
(Plymouth, England: W.H. Luke, 1839).

[113]*The Bazaar; or Fragments of Mind. In Prose and Verse* (Lancaster, England: Holme
& Jackson, 1831), 4-5.

[114]Hedgehog (John Agg), 'The London Bazzaar,' 7.

[115]Holland, *The Bazaar*, 16.

allegory of a charity bazaar that suggested that the 'sham goods' sold at these bazaars were not used but recycled for the next bazaar: 'Your lady wife will lay these tea-cosies and pen-wipers aside in a safe place, until she is asked to contribute to another Charity Bazaar. There the tea-cosies and pen-wipers will be once more charitably sold. . . . In short, Sir, the whole affair is a cycle of operations.'[116] Why wealthy ladies had to threaten traditional tradesmen by retailing useless goods for charity puzzled many observers.

Some of the criticism is apt: the bazaars often appeared to be more for the benefit of the ladies hosting them than the various refugees and orphans in whose honor they were held. In charity bazaars, ladies of the upper-classes found opportunities to demonstrate artistic talents that would otherwise have remained in the privacy of the domestic sphere. A Ladies' Bazaar of the Royal Ophthalmic Hospital in Westminster held in June 1832 boasted: 'most elegant fancy articles, including drawings, executed in a very superior style, by the lady-contributors. A wax model of horses and a foal, by Lady Dacre, attracted much notice.'[117] The next year, the fancy fair for the Society of Foreigners in Distress promised: 'a carpet worked by 29 ladies, for which £60 has already been offered. Her Royal Highness the Duchess of Kent has presented the committee with various articles, the work of her own hands and those of the Princess Victoria . . ..'[118] In George Eliot's 1860 *Mill on the Floss*, the heroine, Maggie Tulliver presides over a stall at a charity bazaar selling objects ranging from her knitted wrist warmers to a 'scarlet fez' embroidered by her cousin.[119] Even if it had something of the taint of commerce, the fancy fair provided these women with a very public gallery of artistic and domestic accomplishments. The women helped to arrange the fairs, contributed works to be sold, and staffed the stalls to sell the wares.

For some women charity bazaars became a sort of vocation. While critics found the participation of women in the commercial world distasteful, the women took pride in their finesse in the art of selling. Mary Thompson, a member of the Ladies Committee raising money for a political organization, took on a supervisory role at the bazaar held in 1845. Thompson suggested that lists of articles sold by each stall should be posted by the ladies hosting that stall. This way purchasers could 'browse' without having to search through every knick-knack. Thompson also suggested that whenever an article was sold, it should be marked off the sales board.[120] Women, young and old, and sometimes several generations of a family worked at these bazaars to produce profits for selected charities. The business-like

---

[116]Stevenson, 'The Charity Bazaar,' 3. Stevenson actually wrote this short play to be sold at his mother's own charity bazaar.

[117]*Times*, 1 June 1832. Another bazaar in the same year managed to obtain the drawings of Princess Victoria to sell. *Times*, 26 October 1832.

[118]*Times*, 19 June 1833.

[119]George Eliot, *The Mill on the Floss* (New York: The New American Library of World Literature, Inc., 1981), 450-452.

[120]Mary Thompson, Anti-Corn Law League Ladies Committee, *Anti-Corn Law Leaugue Bazaar Gazette*, no. 8 (London: 1845).

seriousness of this selling by women along with the inevitable public mixing of the genders that resulted from these bazaars frightened observers. Holland berated the 'Matrons, maiden daughters, and young wives . . . comingled with the bustling crowd . . . .'[121] An article that appeared in a newspaper of commercial traders, *The Draper*, likened the hard sell of the bazaar ladies to the Spanish Inquisition:

'Torquemada might have learnt something at the Wellington Barracks Riding School yesterday—a moral torture . . . it was to plunge shivering and shrinkingly into the chaos of flags, ribbons, flowers, muslin-covered stalls . . . .I marked a young lady in tricolour ribbons. . . . She gloated over the sufferings of her victims. She marked them from afar. Piteously, and with much pleading for mercy, did the wretched creatures retire, and . . . take refuge in Mrs. Thomas Taylor's 'Fine Art' corner. All to no purpose . . . .Circe had them, and they paid. . . .'[122]

Another article in *The Draper* in July 1872 sarcastically remarked that the women's 'time spent at the silk mercer's or the draper's in being served of an afternoon is not thrown away as an educating influence . . . .'[123] Holland had also compared ladies at bazaars to apprentices in retail shops.[124] The younger women sold flowers and boutonnieres while older women were the vendors of smoking caps, suspenders, cigar-cases and other items aimed at a male clientele. *The Draper* complained, 'When your purse is empty they will no longer even talk to you, but run up and smile upon a complete outsider . . . .'[125]

The public nature of the fancy bazaars, along with their commercial flavor and 'un-Christian' self-indulgence, brought criticism. The mixing of sexes at the bazaars with ladies behind the counters conversing with gentleman customers brought the most censure. Seeing and being seen, display of oneself, ranked in importance with display of one's artworks or fancy articles, and for younger women it was especially important as an acceptable way to 'interview' various gentlemen. In the July 1837 *Comic Almanack*, a journal to which Thackeray contributed, a poem appeared titled, 'Fancy Fairing:'

I saw her at the Fancy Fair:
  'Twas there my heart she won
Within the sweet, romantic grounds
  Of Mr. Jenkinson.

    . . .
To cure Diseases of the Ear,
  They say they've oped the mart:

---

[121]Holland, *The Bazaar*, 16.
[122]'A Fancy Fair,' *The Draper* (London) 7 June 1872. Originally published in *The Echo*.
[123]'The Fancy Fair,' *The Draper* (London) 12 July 1872.
[124]Holland, *The Bazaar*, 15, f.n.
[125]'The Fancy Fair,' *The Draper*, 12 July 1872.

But I think it's to propagate
    Diseases of the heart.[126]

Holland sarcastically compared the obvious display of respectable young women at bazaars to that of bar-maids in a public house.[127]

The classes attending and exhibiting at charitable bazaars, however, ranked much higher on the social scale. The best classes in their best dress, both men and women, were at the core of the exhibition. Even gentlemen sold a part of themselves in the form of autographs, one of the most popular items.[128] Also, reports of charity bazaars contained long lists of the upper-class attendees: 'distinguished personages we observed [were] Marchioness and Ladies Cornwallis, Countess Manvers, Lady Hawarden, Lady Radstock, Lady Katharine Stewart, Lady Rawsen, . . .' is only one example.[129] *The Draper* sarcastically reported 'that truly first quality charity bazaars had duchesses serving refreshments.'[130] The greatest display of all was a view of Royalty, and charities clamored for the attention of the royal family. The best fairs merited an appearance by the Queen herself.[131]

Thackeray begins his novel *Vanity Fair* with a vision of the traditional fair and ends it with a critique of the fancy bazaar. '[Becky Sharp] goes to church, and never without a footman. Her name is in all the Charity Lists. The Destitute Orange-girl, the Neglected Washerwoman, the Distressed Muffin-man, find her a fast and generous friend. She is always having stalls at Fancy Fairs for the benefit of these hapless beings.'[132] In one of his 'Sketches by Boz,' Charles Dickens complains that the middle classes were beginning to imitate this institution of the upper class: 'Aspiring young ladies, who read flaming accounts of some 'fancy fair in high life,' suddenly grow desperately charitable; visions of admiration and matrimony float before their eyes . . . Johnson's Nursery ground, is forthwith engaged, and the aforesaid young ladies . . . exhibit themselves for three days, from twelve to four, for the small charge of one shilling per head.'[133]

In response to what they viewed as the economic, social, and moral threat of charity bazaars, critics warned that the women staffing the charity bazaars were as false as the economy of impractical, decorative goods they helped to create. In *The Comic Almanack*'s July 1837 poem spoofing the Fancy Fair, the hero wooing the

---

[126]'Fancy Fair,' *The Comic Almanack: An Ephemeris Containing Merry Tales, Humorous Poetry Quips and Oddities.* First Series, 1835-43 (London: Chatto & Windus), 97.

[127]Holland, *The Bazaar*, 15, f.n.

[128]*Times*, 30 October 1859.

[129]*Times*, 9 July 1840.

[130]'The Fancy Fair,' *The Draper*, 12 July 1872.

[131]Prochaska, *Philanthropy*, 13. See also *Times*, 28 April 1831; *Times*, 23 June 1853.

[132]Thackeray, *Vanity Fair*, 753-754.

[133]'Sketches of London, No. 6,' *Evening Chronicle* (London) 17 March 1853. For a valuable collection of reprints see *Sketches by Boz and Other Early Papers, 1833-39,* ed., Michael Slater (London: J.J. Dent, 1994). See also Dyer, 'Vanity Fair,' 209.

lady at the stall discovers she is not only false, but criminal. She steals his £5 note, and when he complains, she has him arrested.[134] Holland also warned his male readers about courting a woman from a charity bazaar in his revised version of a popular ballad:

> I woo'd and won, and wed those charms;
>   Bright flash'd the nuptial taper;
> Alas! I clasp'd with loving arms
>   A wife of gilded paper,
> . . .
> Her brain with crochet-work was full:
>   Her tongue, no more it wheedles!
> Her heart, a clew of Berlin wool;
>   Her fingers, netting needles.[135]

For Holland, the ladies of the bazaar, like the articles they sold, were attractive, but without substance and a threat to the values of English society: '[P]retty, indeed, it must be admitted they are, like their feminine producers, but too often like them also, deserving of no higher appelation. . . .'[136] The upper-class ladies of the charity bazaars were threatening to men like Holland both for daring to enter the sphere of commerce and because they gave that commerce a character emphasizing display over quality or usefulness. Critics, however, did not succeed in squelching the phenomenon, and fancy fairs' association with the upper classes brought the admiration and imitation of the middle classes.

The fashion and frippery of the fancy fairs and commercial establishments provided a different kind of temptation—the desire for goods and status. The 'shopping mania' that made bazaars so popular was fueled in part by the dizzying changes in nineteenth-century fashions for women. As Victoria's reign progressed, changes in fashion accelerated. A poem in the 1845 Comic Almanack titled 'Ode to Fashion' bemoaned:

> Oh, Fashion! it were vain, indeed,
>   To try your wondrous flights to follow;
> Onward at such a pace you speed,
>   Beating the *Belle Assemblée* hollow.[137]

In vain Adam Blenkinsop advised in his 1850 shilling pamphlet *A Shilling's-Worth of Advice, on Manners, Behaviour & Dress* for women to reign in their love of fashion for more practical and inexpensive styles. He addressed those women of the

---

[134]'Fancy Fair,' *The Comic Almanack*, 97.
[135]Holland, *The Bazaar*, 17-18.
[136]*Ibid.*, 16.
[137]'Ode to Fashion,' *The Comic Almanack*, Second Series, 1844-53, 57. Note: the *Belle Assemblée* was a popular fashion magazine.

lower classes tempted to mimic the wealthier ladies who staffed the stalls of benefit bazaars: 'Never wear cheap and gaudy things. . . Choose sober colours and shew your taste by the way the dress is put on. A handsome scarf of some chastened pattern, suitable to your age, complexion and style, may, if you can afford it, be worn . . ..'[138] Blenkinsop also complained that domestic servants tried to imitate the dress of their lady employers by buying 'satins and silks' with surplus income instead of wisely saving their money.[139] An anonymous pamphlet from 1857 on *The Science of Dress* lauds the 'plain woman' who 'attired gracefully, richly, and becomingly will attract more attention than a pretty woman badly and carelessly dressed.'[140] Fancy articles in bazaars were directed at the women whose purchases were increasingly driving specific aspects of the English economy, the women of the middling classes and those aspiring to the middling classes who provided the market for fashionable, clothing, novelties, and accessories. Despite critics, women announced their status by following fashion.

Gender, Class, and the Bazaar in the History of Retail

Just as complex as the relationship of bazaars to class was their relationship to the gender with which they are most associated—women. In many ways, they were attempts to control women, 'safe' outlets that kept them out of harm's way. For upper-class women the charity bazaars fulfilled a social welfare function while occupying the time and expending the energy of a large class of leisured women. Yet, they also gave women the freedom to move outside their immediate social and domestic circles, and to participate in a kind of work. Some even utilized the fancy fair as a showplace for their painting and sculpture. For the working women in the bazaar, it gave them a chance at livelihood and a 'career.' Some of them were also contributing to the crafts they sold at their stalls.[141] Although still only a small part of the overall retail trade, bazaars helped to feminize the consumer experience as well as make way for consumer culture on an even larger scale at the end of the nineteenth century. The ladies who frequented bazaars were the forerunners of the West End shopping ladies so familiar later in the century.[142] Despite accusations of prostitution, and biting satires of the 'shopping mania,' women carved out a public and economic space for themselves in bazaars.

---

[138] Adam Blenkinsop, *A Shilling's-Worth of Advice, on Manners, Behaviour & Dress* (London: Blenkinsop, 1850), 22-23.

[139] *Ibid.*, 32.

[140] *The Science of Dress* (London: Groombridge and Sons, 1857), 14.

[141] John Holland notes the irony that the upper-class ladies who worked in charity bazaars looked with contempt on the working-class women of retail trade doing precisely the same kind of work like "shop girls,' . . . 'warehouse women,' 'seamstresses.' Holland, *The Bazaar*, 15, f.n.

[142] See Walkowitz, *City of Dreadful Delight*, 47.

Some of the innovations credited by historians of the latter nineteenth-century to the department stores developed first in the bazaars. In discussing the advent of the department store, William Leach claims, 'Had they been alive to witness it, the merchants of the 1840s would have blinked at such a transformation. What, they would have asked, is an auditorium doing in a retail store? a restaurant? a roof garden?'[143] Yet all of these innovations had been pioneered in bazaars. In one of England's earliest department stores, Manchester's *Lewis's*, goods were displayed openly 'in square boxes, from which customers could help themselves' just as they were in the bazaars like Soho.[144] If the bazaar is part of what Bennett refers to as the 'exhibitionary complex,' then surely it is closer to the department store end of that spectrum even with the bazaar's associations with dioramas and panoramas. Like the earlier bazaars, department stores attempted to give a controlled, English version of the exotic East. By placing women behind the counter, bazaars and department stores helped to feminize consumer culture.[145] Bazaars also hastened the approach of conspicuous consumption. Almost all the critics agreed that bazaars sold 'useless' items, yet the English flocked to them with gusto and women especially bought. The bazaar stands undeniably as a flashpoint in the development of consumer culture, and an important ancestor of the dream world of the *fin de siècle grand magasins*.

Although charity bazaars remained popular into the next century, one by one the popular commercial bazaars of London fell victim to the auctioneer's block, or to the vagaries of fashionable entertainment and found themselves eventually reborn as theaters and dance halls. The first to suffer, possibly due to increased competition of charity fairs, but also because they could not compete with larger bazaars like Soho, were those imitations built in the wave following Trotter's establishment. Despite a lavish rebuilding after the fire in 1829, the Queen's Bazaar in Oxford Street had to re-open as a the Princess Theatre in 1839.[146] The effects of the bazaar at Leicester were auctioned off in 1844 after the death of its

---

[143]Leach, 'Transformations in a Culture of Consumption,' 326.

[144]Asa Briggs, *Friends of the People: The Centenary History of Lewis's* (London: B.T. Batsford, 1956), 66.

[145]Dyer, 'Vanity Fair,' 197. See also *Ibid.*, 199; Walkowitz, *City of Dreadful Delight*, 48-49. See also Rosalind Williams, *Dream Worlds: Mass Consumption in Late Nineteenth-Century France* (Berkeley: University of California Press, 1982) and Michael Miller, *The Bon Marché: Bourgeois Culture and the Department Store, 1869-1920* (Princeton: Princeton University Press, 1981).

[146]Queen's Bazaar, 13 April 1836, 'London Play Places,' John Johnson Collection; The Queen's Bazaar, 23 October 1836, 'London Play Places,' Box I, John Johnson Collection, Bodleian, Oxford; The Queen's Bazaar, Oxford Street, 18 October 1838, 'London Play Places,' Box I, John Johnson Collection, Bodleian, Oxford; Queen's Bazaar, 20 February 1837, 'London Play Places,' Box I, John Johnson Collection, Bodleian, Oxford; The Queen's Bazaar, Oxford Street, 22 October 1837, 'London Play Places,' Box I, John Johnson Collection, Bodleian, Oxford. See also Shaw, *London in the Sixties*, 229.

proprietor.[147] By the end of the century, Soho became an area of tenement houses and struggling tradesmen—mostly those of the boot and tailoring trades.[148] Closing in 1889, the Soho Bazaar itself was replaced by the newest innovation in consumer culture—the department store.

The reign of the department store, however, as the undisputed Queen of English consumer culture did not occur until the end of the century, and although *commercial* bazaars began to decline after mid-century, their retail innovations overtook traditional English shopkeeping. The feminization of shopping with lavish displays and an emphasis on appearance over utility encouraged by the bazaars also, according to critics, undermined English trade as a whole. Critics accused bazaars, emporiums, and discount drapery shops, of corrupting English trade and English consumers with a false retail culture.

---

[147]The Bazaar, Leicester Square, 1844, 'London Play Places,' Box I, John Johnson Collection, Bodleian, Oxford.

[148]Shaw, *London in the Sixties*, 229-230; *The Story of Old Soho* (London: T. Pettitt & Co., 1893), intro.

Chapter 3

'Mothers Beware!':
Fraud by the Retailer

'When we come to have a crowd, they won't get in and out,' said Jones.'If only we could crush a few to death in the doorway our fortune would be made,' said Robinson.

—Anthony Trollope, 1870

A Retail Culture of Fraud

The following advertisement by a St. Paul's Churchyard drapery firm appeared in 1853:

> 'FIRE! . . .£80, 794 Worth of DRAPERY GOODS, damaged (chiefly by Water), immense Stock of West of England Woollen CLOTHS Of every shade and Color; Cassimeres, Kerseys, Carpetings, &c., &c. In consequence of the late extensive FIRE which took place on the Premises of Messrs. PAWSON & CO., of London, a portion of their valuable and varied Stock saved from the Fire) has been consigned . . . for the purpose of affecting speedy Sales. . . . Many of the Goods being stained and soiled by water, are rendered unfit for the Wholesale Trade, but no worse to the retail purchaser or wearer, . . . The goods are therefore warranted perfect, although OFFERED TO THE PUBLIC AT ONE HALF the customary Trade Prices.[1]

Pawson & Co.'s 'extensive fire' seemed to leave many of their goods in perfect condition and provided them with an opportunity for a mass sale to the public. Such methods left many nineteenth-century critics suspicious of the honesty of retail dealers. Innovations like bazaars and large drapery shops helped usher in the golden age of retail trade during which small, stall-sized conventional shops made way for grand shopping palaces. The transformation from traditional shop to grand department store was complex, and retail trade was criticized for its deficiencies as often as it was lauded for its successes. The ideal split between the traditional shop and discount emporium was less clear in reality than in the writings of critics. Critics found the golden age of retail to be merely brass.

---

[1] Pawson & Co., 'Bazaars & Sales,' Box I, John Johnson Collection, Bodleian, Oxford; This business was founded as Leaf & Sons wholesale haberdashers of Old Change and then moved to St. Paul's Churchyard becoming Pawson & Leaf and by 1853 Pawson & Co. See figure 3.1 page 91 for the full advertisement. See also Alison Adburgham, *Shops and Shopping: 1800-1914* (London: Barrie and Jenkins, 1964), 151.

Once the pride of a 'nation of shopkeepers,' English retailers found themselves in the new century increasingly accused of fraud. Although worried about the thieving small dealer or 'cheap shopkeeper,' commentators like Anthony Trollope were more concerned with the growing retail culture of 'fraud' typified by the large, discount, drapery emporiums. Much of the criticism of fraud or falseness in English trade did not involve cases of actual criminal frauds committed by shopkeepers but was, in essence, a condemnation of new retailing methods that were based on advertising, display, and bargain sales. As traditional, smaller, family-run shops were replaced with larger businesses, buying and selling became more impersonal. Critics like Percival Leigh and Richard Doyle depicted this new wave of retail businesses as depending on false sales, advertising puffery, trickery, and outright fraud as large quantities of below-standard goods were sold at 'bargain' prices. With their plate-glass windows, brass fixtures, bright paint, and ornate window-dressing, these large shops emphasized display over substance. Their innovative business methods seemed to many to be based on false principles and undermined the character of English trade. The new shopping that so frightened critics, satirists, and older style retailers was a combination of the luxurious shopping experience of the aristocracy of the eighteenth century with a new, more democratized large-scale element of cheaper goods affordable to the middle classes. Seen by many in their time as encouraging a retail culture of fraud, 'cheap shops' and discount emporiums outlived their critics in the success of later department stores; however, these new 'hard sell' emporiums with their emphasis on customer-attracting displays and advertisements and their adherence to ready money, opened the way for the department stores of the end of the century and modern consumer culture.

The 'Cheap Shopkeeping' Debate

The 'cheap shopkeeping' debates of the mid-nineteenth century supports Lancaster's view of an evolution over the course of the nineteenth century rather than a revolution in English consumer culture in the modern era.[2] Although many studies have been written on the modern love affair with consumption from Marx and Veblen to recent studies by scholars like William Leach, much of this analysis rests on the original nineteenth-century criticisms of the hollow nature of the new methods of retail.[3] These theories of consumption are also burdened by nineteenth-

---

[2] William Lancaster, *The Department Store: A Social History* (London: Leicester University Press, 1995), 3. See also John Brewer and Roy Porter, *Consumption and the World of Goods* (London: Routledge, 1993).

[3] For a useful discussion and summary of the historiography of consumption in the nineteenth century and the effects of both Veblen's theory of conspicuous consumption and Marxist theories of commodification, please see Lancaster, *The Department Store*, 159-168.

century concepts of gender, but, unlike Victorian critics, they allow women to be led to their own destruction by the evils of mass consumption, rather than accusing the women of happily pushing their country's shopkeepers towards that destruction. Nineteenth-century admonitions against the dangers of consumption in such places by critics ranged from novelists to other shopkeepers; they attempted to enforce a check on consumption while criticizing what they saw as fraudulent methods of retail. One of the oldest and most frequent cries warning shoppers of the dangers of participation in consumption was the 'cheap shop.'

Alison Adburgham characterizes the late 1830s and 1840s as 'The Era of Retail Adventurers' due to the phenomenal growth in English shops, but this period may just as well be called the 'Era of Cheap Shops.' Although the idea of the disreputable 'cheap shopkeeper' existed long before the 1840s, a new wave of concern about 'cheap shops' swept through the 1840s. The concern rose along with the growth in English retail, or rather the adoption of new methods of retail. When English commentators criticized 'cheap shops', they meant either an older form of small shop that sold bargains and coarse inexpensive goods, usually to a poorer clientele, or a new larger scale shop that claimed to sell goods at or below wholesale. These larger scale shops, often drapery shops, began threatening older, established businesses near mid-century.

The association of the term 'cheap shop' with emporium-type establishments does not mean that all emporiums claimed to be bargain basements. Like any other type of shop, there were various levels of respectability, but all claimed to sell in bulk at minimum profit. William Ablett, a draper who wrote his memoirs in the 1870s, was apprenticed around this time at one of the smaller, 'cheap shops' catering to a lower income level customer in Whitechapel before moving on to more respectable firms like Waitham's and Everington's.[4] Even more disturbing than the small, 'cheap shops' like Ablett's master's were the larger inexpensive drapery establishments of the late 30s, 40s, and 50s that threatened the business of an entire neighborhood. In a short story in *Tait's Edinburgh Magazine* in 1859, the author describes one such fictional establishment: 'Hilton Hall undersold, and the public took advantage of its folly.'[5] In this story, Hilton Hall, like many of its non-fictional counterparts, was unable to sustain business on this large-scale, small profit operation.

Although many criticized the plague of 'cheap shops' overtaking London in the 1840s, few described them accurately. A writer representing himself as C.B.C. Amicus wrote a treatise on *How to Rise in Life* in which he described 'cheap shops': 'It constantly occures in London and in other towns to see shops inscribed 'selling off at prime cost,' 'awful sacrifice,' 'tremendous failure,' and goods ticketed at prices so low as to be a certificate that they are either good for nothing dishonestly come by, or are to be got rid of for a dishonest purpose . . ..' He also

---

[4] William Ablett, *Reminiscences of An Old Draper* (London: Sampson Low, Marston, Searle, and Rivington, 1876), 75-76.
[5] 'Shoppers and Shopping,' *Tait's Edinburgh Magazine*, 26 N.S (May 1859), 294.

noted that common purchases at these shops were ready-made clothing like 'shirts and other made-up articles of dress.'[6] The year before Amicus's work was published, an article appeared in *Bentley's Miscellany* that more precisely detailed London's 'cheap shops'.

> a ticket-shop, or pretended cheap shop, a lying, Jeremy Diddler shop, that pretends to be always selling off at a great sacrifice, as if its sole ambition were to ruin itself for the benefit of a discerning public. There is something of the cut of the swell-mob about one of these cheap shops; it looks as if it had stolen its commodities, or had obtained them upon false pretences, which, in truth, is usually the case; . . .. You are attracted, if you know no better, to the low prices of articles ticketed in the window, and you enter . . ..[7]

The author of this article, 'Shopping in London,' applied his cautions against not only cheap clothing shops, but an entire range of such businesses that claimed to sell on minimal margins of profit including 'cheap tea-shops, cheap tailors, cheap jewellers,' and 'cheap haberdashers.'[8] The message was clear. 'Cheap shops' were a bane to respectable English trade.

In a letter to the *Times*, 'A London Tradesman' cited a specific case of how such shops undermined English retail and turned it into a culture of fraud ranging from the people who purchase the goods to the men who sell them. Here the meaning of the term 'cheap shops' is unmistakable: they are the discount houses that sell in quantity for ready money to London retail customers. He lashed out against two of the most successful competitors, Hodge and Lowman—a large drapery firm in Regent Street, and Moses and Sons, a sizable establishment in Aldgate. Hermione Hobhouse describes Hodge and Lowman as 'substantial pioneers' establishing themselves in the northern circus, Piccadilly, in the same neighborhood with such giants as Swan and Edgar.[9] In 1834 Hodge and Lowman claimed that from their location at Argyll House, they served as linen drapers, haberdashers, hosiers, glovers, lacemen and also provided silk mercery and family mourning.[10] Both of these commodious establishments, Hodge and Lowman and Moses and Sons, held the distinction of being on the forefront of commercial innovation in their shop-fronts and display methods. Although both were discount

---

[6] C.B.C. Amicus, *How to Rise in Life* (London: Longman, Brown, Green, and Longmans, 1845), 43.

[7] 'Shopping in London,' *The Living Age*, 1, no. 4 (June 1844), 250. Note: originally appeared in *Bentley's Miscellany*.

[8] *Ibid.*, 251.

[9] Hermione Hobhouse, *A History of Regent Street* (London: Macdonald and Jane's, 1975), 50.

[10] Hodge & Lowman, 1834, 'Bill Headings,' Box 16, John Johnson Collection, Bodleian, Oxford.

houses, they boasted the most spectacular plate-glass windows and brass shop-fronts in all of London.[11]

The False Retailer

In his November 8, 1844 letter to the *Times*, the disgruntled 'London Tradesman' drew attention to a previous *Times* article on the bankruptcy of Robert Bannister and disparaged the cheap if innovative trading methods of Hodge and Lowman and Moses and Sons. Robert Bannister was one of the many tradesmen whose businesses failed in 1844. Forced to declare bankruptcy, Bannister admitted in his trial that he had sold his creditors' goods for less than half of their value in order to pay immediate debts. He sold £750 worth of goods to Messrs. Moses and Sons for only £269 and to Hodge and Lowman he sold £200 worth of goods for only £100. Bannister sold the goods to Hodge and Lowman from a rented cab under a false name. The tradesman writing to the *Times* asked that the names of such dishonest tradesmen be published to prevent unfair, fraudulent competition against regular traders.[12] Hodge and Lowman immediately leapt to their own defense declaring they were taken in by Bannister's false name, and that they paid only 20 per cent and not 50 per cent under cost for the goods;[13] however, as the tradesman points out in his later letter, 'It must be supposed, as tradesmen, that they must have known that goods offered to them even at 20 per cent. under the manufacturer's price could only be done so for some dishonest purpose; and the circumstance of a stranger bringing goods for sale in a cab ought to have excited suspicion . . ..' He wryly added that 'buying goods in this manner is most unusual with respectable tradesmen, although not perhaps so with large shops professing to sell cheap.'[14]

The exposure of the Bannister bankruptcy case and his involvement with two successful London drapery firms demonstrates how the term 'cheap shop' stretched to cover innovative discount houses as well as small fraudulent shops. It became something of a catchall term to describe suspicious new methods in retail. These cheap discount houses were expanding despite the suspicions of critics and businessmen like the author of *A Handy Guide for the Draper and Haberdasher* who warned that 'the system adopted by some, of selling tolerably good articles, and such as would allow of a moderate profit, at cost, or less than cost price, is not to be commended . . ..'[15] 'cheap shops' represented everything that traditionalists

---

[11] 'The London Shop-Fronts,' *Chamber's Journal of Popular Literature, Science and Art* (October 15, 1864), 670-672.

[12] A London Tradesman to the Editor of the *Times*, 8 November 1844, *Times*, 9 November 1844.

[13] Hodge and Lowman, Argyle-house, Regent-street to the Editor of the *Times*, 9 November 1844, *Times*, 11 November 1844.

[14] A London Tradesman to the Editor of the *Times*, 11 November 1844.

[15] *A Handy Guide for the Draper and Haberdasher* (20 Paternoster Row, London: F. Pitman, 1864), 27.

thought was going awry in the land of shopkeepers. From small 'cheap shops' to larger discount emporiums, fraud seemed rampant in English retail trade.

As Bannister's case illustrates, fraud was an elastic category in the nineteenth century. Critics not only attacked actual criminal fraud, cases that qualified as fraud under the law, practiced in English business, but also charged the new retailers like emporium operators with practicing unethical, 'fraudulent' trade. In critics' debates, overall fears of the changing nature of English trade intermingled with reports of criminal frauds. Newspapers, trade papers, and trade protection society circulars reveal that many dealers in London shops in the nineteenth century were either fraudulent, or perhaps formerly honest dealers forced into fraud by the threat of bankruptcy.

In 1829, an author identifying himself only as 'A Bow Street Officer' described one of the most common methods of fraud practiced by a group one might call fake retailers. The method he described required a group of swindlers. One posed as a honest tradesman who rented out a respectable place of business while his friends posed as clerks. Female friends pretended to be ladies patronizing the shop. Sometimes the swindlers even rented a carriage for the ladies to visit the shop. After setting up the business, the fraudulent retailers obtained goods on credit from respectable dealers, which they immediately pawned or sold for ready cash. According to the author, they also printed up fake bills that they used to receive better terms from their creditors and even used as a sort of collateral for loans. Soon the fake retailers left town and when the fraudulent bills were due, the money and the goods were nowhere to be found.[16]

As the scheme described by 'A Bow Street Officer' illustrates, nineteenth-century consumers, as well as suppliers, had good reason to be suspicious of new retail dealers. For a shopper there were few protections against unscrupulous dealers and 'cheap' shopkeepers. Consumers had to trust their judgement as to the respectability of an establishment. In London it was especially difficult to find this kind of information outside of one's immediate neighborhood. For people coming into London from the countryside, it was even less possible to distinguish between the borderline and the truly respectable establishment.

Although the government took no real part in keeping businesses honest, self-policing private organizations evolved in the late-eighteenth and early nineteenth century that were supposed to protect their customers and protect their trades from other dishonest dealers. In reality, these business organizations or 'trade protection societies' functioned to protect their members and only secondarily the consumers. These societies sought to expose fraudulent retailers like the ones described by the Bow Street Officer along with tracking down customers who had problems paying

---

[16] Bow Street Officer, *The Frauds of London: Displaying the Numerous and Daring Cheats and Robberies Practised Upon the Stranger and the Unwary* (No. 10, Newgate Street, London: William Cole, 1829), 11.

their debts, or criminals who stole from them.[17] Trade protection societies and trade papers provide numerous records of retail frauds who cheated their creditors, particularly the wholesalers, and set up their shops on false pretences.[18]

In the 1830s Thomas Miller, Secretary for the Society for the Protection of Trade in London, circulated the organization's private newsletter forewarning members of untrustworthy fellow traders and consumers. Some of these fraudulent retailers appear more than once in the newsletter. Richard Sheldrick obtained goods on credit for his shop in Cambridge Road in March of 1831 and left the premises without paying for any of the goods. He accomplished a repeat performance in June of the same year in Kingsland Road.[19] Although Sheldrick's particular area of retail is not specifically named, there was no limit to the areas invaded by fake retailers as this notice from the Trade Protection Society demonstrates:

RICHARD WITTINGHAM, . . . formerly of Southampton Street, Camberwell, Surrey, Baker, . . . —then of Aldersgate Street, near Jewin Street, Umbrella Manufacturer, —then of Chapel Street, Salford, Manchester, Boot & Shoe and Hat Warehouse, . . . then of West Street, Reading, Berks, Brewer, —then of Belmont Row, Wandworth Road, Surrey, Grocer & Cheesemonger, . . . has given notice of his intention to apply for his discharge under the Insolvent Debtor's Act, at the Court House, Portugal Street, Lincoln's Inn Fields, on the 16th of May next, at 10 o'clock in the Morning precisely.[20]

Wittingham was either an accomplished fraud or had very little talent in a variety of careers. He was not alone in his list of frauds in various trades in London and other thriving nineteenth-century English cities. Similar records were held by James Cant whose latest address was given as Newington Causeway, Surrey in 1830[21] and John

---

[17] For a specific example of such a case, see the case of Robert Waters a.k.a. John Hamilton in the papers of the Society for the Protection of Trade. Posing as a respectable dealer, 'John Hamilton' even placed newspaper advertisements in the *Courier* to help complete his fraud scheme. PRO C114/34, Thomas Miller, Society for the Protection of Trade to [members] Society for the Protection of Trade, 22 Ely Place, London, 28 February 1831, 6th notice 1831.

[18] These societies appear to have developed from the late eighteenth- and early nineteenth-century societies for the prosecution of felons in England. See David Philips, 'Good Men to Associate and Bad Men to Conspire: Associations for the Prosecution of Felons in England 1760-1860,' in *Policing and Prosecution in Britain 1750-1850*, ed. Douglas Hay and Francis Snyder (Oxford: Clarendon Press, 1989), 113-169.

[19] PRO C114/34, Thomas Miller, Society for the Protection of Trade to [members] Society for the Protection of Trade, 22 Ely Place, London, 8 March 1831, 7th notice 1831; PRO C114/34, Thomas Miller, Society for the Protection of Trade to [members] Society for the Protection of Trade, 22 Ely Place, London, 7 June 1831, 12th notice 1831.

[20] PRO C114/34, Thomas Miller, Society for the Protection of Trade to [members] Society for the Protection of Trade, 22 Ely Place, London, May 1831, 11th notice 1831.

[21] PRO C114/34, Thomas Miller, Society for the Protection of Trade to [members] Society for the Protection of Trade, 22 Ely Place, London, December 1830, 16th notice 1830.

Danks who practiced trades ranging from Bonnet dealer to slop and shoe warehouseman.[22] The fears of anonymous, urban retail and the changes it wrought in the style of English trade were not unfounded. Even as they were, according to contemporaries, duping their own customers, larger retailers feared being ruined by smaller dealers who did not pay them for goods sold on credit. Competition was so fierce that turning down a customer, shopper or small retailer who seemed less than respectable was an option open to only the most well-established and wealthy businesses. One of the most competitive of all nineteenth-century retail businesses—drapers—faced some of the worst competition, fraud, and demanding consumers of all English retail shops.

Fraud and the English Draper

Drapery and the clothing trade were big money businesses in the nineteenth century. Drapery was also a favorite trade for fraud against the customer and for duping one's suppliers. In 1830, the London Society for the Protection of Trade cautioned its members about John Jenkins Kimpton, a Lesson Grove draper who obtained goods from other traders and then escaped;[23] however, even respectable tradesmen could be tempted into a fraudulent course of business when that constant threat to Victorian businesses, bankruptcy, knocked at the door. Robert Wilson Brookes, a hosier in Shoreditch had already been forced to declare bankruptcy when he saw an opportunity of quickly paying his creditors. The Great Eastern Railway needed to buy his premises for new construction. To make his compensation even greater from the railway, Wilson Brookes started buying large quantities of drapery and silk from suppliers to give the appearance of an extensive business. He was caught before the scheme paid off and sentenced to four months in prison.[24] In 1870, another hosier in Manchester, John Magee, stocked his warehouse with sawdust-filled parcels to make his business look more extensive and encourage others to give him credit.[25] Stocking a warehouse with false goods, acquiring credit on false pretenses, or simply running a false business and absconding with the goods all served as methods for the fake retailer.

Some fake 'retailers' did not even require a warehouse or place of business to commit their frauds. John Gardner worked as a draper for Messrs. Ellis, Howell & Co., a respectable firm in St. Paul's Churchyard. In the spring of 1871 he lost his

---

[22] PRO C114/34, Thomas Miller, Society for the Protection of Trade to [members] Society for the Protection of Trade, 22 Ely Place, London, 7 December 1830, 14 notice 1830.

[23] PRO C114/38, Thomas Miller, Society for the Protection of Trade to [members] Society for the Protection of Trade, 22 Ely Place, Holborn, London, 19 February 1830, 2nd notice 1830. Fraudulent drapers were no less a problem in the 1840s when a London firm swindled into providing a supposed firm in Brighton with 'superfine cloth' discovered their mistake too late. See London Firm to the Editor of the *Times*, 12 March 1844, *Times*, 14 March 1844.

[24] 'Fraudulently Obtaining Goods,' *The Draper* (London) 1 October 1869.

[25] 'A Sawdust Stocked Shop,' *The Draper* (London) 22 July 1870.

employment with Howell & Co; however, using the name of the dress buyer at his old company, Gardner claimed he was sent for fabric to Murdock Nephew's general merchant warehouse. He carried away piece goods and came back later in the same week for more fabric. Finally, the suspicious merchant contacted Howell & Co. and had Gardner arrested for obtaining goods on false pretences. Gardner had pawned the fabric on the same days that he acquired them.[26] Gardner was on the small end of retail fraud—probably driven by lack of employment to steal in the name of his old employer.

One of the most spectacular drapery frauds of the same period was a widowed woman, Madame Doodewaarde. The widow of St. Leonard's Terrace, Maids Hill, left England in December of 1869 owing creditors between £20,000 and £30,000. Doodwaarde ran a respectable firm after the death of her husband, but secretly married a man named Laars in the late 1860s. With Laars' and her son-in-law's help, she sold off the goods given to her on credit at public auctions in various parts of England. Punctual in her payments until she left the country, the once respectable tradeswoman and her new husband were thousands of pounds richer in Holland thanks to duped general merchants and other creditors in England.[27] From Madame Doodewaarde's £30,000 to John Gardner's inexpensive poplin, the fraudulent retailer covered a wide range of respectability and levels of deception.

According to critics, the same falseness in retail that allowed people like Richard Wittingham and Madame Doodewarde to flourish and commit acts of criminal fraud also led to fraud and trickery in other aspects of trade. If retailers used false records and sawdust goods to fool their creditors and discount houses supplied themselves underhandedly by feeding off the misery of bankrupt shopkeepers, they also used dubious methods to sell the goods to the customer. Retail trade seemed rife with deception. The 'cheap' shops selling shoddy goods and the larger 'cheap' discount houses were accused of shady sales methods. Marked by aggressive advertising and promises of unbelievable bargains, retailers, especially in the competitive drapery and haberdashery trades, offered fraudulent sales.

Richard Doyle and Percival Leigh in their 1849 *Manners and Cvstoms of ye Englyshe*, entered a section in 'Mr. Pips's' diary titled 'Trycks of ye London Trade' that caricatured the haberdashery, drapery and mercery trades. In this entry Pips humored his wife by taking her on a walk down Regent Street and Oxford Street. He derided their plentiful window advertisements:

> . . . 'Tremendous Sacrifice!' in another of an 'Alarming Failure!!', in a third of a 'Ruinous Bankruptcy!!', by reason whereof, the Goods within were a-felling off at

---

[26] 'Frauds on Warehousemen,' *The Draper* (London) 21 April 1871.
[27] 'Extraordinary Frauds in the Drapery Trade,' *The Draper* (London) 14 January 1870.

50, 60, or 70 per cent under prime cost, . . . if their notices do tell true: which made
my heart ache, I mean, through laughing at their roguery. [28]

Once a customer was enticed into a store by such advertisements, the methods of
fraud and high-pressure sale continued.

Punch writer Douglas William Jerrold wrote a scathing commentary on the
drapery trade in his sketch of 'The Linen-Draper's Assistant' in the same period.
According to Jerrold, the job of the draper's assistant was to unload as much of his
master's stock as possible on whatever customer he happened to be serving. He
described a typical visit to a linen-drapers in which a lady had been served with the
item she required, but was convinced to purchase more by the drapery assistant's
insistence on asking if she needed anything else:

'N-o; N-othing else,' replies the lady; and ere she has deliberately pulled on her
glove, there is something else unrolled before her.
  'A beautiful thing, madam; and' (this is said half-confidentially) 'the first of the
season.'
  . . . and the lady begins to melt; and her husband's pocket . . . must shrink with
apprehension . . . .[29]

Jerrold contended that the linen-draper's shopman created want were there was
none by repeatedly pressuring his customers: "Nothing else?' is, in matters of
trade, the peculiar weapon of the linen-draper. . .."[30] Lured into shops with
fraudulent or, at least, exaggerated sales, women then faced the pressuring
technique of the linen-draper's assistant tempting them with low-prices and
beautiful fabrics. Husbands, as Doyle, Leigh, and Jerrold were quick to point out,
knew and resisted the false methods of the ostentatious linen-drapers. According to
these critics, women were especially vulnerable to the baits of the clothing retailer.

In an age in which linen-drapers expanded into haberdashery and haberdashers
also vended linen-drapers' fabric, critics and satirists also attacked the haberdasher
as a tempter of shopping ladies:

Count of the Counter! graceful swell!
  The winning smile the ladies wheedles.
Tis thine, accomplished youth, to sell
  Bobbin and tape, and pins and needles,

Persuasion plays upon your face;
  We watch your movements with delight;

[28] Richard Doyle and Percival Leigh, 'Mr. Pips His Diary, Trycks of ye London Trade,
[Tuefday, September 4, 1849],' *Manners and Cvstoms of ye Englyshe* (London,
Bradbury & Evans, 1849).

[29] Douglas William Jerrold, 'The Linen-Draper's Assistant,' *Sketches of the English*, in
The Writings of Douglas Jerrold, vol. 5 (London: Bradbury and Evans, 1853), 236.

[30] Jerrold, 'The Linen-Draper's Assistant,' 237.

And in your finished figure trace
A Haberdasher Exquisite!'[31]

In 1869 the *Girl of the Period Miscellany* was no less clear about the haberdasher in its feature 'Miss Polly Glott's Dictionary of the Future:'

HABERDASHER, n. a siren in the shape of a male human being, possessed of strange powers of fascination, which few women can resist, and by means of his emporium to purchase innumerable articles for which they have not the slightest necessity; in the opinion of husbands, a tempter, a demon.[32]

Described as using over aggressive sales techniques and false claims, the new linen draper and haberdasher in 'his emporium' tempted ladies to purchase shoddy goods and spend beyond their means. They 'seduced' women not for sexual favors—but for the favor of their pocketbooks. Like Doyle, Leigh and Jerrold, 'Miss Polly Glott' agreed that only women were susceptible to the wiles of the cloth retailer. Husbands were represented as above such temptation and trickery.

Bankruptcies, Convenient Fires and Fortuitous Floods

Just as women had begun to enjoy their participation in consumption in the new shops, they were warned of traps at every turn in their enjoyment of pleasure shopping and the power to consume. For the most part, descriptions of the fraudulent methods of sales of drapers and haberdashers came from critics, and the reality of these accusations is difficult to judge. Retailers who used such methods to entice customers did not, for the most part, leave diaries recording their trickery on the English public. However, when William Ablett published his memoirs in 1872, he was well past retirement age, and felt comfortably distanced from his youthful career to discuss some of these methods.

Methods of false sales ranged from 'selling off at a sacrifice' to inaccurately claiming to be victims of fire and flood. Ablett aptly detailed how his master's shop in Whitechapel came to sell by such methods. Like most apprentices in the early nineteenth-century, Ablett began working at a young age. When he was still a teenager, another boy accidentally burned some netting hung up for display in the shop window. Only the netting was damaged, but the young Ablett suggested to his boss that they have a fire sale to drum up business. They printed up bills bemoaning the fire and how goods must be sold at a loss and even 'burnt great holes in a few lengths of common prints and calicoes, which we strung up from the

---

[31] This poem of unknown origin is accompanied by a sinister looking illustration of the well-dressed haberdasher. The Haberdasher, 'Trades & Professions,' Box IV, John Johnson Collection, Bodleian, Oxford.

[32] 'Miss Polly Glott's Dictionary of the Future,' *Girl of the Period Miscellany*, 7 (September 1869), 240-241, 'Fashion,' Box 14, John Johnson Collection, Bodleian, Oxford.

ceiling to the floor inside, which had a very marked and striking effect.'[33] A few days before the well-advertised sale commenced, Ablett and his fellow assistants burnt only one edge of piles of stock with lighted paper so that the damage would not deteriorate the value of the fabric:

> Long before the doors were opened, . . . a dense mob surrounded the shop and blocked up the pavement. . . . Critical old women, that under ordinary circumstances would have spent a long time, . . . examining a pair of stockings, bought the same goods, instantly, at full prices, when slightly singed at the tops, and every class of goods was in request.[34]

The fire sale was such a success that Ablett and his fellows had to close up shop in the middle of the day to rearrange stock and to purchase secretly more 'fire damaged' goods.

Ablett called this successful sales method the 'selling off' system. After the false fire sale, his master adopted this system wholeheartedly and continued such sales: 'whether we were selling the remains of a 'burnt stock' or the salvage of a vessel, that had conveniently sunk for our purpose, when we disposed of wet drapery goods, that had been dipped in salt and water . . ..'[35] He noted that during the earlier half of the century the selling off system grew to be one of the most popular sales methods in London. Ablett's service to his master in this process earned him a salary increase to £80 a year all before the age of sixteen.[36] This selling off system, in which tradesmen claimed to experience disasters ranging from bankruptcy to conflagration, met with criticism from Victorian commentators like Doyle and Leigh and Anthony Trollope. Doyle and Leigh described the fictional draper's shop of Ragge and Rip, 'who have been . . . making a tremendous sacrifice any time the last two years; . . .. But I do not pity such gudgeons a whit as are caught by these tricks of the drapery trade; and methinks they are rightly served by being cheated in seeking a profit . . . by fraud and dishonest bankruptcy.'[37] In other words, anyone who would make a profit off another man's misery, in this case Ragge and Rip's customers, deserved what they got. The customers were as guilty as the cheating drapers.[38] In fiction and satire, drapers represented the worst of

---

[33] William Ablett, 'Reminiscences of an Old Draper,' *Warehousemen and Draper's Trade Journal* (London) 15 May 1872, 53-54; Ablett, *Reminiscences of an Old Draper*, 31-32.

[34] William Ablett, 'Reminiscences of an Old Draper' *Warehousemen and Draper's Trade Journal* (London) 1 June 1872, 79; Ablett, *Reminiscences of an Old Draper*, 37-38.

[35] William Ablett, 'Reminiscences of An Old Draper,' *Warehousemen and Draper's Trade Journal* (London) 1 July 1872, 126. See also Ablett, *Reminiscences of an Old Draper*, 41-47.

[36] *Ibid.*

[37] Doyle and Leigh, 'Mr. Pips His Diary, Trycks of ye London Trade, [Tuefday, September 4, 1849].' Note: spelling modernized.

[38] See also Anthony Trollope, *The Struggles of Brown, Jones, and Robinson: By one of the Firm* (London: Smith, Elder & Co., 1870), 231 for another satirical example of an exaggerated bankruptcy sale advertisement by a drapery firm.

English retail. Thriving like vultures on the misfortunes of other businesses in the volatile nineteenth-century clothing trades, drapers claimed to save consumers money by either mimicking or taking advantage of other people's bankruptcies.

Even respectable firms like Thomas Christie & Sons auctioneers were not above feeding in the selling off system frenzy. In 1857 they advertised their good fortune in selling off the effects of several bankrupt firms including Houghton & Co., Merchants and Warehousemen, Harding & Co., Silk Mercers to the Queen, and Hunt & Co., Linen Merchants and Warehousemen:

> The recent extensive BANK and MERCANTILE FAILURES, . . . have induced COMMERCIAL DISASTERS in this Country, within the last month, to which no antecedent period can bring a parallel. The panic pervading the mind of the wealthy London Merchant deters him, for the moment from embarking in further speculations, or the advantages now accruing to the Public from the above Estates, would be withheld in their primary efficacy; . . . N.B.—What follows, though RUINOUS and STARTLING, is issued with the sanction and by the command of the Highest Mercantile Tribunal in the Land, namely, —the Court of Bankruptcy.

This 'startling' announcement was followed by a general catalog including 'SOILED GOODS . . . Uninjured,—at One Tenth their Cost!!!'[39] This advertisement illustrates that satire such as Doyle and Leigh's had a basis in the reality of English retail. Although it received its harshest criticisms in fiction, the selling off system was an indisputable part of nineteenth-century business practice, especially for the competitive clothing trades.

False bankruptcy and fire sales, high-pressure salesmen, and outlandish advertisements brought criticism on the new retailers. Other businessmen tried to separate themselves from this culture of retail fraud by claiming to respect older, honest, more traditional methods of business. Ribbans' shop in Lavenham, Suffolk was an extensive retail and wholesale business dealing in goods ranging from drapery to grocery items. In Ribbans' poetic advertisement he distanced himself from such shady shop methods: 'Like some vain pretenders he dares not to boast, Of selling articles under prime cost; Nor vaunting his bargains from Bankruptcy's sales, Amuses the Public with fictitious tales; He scorns such deception,—but makes it his care To deal upon terms that are honest and fair.'[40] Some shopkeepers joined nineteenth-century critics of the new retail in romanticizing older traditional methods of trade in an attempt to compete with the overwhelming success of the new larger drapery houses and discount houses.

---

[39] Thomas Christie & Sons, 'Bazaars & Sales,' Box I, John Johnson Collection, Bodleian, Oxford.

[40] Wholesale and Retail Linen Draper, Haberdasher, Hosier, Dealer in Hats, Grocery, &c. &c. &c., 'Women's Clothing and Millinery,' Box I, John Johnson Collection, Bodleian, Oxford. A similar statement is made by E. Reeve, Tailor and Draper, in his advertisement. See E. Reeve, 'Women's Clothing and Millinery,' Box I, John Johnson Collection, Bodleian, Oxford.

Adulteration

Despite the protestations of Ribbans and other shopmen vowing their respectability, critics in satire, in magazine articles, and in newspapers lambasted every aspect of English retail they deemed harmful. Not only were false shopkeepers holding false sales on false premises, sometimes the goods themselves were false or at least below standard. The fictional Mr. Pips' after a trip to Regent Street complained of his wife's desire to purchase cheap muslin at Ragge and Rip's tremendous sacrifice sale: ' a Muslin she did say was dirt-cheap, and I knew was dirt-worth. I plainly refused to let her buy it . . ..'[41] A woman in Jerrold's story, 'The Linen-draper's Assistant,' had no discerning spouse to prevent her from buying a piece of substandard cloth. In this supposedly true story a gentlewoman purchased some cloth from a draper after he assured her that it would wash. The lady angrily returned the item two weeks later and the shopman replied: "I said it would wash—I pledged myself to the fact—but I did not say it would keep its colour."[42] Occasionally such substandard goods threatened more than the buyer's pocketbook. Worse than substandard, some clothing goods were adulterated with harmful chemicals that sickened the wearer.

Adulteration, making products look larger or more attractive by mixing them with something else, is a practice much older than the nineteenth-century. Concerns over adulteration reached a fever pitch in this era of industrial production and anonymous urban environments. Originally, adulteration was associated almost exclusively with food products, but by mid-century the concept was expanded to cover other harmful items like adulterated wallpapers and clothing dyes.[43] A writer in 1855 in *Chamber's Edinburgh Journal* began his article on adulteration by comparing English shopkeepers to the thugs of India: 'Our Thugs manage differently. They converse with their men with the shop-counter between; plunder them of a trifling sum by mixing with the goods they wish to purchase something that is both worthless and deleterious; and then take leave of their victims with a bow and a smirk, indifferent to whether they live or die.'[44] This picture of English shopkeepers makes the satires of Jerrold, Trollope, and Doyle and Leigh seem generous by comparison.[45] This criticism of the increasingly competitive nature of

---

[41] Doyle and Leigh, 'Mr. Pips His Diary, Trycks of ye London Trade, [Tuefday, September 4, 1849].' Note: spelling modernized.

[42] Jerrold, 'The Linen-Draper's Assistant,' 239.

[43] For an overview of the problem of adulteration in English shops and the failure to pass effective legislation in the nineteenth century see Clive Emsley, *Crime and Society in England, 1750-1900* (New York: Longman, 1996).

[44] 'The English Thugs,' *Chamber's Edinburgh Journal*, 23, 70 (1855), 274. See also Amicus, *How to Rise in Life*, 42 for an earlier reference to the harmful practice of adulteration.

[45] 'The English Thugs,' 274-275. For similar observations on the 'decline' of traditional English shopkeeping in the face of cheap shops and emporiums, see 'Shopping in London,' 254 urging customers to avoid cheap shops and deal with 'an honest

English retail may be related to the growing disdain in the nineteenth century for English capitalism and the day to day struggle for material wealth.[46] Once proud to be a nation of shopkeepers, the new views of shopkeeping as a dirty, fraudulent business reflects a sea change in English attitudes towards trade as well as fears of adulteration and trickery in business.

Such charges of adulteration upset retailers. Drapers protested their inclusion in the group of English retailers eager to adulterate goods for profit. A writer in *The Draper* complained of the unfair description of drapers as adulterators. In 1871 a doctor's patient purchased some new pairs of green gloves from a respectable firm that caused eruptions on her skin after she had only worn them a few times. When she stopped wearing the gloves the rash ceased, but the rash returned when she put them on again. The author in *The Draper* blamed the lady herself for 'not keeping her hands clean and proper state.' According to this trade paper author, the accusations of adulteration against drapers was merely a vicious fad. He asked jokingly: 'What became of the attempted agitation against the wearing of striped stockings we know no further than its abortive termination, and hose so dyed was worn since without causing ulcerated legs to either man, woman, or child.'[47] Only seven months later, the adulteration issue returned to current topics, and *The Draper* retracted its earlier statement claiming that some red dyes did have deleterious effects on their wearers and advised plain 'white lambswool socks' instead.[48] Once again, English clothing merchants found themselves accused of selling substandard articles as false bargains, or worse yet, of attracting customers with brightly colored articles of green or magenta that were attractive to the eye, but which the shopkeeper knew to be poisonous to the wearer.

Display: Science, Art or Fraud?

Shopkeepers were constantly accused of committing fraud for profit. If they were not condemned for selling adulterated or substandard articles, they were said to dupe the consumer by displaying one article and selling them another, or perhaps for luring the customer with one item displayed at a real bargain to entice her to buy more expensive ones. For critics, 'fraud' was an elastic category in the nineteenth century and included methods of sale now standard practice such as using a well-advertised, low-priced sale item to attract customers into a shop.

[business] man.' See also 'Old London Shops and Shopkeepers,' *Chamber's Edinburgh Journal* 31 (Saturday, June 1859), 371 complains of the disappearance of courtesy in modern shopkeeping. By contrast 'London Shops, Old and New' in the *Chamber's Edinburgh Journal* 20 (1853), 250-253, seems to be a weak attempt to defend English shopkeepers in the face of current criticism.

[46] See especially Martin J. Wiener, *English Culture and the Decline of the Industrial Spirit, 1850-1908* (New York: Cambridge University Press, 1981), 13-15.

[47] 'Leading Article,' *The Draper* (London) 27 January 1871, 39.

[48] 'Poisonous Stockings,' *The Draper* (London) 18 August 1871, 413.

Advertising was only one way such customers could be lured into stores. Expensive, grand plate-glass windows also served to tempt the consumer into the new retail shops. Although most English shops were moving toward this more modern method of display in the nineteenth century, large display-filled windows were particularly associated with emporiums and cheap drapery shops, and targeted by their detractors.

Display windows were not new to the nineteenth century, but the grandeur of plate-glass windows with their expanse of exhibition space was particular to the 1800s. Even after the rebuilding of London after the great fire of the seventeenth century, shops did not have glass windows. The glazed window with its many panes was slowly adopted in the eighteenth century. As late as the 1820s, clothiers' shops in Cloth Fair were open to the air.[49] During the Napoleonic Wars, English shopkeeping was still mired in eighteenth-century methods when evening shoppers were greeted with a street of 'a few blinking oil-lamps' that ' just sufficed to render the darkness visible-the narrow shop-window, with its panes of bulging glass, twenty inches by twelve, lighted by a couple of tallow candles . . ..'[50] Such small shops only had one or two people behind the counter who waited for the shop bell to ring to announce the entrance of a customer.[51] When Sir Robert Peel removed the duty on plate glass in 1844, he opened up new vistas in English trade. By the 1860s plate-glass windows in Oxford Street and Regent Street worth, in some cases, over £600 graced the storefronts of the most prestigious establishments.[52] For traders, the great display windows of the nineteenth century were a boon to trade. An 1864 guide for the draper and haberdasher cautioned shop owners about the importance of display and shop visibility: 'If the materials sold are chiefly of a fancy kind, and dependent on accident or chance, the more public the situation the better . . ..'[53]

A writer in *Chamber's Edinburgh Journal* at mid-century noted that although England had long been known as a nation of shopkeepers, only his generation had made 'the greatest discoveries in the science of Shopkeeping.'[54] The plate-glass window was the greatest of these discoveries. Londoners especially prided themselves on the splendor of their shop fronts of highly polished plate glass protected by chest-high brass bars to prevent pedestrians from walking through them. In the evenings, these window displays were brightly illuminated with exterior gas lamps.[55] The contents of the windows rather than the actual contents of the shop became the focus of sale. Keeping these windows filled in the latest style required having the newest shop fittings. In 1871 Messrs. Wells and Son, 63, Wood

---

[49] 'Old London Shops and Shopkeepers,' 371.
[50] 'London Shops, Old and New,' 250-251.
[51] *Ibid.*
[52] 'The London Shop-Fronts,' 670.
[53] *A Handy Guide for the Draper and Haberdasher*, 1.
[54] 'London Shops, Old and New,' 250-251.
[55] 'The London Shop-Fronts,' 670; 'London Shops, Old and New,' 250-251.

street in the City specialized in selling shop fittings to drapery and millinery stores including wire mannequins, ribbon-winders, and 'specially constructed glove boxes so that when one glove was taken out the other wouldn't be soiled.'[56] Begun behind the glass panes of the late eighteenth century, display techniques and shop fittings became much more complex after the adoption of plate-glass.

In his 1875 business advice book *Hints on Haberdashery and Drapery*, J. W. Hayes, a draper for 28 years, illustrates the emphasis on presentation and display. He devotes an entire page to the importance of dressing a large shop window, and recommends: 'Every draper, however small the concern, should have a glass case furnished with an assortment of haberdashery, placed in a conspicuous position and easy of access; he should also show it in the windows as often as possible . . .. In shops where there is plenty of room it is a good plan to have a table or stall, after the style of a bazaar, constantly supplied with an assortment [of haberdashery goods].'[57] Plate glass and display was no longer a luxury but a necessity of successful shopkeeping. For critics, on the other hand, a window was another medium through which shopkeepers perpetrated fraud.

Although the wealthiest and most exclusive traders possessed fancy shop fittings and the expansive and expensive glass windows, such methods were even more popular in the new, large discount houses—the shops derogatorily called 'cheap shops' by their critics. Some nineteenth-century observers saw the incongruity between the spectacular shop windows and the claims of such emporiums to be discount houses. It seemed that the cheaper and more discounted the shop claimed to be, the more it was obsessed with display and luxuriant shop fittings. Describing a shopper's experience in such a well-fitted shop in 1853 a writer commented: 'He walks over rich carpets, in which his feet sink as though upon a meadow-sward; and he may contemplate his portrait at full length in half-a-dozen mirrors, while that pair of gentleman's kids at 2s. 10 1/2d. is being swaddled in tissue-paper, and that remnant of change . . . is being decently interred in a sort of vellum sarcophagus ere it is presented to his acceptance.'[58] To many observers this princely treatment simply to buy a pair of gloves was ludicrous. To others it revealed yet more evidence of the lack of substance in nineteenth-century English retail. All of the emphasis was on display and none on the quality of the goods or honesty in trade. The worst offenders were the discount shops.

An 1844 critic of 'cheap shops' described the typical discount shop, 'its plate-glass windows, brass sashes, and full-length mirrors, have an impudent, unpaid-for, expression.'[59] Hodge and Lowman and Moses and Sons, the very stores that had raised the ire of a more traditional competitor in 1844, possessed, along with Copestake's in Bow Church Yard, the most elaborate display windows of the

---

[56] 'Shop and Window Fittings, *The Draper* (London) 24 August 1871, 435.

[57] J. W. Hayes, *Hints on Haberdashery & Drapery* (London: Clements and Newling, 1875), 7 and 19. Quote on page 7.

[58] 'London Shops, Old and New,' 250-251.

[59] 'Shopping in London,' 250.

1860s.[60] The author of 'Old London Shops and Shopkeepers' in *Chamber's* in 1859 unfavorably compared the new shops with the traditional shopkeepers of the previous century who 'considered that the beautiful and costly goods they proffered for sale required no setting off.' He thought that the 'utter trash sometimes to be seen within these splendid shop-windows would have made them stare. 'Flowers, 2 3/4 d. a spray' heaped up behind a square of glass that could scarcely have cost less than twenty guineas!'[61]

Although plate glass found supporters who praised it as the ultimate invention in the 'science' of English shopkeeping, these windows were also associated with shops on the new plan whose cheap goods did not live up to the promise of their elaborate displays. Every tradesman did not rush to embrace the new methods of shopkeeping. Like the writer in *Chamber's*, William Ablett's new boss in Bristol was suspicious of Ablett's method of displaying goods in elaborate window-dressing. Ablett's new boss feared that the display goods would become soiled and unsaleable. Ablett noted, however, that by the time he wrote his memoirs in the 1870s this was a common practice, but when he was a young man, fifty years' earlier, traders still found it somewhat suspicious and newfangled.[62]

In spite of the resistance of traditionalists and critics who associated elaborate display with the aggressive, false practices of the cheap emporiums, window displays stayed because they drew customers into English shops. An 1853 writer described them as 'the city's principal attraction to strangers and visitors.' He further stated that museums and picture-galleries could not compete with the displays of London's shops.[63] London shop windows possessed such a strong attraction that they left the fictional Mr. Pips 'trembling' as he watched his wife constantly looking at the window displays in Regent Street and Oxford Street.[64] Windows fascinated the casual shopper, usually a woman, and drew her into a culture of English retail that prized appearance above all else; a place where cheap flower sprays were sold with the pomp and pageantry of princely gems.

A Shrinking 'Nation of Shopkeepers'

For critics, particularly middle-class men, windows were baits luring lady shoppers. In the writings of the satirists and journalists, men seemed to resist the magic of shop display, and supported older shop methods and identified with those

---

[60] 'The London Shop-Fronts,' 671.

[61] 'Old London Shops and Shopkeepers,' 370. See also Trollope, *Brown, Jones, & Robinson*, 37 in which Mr. Robinson says of plate glass, 'I regard the tradesman who can surround himself with the greatest quantity of it, as the most in advance of the tradesmen of his day.'

[62] Ablett, *Reminiscences of An Old Draper*, 164 and 142.

[63] 'London Shops, Old and New,' 252.

[64] Doyle and Leigh, 'Mr. Pips His Diary, Trycks of ye London Trade, [Tuefday, September 4, 1849].' Note: spelling modernized.

shopkeepers of yesteryear who needed no costly display mechanisms to sell their goods. In the criticisms of fraud and falseness in English retail, the respectable retailer of old serves as the foil to the nineteenth-century cheap draper or other shopkeeper. The criticism of cheap shopkeepers and discount drapers contrasted markedly with the cherished ideal of British shopkeeping in which English merchants are the last and best link in the chain of global capitalism—a view summed up in 1853 in *Chamber's*:

> It is for the shopkeeper that the navigator ploughs the seas, the traveler braves the African Desert, the Mexican labours in the mine, the swart Indian dives for pearls in the ocean depths. . . . He stands before the face of the world—the exponent of the world's worth, of all that it has done and can do, of all that it has and is. He is the index of a nations industry, enterprise, and progress—the honoured and the honourable depositary of the last and best creations of the divinest faculties with which God has endowed his human race. To be a nation of shopkeepers, then, is no dishounour, because it is to be a nation pre-eminent above all others in the possession and appreciation of all that man was formed to produce and to enjoy.[65]

The same men who criticized cheap shopkeepers and female purchasers supported its virtuous counterpart—that supposedly dying breed of traditional English shopkeeper who prized reputation and fairness above all else. This gender division among English consumers and critics is well illustrated by the consumption preferences of the fictional Pips' family. Under the protestations of his wife, Mr. Pips showed her the true meaning of English retail by refusing her purchase at Ragge and Rip's discount house so that he could take her to a respectable, traditional shop—'FAIRCLOTH and PRYCE's, who do carry on Business without the roguish Puffery, ...'[66] 'Roguish Puffery' like the grand advertisements of Ragge and Rip, however, was the key to nineteenth-century English retail and its future development.

Advertising

Between mid-century and 1880 advertising grew phenomenally due to a variety of factors, including expansion of the press, a growth in middle-class markets, and the professionalization of the advertising trade. In the earlier period, before mid-century, advertising, especially illustrated advertising, was so much associated with false bargains and 'cheap shops' that it only made its way consistently into the working-class press. Slick professional advertising with beautiful illustrations touting late Victorian commodities replaced the older, cruder advertising dependent on exclamation-laden texts exclaiming 'wonderful bargains.' The perception of advertisement rose from fraudulent puffery to the herald of middle-class luxury.

---

[65] 'London Shops, Old and New,' 253. One wonders if the pearl divers shared the same views of British commerce.

[66] *Ibid.*

Whiteley's and other famous, respectable English stores saturated the pages of middle-class newspapers and magazines with their ads without facing the criticism directed at earlier aggressive advertisers like cheap drapery shops.[67]

This suspicion of advertisement and the shop methods it represented, however, reverberated throughout the period surrounding mid-century. In 1855 a journalist from *Chamber's* noted: 'It is the detestable system of puffery, which seems to have completely beridden our trade and manufacture, and which is, we are bold to say, an ill omen for the future. A puff is an organized lie, and in ninety-nine cases out of a hundred, a cloak for deliberate fraud . . .. Advertising is one thing, lying is another . . ..'[68] For the first three-quarters of the nineteenth century, exaggerated advertising whether in a poster in the window or a bill posted down the street, was viewed as the first step to fraud. Sales methods commonly used by the most respectable shops and department stores in the twentieth century were, in their earliest days, viewed as false—almost criminal.

The innovations in English advertisement changed the relationship of English consumers to their retailers. After mid-century, advertising became increasingly sophisticated. As the main consumers in Victorian society, women, found themselves especially targeted by this new mass media.[69] Advertisement and a proliferation of shops brought the message to women and men that 'fashion' was attainable and affordable to those who had not been able to worship at its altar before.[70] Advertising, ranging from temptingly cheap products displayed behind plate glass to the method of newspaper ads and handbills promising the most up-to-date materials at unbelievably low prices gave the same message to shoppers: consumers, even of smaller means, could join the ranks of fashion. With prices so low and such an abundant selections of cheap drapery shops and emporiums, remaining fashionable seemed a duty rather than a luxury.

The shift from the basically 'factual' advertisement of the early nineteenth century to the screaming paragraphs aggressively urging the low cost of fashionable goods occurred gradually. Like Ribban's shop in Suffolk, most respectable dealers offered little more than bad poetry in the first half of the century. Ribban's ad said

---

[67] Lori Anne Loeb, *Consuming Angels: Advertising and Victorian Women* (New York: Oxford University Press, 1994), 5; Thomas Richards, *The Commodity Culture of Victorian England: Advertising and Spectacle, 1851-1914* (Stanford: Stanford University Press, 1990). See also Virginia Berridge, 'Popular Journalism and Working Class Attitudes 1854-1886: A Study of Reynold's Newspaper and Lloyd's Weekly Newspaper,' University of London, Ph.D. diss., 1976, and E.S. Turner, *The Shocking History of Advertising!* (London: Michael Joseph, 1953), for details of the development of the profession.

[68] 'The English Thugs,' 274-275.

[69] Richards, *The Commodity Culture*, 1-7. See also Judith R. Walkowitz, *City of Dreadful Delight* (Chicago: University of Chicago Press, 1992), 46-50; Women continue to be favored targets of advertising today. See Blanche B. Elliot, *A History of English Advertising* (London: B.T. Batsford Limited, 1962), 213.

[70] Asa Briggs, *Victorian Things* (London: B.T. Batsford, 1988), 273-288.

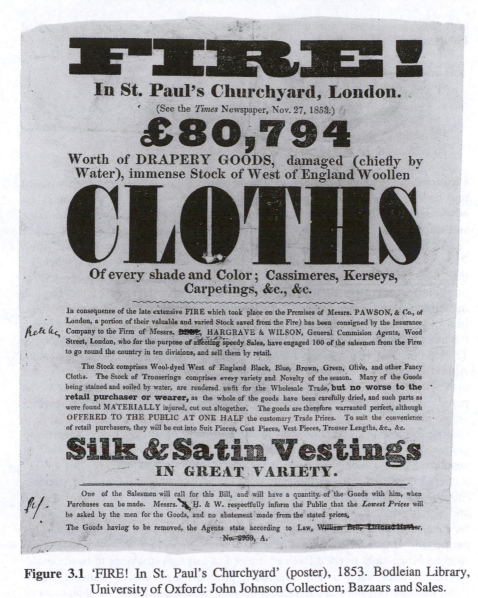

FIRE!

In St. Paul's Churchyard, London.

(See the *Times* Newspaper, Nov. 27, 1853.)

£80,794

Worth of DRAPERY GOODS, damaged (chiefly by Water), immense Stock of West of England Woollen

CLOTHS

Of every shade and Color; Cassimeres, Kerseys, Carpetings, &c., &c.

In consequence of the late extensive FIRE which took place on the Premises of Messrs. PAWSON, & Co., of London, a portion of their valuable and varied Stock saved from the Fire) has been consigned by the Insurance Company to the Firm of Messrs. BELL, HARGRAVE & WILSON, General Commision Agents, Wood Street, London, who for the purpose of affecting speedy Sales, have engaged 100 of the salesmen from the Firm to go round the country in ten divisions, and sell them by retail.

The Stock comprises Wool-dyed West of England Black, Blue, Brown, Green, Olive, and other Fancy Cloths. The Stock of Trouserings comprises every variety and Novelty of the season. Many of the Goods being stained and soiled by water, are rendered unfit for the Wholesale Trade, but no worse to the retail purchaser or wearer, as the whole of the goods have been carefully dried, and such parts as were found MATERIALLY injured, cut out altogether. The goods are therefore warranted perfect, although OFFERED TO THE PUBLIC AT ONE HALF the customary Trade Prices. To suit the convenience of retail purchasers, they will be cut into Suit Pieces, Coat Pieces, Vest Pieces, Trouser Lengths, &c., &c.

Silk & Satin Vestings
IN GREAT VARIETY.

One of the Salesmen will call for this Bill, and will have a quantity of the Goods with him, when Purchases can be made. Messrs. B. H. & W. respectfully inform the Public that the *Lowest Prices* will be asked by the men for the Goods, and no abatement made from the stated prices,

The Goods having to be removed, the Agents state according to Law, William Bell, Licensed Hawker, No. 2959, A.

Figure 3.1 'FIRE! In St. Paul's Churchyard' (poster), 1853. Bodleian Library, University of Oxford: John Johnson Collection; Bazaars and Sales.

only that his 'Goods are selling remarkable low.'[71] A clothing shop called Lambert's mildly exclaimed:

> Ladies, to you I first address
> Myself, in humble thankfulness,
> . . .
> I've very much enlarged my shop;
> Intending, by this alteration,
> To better your accommodation.[72]

Characteristic of this earlier period, Lambert and Ribbans' advertisements would not have been considered puffery. Such methods were soon superseded by advertisements filled with more superlatives than factual quotations on available stock and prices.

As the various examples of mid-century advertising ranging make clear, from Pawson and Company's 'fire' sale to the Christies' auction of bankrupts' stock, by the 1840s, 50s, and 60s 'puffing' advertisement based on the promise of goods at far below average prices became one of the defining features of the English haberdashery and drapery trade. Although other journalists and writers in this era, like Doyle and Leigh, condemned the fraudulent practices of cheap drapery firms, the most lacerating criticism of drapery advertising techniques came from Anthony Trollope in his 1870 novel *The Struggles of Brown, Jones, and Robinson*. Although some of the techniques like false bankruptcy sales, leading articles, and displaying high quality goods while selling cheap counterparts were as old as the parody of 'Ragge and Rip,' really ostentatious advertisement had only come into vogue after mid-century, a vogue that Trollope despised. The hero of his satire is George Robinson, a poor boy who rose from lowly billsticker to the advertising genius of a new drapery firm describes his business methods: 'In the way of absolute capital,—money to be paid for stock,—4,000*l.* was nothing. But 4,000*l.* scattered broadcast through the metropolis on walls, omnibuses, railway stations, little books, pavement chalkings, illuminated notices, porter's backs, gilded cars, and men in armour, would have driven [his shop's address] into the memory of half the inhabitants of London.'[73] In the novel, Robinson wastes the entire fortune of his partner Mr. Brown in creating a modern drapery emporium. Robinson opens the shop by hiring eight liveried footmen dressed in magenta stockings to hand out the businesses trade card, which was itself, printed on expensive magenta paper. Robinson's heroes were the nineteenth-century tradesmen who made thousands of

---

[71] Wholesale and Retail Linen Draper, Haberdasher, Hosier, Dealer in Hats, Grocery, &c. &c. &c. corner of market-street, Lavenham, Suffolk, 'Women's Clothing and Millinery,' Box I, John Johnson Collection, Bodleian, Oxford.

[72] Lambert's Address, 'Tradesman's List Exhibition,' Box I, John Johnson Collection, Bodleian, Oxford. Note: spelling modernized.

[73] Trollope, *Brown, Jones, & Robinson*, 35.

pounds through advertising such 'useful' products as Holloway's Pills and Macassar Oil.[74]

Heralding the advertising maxims of the future, Trollope's George Robinson believed that there was no such thing as bad press. When the horse of one of the firm's advertising knights accidentally trampled on a small boy, Robinson capitalized on the accident: 'The Jupiter daily newspaper took the matter up, and lashed out vigorously at what it was pleased to call the wickedness as well as absurdity of such a system of advertising; but . . . the firm was able to make capital out of the Jupiter, by sending a daily bulletin from Magenta House as to the state of the child's health. . . . and the whole thing had acted as an excellent unpaid advertisement.'[75] When a young baby was jostled by the crowd in front of the store, Robinson inserted this newspaper notice:

> CAUTION TO MOTHERS!—MOTHERS, BEWARE! Three suckling infants were yesterday pressed to death in their mother's arms by the crowd which had congregated before the house of Brown, Jones, and Robinson, at Nine times Nine, Bishopsgate Street, in their attempts to be among the first purchasers of that wonderful lot of cheap but yet excellent flannels, which B., J., and R. have just imported.[76]

In the competitive atmosphere of London clothing retail, Trollope's character preferred negative notice to no notice at all. In this satire of the connection between puffery and English retail, Trollope echoed the sentiments of critics who had been distrustful of these 'false' retailers since before mid-century.

The Abuse of Employees

Based on a system of puffery, fraud, and display, the new stores also changed the nature of retail employment. The advent of larger and larger premises required a crowd of assistants to fill that new space. By destroying the older close relationship between a shopkeeper and his or her few employees, critics claimed that retailers created a new class of poorly paid workers desperate to sell by any means and produce the profit that would prove their worth to their employers. Eventually this less personal system of employing a large staff broke down the older arrangements of apprentices living in or near the shop, but the long hours common to the drapery trade remained. Linen Drapers' assistants often worked twelve to fourteen hour days at mid-century.[77]

---

[74] *Ibid.*, 49-50 and 249. It is also likely that Trollope knew of the association between the newly discovered dye shade and cheap, adulterated goods.

[75] *Ibid.*, 93-94.

[76] *Ibid.*, 200.

[77] Lancaster, *The Department Store*, 126. See also Jerrold, 'The Linen-Draper's Assistant,' 138.

When this new army of workers ventured to complain of their conditions, they met with reproofs regarding the deceitful nature of their work. Moreover, some critics ike Douglas Jerrold did not take draper's assistants seriously since they spent most of their day displaying rich fabrics to shopping ladies—something Jerrold viewed as not the most manly of occupations. A writer in 1844 complained of the swarms of these poorly paid assistants in 'cheap shops', the larger discount firms: 'There are no shopmen in these places, but only somethings between young men and boys; raw, twenty pounds a-year counter-jumpers, in sallow, half-starched cravats, and seedy blackcoats ; . . . the shop-boys have a servile, insolent manner, and an open, undisguised desire of cheating and taking you in.'[78] In an 1859 short story in *Tait's Edinburgh Magazine*, the author describes a draper's assistant: 'He was a draper's assistant, who spent the best part of his existence in displaying ribbons and silks; and, without compunction, I placed him amongst those gallants who flutter around the gay butterflies of fashion, where the business of life is to discern betwixt a shade or to decide a colour, ...'[79] Perhaps most revealing of the prevailing opinion of draper's assistants and the women they served is Douglas Jerrold's description in which he refers to shoppers as 'Eves' and assistants as constant reminders of the Fall—forcing more and more clothes upon them.[80]

In reality, the work of a draper's assistant was heavy and grueling. The hard sell that marked their profession and, in the eyes of critics, wounded their reputation as honest workers was often a necessity of business. In some houses, especially less-established ones that sold cheaper goods, the rule was that an assistant who let a customer walk out without purchasing was fired immediately afterward.[81] Doyle and Leigh pointed out that the pale, almost effeminate stereotype of the draper's assistant came from 'the want of sufficient air and exercise; which is a sad consideration.'[82] Later in the century, Copestake and Moore, known for one of the showiest shop displays in London,[83] found itself consistently accused of mistreating staff. In January of 1870 even *The Draper* found them guilty of overstepping employer boundaries when they dictated that all of their assistants had to be clean-

---

[78] 'Shopping in London,' 250. For an illustration of this stereotype of the seedy draper's assistant see the sketch of The Linen Draper's Assistant, 'Trades and Professions,' Box 3, John Johnson Collection, Bodleian, Oxford. See also *Times*, 26 September 1844 reprint of a *Punch* article on ladies shopping. See also Lancaster, *The Department Store*, 190. See also the scene between Mr. Pips' wife and such an assistant in Doyle and Leigh, 'Mr. Pips his Diary. A Prospect of a Fashyonable Haberdasher hys Shoppe. [Tuesday, Auguft 7, 1849],' in *Manners and Cvstoms of ye Englyshe.*

[79] 'Shoppers and Shopping,' 291.

[80] Jerrold, 'The Linen-Draper's Assistant,' 138.

[81] *Ibid.*

[82] Doyle and Leigh, 'Mr. Pips his Diary. A Prospect of a Fashyonable Haberdasher hys Shopre.[Tuesday, Auguft 7, 1849].'

[83] The London Shop-Fronts,' 670.

shaven.[84] More seriously, Copestake's was accused of practically starving their overworked assistants in 1871.[85] In a sort of exposé, a melodramatic piece of fiction in *Tait's Edinburgh Magazine* in 1859, the assistants in the story were killed by their work in the drapery trade. 'Harry' dies of a consumptive illness from his lack of fresh air and his friend 'Barty' has a nervous breakdown and dies imagining that he is being choked by cobwebs.[86]

Notwithstanding the exaggeration, the almost mythical cheap shop or discount emporium of Trollope's fiction and the *Edinburgh Magazine's* short story, with their pushy, half-starved salesmen, puffing advertisements, and gaudy displays were based on some real changes in British trade in the nineteenth century. The lower prices of the 'cheap shops' and vast drapery firms came not only from the plentiful production of English factories, but also from keener competition and new methods of trade. An innovation of the late eighteenth century, by the nineteenth century, 'ready-money,' immediate cash payment, was the religion of the English haberdashery and drapery trades.

Credit and Cash

The changes in credit in nineteenth-century England is still a much-debated process; however, there was an attempt, at least in London trade, to shift from a dependence on long-standing credit accounts to a base of ready money for profit. This ready-money revolution was made possible in London by not only its own population base, but also the improvements in transportation that brought in money from outside the city. London was not just a collection of sub-villages; it became an urban monolith. These special circumstances allowed London retailers to offer discounted or reasonably priced goods for ready money only. One of the first types of establishments to adopt this method was the shopping bazaar. In Joseph Nightingale's 1816 treatise on the Soho Bazaar he noted: 'But the great advantage, both to authors, and to all other persons . . . of this Bazaar, is that of a quick and READY MONEY SALE. Those who give no credit need take none; . . ..'[87] In an article on London shops in 1853, *Chamber's* pointed out that although shop rents had risen an average of ten percent in London over the past few years, and London shopkeepers paid heavy taxes, they had an advantage that dealers in the country and smaller cities did not possess: 'Credit, which in many small towns is the rule of the majority of commercial transactions, is in London the rare exception. Of a hundred faces that stand at his counter in the course of the day, it is likely that the

---

[84] 'Petty Tyranny,' *The Draper* (London) 28 January 1870. This no beard rule is reminiscent of modern-day debates over the dress and hygiene codes of such corporate giants as Disney.

[85] See 'Hungry Drapers,' *The Draper*, London, 29 September 1871.

[86] 'Shoppers and Shopping,' 296-297.

[87] Joseph Nightingale, *The Bazaar, Its Origin, Nature, and Objects Explained, and Recommended as an Important Branch of Political Economy; In a Letter to the Rt. Hon. George Rose, M.P.* (London: Davies Michael and Hudson, 1816), 40.

shopkeeper in a frequented thoroughfare is hardly familiar with one, or knows them but as occasional customers . . .."[88] Those provincial shopkeepers with their stale accounts must have envied the London retailer and his instant profit.

Today we associate credit with the evils of overspending and consumption beyond one's means. Some nineteenth-century critics held a similar view and were happy to see the old credit system fall by the wayside. The Rev. Archdeacon Paley stated, "I never let my women (be it understood he spoke of Mrs. Archdeacon Paley and the Misses Paley)—I never let my women, when they shop, take credit; I always make them pay ready money, sir: ready money is such a check upon the imagination!"[89] Rather than serving as a 'check upon the imagination,' however, the switch to ready money often seemed to encourage shoppers to stretch their pound as far as it would go—just the sort of bargain shopping that angered middle-class male critics. For their part, shopkeepers claimed that for the convenience of ready money they would forego a significant mark-up and survive on the minimum of profit. Even the tailor E. Reeve, who distanced himself from 'cheap shops' in his advertisement, claimed to follow the new religion of small profits and ready money.[90] Hodge and Lowman, the discount emporium, proudly announced their adherence to READY MONEY in bold print in their 1834 bill heading on their receipts.[91] Trollope's fictional cheap emporium, Brown, Jones and Robinson, claimed to charge only a ½ per cent profit on goods sold. Painted boldly over an archway of their shop was 'an edict of trade against which retail houses in haberdashery line should never sin,—'Terms: Ready cash.'"[92] However, critics warned that it was this very adherence to ready cash that tempted 'unprincipled men' to open up shops in London to make a fast pound. The quickness of ready cash took some of the honor out of the trade of shopkeeping.[93]

Ready cash was described as both the savior of London retail trade and one of the ingredients in its fall into trickery and fraud. It encouraged bargain shoppers to compare prices, and search for the lowest of the low to get the maximum effect out of the immediate pound rather than to establish a relationship with one neighborhood store. To complicate matters further, the very 'cheap shops' that offered no credit to their customers depended on credit themselves from wholesale and other dealers. The temptation to overextend your credit to the larger dealer was complicated by the new business practices of higher volume, lower profit trade. E.E. Perkins warned in 1830: '[A] young man, on entering the trade, may be induced to make purchases beyond his capital, in the hope that by forced sales he

---

[88] 'London Shops, Old and New,' 252.
[89] Jerrold, 'The Linen-Draper's Assistant,' 236.
[90] E. Reeve, 'Women's Clothing and Millinery,' John Johnson Collection.
[91] Hodge & Lowman, 1834, 'Bill Headings,' John Johnson Collection.
[92] Trollope, *Brown, Jones, & Robinson*, 50 & 58.
[93] See 'London Shops, Old and New,' 252.

may be enabled to meet his engagements . . .'[94] Trollope's 1871 satire stated: "British commerce is not now what it was. . . . That bugbear Capital is a crumbling old tower, and is pretty nigh brought to its last ruin. Credit is the polished shaft of the temple on which the new world of trade will be content to lean. That, I take it, is the one great doctrine of modern commerce."[95] 'Cheap shops' that made their profits from fast, ready cash cheated their own creditors by overextending themselves.

Despite the worship of 'ready money', the older view of classical economists that capital rather than credit drove the industrial revolution does not hold true. Shoppers, especially working-class shoppers, still relied heavily on the credit granted by shopkeepers throughout the century.[96] Margot Finn has found that credit remained an integral part of nineteenth-century business transactions for both retailers and consumers.[97] In other words, the claim of 'ready money' was not always followed up in reality, and the dependence or overdependence on credit often led many to fall under that constant shadow threatening nineteenth-century businesses—bankruptcy.

The Specter of Bankruptcy

Trollope estimated that of all shops opened in London, only half survived for a year and only half of those ever turned a profit for the shopkeepers who opened them.[98] Vicious retail competition made bankruptcy a constant threat. Losses from bankruptcy averaged £4 and £5 million per year throughout the nineteenth century.[99] To control bankruptcy, the English attempted a series of legal and government reforms with direct government participation in bankruptcy proceedings falling in and out of favor throughout the century. Despite such reforms as abandoning imprisonment for debt in 1869, bankruptcy held numerous

---

[94] E.E. Perkins, *Haberdashery, Hosiery, and General Drapery; Including the Manchester, Scotch, Silk, Linen, and Woollen Departments, Foreign and Domestic* (London: William Tegg, 1830), 138.

[95] Trollope, *Brown, Jones & Robinson*, 4.

[96] Christopher Hosgood, 'The 'Pygmies of Commerce' and the Working-Class Community: Small Shopkeepers in England, 1870-1914,' *Journal of Social History*, 22, 3 (1989): 439-450. This reliance of the working classes on credit is also well documented in Melanie Tebutt's study of pawnbroking. See Melanie Tebutt, *Making Ends Meet: Pawnbroking and Working-Class Credit* (London: Methuen, 1984).

[97] Margot Finn, Emory, 'Fair Trade and Foul: Swindlers, Shopkeepers, and the Use and Abuse of Credit in the Nineteenth Century,' (paper presented to the North American Conference on British Studies annual meeting, Washington, DC, October 1995), 4.

[98] Trollope, *Brown, Jones, & Robinson*, 228.

[99] See V. Markham Lester, *Victorian Insolvency: Bankruptcy, Imprisonment for Debt, and Company Winding-up in Nineteenth-Century England* (Oxford: Clarendon Press, 1995), 3.

horrors for the Victorian trader as debtor and creditor. Poverty was still viewed as a moral failing even by later Victorians.[100]

Drapery firms, due to the expensive goods sold such as fine dress fabrics, were the most profitable, but also the most risky retail enterprises in the nineteenth century. If a firm did not move their expensive fabrics fast enough, they were in danger of not paying creditors. The circulars of the Society for the Protection of Trade in the 1830s contain numerous examples of such failed drapers. In 1830 a reward was offered for the capture of Augustus Neve: '[A] reward has been offered for the apprehension of AUGUSTUS NEVE, Linen Draper, late of Portsea, for not having duly surrendered himself to a Commission of Bankruptcy issued against him. He is about 26 years of age, 5 feet 7 inches high, dark hair and sallow complexion, stoops in his walk, and has a slight impediment in his speech . . ..'[101] Earlier that same year, James Butler Ridgway, a linen draper in Cleveland Street was accused of conspiring to defraud his creditors.[102] As businesses became larger, risks became greater and bankruptcy was no less a problem later in the century.

In January of 1871, a woolen draper in Wakefield named Caleb Barkworth left his home, taking with him his horse and gig. Later that day he sent the gig and horse home with a message that he was going to Barnsley and would return the next day. Barkworth's shop foreman received a note the next day that his boss had poisoned himself and the body could be found at Newmillerdam. Barkworth's coat was found on the bank of the dam, and a hole cut in the ice near the spot had finger marks around it. Just as his creditors gathered to mourn the irrevocable loss of their money, Barkworth's father sent a message to the constabulary informing them that his son was still alive.[103] Apparently Barkworth hoped that by faking his death, he would not have to suffer the indignities of bankruptcy.

Although bankruptcy threatened all of English business, it particularly worried those in the highly competitive drapery trade. Bankruptcy also had special connections to the cheap shopkeeping aspect of the clothing trades. As mentioned before, discount houses often claimed to present their customers with a bankrupt's stock that they had acquired at far below retail prices.[104] The journalist who penned

---

[100]See especially, *Ibid.*, 155-169. See also Barbara Weiss, *The Hell of the English: Bankruptcy and the Victorian Novel* (Lewisburg, Pennsylvania: 1986).

[101]PRO C114/34, Thomas Miller, Society for the Protection of Trade to [members] Society for the Protection of Trade, 22 Ely Place, London, 13 December 1830, 15th notice 1830.

[102]PRO C114/34, Thomas Miller, Society for the Protection of Trade to [members] Society for the Protection of Trade, 22 Ely Place, Holborn, London, 17 June 1830, 7th notice 1830. See also the case of Strain Stevenson of Ramsgate, draper who gave a bad note to his creditors PRO C114/34 Thomas Miller, Society for the Protection of Trade to [members] Society for the Protection of Trade, 22 Ely Place, Holborn, London, 14 May 1834, 5th notice 1834).

[103]'Mysterious Disappearance of a Draper, *The Draper* (London) 27 January 1871, 41.

[104]Brooks & Company of 105 and 106 High Street, Borough claimed: 'Brooks & Co are purchasers of Bankruptcy Stocks, & however cheaply bought, sell at a fixed Profit, thereby insuring to their customers the full benefit of these purchases.' See Brooks &

'Old London Shops and Shopkeepers' told a similar tale of a business driven to bankruptcy by the competition of another cheap shop in the immediate neighborhood: 'Another 'emporium' was evidently about to be opened . . . and little boys stood on the pavement thrusting lists of these bargains into everybody's hands. From henceforth there was bitter strife between the rival shops . . . erelong on both houses, 'These Desirable Premises to Let' told the neighborhood the result of the reckless game of competition.'[105] Sometimes even the most respectable of businessman failed when their dreams of large emporiums overstepped the boundaries of their customer and financial base. In 1871, an immense drapery firm in Liverpool specializing in silk failed with liabilities exceeding £400,000. This emporium built by the successful Jeffrey brothers promised to become a department store if it had survived. J.R. Jeffrey's sudden death in July of 1871 prevented him from experiencing the final degradations of the bankrupt, and his shop, which cost £250,000 to build, never became the palatial department store he envisioned. His brother and partner in business had already died of 'apoplexy' during the construction.[106]

Shopkeepers faking their own deaths to avoid creditors, drapers building enormous discount palaces in hopes of making mammoth profits, retail trade rife with bankruptcy and bad credit, all of these changes in trade left the observers to declare: "Is there no honesty left in the world, Mr. Brown? . . . Ah me, what an age is this in which we live! Deceit, deceit, deceit,—it is all deceit!"[107] Perhaps only 'a few disreputable traders . . . brought discredit on [the] trade'[108] as one retailer claimed, or the cheap shopkeepers and discount emporiums were actually a sign of a greater decline in English trade. The anxiety over the ethics of English retail and its corruption in a competitive, global marketplace reflect greater Victorian concerns about English national identity and the loss of 'traditional' values in the face of rampant capitalism.[109] For some the ideal English shopkeeper still existed in the nineteenth century even if only on some Platonic level of perfection that never saw its reality in London shops. For others, the system was so corrupted by the false sales, fraudulent firms, and discount houses that there was no going back to that ideal heaven of traditional shopkeeping with the well-known, honest proprietor individually greeting his customers.

Co., 'Trade Cards,' Box XII, John Johnson Collection, Bodleian, Oxford. From the illustration, this advertisement appears to date from around mid-century. The firms in the fictional tale of 'Shoppers and Shopping,' 292 also went bankrupt.

[105]'Old London Shops and Shopkeepers,' 372.

[106]'Failure of Messrs. J. and W. Jeffrey and Co., Silkmercers,' *The Draper* (London) 3 March 1871, 101; 'Sudden Death of Mr. J.R. Jeffrey of Liverpool,' *The Draper* (London) 7 July 1871, 317.

[107]Trollope, *The Struggles of Brown, Jones & Robinson*, 207.

[108]*A Handy Guide for the Draper and Haberdasher*, 34.

[109]See Martin J. Wiener, *English Culture and the Decline of the Industrial Spirit, 1850-1980* (Cambridge: Cambridge University Press, 1981), 27-40.

Fraud in Retail History

Placing the fraudulent retailer, the cheap shopkeeper, in retail history is challenging. On the one hand, they seemed to evolve from a tradition of older, small 'cheap shops' like the one in Whitechapel where Ablett started his career. On the other, they possessed new qualities. As the century progressed, the term 'cheap shop' was increasingly linked not to older shops, but to the new discount houses, the Hodge and Lowman's of London—some of which had an imminently respectably clientele. Yet, these shops were not quite department stores. They did not possess the vastness or the organization of a Bon Marché, let alone the later Selfridge's. They were only partially departmentalized and most did not stray far from drapery and haberdashery products. They shared with the earlier bazaars the adherence to (or claimed adherence) to a ready money policy along with an emphasis on display from their over-stuffed display windows to their brass and mahogany fittings. They also shared with bazaars an almost exclusively female customer base; however, drapery and haberdashery firms had long held such a base. Like arcades, they prided themselves on obsequious service, but did not have the same snobbery regarding their clients. Overall, I agree with Bill Lancaster's view of such emporia as proto-department stores. However, Lancaster cites only the successful firms in the north of England as the prototypes for these stores, and neglects the sometimes-unsuccessful London discount houses as models for this phenomenon.

Although there is ample evidence that there were fraudulent practices such as faulty merchandise, and false-ticketing in nineteenth-century shops, other practices such as ready-money sales, large-scale discount sales, display windows and advertising were merely part of the changes ushering in the future of English retail. Despite being declared suspect by critics, improvements like plate-glass and brass with an emphasis on color, fashion, and display were just another step in the evolution of British retail. Nineteenth-century critics recognized the threat they posed to older shopkeeping methods, and those uncomfortable with the change pitted these 'honest' methods against the newer cheap shops. Mr. Pips claimed that the maxim of the old style shopkeepers that "Good Wine needs no Bush," still held true in the late 1840s; however, in an increasingly anonymous society even the best wine might remain unsold if the masses never knew of its existence.[110] Reputation and word of mouth was no guarantee of success.

The early century shifts in methods of retailing created anxiety that nineteenth century English shopkeeping fostered a culture of fraud, an anxiety only heightened by the introduction of 'cheap shops' and discount shopping emporiums directed at the non-genteel, female shopper. According to critics, the 1830s, 40s, and 50s

---

[110]Doyle and Leigh, 'Mr. Pips His Diary, Trycks of ye London Trade, [Tuefday, September 4, 1849]'. See also 'Old London Shops and Shopkeepers,' 370 which also brings up this phrase in its comparison of older traditional shops with flashy new ones.

introduced an era of dishonest retail: false bankruptcy and fire sales, fraudulent merchandise, and cheap shopkeepers. The criticisms of 'cheap shopkeepers' in newspapers, periodicals, satire, and fiction were a mask for English fears of the changes in nineteenth century retail. Due to fierce competition, drapery and haberdashery firms were the first to implement the new techniques. Critics feared that business was no longer built on cold, hard capital, but instead on shaky credit and sensational advertising—words instead of deeds or money. A common fact of business, bankruptcy was not taken seriously by these firms that used the misfortunes of bankrupts to promote their sales. Traders like Jeffrey risked big to draw high profits rather than starting traditional smaller shops. As the older shops slowly died away, and even the arcades suffered in an age of democratizing luxury, new emporiums sprang up—many to die quick deaths like Jeffrey's shop and Trollope's fictional Magenta House, but others as the progenitors of department stores like Whiteley's. These businesses built their reputations on ready money, small profits on a large scale, heavy advertising, and catering to a mostly female clientele. They emphasized display in their large windows and risked fading their merchandise in order to attract customers. Detractors saw this emphasis on show over substance as undermining a once respected branch of English trade. They also argued it created a gender divide between English consumers with women participating in the retail culture of fraud and middle-class men supporting the honest, traditional shopkeeper.

Chapter 4

The Culture of Fraud and the Female Consumer

Men made money, either in business, or in a profession, or by an art.
Women spent it. That was all she knew.
—*Mabel Collins, 1881*[1]

False Finery or Necessity?

At the popular commercial and charity bazaars a female staff sold goods to a mainly feminine clientele, and by the advent of the emporium, large retailers had also added to their stores with sumptuous décor, display windows, and a staff to cater to the female shopper. Rather than turning away from these innovations as many male critics urged them to do, nineteenth-century women embraced the new changes in retail and the large retail houses with their vast selections, mirrors, comfortable chairs, and armies of assistants. Even more disturbing to commentators were the ways English women used bargain hunting and various other unscrupulous methods to purchase status through finery.

Advertisements, periodicals, novels, and even ballads illustrate the mixed message of consumption experience by nineteenth-century women. Retail traders encouraged women to enjoy the fruits of capitalism by exercising their right to shop in the establishments of linen-drapers, silk mercers, hosiers, bazaars, and haberdashers of nineteenth-century England. Inspired by fashion magazines such as *La Belle Assembleé* and its many imitators, and aided by handy shopping guides such as Perkins', women heartily participated in the growing consumer culture. However, just as they were being encouraged to shop and buy to the limits of their pocketbooks, they were also warned against going too far in their search for shopping pleasure. Middle-class magazines and newspapers warned women of false or low-quality goods masquerading as worthy items, shady shopkeepers who took advantage of female pocketbooks and persons, and "bargain" sales luring unwary customers to make unwise purchases. Most importantly, they cautioned women not to be fooled by the world of plate-glass windows and sumptuous display that increasingly characterized the largest English shops. These warnings and criticisms

---

[1] The thoughts of Mrs. Harcourt in Mabel Collins, 'A Woman of Fashion,' *Tinsley's Magazine*, 29 (1881), 137-168.

of 'cheap shops' and 'cheap shopkeepers' were also a way to criticize those who most often frequented them—English women.

Were the nineteenth-century critics' accusations of the feminization of shopping just a way to denounce the real victims of the nineteenth-century's drive toward conspicuous consumption—women? Rachel Bowlby's study of women and the creation of desire for commodities points to a process in which women are the victims of the giant stores in league with the industrial mass-producers. William Lancaster, however, questions this view of women as passive economic actors. He recognizes, just as the Victorians did, women's active participation and encouragement of the new retail culture.[2] For their part, nineteenth-century English commentators were less generous in their recognition of this active role. Trollope noted the key difference between the older, traditional English method of shopping and the new, false, feminized version:

> Send a man alone out into the world to buy a pair of gloves, and he will go to some discreet and modest glove shop . . .. But his wife having to make the purchase for him will probably go into an emporium at one door and pass out, when she has spent her pleasant half hour, at another, having, with great satisfaction to herself, been referred to the cashier when she has completed her purchase.[3]

Erika Rappaport asserts that the shopper like the kleptomaniac "metaphorically stood for a class abandoning itself to consumer desires and giving new meanings to consumption."[4] This shopper was, of course, female. Rappaport cites an 1875 *Saturday Review* article on shopping she attributes to Eliza Linton, "'its mystical feminine meaning, to shop is to pass so many hours in a shop on the mere chance of buying something . . ..'"[5] Feminized shopping was shopping for sport. It represented wasted hours, money, and effort on the part of the shopper, the employees, and, of course, the shopper's suffering male supporter.

What might seem to be extraneous luxury to modern eyes, were badges of station for middle-class women. Examining the defendants in Bath's Court of Requests, Margot Finn found the purchases of such women to be "[s]econd in diversity" only to the gentry ranging from cutlery to pianofortes. Although seemingly economically powerless, the "law of necessaries" in the common-law not only allowed married women to make contracts on their husband's behalf, but

---

[2] William Lancaster, *The Department Store: A Social History* (London: Leicester University Press, 1995), 172. See also Rachel Bowlby, *Just Looking: Consumer Culture in Dreiser, Gissing, and Zola* (New York: Methuen, 1985).

[3] Anthony Trollope, *London Tradesmen* (London: Elkin Mathews & Marrot Ltd. , 1927), 93. Note: 'The eleven sketches which compose this volume appeared at intervals in the *Pall Mall Gazette* from July 10th to September 7th, 1880.'

[4] Erika D. Rappaport, ''The Halls of Temptation': Gender, Politics, and the Construction of the Department Store in Late Victorian London,' *Journal of British Studies*, 35, 1 (January 1996), 75.

[5] *Ibid.*, 76.

allowed wealthier women great leeway in contracting for goods "suitable to their station." In nineteenth-century England this could be interpreted to mean anything from expensive dresses to a parlor piano.[6] Since the reign of Henry VI, women were able to contract for goods under their husband's name in order to supply the materials befitting someone in their station of life. Widely interpreted, the law of necessaries allowed later eighteenth-century and nineteenth-century women of the middle and upper classes to contract for luxury goods with or without their husband's knowledge. The law also allowed women of the lower classes who were separated from their husbands to enforce monetary support.[7] Finn's study reveals not only women's depth of involvement in everyday transactions of debt and credit, but also women's participation in these transactions due to their crucial role as consumers. Women were not passively accepting the financial rule of their family patriarchs.[8] This widening interpretation of the law of necessaries by judges allowed a further feminization of shopping.

The Pursuit of Fashion as Vocation

The Middle Classes

The shopping that seemed to many critics to be a purposeless accumulation of unnecessary goods was for many women an important vocation—the pursuit of fashion. Women found themselves in a distressing position in the nineteenth century. On the one hand, the pressures of class and status kept them scrambling for more fashionable and expensive clothing. On the other, women were warned that an excessive love of finery would lead to their and their society's moral

---

[6] Margot Finn, 'Debt and Credit in Bath's Court of Requests, 1829-1839,' *Urban History* 2 (October 1994): 235; Margot Finn, 'Victorian Women as Consumer Debtors: Theory and Practice' (paper presented to the North American Conference on British Studies, 1993), 3-8. See also *Times*, 6 August 1892 for a later case.

[7] Margot Finn, 'Victorian Women as Consumer Debtors: Theory and Practice' (paper presented at the North American Conference on British Studies, Montreal, Canada, 1 October 1993), 4. Finn also examines some cases of debt which take place in county court in the 1840s, page 11; Margot Finn, 'Women, Consumption and Coverture in England. c. 1760-1860.' *The Historical Journal* 39, 3 (1996): 703-722. See also Leach, 'Transformation in a Culture of Consumption,' 334 who brings up this point in American cases around the turn of the century. Some judges widened the interpretation of 'necessaries' and made husbands pay for whatever luxury goods their wives had contracted.

[8] In America, similar interpretations were made of the law of necessaries at the turn of the twentieth century. William Leach has found that some judges were willing to expand the concept of necessaries and force husbands to pay on the wives contracted debts. William R. Leach, 'Transformations in a Culture of Consumption: Women and Department Stores, 1890-1925,' *The Journal of American History* 71, 2 (September 1984): 334. See also Finn, 'Victorian Women as Consumer Debtors.'

degradation. Finery was falseness—pretending to be something you were not. Prostitutes would be the most extreme case of the nineteenth-century correlation between excess in dress and immorality.[9] Just as powerful as this warning against finery was the desire to appear to be the best and most tastefully dressed as one's class permitted. Sometimes a command of fashion might even lead to an elevation in status. The importance of such minor details of dress is illustrated by Mrs. Warren's description of her own mastery of fashion in 1866:

> If I purchased an inexpensive material, I did not call attention to the fact by overloading it with trimming and paltry lace, but it was well shaped, and well made, and simply trimmed so that by this means it escaped particular notice. I also avoided buying anything with otherwise than the most simple pattern on it. I had no desire to beknown at any distance by my dress. The plainest, rich silk—generally black—was my best dress; and the exquisite, fine soft silky black alpaca my home and evening dress. There is no pretention about the latter material—it is at once suitable and pleasing to the eye, and may be worn by a duchess without deteriorating from her acknowledged good taste.[10]

Plain, but not too plain, rich enough for a duchess, but not pretentious—the tension between respectability and finery defined the nineteenth-century Englishwoman's relationship to clothing.

Nineteenth-century women and retailers did not create fashion; however, in the nineteenth-century increased production, greater competition, and discount emporiums helped to democratize it. In the eighteenth century England's middling folk experienced an increase in prosperity and became more interested in the pursuit of fashionable goods. This is the era of the beginning of the "consumer revolution." Fashion, especially female consumption of apparel, was readily adopted by non-aristocrats as a way to display wealth and "taste." The desire for fashionable goods firmly established in the 1700s was connected to the idea of the middle-class woman as cultured lady rather than as fellow worker in the household economy.[11] The difference between fashion in the eighteenth century and in the nineteenth century was not one so much of a desire for fashionable goods as it was

---

[9] See Judith Walkowitz, *City of Dreadful Delight: Narratives of Sexual Danger in Late-Victorian London* (Chicago: University of Chicago Press, 1992), 50-52: Lancaster, *The Department Store*, 178-179.

[10] Mrs.Warren, *How I Managed My House on Two Hundred Pounds a Year* (London: Houlston and Wright, 1866), 87.

[11] See especially G. J. Barker-Benfield, *The Culture of Sensibility: Sex and Society in Eighteenth-Century Britain* (Chicago: The University of Chicago Press, 1992), 155-214; Jennifer Jones, 'Coquettes and Grisettes: Women Buying and Selling in Anacin Régime Paris,' in *The Sex of Things: Gender and Consumption in Historical Perspective*, Victoria de Grazia and Ellen Furlough, eds. (Berkeley: University of California Press, 1996), 30. See also Hoh-cheung and Lorna H Mui, *Shops and Shopkeeping in Eighteenth Century England* (Montreal: McGill-Queen's University Press, 1989), 234.

the means to purchase those goods and a grander scale of consumption that came in the nineteenth century.

In "Going Out A Shopping," a canting ballad from the mid-nineteenth century, the male protagonist complains of his wife's expenditures on fashionable clothes and accessories. When the ballad begins, the husband intends only to take his wife to the famous drapery establishment of Swan and Edgar in Piccadilly Circus; however, the wife shops her way through the West End before the couple even reach Swan and Edgar's:

> A Polka scarf her fancy caught,
> 'Twas quite a bargain-so she thought,
> That was the first thing that she bought
>   When we went out a shopping.
>
> . . .
>
> To Swan and Edgar's when we got,
> Of things she purchased such a lot,
> A shot of silk, would it had been shot,
>
> . . .
>
> When we went out a shopping.[12]

This satiric ballad gives some idea of the scale of London shops, especially the emporium shops that evolved from the drapery and haberdashery trades. The couple is obviously one of well-to-do upper-middle class people. Along with the "bargain" polka dot scarf and the ribbons and other haberdashery items, the lady in the ballad buys not one, but eight different types of fabric at Swan and Edgar's. Although the voracious appetite of the shopping lady is exaggerated in this ballad, all of the varieties of fabric were "real" and popular for fashionable clothing. Shawls, mantles, lace, trimmings, and especially the lighter cotton fabrics formed the foundation of nineteenth-century women's fashions.

For the middle-class woman in the 1800s, what was once frippery became necessity. Despite suffering briefly during the bare shouldered fashions of the first two decades of the century, in the nineteenth century rich shawls from India wrapped the best-dressed ladies of England. The center for this shawl trade was London. The highest quality and most expensive shawl shop was the India Depot on Ludgate Hill. In the 1830s, a single shawl from the India Depot could easily exceed £6.[13] These shawl shops specialized in display, eschewing counters for rosewood tables:

---

[12] 'Going Out A Shopping,' (Dudley Street, 7 Dials, London). Dated from references in the text.

[13] E. E. Perkins, *The Lady's Shopping Manual and Mercery Album Wherein the Textures, Comparitive Strengths, Lengths, Widths, and Numbers, of every description of Mercery, Hosiery, Haberdashery, Woollen and Linen Drapery, are pointed out for Domestic Economy, and which will be found of great advantage to the Heads of Families and Charitable Institutions for Clothing the Poor* (65 St. Paul's Churchyard, London: T. Hurst, 1834), 81. For a description of shawls in fashion see Alison Adburgham, *Shops*

Rich carpets conceal the floor of these establishments, vases of rare and costly china are dispersed about the room, whose great size is relieved by rows of pillars; lustres of brilliant crystal descend from the painted ceilings, and the rosewood tables (for here you see no vulgar counters) dispersed throughout the vast apartment are heaped with costly velvets, and piles of cloth of gold.[14]

As skirts widened in the crinoline craze of the 1860s and fitted jackets became impossible, shawls became even more popular. Arthur Liberty, founder of one of England's most famous department stores, began his career at a shawl emporium called Farmer & Roger's in Regent Street. True Indian shawls could only be afforded by the wealthy; however, factories at Paisley and Norwich produced bright, more affordable patterns.[15] In Wilkie Collins' 1860s novel *Armadale*, the lower-class character Lydia Gwilt is identified by one of these cheaper Paisley shawls, a bright imitation of the true Indian shawl.[16]

The rich, delicate patterns of imported and imitation shawls had to be purchased because nineteenth-century English women could not make such items at home— even if they wished to. Likewise, the yards and yards of lace decorating women's fashions in this century made home-production impossible. The intensity of labor required by lace production made it very expensive even when demand was high: "The finest specimen of Brussels lace is so complicated as to require the labour of seven persons on one piece . . .. The thread used is of exquisite fineness, which is spun in dark, underground rooms, where it is sufficiently moist to prevent the thread from separating."[17] Two of the most famous vendors of lace in London were Urling's and Hayward's. Founded in 1770, Hayward's began as a large, lace shop and then expanded into a drapery type emporium. By the 1860s, Haywards had become a shop specializing in a variety of wares including wedding linen, embroidered robes, frocks, and silk, muslin, and velvet ready-made mantles.[18] Urling's lace shop in Regent Street was famous for its advertising innovation of including actual samples of its lace in ladies magazines.[19] Until about 1830, artisan production and specialty shops kept lace a luxury; however, in the early 1830s more complex machine-made laces were produced and by the 1840s, machine-

---

and Shopping: 1800-1914: Where and in What Manner the Well-Dressed Englishwoman Bought her Clothes (London: Barrie and Jenkins, 1964), 54, 98.

[14] 'Shopping in London,' *The Living Age*, 1, 4 (June 1844), 253.

[15] Adburgham, *Shops and Shopping*, 98-100.

[16] See Wilkie Collins, *Armadale* (New York: Dover, 1977), 88, 115. Originally published in the *Cornhill Magazine* November 1864-June 1866.

[17] E.E. Perkins, *Haberdashery, Hosiery, and General Drapery: Including the Manchester, Scotch, Silk, Linen, and Woollen Departments, Foreign and Domestic* (London, William Tegg, 1830), 106. Although dated 1830 this text has references to later dates up to the 1850s and must be a later edition of the original.

[18] 'Hayward's,' Trade Cards, John Johnson Collection, Box XII, Oxford.

[19] Peter Jackson, *George Scharf's London: Sketches and Watercolours of a Changing City, 1820-50* (London: John Murray, 1987), 130.

made lace came in a variety of complicated patterns.[20] Demand for lace, like the demand for richly patterned shawls, was already high in the 1800s; however, imitation Indian shawls from Paisley and patterned lace produced in native factories met the high consumer demand and made cheaper fashion possible.

Changes in production coupled with the changes in distribution expanded the market of fashionable clothing. The lace and shawl shops that thrived early in the century either lost business to the increasing scale of the "monster shop" emporiums, or, like Hayward's, became emporiums. Lace, shawls, hats, and hosiery were all once sold by specialists in smaller shops, but in the second half of the nineteenth century, emporiums eroded that business. An 1869 bill heading from Hayman, Pulsford & Company, previously Youngman and Hayman, of Sloane Street demonstrates the shift:

HAYMAN, PULSFORD & COMPANY
Silk Mercers, Family Linen Merchants,
Shawls and Mantles, Gloves and Haberdashery, Lace, mourning
FAMILY MOURNING OF EVERY DESCRIPTION[21]

In the same era, William Whiteley's store had at least seventeen separate departments including ones for lace, ribbons, linens, and haberdashery.[22] Throughout the changes in English retail from specialty shop to emporium to department store, women shopped for the best quality at the lowest price. The individual dealer of gloves, hosiery, hats, and shawls felt the squeeze of the new competition.

Nineteenth-century women's fashions continued the trend of democratized luxury from the eighteenth-century in which the women of the middle classes began to enjoy the elaborate trimmings once relegated to the highest levels of society, and it also democratized on a greater scale beyond the wealthiest of the middling classes. "Indian" shawls made in Scotland, machine-made lace, and mass production of affordable cotton-based clothing allowed greater numbers of women to join the ranks of the fashionable. The availability of cheaper clothing did not melt away all class distinctions in fashion or in English society; however, the spread of fashion increased the scale of consumer culture and the number of women experiencing it. It created anxieties about preserving class distinction in the face of fashionable "pretenders" and accelerated the gendering of consumer culture.[23]

---

[20] Perkins, *Haberdashery, Hosiery, and General Drapery*, 101-102.

[21] 'Hayman, Pulsford & Company,' Bill Headings, John Johnson Collection, Box 18, Oxford.

[22] Adburgham, *Shops and Shopping*, 153.

[23] See especially Georgiana Hill, *A History of English Dress*, Vol. II (London: Richard Bentley and Son, 1893), 310-342 for the changes the new production and availability made in English fashion.

Democratizing Fashion: Lower Middle Class and Working Women

For women of the middling classes, shopping emporiums and factory imitations of luxury accessories made fashion an attainable ideal. However, for women of the lower middle and upper working classes, the most important innovation in English fashion was the shift in production from linens and heavy wools to fashionable, colorful, and cheap cotton fabrics. The brightly colored cotton cloth destined to clothe middle-class and working women in the later nineteenth century was introduced from India—calico. In the late 1700s, new steam-driven production in the weaving industry helped England to produce this popular fabric to satisfy increasing demand without relying on finished imports. Cotton became so rapidly popular in the eighteenth century that a series of statues were passed imposing penalties and duties on the wearing and selling of calico. The mass production of native calicoes in the late eighteenth-century led to the repeal of these statutes.[24] The most competitive and innovative drapery shops of the late eighteenth century, especially in London, targeted the "middling orders and below" and sold to them the new cheaper cotton fabrics. Hoh-cheung and Lorna Mui link the new retail techniques in drapery establishments directly to the increasing sale of cotton goods.[25] This trend continued into the nineteenth century when such fabrics become the basis of trade of 'cheap shops' and discount emporiums. The new accessibility of "fashion" created class tensions and confusion.

Fashion was a badge of class status, wealth, and a particularly important starting point to judge character and respectability, those treasured belongings of the Victorian age. In the nineteenth century, the burden of fashion rested increasingly on women. In France the value of women's wardrobes began to outpace the value of men's wardrobes across class lines by the end of the 1700s.[26] This gendering of fashion took place in England and reached below the upper and upper middle classes. Critics contended that for the benefit of appearing slightly better than their means allowed them, women sacrificed honesty in English trade and their own morality. In the novel *Brown, Jones and Robinson*, Trollope's athletic Mrs. Morony was willing to physically fight for the silk mantle she could not have afforded in a respectable shop. The mantle was placed in the window and was meant as an enticement for shoppers who would actually be sold a more poorly made but similar mantle. In the novel, Mrs. Morony fights with Mr. Jones because she is aware of the trick, known in the drapery trade as a "leading article," and wants the display instead of the cheaper stock article. In the end Morony wins the ensuing fight and neglects to pay even the low-ticketed price.[27] Morony's character

---

[24] Perkins, *Haberdashery, Hosiery, and General Drapery*, 40-41, 46-47.

[25] See Mui and Mui, *Shops and Shopkeeping in Eighteenth Century England*, 236-237.

[26] Jones, 'Coquettes and Grisettes,' 30-31.

[27] Anthony Trollope, *The Struggles of Brown, Jones, & Robinson: By One of the Firm* (London: Smith, Elder & Co., 1870), 143-150.

desires fashion even if she does not possess the means necessary for purchasing fashionable goods.

Although they were satirized by Trollope and others, an 1864 draper's guide warned shopkeepers not to drive away these possibly profitable lower-class customers who desired their goods: "Do not allow a similar mistake to be made as it regards the appearance of a person. Many an intended good customer has been bowed out, or allowed to go without so much courtesy, because it was conjectured that his or her circumstances would not allow of any important purchase."[28] Desiring silk and satin, women below the middling classes bought what was available to them—the colorful calico prints. When Ablett began his career as draper's assistant early in the century, he noted that the "common people" and servant girls wore only cheap dark blue cotton prints of such poor quality that they were kept behind the counter so they would not distract from the finer fabrics. However, at the time of his writing in 1876, he noted that even the servant girls possessed an "abundance of clothing" much improved from the cheap navy prints.[29] In 1866, a beauty advice book writer noticed the shift:

> The perfection and enormous power of our machinery, and the consequent immense production of our looms, have so reduced the price of all the ordinary materials of dress, as to place them within the reach of almost every individual . . ... The wife of a labouring man may now purchase a dress of cotton, muslin, or woolen, richly printed with a beautiful pattern, and in brilliant and permanent colours, for a few shillings . . ... A country wake in the nineteenth-century may display as much finery as a drawing-room of the seventeenth . . .."[30]

Participation in the consumer culture of clothing—fashion—did not occur for these women until the nineteenth century, when increased production and a new way of selling made these purchases possible and met the demand kindled in the 1700s.

The middle-class reaction to this working-class incursion into their consumer revolution demonstrates how the new retail culture with its cheap fabrics and 'cheap shops' threatened class boundaries. In the 1860s, the era of bright aniline dyes and Madame Rachel's cosmetics, middle-class critics refer to reinstating the sumptuary laws of the sixteenth century to prevent working women from pushing back the envelope of respectability by donning fashionable clothes. The sumptuary

---

[28] *A Handy Guide for the Draper and Haberdasher* (20 Paternoster Row, London: F. Pitman 1864), 33.

[29] William Ablett, *Reminiscences of An Old Draper* (London: Sampson Low Marston, Searle, and Rivington, 1876), 102-103. Phillipe Perrot finds a similar trend away from the dark blue cloth to brighter colors in working women's fashions in mid-century France. See Philippe Perrot, *Fashioning the Bourgeoisie: A History of Clothing in the Nineteenth Century* (Princeton: Princeton University Press, 1994), 73-75. See also Jones, 'Coquettes and Grisettes,' 30.

[30] Arnold James Cooley, *The Toilet and Cosmetic Arts in Ancient and Modern Times* (192, Piccadilly, London: Robert Hardwicke, 1866), 80.

laws passed in the 1500s in the reign of Elizabeth were meant to prevent the *nouveau riche* from aping the aristocracy by wearing the ostentatious and gaudy fashions of this era. Finally, in 1604 the government had given up these unenforceable laws by taking them off the books.[31] Writing on domestic management, Mrs. Warren, herself trying to keep up appearances with cheap but well made clothing, condemned her servant girls for their ruinous love of finery: 'I have often wished sumptuary laws were in force to compel them to attire themselves in a manner becoming to their station, or that their wages might be partially devoted to the savings banks . . ..'[32] In an excerpt from a current novel titled 'Must We Revive the Sumptuary Laws?' *The Young Englishwoman* in 1865 drew attention to the "problem" of working women attaining fashion:

> 'To know a gentleman from a snob is easy enough, but to discriminate between two lovely females, . . . is altogether beyond this present writer. I have seen such elegantly dressed and graceful creatures flirting in Kensington Gardens, upon a Sunday, with Her Majesty's foot-guards, as have excited the liveliest apprehensions in my breast with respect to the morals of our female aristocracy. They were, doubtless, only ladies' maids, at highest, a natural aptitude for making the best of themselves; they are so ingenious in the provision of ornament; and beauty itself although so common, is so dainty and glorious a possession, that I conclude the whole sex to be ladies?'[33]

The pressure to dress well reached far below the middle-classes and fueled the nineteenth-century clothing industry, which angered middle-class critics who viewed these women as pretenders to the better classes.

The sale of fashionable clothing at cheaper prices in the new retail emporiums threatened not only the stability of the middling classes by increasing the competition from below, it also threatened the respectability of the middle classes by encouraging middle-class women to participate in a fraudulent culture of consumption. 'Cheap shops' promised more goods for less money and used the techniques of display to spread the gospel of the bargain. According to critics, this creed of cheapness destroyed middle-class morality by creating greedy, bargain shopping women who were as dishonest as the drapers who lured them in with their false sales and ostentatious displays. Critics noted that the new retail culture depended on appearance—show—over substance: the new shopping was based on a firm foundation of fraud.

---

[31] See Frank Whigham, *Ambition and Privilege: The Social Tropes of Elizabethan Courtesy Theory* (Los Angeles: University of California Press, 1984) 155-169.

[32] Warren, *How I Managed My House on Two Hundred Pounds a Year*, 87.

[33] 'Must We Revive the Sumptuary Laws?,' *The Young Englishwoman* (January 1865), 47 in 'Fashion,' John Johnson Collection, Box 15. Oxford. Quote from *Married Beneath Him*.

The Cost of Bargain Hunting

'Cheap Purchases': 'A Female Mania'?

In 1853, *Chamber's Edinburgh Journal* described a conspiracy of 'cheap shops' whose enticing displays and unscrupulous methods rivaled the criminal underworld. According to this writer, it was the anonymous nature of shopping in London that tempted these corrupt proprietors: 'gangs of unprincipled men, which infest some of the main channels of commerce with specious establishments, which are actually nothing more than dens of villainy; where, under the pretence of unheard-of bargains, the public, and the sex in particular, are bamboozled and bullied out of their cash.'[34] Whether it was in the ominous warning of a magazine article or in a satire of modern English life, women received criticism for their participation in the 'cheap shop' system. Richard Doyle and Percival Leigh's satire *Manners and Cvstoms of ye Englyshe* published in 1849 has an entry describing a husband and wife's trip to Regent Street where the wife is drawn into a 'cheap shop' by an inexpensive scarf displayed in the window: "my wife . . . would stop to look at it with a crowd of other women gazing at the finery, which MR. SKITT do call baits, and a draper's shop, a lady-trap." After she buys some items the shopman offers her, "'a love of a robe, a barege, double glacé, brocaded in the flouncings, and reduced to twenty-one-and six from forty-five.' . . . saying that it was indeed a bargain, which I find is a woman's word for anything cheap whether wanted or no . . .."[35] In satire and in the press, 'cheap shops' and the women who went to them were inextricably tied together. In March of 1844 a writer to the editor of the *Times* told a harrowing tale of a respectable woman wrongly accused of theft by a hosiery retailer when she refused to buy the goods he displayed.[36] Women were either chided for succumbing to the lures of these shopping emporia, especially the displays of bargain goods and prices, or they were severely warned against their dangers.

In the mid-century ballad, 'Going Out a Shopping,' the husband tries to physically separate his wife from the attractive window displays by walking between her and the shop windows on Regent Street:

Again I started with my bride,
And placed her on my outer side,
Because I wished the shops to hide,
But, ah, she was awake too wide—
She fell in love with a pelise,
And though I wish'd the fun would cease,

---

[34] 'London Shops, Old and New,' *Chamber's Edinburgh Journal*, 20 (1853), 252.
[35] Richard Doyle and Percival Leigh, 'Mr. Pips his Diary. A Prospect of a Fashyonable Haberdasher hys Shopre [Tuesday, Auguft 7, 1849], *Manners and Cvstoms of ye Englyshe* (London: Bradbury & Evans, 1849).
[36] An Old Subscriber, Letter to the *Times*, 12 March 1844, in *Times* 14 March 1844.

I stretch'd the point to keep the peace,
  When we went out a shopping.[37]

Throughout the ballad the shopping wife is consistently enticed into purchasing more and more items by the window displays of shops whether they promise especially beautiful and fashionable products or bargain prices. Criticisms of women lured by extravagant displays of consumer goods and the dreamlike atmosphere they create far predate the emergence of the Parisian style department store.[38] In England women are described as being enticed by such displays throughout the nineteenth century, especially after the widespread use of plate-glass.

Sometimes the displays were themselves false. "Leading articles" were expensive, quality items prominently displayed in the shop windows for ticket prices well below their value. Coaxed into the store by these decoy goods, the customer, like Trollope's fictional working-class Irish woman, was told that the items in the window were not for sale, but that the shop had similar goods. These similar goods were, of course, substandard and some customers were fooled into buying them.[39] Trollope's description of this practice in *The Struggles of Brown, Jones and Robinson* is illustrative of the relationship between window displays, fraudulent retail, and the female shopper:

> At first, the other partners had not objected to this ticketing, as the practice is now common . . . .. A lady seeing 21s. 7d. marked on a mantle in the window, is able to contemplate the desired piece of goods and to compare it, in silent leisure, with her finances. . . . But it has been found by practice that so true are the eyes of ladies that it is useless to expose in shop-windows articles which are not good of their kind, and cheap at the price named. To attract customers in this way, real bargains must be exhibited; and when this is done, ladies take advantage of the unwary tradesman, and unintended sacrifices are made. . ..[40]

There must have been hundreds of shoppers who were fooled by this practice of display.

Tradesman did not shoulder the blame alone for this fraudulent system in English retail. They shared it with the wives who wanted their families to possess the maximum material possessions as well as the maidservants who wanted to appear a notch or two above their class. Novelist, journalists, ballad writers, and other male, middle-class commentators castigated these female demon shoppers for

---

[37] 'Going Out A Shopping,' (Dudley Street, 7 Dials, London).

[38] Jennifer Jones finds such references in late eighteenth-century Paris.   See Jones, 'Coquettes and Grisettes,' 27.

[39] For a description of this practice see 'Shopping in London,' 250. How far this method predates the Victorian age is unknown; however, since the practice of ticketing goods at all was not widespread until the nineteenth century, it is unlikely that the ruse dates far beyond 1800.

[40] Trollope, *Brown, Jones, & Robinson*, 139-141.

bringing English trade into a state of corruption. In the final analysis the burden for this plague of cheapness rested on feminine shoulders. Trollope's character, Robinson, bemoaned, "'Is not the passion for cheap purchases altogether a female mania? . . . Would that women could be taught to hate bargains! How much less useless trash would there be in our houses, and how much fewer tremendous sacrifices in our shops!'"[41] Amicus contended in 1845 that those who recognized quality work and were willing to pay a fair price could mitigate the "evil" of competition and admonished ladies to seek 'what is good instead of what is cheap.'[42] Doyle and Leigh were less generous in their depiction of female participation in 'cheap shops.' They portrayed Mr. Pips' wife as knowing exactly how and why she was participating in the system. She responded to Pips criticism of Rip and Ragge: "But my wife did say, very serious, and that we were not to judge, or to know of their tricks and cozenage, and, that it was no matter to us if they did cheat their creditors, provided we could buy their wares at a bargain, and besides, if we did not, others would."[43] For these nineteenth-century commentators, women were not only participating in the system of 'cheap shops' and fraudulent retail, women were the driving force behind the evolution of English 'cheap shops' and discount emporiums.

According to critics, female bargain hunters were morally bankrupt in their passion for cheap goods. In this criticism of bargain hunters from *The Living Age*, the new bugbear of the bargain hunter is included with the older stereotype of the greedy, Jewish commercial trader: 'Time, temper, and shoe-leather, these people submit to the loss of, for a bargain; will stew themselves in an atmosphere of odoriferous perspiration among greasy Jew-brokers at an auction. For a bargain, will bid against their best friend for a thing which he wants, and which they don't want, for the lure they hear a bargain.'[44] The fraudulence of women shoppers was compared with that of criminals. Trollope's later equation of bargain shoppers and lady thieves was more pointed when his character explained:

'. . . our strong abhorrence of ladies who are desirous of purchasing cheap goods to the manifest injury of the tradesmen from whom they buy them. . . . The lady who will take advantage of a tradesman, that she may fill her house with linen, or cover her back with finery, at his cost, and in a manner which her own means would not fairly permit, is, in our estimation,—a robber.'[45]

---

[41] *Ibid.*, 142.

[42] C.B.C. Amicus, *How to Rise in Life* (London: Longman, Brown, Green, and Longmans, 1845), 43.

[43] Doyle and Leigh, 'Mr. Pips his Diary. Trycks of ye London Trade' [Tuefday, September 4, 1849], *Manners and Cvstoms of ye Englyshe.*

[44] 'Shopping in London,' 250.

[45] Trollope, *Brown, Jones, & Robinson*, 141.

By refusing to pay market price, the English woman shopper could be blamed for what critics saw as the cheapness and falseness of English retail that undermined traditional business practices as well as English morality.

Bargain Hunters, Starving Seamstresses and Dead Shop Assistants

Not only bargain emporiums, but also bargain shoppers were seen as being responsible for degrading English retail and destroying the lives of those laborers connected with the trade. In magazine articles, newspapers, and novels, women were chastised for their thoughtless pursuit of bargains, which profited unethical shop owners, but led to long hours and poor pay for assistants and seamstresses. Drapers' assistants and other shop assistants, male and female, along with a particularly poor class of women needleworkers, starved and worked themselves to death to please the new shoppers. William Lancaster has asserted that because department stores were dominated by female workers throughout much of their history, labor historians have overlooked this section of labor history in favor of that of more male dominated labor forces like factory work.[46] I would argue that even the earlier retail male workers, the famous draper's assistants, were overlooked because they participated in a "feminized" workplace. However, some contemporary commentators did concern themselves with the plight of the English retail worker and clothing producer, and denounced the woman shopper as the cause of their woes.

In 1844 a writer in the middle-class magazine *The Living Age* directly connects the bargain hunter to the starving seamstress and infers that a continued trend of bargain retail will lead to England's decline as it depends on poorly paid workers from less industrially developed regions:

> Now, what is a bargain? Something purchased for less than its fair marketable value. Who is the sufferer by this? Either the vendor, the owner, or the poor artizan, ...
> Alas! How many tears may not the poor worker of that precious bargain have shed, while wearing her fingers to the bone for, wages, mayhap barely enough to keep body and soul together !
> . . Ay, ladies of Britain, go bargain-catching, and, give to South Sea islanders and nasty niggers the accumulated produce of your savings from the sweat and life-blood of your distressed country-women![47]

Steeped in patriotism and racism, this appeal warns of the effects of bargain shopping in England. England's workers will suffer and English wealth will drift into other corners of the globe to provide material possessions for one section of the English public—female shoppers.

Throughout most of this period the demand for inexpensive but fashionable clothing also assured a demand for cheap needleworkers. The contrast of the

---

[46] Lancaster, *The Department Store*, 125.
[47] 'Shopping in London,' 250-251.

fashionable lady and her overabundance of finery with the poor needleworker who produced this clothing is represented throughout the nineteenth century. The image of the pale, thin nineteenth-century seamstress bent squinting over her work is well known.[48] A trade that had once been lucrative for some women earlier in the century became increasingly less so as the work of the independent dressmaker was taken over by the mass-produced clothing of the ready-to-wear market.[49] The Milliner's and Dressmaker's Provident and Benevolent Institution was founded in the late 1840s to help stem the tide of starving dressmakers and was still flooded with requests for assistance in the 1870s.[50] In 1870, A Mrs. Elizabeth Street, a court dressmaker in London, was taken to trial for breaking the Workshops Act of 1867 for the treatment of her young workers. Assistants were not supposed to work after four on Saturday or later than nine on other nights, but the Act was often ignored because, "If a lady was going to a ball she must have her dress . . .." The judge in the case condemned the lady who ordered the garment: "Any lady who knew the Act and its consequences and still gave the class of order [rush] the defendant had, deserved to be held up to public shame. . .."[51] Just as the draper's assistant toiled for his greedy bosses and the unappreciative female shoppers, so too did the young dressmaker's assistant waste her youth for the vanity of a woman who wanted a ball gown. According to commentators like this judge, the changes in English retail and consumption were much more than just dangerous to the character of British shopkeeping, these changes corrupted the shopper as well as the shop, and ruined the health and morality of the employees.

Although the drapery trades remained male-dominated until later in the century, the women who were employed in retail shops did not even have the protection provided to the dressmakers. Shop assistants were not covered in the 1867 Workshops Act, and the law did not limit their hours. Like the men in the trade, fourteen hours was not an unusual workday. Even after the Early Closing Movement led wealthy drapery shops in Regent Street and Oxford Street to close in the early afternoon, the small shops remained open.[52] As early as 1817, Priscilla Wakefield urged women shoppers to support the female worker by patronizing shops that were run by and employed women. She also urged shoppers to pay these female needleworkers and assistants equal wages to males in the same

---

[48] See Adburgham, *Shops and Shopping* and Lancaster, *The Department Store*. See also 'The Dressmaker,' Trades and Professions, John Johnson Collection, Box 3, Oxford—an illustration of the nineteenth-century image of a young woman worn out by close needlework and poor pay—pictured working by her candle at night.

[49] See Adburgham, *Shops and Shopping*. Also, see the elaborate and well-articulated advertisement of Miss Smart, a successful Islington dressmaker. 'Miss Smart,' Trade Cards, John Johnson Collection, letter advertisement, Box XII, Oxford.

[50] Milliner's and Dressmaker's Provident Fund, *The Draper* (London) 3 March 1871.

[51] 'Overworking at a Dressmaker's,' *The Draper* (London) 24 June 1870.

[52] See Lancaster, *The Department Store* on Early Closing. See also 'Shop Girls In London,' *The Draper* (London) 10 June 1870.

employment.[53] In his series on "London Tradesmen" in the *Pall Mall Gazette* over sixty years later, Anthony Trollope criticized those who bemoaned the proliferation of men in the clothing trades that once employed more women. Trollope said that women simply did not possess the 'patience, continuity, and strength' required by the trade.[54] Female assistants, said Trollope, 'show their impatience and their weariness, and, not having the difference of sex to add a something of gallantry to their intercourse, they are apt to show that they are put out, and to entail upon the house a feeling that incivility may be met there.'[55] Trollope seemed to fear that shop employment, like shopping itself, would become feminized and employ only cheap female workers.

If the woman shopper's love of a bargain destroyed the lives and wages of English workers, so too did the new attitude toward shopping as entertainment. Contributing to the new hollowness, the cheap greediness that prized quantity over quality and display over substance, was the English woman's use of shopping as entertainment. Although men also enjoyed this new shopping experience, women were the main consumers in the nineteenth century and shopping was their "sport." Visible reminders of the changing consumer culture, female shoppers met with criticism in the press—sarcastic commentaries on their irresponsible participation in a retail culture of fraud.

In *Punch*'s 1840s lampoon, "Directions to Ladies for Shopping," we find the sport of nineteenth-century shopping sarcastically well detailed:

> Ride all the way till you come to the shopping-ground in a coach, if you can; in an omnibus, if you must; lest you should be tired when you get there. . . . The best places for shopping are fashionable streets, bazaars, and the like. Street-shopping principally relates to hosiery, drapery, and jewellery of the richer sort. . . . In street-shopping walk leisurely along, keeping a sharp look-out on the windows. . . . You will find, too, as you go on, that one thing suggests another; as bonnets-ribands for trimming, or flowers; and handkerchiefs—perfumery. . . . See if there is anything before you superior in any respect to a similar thing which you have already; if so, get it instantly, not reflecting whether your own will do well enough.[56]

No longer limited to local shops, women utilized the fastest urban transportation to take advantage of a variety and range of shops from the vast bazaars to the larger drapery shops. This version of shopping as entertainment encouraged window displays and other enticements to the casual shopper. Once the casual shopper was convinced to buy an item, she initiated a domino effect of shopping by purchasing the accessories to that item—a dress might require a hat, ribbons, and hose for example. Instead of coming to London to purchase a black wool dress, a woman

---

[53] Priscilla Wakefield, *Reflections on the Present Condition of the Female Sex* (London: Barton, Harvey, and Darton, 1817), 114-116, 123.
[54] Trollope, *London Tradesmen*, 97.
[55] *Ibid.*, 93.
[56] *Punch*, 1844. Reprinted in the *Times*, 26 September 1844.

came to London to "shop" and perhaps would buy a black wool dress along with various other items, or just as often shopped without buying anything. Anthony Trollope complained in the *Pall Mall Gazette* of 1880, "[T]hat shop customers generally are chiefly women, that 'shopping' is a woman's term and a woman's practice, and that, all the world over, though the money is made by the men, it is spent by the women."[57] Critics were incensed that for their own pleasure and entertainment, women encouraged this buying without need along with browsing without buying and the retail methods that supported such sport shopping.

Along with critics of women's participation in shopping were some supporters especially tradesmen. E.E. Perkins, whose successful *Treatise on Haberdashery* helped implement more modern trading methods among haberdashers, published another treatise in the 1830s entitled *The Lady's Shopping Manual and Mercery Album*. This book gave women tips on getting the best quality haberdashery goods and explained the complicated varieties available. However, this avid supporter of the trade warned women of the dangers of shopping: "Three fourths of the male assistants in the trade know nothing of the goods which it is their business to exhibit. Their object too frequently is to sell by any means, and in many cases the daily amount of sales is the tenure by which they retain their situations."[58] Male draper's assistants were accused of possessing the worst of female traits—vanity in their clothing and appearance and a tendency toward duplicity. Perkins warned women not to be taken in by the finery displayed to them. The same writer in the *Times* who admonished magistrates for not considering ladies possible thieves also warned ladies that shopping was not their right as an entertainment: "As, however, there are innumerable instances of politeness on the part of vendors even under the greatest trials of patience, ladies should also remember that the time of every man of business is his estate, and that they have no right to cause unnecessary, unremunerated trouble . . .."[59]

Perhaps the most revealing treatment of the dangers of the sport shopper appears in the *Edinburgh Magazine* in 1859. In this short story, "Shoppers and Shopping," lady shoppers are the real villains of the piece even though the new retailers cause the hardship of the two drapery assistant protagonists. The narrator of the tale describes his horror when two ladies he was on an outing with chose to spend an idle hour at the "warehouse of Jenkins and Jones." After chatting and examining the costly fabrics brought to them for over an hour, the ladies left the store: "significant glances were exchanged betwixt the friends . . . without a word

---

[57] Trollope, *London Tradesmen*, 93. See also Doyle and Leigh, 'Mr. Pips his Diary. A Prospect of a Fashyonable Haberdasher's Shopre,' in *Manners and Cvstoms of ye Englyshe, London*. In this satire of English life a shopping trip to Regent Street begins with a woman buying lace collars and ends with her buying numerous accessories before the husband is able to entice her away from the store.

[58] Perkins, The Lady's Shopping Manual and Mercery Album, v-vi.

[59] An Old Subscriber, Letter to the *Times*, 12 March 1844, in *Times*, 14 March 1844. See also Rappaport's mention of much later complaints of this practice in draper's journals. Rappaport, 'The Halls of Temptation,' 76.

of thanks or any apology for the trouble given, the fair shoppers swept out of the 'Department' evidently well-pleased at the attention shown and the entertainment afforded them, indifferent as to whether they had not caused one fellow creature an additional hour's labour and another a waste of time . . . ."[60] The author of the story calls such women "pricers" and blames these pleasure shoppers for the death of his two heroes, both young assistants in clothing retail. Before he too is killed by these shopping practices, Barty explained to the narrator why his friend Harry died so young. He was worked to death by "pricers":

> 'Then I suppose that shoppers kill half the assistants in London.'
> 'One class, perhaps unconsciously.'
> 'Are Shoppers divided into classes ?'
> 'They may be into two, those who believe with Johnson that a shop is a place for sales, and those who are of a different opinion, and seem to think that shops are opened, stocked, and kept up for their accommodation and amusement, and who look upon assistants as mere machines, constructed, and warranted to keep in perpetual motion for fourteen hours a day . . .. They are the terror of the assistants, though they must meet them with smiling face in the warehouse—aware that they have come there with no intention to buy, but to fill up the time between two engagements, or to rest when the promenade becomes fatiguing . . ..'[61]

These pricers killed Barty too, in the end, when he goes mad from the pressure and long hours of the drapery business. For women in the nineteenth-century shopping became more than an errand to acquire family goods. It was an entertainment, a pastime, or as Barty styled it, "a right."

'No Spirit of Logic': Men, Women and the New Retail

His 1880 sketches of tradesmen in which his estimate of lady shoppers was little changed followed Trollope's 1871 criticism of shoppers and 'cheap shopkeepers' in his novel *Brown, Jones, and Robinson*. Trollope summed up the nineteenth-century complaint that women had turned shopping into a hollow pastime instead of participating in a respectable, traditional transaction of quality trade. Like Doyle and Leigh's contrast between the fictional Mr. Pips and Mrs. Pips in 1849, Trollope's discussion of the clothing retail shop highlights the gendering of traditional shopkeeping as male and the new, emporium, 'cheap shopkeeping' as female:

> There is, we think, nothing in which the difference of taste between the two sexes is more visible than in the reputation in which these shops are held by men and women. The man's idea is that the mercer should sell cloth, and the silk-merchant

---

[60] 'Shoppers and Shopping,' *Tait's Edinburgh Magazine*, 26 n.s. (May 1859), 291.
[61] *Ibid.*, 294-295.

silk, and the upholsterer tables. He may be beaten from it by the alleged greater cheapness of the 'Store'; but the spirit of logic, of which he is unconscious, tells him that the man who deals in gloves only will know most about gloves. His wife has no spirit of logic, consciously or unconsciously. It is a trouble for her to find out the really good glove shop, and in the long run she is satisfied with gloves from Marshall and Snelgrove's.[62]

By 1880, the drapery emporium had been replaced by the even grander department store. Perhaps it is more appropriate to say that the drapery and haberdashery emporiums often became the grander department stores of the later nineteenth century. Trollope further described this shopping as comparable to the men's clubs of the same era: 'And, moreover, the plan offers to the lady some of those club attractions which her husband has at his disposal. She can lounge there, and talk, and be surrounded by pretty things. She can meet her friends, and she will always be treated with courtesy . . ..'[63] This women's club version of shopping in 1880 is similar to the description of the emporium "pricers" of the late 1850s; except that Trollope did not accuse these women of killing anyone in their search for pleasure.

Women's participation in and encouragement of the retail culture of fraud that permeated mid-century shops and shopkeeping only served to further lower critics' estimation of the new shop practices. From the purchases of useless frippery at bazaars to the buying of bargain fabric at the 'cheap shops' and discount emporiums, women were gendering consumption. Although in theory the man possessed the family pocketbook, the women wielded it, and were increasingly identified with this role. Beginning in the eighteenth-century, English commentators chastised women for their pursuit of consumption and ruinous overspending.[64] They were frequently criticized for spending above their means. In the late 1860s, *The Draper* inserted this poem that posed the question "Why Don't I Marry Mary Anne?":

'Why not for worse or better take her?

. . .

For though her days would all be spent
From shop to shop in visits ambling,
Whereby she'd swallow up the rent,
And I perhaps should take to gambling.'[65]

Middle-class men and their pocketbooks were not safe from the depredations of shopping wives, daughters, and girlfriends. Critics seemed exasperated by women's participation and encouragement of this retail madness that threatened even well-

---

[62] Trollope, *London Tradesmen*, 93.

[63] *Ibid.*

[64] See especially Margot Finn, 'Women, Consumption and Coverture in England, c. 1760-1860,' *The Historical Journal*, 39, 3 (1996): 703-704.

[65] 'Why Don't I Marry Mary Anne?,' *The Draper* (London) 24 December 1869.

padded bank accounts and the respectable men who owned them. The women acted as if it were they who controlled the family purse.

Middle-class men, particularly husbands, are always portrayed as more sensible than women in their attitude toward shopping and their knowledge of the "tricks" of the trade. The critics of lady shoppers paint a very different picture of men and consumption. Men realized the importance of the traditional, specialized, English shopkeeper. Men paid fair prices for quality goods from reputable dealers. Men did not use shopping as a form of entertainment, but only shopped to actually buy goods. However accurate or inaccurate this picture of middle-class male shoppers may be, their refusal to participate in the new retail did not affect its success, because women increasingly controlled consumption. To "sensible" middle-class men, this consumer culture must have seemed like a conspiracy between the shopkeepers and their female family members:

> For Swan and Edgar we were bound,
> But, ere we walked five yards I found
> My purse the lighter by a pound,
> For going out a shopping.[66]

Like the husband in the ballad, men were able to resist the onslaught of the larger scale, cheaper retail trade unlike the women shoppers who frequented these shops.[67]

Although male commentators distanced themselves from this feminized, false retail culture by criticizing it, or claiming to be its victims, they were also participating in and supporting it. First of all, most of the shopkeepers adopting the new methods of trade were male and middle-class. Secondly, men participated in the nineteenth-century scramble for status. They could not be unaware of the connection between status and possession of the requisite goods. Wilkie Collins' 1852 novel *Basil* satirizes middle-class consumption in the house of a London linen-draper:

> Everything was oppressively new. . . . the paper on the walls, with its gaudy pattern of birds, trellis work, and flowers, in gold, red, and green on a white ground, looked hardly dry yet; the showy window-curtains of white and sky-blue, and the still showier carpet of red and yellow, seemed as if they had come out of the shop yesterday; . . . the paper, the curtains, the carpet glared on you: the books, the wax-flowers in glass-cases, the chairs in flaring chintz-covers, the china plates . . . the over-ornamented chiffoniers with Tonbridge toys and long-necked smelling bottles on their upper shelves—all glared at you.[68]

---

[66] 'Going Out A Shopping,' (Dudley Street, 7 Dials, London).

[67] For an examination of the representation of the male shopper as 'rational' and the female shopper as 'irrational,' see Jennifer Jones discussion of the female consumer in eighteenth-century France. Jones, 'Coquettes and Grisettes,' 35.

[68] Wilkie Collins, *Basil* (New York: Dover Publications, Inc., 1980); reprint: (London: Sampson Low, Son & Co., 1862); See also Lancaster, *The Department Store*, 162.

Such overstuffed display announced a family's wealth and status. Although purchased by women, this bric-a-brac provided visible proof of the position of a middle-class man and his family. The middle-class man also knew that his wife's fashionable appearance increased his status. In Doyle and Leigh's 1849 satire, even the practical Mr. Pips admits of his wife's new bargain dress that "the pattern was pretty, and my wife being well-dressed do please my taste, and also increase my consequence and dignity."[69] That consumption was part of everyday Victorian living did not prevent novelists, journalists, and others from complaining about this new "women's" shopping culture.

In the evolution of English retailing, female shoppers remained far ahead of their male counterparts. The pleasure women took in frequenting cheaper shops and taking advantages of their discounts and the leisure time women spent in these pursuits angered male contemporaries. To men like Trollope, the whole process of shopping, the polite attentiveness of the assistants, the comparisons in ambling from shop to shop looking for sales, seemed a wasteful and ridiculous process. That women went alone in public and dealt with such fraudulent men also made the process suspicious. Shopping itself was becoming feminized, by women and for women, and after the advent of the department store women often also staffed the stores.[70] For some there was little difference between these shopping ladies and the shoplifting ladies who sometimes found themselves on trial throughout the nineteenth century.

In *Brown, Jones and Robinson*, Trollope sarcastically explained that the position of ladies in retail culture was not one of a helpless consumer:

'If a tradesman can induce a lady to buy a diagonal Osnabruck cashmere shawl by telling her that he has 1,200 of them, who is injured? And if the shawl is not exactly a real diagonal Osnabruck cashmere, what harm is done as long as the lady gets the value for her money? And if she don't get the value for her money, whose fault is that? Isn't it a fair stand-up fight? And when she tries to buy for £4, a shawl which she thinks is worth about £8, isn't she dealing on the same principles herself? If she be lucky enough to possess credit, the shawl is sent home without payment, and three years afterwards fifty per cent. is perhaps offered for settlement of the bill. It is a fair fight, and the ladies are very well able to take care of themselves.'[71]

Throughout the nineteenth century, journalists, judges, novelists, short-story writers, and ballad composers revealed anxiety over the female shopper. Women were the co-conspirators with the drapers.

Urged on by the growth in women's fashions and the desire for status, female shoppers of the middle-classes and below accumulated fashionable goods.

---

[69] Doyle and Leigh, 'Mr. Pips his Diary. A Prospect of a Fashyonable Haberdasher hys Shopre [Tuesday, Auguft 7, 1849], *Manners and Cvstoms of ye Englyshe*.

[70] See Erika Rappaport's description of shopping as a 'gendered' and 'female urban pleasure.' Rappaport, 'The Halls of Temptation,' 82.

[71] Trollope, *Brown, Jones, & Robinson*, 42. Note: abbreviation for pounds modernized.

According to their critics, they encouraged fraud by responding to advertisements, shopping alone and unprotected, and refusing to pay market price in hopes of bettering their status with finery beyond their means. Women even stole literally from the tradesman as he was defrauding her by secreting ribbons, silks, and lace or even entire rolls of fabric. English women turned shopping into their new leisure past time forcing more brass, glass, display, and attendants on shopping emporiums without providing returns. Female shoppers encouraged the shopkeepers to make money in less legitimate ways and endangered the lives and health of overworked employees. In the eyes of the critics, women encouraged the new culture of fraud in retail and participated willingly in it. Male, middle-class critics distanced themselves from this shift in consumption and contributed to the gendering of the act of buying itself, the feminization of English shopping.

Although nineteenth-century female consumers were not as dishonest or as powerful as contemporaries describe them, neither were they the victims of a system of mass consumption. What seemed to many male commentators as a wasteful and costly new attitude of shopping as *entertainment* that rested on false pretenses—buyers feigning interest in a large number of goods while sellers emphasized display and pretended to offer only bargains—was in reality nineteenth century women's recognition of a new style of consumption that required both seller and buyer to be conscious of display and the larger scale marketing of goods. New production methods and the spread of fashion to the middle and some members of the working classes intensified the bargain hunting competition and led to the publication of carefully worded etiquette and how-to manuals for middle-class women on tight budgets as well as satirical writings on the *nouveau riche* and the class-climbing servant girl. Carefully striving to balance between obtaining status for themselves and their families with the right sort of goods at the right price and 'overdoing' it by buying ostentatious or poorly made goods, women experienced pleasure in their widening powers of consumption and used that power to create a leisure world for themselves. This shopping 'demon' of short stories, satires, and serious reports on English shopping contrasts with the role of women, especially middle-class women, as moral defenders of home and hearth in the nineteenth-century. The tension between aggressive consumer and passive homemaker shapes the debate not only of the female shopper, but of the true bargain hunter—the criminal consumer.

PART II
CRIMINAL CONSUMPTION

Chapter 5

Shoplifting in Early Nineteenth-Century England

There's one law for the Rich,
And another for the Poor now.
—'Ladies Don't Go Thieving!,' 1855[1]

Shoplifting Before Kleptomania

In his study of shoplifting in England, Daniel Murphy states: 'This is not the place to delve into feminist literature . . ..'[2] Yet shoplifting is precisely the place to delve into feminist literature—to search for the roots of the gendered nature of this crime and discover how women came to be associated with it. Shoplifting cases in England prior to the mid-nineteenth century reveal not only England's treatment of petty female criminals, but also how society interpreted the scourge of light-fingered ladies. Before the availability of the kleptomania defense, middle-class women only had the option of denying their crime or of blaming the 'cheap shopkeeper' of falsely accusing them. Women's role as demanding, aggressive shoppers terrorizing assistants and pauperizing store owners in their search for bargains contrasted with their representation as icons of the nineteenth-century domestic ideal.[3] Faced with evidence of shoplifting, among non-working-class women, some English critics blamed the new consumer culture for encouraging and creating the problem of middle-class shoplifting long before the rise of the department store.

For women of all classes, the opportunities for crime evolved along with the progress of English consumption. The growth of commercial bazaars and other

---

[1] 'Ladies Don't Go Thieving!,' Johnson Ballads 1308, John Johnson Collection, Bodleian, Oxford. See also also 'Rich & Poor Law,' Street Ballads, Box 9, John Johnson Collection, Bodleian, Oxford. See illustration page 165.

[2] Daniel J. I. Murphy, *Customers and Thieves: an Ethnography of Shoplifting* (Brookfield, Vermont: Gower, 1986), 39.

[3] For a discussion of the rise of the representation of the middle-class woman as the defender of home and hearth see Leonore Davidoff and Catherine Hall, *Family Fortunes: Men and Women of the English Middle Class 1780-1850* (Chicago: The University of Chicago Press, 1987), 335-415. See also Bram Dijkstra, *Idols of Perversity: Fantasies of Feminine Evil in Fin-de-Siècle Culture* (New York: Oxford University Press, 1986), 3-24.

indoor markets like arcades marked the late eighteenth and early nineteenth centuries. In William Lancaster's study of the phenomenon of department stores in Britain, he notes a change in the mode of selling especially by linen drapers and haberdashers between the 1830s and 1850s. As chapters one and three showed, the traditional eighteenth century shop with its specialized market, custom of credit, high profit margin, and slow turnover faced new competition in the 1830s from stores like linen drapers in urban centers who were expanding and selling a greater variety of items, usually for cash only. As mid-century approached, these larger linen draper emporiums reached out to new classes of shoppers below the old elites and into the middle classes and lower classes. People who had once depended on 'pedlars, Scotch travellers, visiting fairs and other itinerants' for their clothing and other non-grocery items were now coming to the expanded city establishments.[4]

Although not on the same scale as later shoplifting with its grand department stores and perfection of consumer culture, the commercial expansion of the early Victorian period brought forth similar trepidations about women and the crime of shoplifting. In the 1840s and 1850s, the people of England saw what they thought were increasing waves of crime.[5] Londoners especially worried that the metropolis had metamorphosed into a city of thieves.[6] Frederic Hill, a former Inspector of Prisons, noted in 1853 that 'In Great Britain the large majority of the offences now committed consist of thefts, unaccompanied with violence . . ..'[7] Petty thefts like shoplifting were becoming the typical criminal offense.

However, the incidence of shoplifting in the nineteenth century is difficult to trace for several reasons. Shoplifting, even when reported, was statistically lumped with other common thefts. Shoplifting could be treated as either an indictable offense tried in front of a jury of the assizes or quarter sessions, or a non-indictable offense dealt with summarily by a magistrate. Sometimes shoplifters would appear before a magistrate only to be sent to a jury trial.[8] Moreover, undetected offenses probably far exceeded detected ones. Shoplifting is by definition a crime of deception and its most practiced professionals make items disappear without attracting the slightest attention. Even in the smaller shops of the eighteenth and

---

[4] William Lancaster, *The Department Store: A Social History* (London: Leicester University Press, 1995), 8.

[5] See especially V.A.C. Gatrell, 'Crime, Authority, and the Policeman-State,' *The Cambridge Social History of Britain 1750-1950*, ed. F.M.L. Thompson (Cambridge: Cambridge University Press, 1990), 250-254.

[6] See Mansfield, 'The Causes of Crime in the Metropolis,' *Tait's Edinburgh Magazine*,' n.s., 17 (June 1850): 330-331.

[7] Frederic Hill, *Crime: Its Amount, Causes, and Remedies* (London: John Murray, 1853), 37. Martin Wiener in *Reconstructing the Criminal* attributes part of this heightened concern to the availability of more accurate national criminal statistics that gave an impression of soaring criminality. Martin Wiener, *Reconstructing the Criminal: Culture, Law, and Policy in England, 1830-1914* (New York: Cambridge University Press, 1990), 14-26.

[8] Murphy, *Customers and Thieves*, 5.

previous centuries, shopkeepers commonly suffered from the crime of shoplifting despite their precautions of keeping goods out of public reach.[9] Detection became if anything more difficult as stores switched to more open displays. In the nineteenth century critics chided linen drapers shops for their tendency to display goods at their shop doors within easy reach of criminals.[10] Linen drapers' shops, like commercial and charity bazaars, lured customers in with open displays of their goods. These innovative retail methods also attracted shoplifters. Yet due to problems of prosecution and fears of upsetting middle-class customers, many official arrests were never made.[11] The problems in detecting and prosecuting shoplifters made the so-called 'dark figure' of unreported crime or shoplifters who were never caught particularly large.[12]

Although one cannot be sure if the number of shoplifters in the early Victorian era actually grew, the concern about shoplifting in the press and in fiction certainly increased. However, those participating in the shoplifting debates prior to mid-century did not have access to the easy answer to middle-class women's crime provided by the kleptomania diagnosis in the later years of the century. Until the mid-nineteenth century, Victorians sought moral explanations of crime.[13] A vague notion of 'insanity' in relation to this crime existed, a lapse of reason or attack of absent-mindedness, but there was no clear association between bourgeois shoplifters and a special sort of disease. Middle-class and lower-class shoplifters, however, were treated differently, and the crime was already associated with women. Middle-class observers developed an early version of the later consumer culture theory of female shoplifting by blaming storekeepers for their recklessness and criminal trickery rather than blaming the 'ladies' who may have stolen from them. By the end of the century, the focus on the culpability of retail shops in encouraging middle-class shoplifting shifted from their fraud and trickery to their elaborate exhibition of goods. In the latter half of the nineteenth century, the department store began to shoulder some of the blame for tempting women with sumptuous displays of goods. In 1896 the French alienist[14] Laccasagne accused: "[Department stores] exist in order to arouse desire. They are the preparation of an illusion. They fascinate the client, dazzle her with their disturbing exhibitions."[15] Once again, the retail culture corrupted the shopper and turned her into the

---

[9] See Dorothy Davis, *A History of Shopping* (London: Routledge & Kegan Paul Ltd., 1966), 193.

[10] Mansfield, 'The Causes of Crime in the Metropolis,' 334.

[11] Patricia O'Brien, 'The Kleptomania Diagnosis: Bourgeois Women and Theft in Late Nineteenth-Century France,' *Journal of Social History* (Fall 1983): 66.

[12] Murphy, *Customers and Thieves*, 6.

[13] See Lucia Zedner, *Women, Crime, and Custody in Victorian England* (Oxford: Clarendon Press, 1991), 86, and Wiener, *Reconstructing the Criminal*, passim for the shift in Victorian criminological attitudes.

[14] Mad doctor—an early version of a psychiatrist.

[15] Zedner, *Women Crime, and Custody*, 73. See also Havelock Ellis, *Studies in the Psychology of Sex*, vol. 2, pt. 2 (New York: Random House, 1936), 480.

shoplifter. This nineteenth-century perception of shoplifting which found the stores at least partially at fault for the commission of retail crime constrasts sharply with early modern views of shoplifting.

A History of Shoplifting in England

Shoplifting in the Seventeenth and Eighteenth Centuries

Particularly associated with deception, shoplifters garnered little sympathy for their crime in earlier periods. In the Elizabethan era, shoplifters were simply called 'lifts' and a 'Lifting Law' existed in the very late 1500s.[16] In 1698 an Act of Parliament officially designated it "the Crime of stealing Goods privately out of Shops and Warehouses, commonly called Shop-lifting."[17] Under this Act of William III's reign, execution was the punishment, and the term 'privately stealing goods' appears in later court cases. By the second half of the eighteenth century the term 'shoplifting' reflected modern usage.[18] J.M. Beattie notes that under this 'Shoplifting Act' any theft from a shop up to five shillings was a felony but one *not* covered by the benefit of clergy—automatically a hanging offense. However, due to problems in detection and prosecution and the unpopularity of the death sentence for such a small offense, little use was made of this statute.[19] In his survey of the eighteenth-century Surrey assizes Beattie found on average less than two offenders per year prosecuted for shoplifting as a capital offense. A more common punishment for such thieves was transportation.[20] Despite leniency in the actual punishment of shoplifters, V.A.C. Gatrell notes that Romilly's Bill to abolish the death penalty for shoplifting was rejected six times between 1810 and 1820 by the House of Lords before it was finally approved.[21]

As the 1699 Shoplifting Act of William and Mary demonstrates, by the 1700s, the term shoplift was in common usage and the crime itself had become serious enough to merit special legislation. Although capital punishment was not often enforced for shoplifting, some criminals were executed under the statute and others were transported. A perceived rise in shoplifting in London in the early 1700s led merchants to request a government crackdown especially against the 'professional'

---

[16] Loren E. Edwards, *Shoplifting and Shrinkage Protection for Stores* (Springfield, Illinois: Charles C. Thomas, 1958), 4. See also Murphy, *Customers and Thieves*, 85.

[17] OED, 2nd edition; Murphy, *Customers and Thieves*, 85.

[18] *Ibid.*

[19] Beattie dates the statute 1699, 10 and 11 Wm III, c.23. J. M Beattie, *Crime and the Courts in England, 1660-1800* (Princeton University Press, 1986), 178-179. See also 'Shoplifting Bill,' *Morning Chronicle* (London) 27 March 1813.

[20] *Ibid.* See especially f.n. 87, page 179.

[21] V.A.C. Gatrell, *The Hanging Tree: Execution and the English People, 1770-1868* (Oxford University Press, 1994), 500-501.

shoplifting gangs who worked in teams of two or three and were difficult to catch. Merchants sent a grievance to parliament to ask for assistance:

> The notoriousness and increase of this practice needs no other demonstration than the daily experience of all the shopkeepers . . . against which their strictest diligence cannot secure them, their number, craft, and power, being jointly increas'd and combin'd, by which means they personate all degrees of buyers, in all their respective qualifications . . ..[22]

However, after the 1698 act, the government did little to ensure the punishment of shoplifters. Many traders decided to band together against those who preyed upon their stocks. The trade organizations formed were not official government bodies, but collections of private business people who circulated private newsletters with the names of known offenders, offered rewards, and aided in the prosecution of shoplifters, swindlers, and various other criminals.[23]

Founded largely in the eighteenth century, many continued to be active well into the nineteenth century and beyond. One of the earliest, founded by magistrate and author Sir John Fielding in March 1767, was the Society for Prosecuting Felons, Forgers, Shoplifters, Domestic Thieves and Persons Giving False Character to Servants. Under this lengthy title, bankers, merchants, and tradesmen worked together to increase prosecutions and apprehensions of criminals like shop thieves.[24] Established one decade later, The Guardians: or Society for the Protection of Trade Against Swindlers and Sharpers has an even longer history. In its 'Rules and Orders' of 1816 the society stated:

> That, whenever any Member shall have suffered robbery of any kind, or by shoplifting, and shall have prosecuted the offender or offenders to conviction, he shall be at liberty after such conviction, to lay a state of the facts, in writing, before the Committee . . . of the expenses to which he may have been put in carrying on

---

[22] 'The Great Grievance of Traders and Shopkeepers, by the Notorious Practice of Stealing their Goods out of their Shops and Warehoufes, by Perfons commonly called Shoplifters; Humbly reprefented to the Confideration of the Honourable Houfe of Commons,' London, n.d. [British Library]. Note: Spelling of eighteenth-century texts modernized.

[23] See David Philips, 'Good men to Associate and Bad Men to Conspire: Associations for the Prosecution of Felons in England 1760-1860,' *Policing and Prosecution in Britain, 1750-1850*, ed. Douglas Hay and Francis Snyder (Oxford: Clarendon Press, 1989), 113-170.

[24] Society for Prosecuting Felons, Forgers, Shoplifters, Domestic Thieves and Persons Giving False Character to Servants; also for Defraying the Expenses of Advertisements, Hand Bills, and Rewards, April 1808, 'Police and Public Security I,' Box I, John Johnson Collection, Bodleian, Oxford.

such prosecution, which expenses the Committee shall have power to order the payment of to such Member . . ..[25]

However, in the case of shoplifting, the reimbursement was not to exceed forty shillings.[26] Many of these societies continued to operate well into the nineteenth century. By the mid-nineteenth century, the Guardians had become the City of London Trade Protection Society and in their 1848 circular they warned of a woman going by the name of Madame Desireé or Ribrie who preyed upon silk merchants and drapers: '[She] is calling at wholesale mercers and ordering large quantities of goods, and naming a day when she will call and pay for them, and take them away; she never makes a second appearance, and she is believed to be a shoplifter.'[27] Founded in response to rising concerns over property crime in the late 1700s, these societies attempted to adapt their methods to nineteenth century crime.

In an attempt to better control this crime in the early nineteenth century, Sir Samuel Romilly proposed a bill to remove shoplifting from the list of capital offenses which would not only make the punishment for shoplifting less bloody, but would also increase the conviction rate. For shopkeepers the low conviction rate was disappointing, but MPs feared abandoning the eighteenth-century system that depended heavily on the terror of hanging as a 'deterrent' to would-be criminals. In March 1813 Romilly claimed that out of the 188 people tried the previous year under the law, only 18 were convicted. Juries were not willing to punish a theft under 5 shillings with death.[28] Some MPs feared that Romilly's less severe punishment would increase an already burgeoning crime rate rather than benefiting besieged shop owners. A Mr. Frankland in the Commons opposed the Bill 'on the ground, that since the increase of the commercial system, it was necessary to guard property so exposed as that of shops by the most severe punishments.'[29] Romilly defended his bill and cited the recent Act passed against pick-pocketing that had raised the conviction rate from one in thirty to one-half of those indicted. However, under Romilly's bill a shoplift who took over five pounds

---

[25] The Guardians: or Society for the Protection of Trade Against Swindlers and Sharpers, 'Rules and Orders'(Northumberland Street, Strand, London: G. Sidney, 1816), 25-26.

[26] *Ibid.* See also 'Highworth Association For the Prosecution of Felons and Other Thieves,' (Faringdon, Cotton, Printer, 1810) for a description of a society more concerned with non-commercial property crime.

[27] 'Madame Desire, alias Madame Ribrie,' *City of London Trade Protection Circular (private circular)* (London) 9 August 1848; 'Desiree,' Madame,' *City of London Trade Protection Circular (private circular)* (London) 28 August 1848. See also James Henry Dixon, *A Statement of Facts In Reference to the City of London Trade Protection Society, (13, Swithin's Lane,) and the Mode in Which it Discharges it Pecuniary Obligations* (London: Effingham Wilson, Royal exchange, 1851).

[28] 'Shoplifting Bill,' *Morning Chronicle* (London) 27 March 1813.

[29] *Times* (London) 27 March 1813. For an example of the type of shoplifting Romilly hoped to curb, see the case of Mary Jones *Times* (London) 11 September 1811 and a woman named Roach *Times* (London) 10 January 1812. Note: all following references to *Times* refer to the London *Times*.

worth of goods could still be transported. The debate raged for ten years before the bill's supporters gained the approval of the lords. After 1820 in England, shoplifters no longer faced losing their lives for the offense, but repeat offenders could find themselves on distant shores. Women continued to be transported to Australia until 1852 when Van Dieman's Land refused to accept any more female convicts, and England was forced to find prison space for women instead.[30]

Although both men and women shoplifted in the eighteenth century and contributed to the rise in petty theft, the crime was notable for its many female perpetrators. In her case study of illegitimate male and female trading in Devon and Somerset in the eighteenth century, Amy Williams finds women particularly active in the networks of trade involving stolen goods, especially clothing, and in the actual theft of these goods.[31] In the early eighteenth century traders' grievance to parliament they claimed: 'a late shop-lift before her execution confessed that she (in her calling) had stolen to the value of twelve thousand pounds; by which practice many shopkeepers have been insensibly ruined, ...'[32] In the 1700s, the motive for shoplifting was largely the same as the motive for other theft—poverty. Two women who stole to alleviate their poverty, Mary Robinson, seventy years old, and a younger woman named Jane Holmes went to the noose in 1726 as a result of their shoplifting excursions. A woman named Mary Jones, left to fend for herself and two children after her husband had been taken by a press gang, was executed in 1777 for attempting to steal some coarse linen to provide some income for her family. She was nineteen years old.[33]

'A Favourite Mode of Plunder': Shoplifting in the Nineteenth Century

By the nineteenth century, poor, lower-class women like Jones were especially associated with shoplifting, but emerging evidence of middle-class, 'non-professional' women shoplifters threatened the comfortable image of this theft as a crime of the poor. The rise in middle-class female shoplifting was particularly disturbing, and seemed to be a relatively recent development in female crime. Beattie cites an 1819 House of Commons committee finding that shoplifters were often "not persons who are regular traders in thieving, but are persons in better circumstances, particularly the women."[34] In John Brown's 1855 article 'On Genteel Thieves,' he claimed there were also many gentleman shoplifts, but there is little mention of

---

[30] *Times*, 27 March 1813 and 23 May 1816. See also Zedner, *Women, Crime and Custody in Victorian England*, 174-177.

[31] Amy Williams, 'Illegitimate Male and Female Trading in the Eighteenth Century: a Case Study of Devon and Somerset 1735-1785' (paper presented at the Second Exeter International Gender History Conference: Women, Trade & Business, University of Exeter, U.K., 15 July 1996).

[32] 'The Great Grievance of Traders and Shopkeepers, by the Notorious Practice of Stealing their Goods.'

[33] Edwards, *Shoplifting and Shrinkage Protection*, 5-9.

[34] Beattie, *Crime and the Courts in England*, 179.

or debate over such cases.[35] Along with expanded opportunities for consumption, increase in commerce presented expanded opportunities from crime.

Women's involvement in shoplifting appeared to be on the increase in the early nineteenth century. In London well-dressed women operated in concert to plunder tradesmen:

[I]t had long been a favourite mode of plunder among abandoned females. In order to carry on their depredations, a conspiracy was formed of two or more abandoned women, who, well dressed, went together into shops and, while one bargained and paid for some small articles, the others secreted whatever they could lay their hands upon.[36]

The spread of ornate fashions, with bonnets, mantles, and frills to a greater section of the populace produced an everyday look for women that easily concealed bits of lace, and even larger objects like rolls of fabric. Extra deep pockets in skirts and even special hooks or undergarments gave women shoplifters an advantage.[37] In the 1840s women's fashions included a long, wide, open sleeve for the well-dressed woman.[38] Throughout the century, voluminous women's fashions aided the female shoplifter.

The same shift to ornate women's fashions that abetted the female shoplifter in hiding her plunder also inspired women to shoplift to obtain those fashionable goods. In the early Victorian period the amount and variety of consumer goods available for sale was multiplying, and shopping was becoming a far more complex activity than it had been in the eighteenth century. In London, stores tempted and shop windows sparkled with a dizzying array of goods from patent medicines to ladies' dresses. The open displays of bazaars with their refreshment stands and musical entertainments drew shoppers to the places of purchase. In novels and newspapers, critics and admirers alike commented on the rising tide of goods and their display. Novels themselves carried commercial advertisements as magazines do today.[39] Thomas Richards traces the first extensive manifestation of this growing commodity culture back to the Great Exhibition of 1851 with its fantastic displays at the Crystal Palace; however, the growing commodity culture predates

---

[35] John Brown, 'On Genteel Thieves,' *Tait's Edinburgh Magazine*, o.s., 26, n.s., 22 (1855): 292. See also one such case *Times*, 8 April 1844.

[36] G.T. Crook, ed., *The Complete Newgate Calendar* (London: Privately Printed for the Navarre Society Limited, 1926), 71- 72.

[37] *Ibid.*, 72; Murphy, *Customers and Thieves*, 88-89.

[38] See the front color plates of *The Ladies Pocket Magazine* (November 1842) published by London: Sherwood and Co. Simpkin & Co.

[39] For literary examples of this growing commodity culture see the excerpts from Thackeray and Dickens in Hilary M. Schor, 'Urban Things: The Mystery of the Commodity in Victorian Literature' (paper presented at the Interdisciplinary Nineteenth-Century Studies conference on The Nineteenth-Century City: Global Contexts, Local Productions, Santa Cruz, California, 7-8 April 1995), 4-6.

handkerchiefs at the large firm of Messrs. White and Greenwell in Blackfriars Road. A total of twenty-five assistants were working on the day of the theft and the business employed a total of between seventy and eighty employees. Witnessed by one of these many assistants, the theft of the handkerchiefs led to a search of Nunn's belongings that turned up more of her employer's wares. The shopgirl as shoplifter was frightening because she threatened the trust of employer/employee relations and reached above her class by taking the finery she could not afford legally. Susan Nunn served six months in prison for her crime.[52]

For the poorer, non-middle class women accused of shoplifting, the punishments, although not capital after 1820, remained harsh. Even before 1820, courts too timid to sentence women to death would often sentence them to be transported. Two women, Mary Jones and Elizabeth Paine, browsed at a hosiers shop in Holborn in October 1809 and were caught outside the shop with twelve stolen pairs of stockings. The judge at the Old Bailey sentenced both women to seven years transportation.[53] Two women, who had once been respectable milliners in Hammersmith, were caught in December 1835 for a series of shoplifting excursions and tried at the Middlesex Sessions. The older woman, Hannah Hart, was transported for seven years, but her younger companion, Anne Reason only got a short prison sentence.[54] Also sentenced to transportation for repeated offenses of shoplifting, the short biography of Eliza Smith is one of the few if not only accounts remaining of a lower class woman shoplifter in the nineteenth century. An Irish woman forced to work as a maid to support her family after her alcoholic husband spent all of their earnings, Eliza spent much of her life in legitimate work. Pregnant with her third child, she returned home to find her husband living with his landlady. Forced again on her own, she started shoplifting in 1835 after the death of her third child: 'On the 29th September, I became acquainted with a woman whose line of life was that of shop-lifting, and with her I went into many shops to deprive my fellow-creatures of their property.'[55] Actually it was with a group of such 'abandoned females' that Eliza shoplifted with until her final sentence of transportation in 1839.[56]

The criminal careers of lower class women, like Susan Nunn, and disreputable women like Flash Poll and Saucy Nan were expected; however, there was no easy agreement on the question of 'respectable' women and shoplifting. This seemed to be the question in the minds of many of the people who wrote in to the *Times* in the

---

[52] CCCSP, Third Session, 1841, p. 407-408.
[53] Crook, The Complete Newgate Calendar, 72.
[54] GLRO, Indictment of Hannah Hart, Middlesex Quarter Sessions of the Peace, Middlesex Sessions Papers, 14 December 1835; *Times*, 19 December 1835. See also the case of repeat offenders Ann Bailey and Mary Anne Rutley transported for ten years in 1851. GLRO, Indictment of Ann Bailey and Mary Ann Rutley, Middlesex Quarter Sessions of the Peace, Middlesex Sessions Papers, 31 January 1853.
[55] Eliza Smith, *Memoir of Eliza Smith Who Was Transported for Shoplifting, Written By Herself* (Dublin: Hardy & Walker, 1839), 11.
[56] *Ibid.*, 12-13.

the Exhibition.[40] The responsibility for picking through this confusing world of goods increasingly went to women. In the 1840s and 50s in large cities like London, the separation of domestic activity from waged work left the province of shopping to growing numbers of middle-class women.[41]

In an era in which women have been seen as having little or no control over their own resources, women displayed surprising power in the arena of consumption. Many historians have noted the famous concept in English law—coverture—which precluded women from holding property and subsumed their status under that of their husbands upon marriage. This law made wives' contracts a point of antagonism between the husbands and the storekeepers. The law favored middle-class and upper-class women by empowering them to contract for large, expensive goods while lower class women were only qualified to contract for the very basics of life.[42] The consumer debt lawsuits Finn examines reflect similar tensions between sellers and customers as shoplifting cases in this period. Finn also notices that this increasing exercise of women's economic power led to a flood of 'prescriptive literature of the consumer revolution' condemning women's ruinous participation in that process.[43] These warnings of the dangers of female consumption resonate throughout the nineteenth century in condemnations of retail crime and consumption in general.

In the early Victorian era, crime, like the poverty that helped spawn it, was still associated more with immorality than disease. If middle-class women did steal it was surely a more heinous offense than that of their lesser educated and disadvantaged sisters. Middle-class women were idealized as the moral exemplars of the era. As Victorian gender ideology attempted to push women further into the protected sphere of the home, women's public forays produced severe anxiety. Paradoxically, the ideology of separate spheres with woman as a morally insulated 'angel' rose concurrently with commodity culture and a greater participation by women in the public of retail and consumption of goods. The association of women with shoplifting and later kleptomania came from this change in the Victorian economy in which women became the main family purchasers. Although an expanding consumer culture increased opportunities for shoplifting for female consumers of all classes, the treatment of lower-class women shoplifters continued to reflect older stereotypes of the hardened, professional female criminal.

---

[40] Thomas Richards, *The Commodity Culture of Victorian England: Advertising and Spectacle, 1851-1914* (Stanford: Stanford University Press, 1990), 17-41.
[41] William R. Leach, 'Transformation in a Culture of Consumption: Women and Department Stores, 1890-1925,' *The Journal of American History*, 71, no. 2 (September 1984): 333.
[42] Finn, 'Victorian Women as Consumer Debtors,' 4-13; Finn, 'Women, Consumption and Coverture in England,' 709-719.
[43] Finn, 'Women, Consumption and Coverture in England,' 704.

Older Stereotypes: Shoplifting and Non Middle-Class Women

The treatment of lower class women arrested for the crime of shoplifting exposes the bias of the gendered ideology that both limited and 'protected' middle-class women. In 1844, three lower-class women were taken in for shoplifting, and their cases, unlike middle-class shoplifting cases, elicited no fervent letters to the editor in their defense. These three women put on the mantle of respectability and went shoplifting eighteenth-century professional style. Elizabeth Langthorne, Mary Sullivan and Martha Boyd had been on at least a two-day shoe stealing spree when they were caught with stolen goods in December of 1844. Because they had worked as a team and posed as respectable young ladies, there was no sympathy in the reporting of their case:

> The prisoners affected to cry, but could not squeeze out a tear between them, and they loudly protested their innocence, saying that they never had a key turned upon them in their lives until the present occasion . . . .[44]

At this point in their incarceration, two policemen who had served a beat on the East end of the city recognized two of the ladies as 'Flash Poll' and 'Saucy Nan:' all had records.[45] This lack of sympathy or even an attempt at alternative explanations was typical of shoplifting committed by lower-class women. Also, by working in 'gangs' and demonstrating planning and deliberation in the commission of their crimes, lower-class women, especially those who used shoplifting as a profession, gathered little sympathy in the press.[46]

In July of 1840, two single women were caught in a well-practiced shoplifting operation at a linen draper's in Tothill street. As it often did in shoplifting cases, the newspaper report of the case stresses that the women were well-dressed. It is difficult to determine precisely to what class these women belonged; however, the fact that Mary Clarke and Mary Smith were living together in a lodging room at the time of the crime intimates that they were not middle class. The scam consisted of the women, dressed like respectable ladies, entering a shop and requesting to see a variety of goods. While one woman distracted the shop assistant in conversation, the other secreted a garment 'under her apron.' To complete the ruse the other

---

[44] *Times*, 13 December 1844.

[45] *Ibid.*

[46] *Central Criminal Court Sessions Papers*. The Whole Proceedings on the Queen's Comission of the Peace, Oyer and Terminer, and Gaol Delivery for the City of London, and Gaol Delivery for the County of Middlesex, and the Parts of the Counties of Essex, Kent, and Surrey, Within the Jurisdiction of the Central Criminal Court (Dobbs Ferry, New York: Trans-Media Publishing Co., 1981), microfilm, Second Session, 1844, 293–294. Note: Central Criminal Court Sessions Papers hereafter referred to as CCCSP. Perhaps due to their youth—the women were still in their teens—and their plea that they were only guilty of receiving and not theft, only two of the women, Langthorne and Sullivan, were sentenced to serve three months at the Old Bailey.

woman always left a small 'down payment' on some item she pretended to select and claimed she would be back later for it. When they searched the room of these women, the police found '45 duplicates'[47] for such items. Clarke and Smith took their customer impersonation very seriously with this down payment ploy, which doubtless had saved them from suspicion on other occasions. However, this time they went to the Old Bailey on shoplifting charges. The obvious professionalism of their tactics gained them little sympathy in the dry crime report of the *Times*.[48]

Like Clarke and Smith, many shoplifters disposed of their goods at legitimate pawnbrokers' shops. Pawnbrokers took goods in pledge for short term money loans and gave pawners a 'duplicate' or ticket to reclaim their goods. Pawners forfeited the goods if they could not pay back the loan plus the pawnbroker's interest by the end of the agreed upon period. Pawning, despite its critics, remained a mostly legitimate crucial source of credit for the working class in the nineteenth century. A woman pawning her most expensive goods, a common practice, would arouse little suspicion.[49] For the shoplifter, the advantages of pawning are obvious. The use of the pawnbroker as a fence, knowingly or unknowingly, for stolen goods brought criticism. Horatio Mansfield in his article on crime quotes a contemporary: 'The facilities that offer, or rather, I might add, invite, parties . . . to dispose of stolen property, without reference to value or extent, from the existence of those innumerable receptacles misnamed small 'pawn-shops,' . . . is much more serious and extensive than is generally believed.'[50] Searches of shoplifters' lodgings often produced hoards of pawn tickets.

A much less professional case of shoplifting was that of Ann Smith, a woman who worked alone and stole non-luxury items. Although it is fairly certain that criminal teams such as Clarke and Smith, who had a record of almost fifty crimes in their room, probably sold most of the stolen goods, it is not always clear how much was stolen for personal use. For poorer women, thefts of useful, non-luxury goods may have been for personal use rather than professional sale. In 1844 Ann Smith was charged with the theft of wool stockings from a hosier in Soho. Her method of operation was similar to the other crimes in that she actually paid for one pair and hid the other two. Once again, the woman was respectable in appearance, 'genteel,' but elicited little sympathy in the report of her crime other than that she was 'much affected' by her arrest.[51]

If the temptation of consumer culture was great for women who frequented the shops of London, the shop girls who were exposed to the lure of such merchandise all day may have found themselves more tempted. In December of 1840, a young woman named Susan Nunn was reported by her coworker for stealing two silk

---

[47] Pawn tickets.

[48] *Times*, 15 July 1840.

[49] See Melanie Tebutt, *Making Ends Meet: Pawnbroking and Working-Class Credit* (Leicester University Press, 1983).

[50] Mansfield, 'The Causes of Crime in the Metropolis,' 334.

[51] *Times*, 10 January 1844.

1840s concerning shoplifting cases. For some, respectable women who stole elicited sympathy, but for others, they deserved even more disdain because they should have been upholding society's values instead of transgressing them. In one case, the *Times* demonstrated its sympathy although the court did not. An eighteen year old named Jane George had apparently stolen numerous items at three stores in one day; however, her counsel explained that she had taken these things, 'white ribands and lace,' because she wanted 'to appear rather finer on her wedding day than her means honestly enabled her to do.' George was respectable, but not solidly middle class and with her wedding less than a week away she desired a display of status that in reality she did not possess. Despite her lawyer's protest that she was 'no common shoplifter,' George was sentenced to four months of hard labor in prison.[57] By trying to attain the middle-class ideal, George lost the 'respectable' status given to her under that very same ideal. She was treated like a 'common shoplifter.'

Without proof, such as the corroboration of a policeman, it was difficult to discern the true station in life or the intent of shoplifting women. Shopkeepers faced the dangers of falsely accusing respectable women in their pursuit of the shoplifter. In December 1844, Leah Mary Roper, 'a middle-aged woman, respectably dressed in deep mourning, and appearing to walk lame,' had all the appearances of a real customer. After looking around the store for a time, Roper settled on a few small purchases and left the store saying she would come back later to pick them up. In the meantime 48 yards of fabric were missed by the shop assistant. When the woman returned she was questioned, and after the police were called, she admitted her guilt and even took the police to the pawnbrokers where she had sold the fabric. This 'respectable widow' with her lame leg (probably an affectation that allowed her to carry things unnoticed under her dress) was actually a professional thief of several years running who had '30 or 40 duplicates' for goods taken and hidden under the carpet of her house.[58] Since the appearance of respectability was a prerequisite for successful shoplifting, the difficulty posed by these cases for shopkeepers and prosecutors were endless. Roper turned out to be a professional, but she could have easily have been a respectable middle-class woman.

Respectable Shoplifters

Who is to Blame?

With the rising anxiety over respectable shoplifters, the older view of shoplifters as immoral and lower-class no longer sufficed to explain the crime of shoplifting in England. By the nineteenth century shoplifting was seen as a woman's crime.

---

[57] *Times*, 18 March 1844.
[58] *Times*, 4 December 1844; CCCSP, Second Session, 1844, 251-252.

Lower-class women, especially those who showed signs of deliberation of their crimes by working in gangs and fencing goods in pawn shops could still be easily fit into eighteenth-century definitions of the corrupt, predatory female criminal or the desperate woman stealing as an illegal means of support. However, some women, even working-class women like Jane George, appeared not to steal for cash gain, but instead to take items for personal use—to wear as a sign of higher status. In cases of upper working-class and middle-class female shoplifters the correlation between crime and its cause was even more difficult for nineteenth-century commentators to discover. *Punch* theorized that respectable shoplifting was simply the current 'fashion' in England. Not easily ascribed to either poverty or moral corruption, middle-class shoplifting puzzled nineteenth-century observers who were faced with the difficulty of protecting the ideal of the domestic angel while being forced to admit the existence of middle-class female shoplifting. The search for answers began early in the century.

Between 1800 and 1820, the city of Bath experienced two cases of middle-class and wealthier female thieves that caused debate in the press. The scandalous Perrot case at the turn of the century tested the concept of middle-class feminine moral inviolability. Jane Leigh Perrot's acquittal of the crime of shoplifting an extra card of lace in her parcel from a haberdasher's shop protected her status and reputation, but left many unanswered questions about the nature of women's relationship to consumption and consumer crime.[59] Perrot claimed only that she was falsely accused by the shop keepers; however, a later non-shoplifting case in the 1820s hinted at what would become an acceptable and more frequent explanation of middle-class female crime. In 1820 Mrs. Sarah Bingham, a respectable woman in her 70s living in Bath, brought libel charges against the Reverend John Gardiner for accusing her of stealing a one-pound note from a church collection plate. Bingham claimed she absent-mindedly picked up the note thinking she had accidentally dropped too much money into the plate. Although some thought she had been prompted by 'a momentary temptation of the devil,'[60] Bingham insisted it was an absent-minded mistake and she had returned the note after she realized what she had done. In her defense her counsel brought up the case of another woman who borrowed a gold pencil case to use in a local shop and afterwards stuffed it into her pocket as she would have her own. She later discovered her mistake and returned the box to the shopkeeper who told her 'he had observed her put it in her pocket.' The lady angrily chastised the shopkeeper for not telling her and endangering her reputation, and 'she declared that she never would go to the shop

---

[59] See *The Trial of Jane Leigh Perrot at Taunton Assizes, on Saturday the 29th of March, 1800; Charged with Stealing a Card of Lace, in the Shop of Elizabeth Gregory, Haberdasher & Milliner, of the City of Bath* (Bath: W. Gye, 1800), reprint in *British Trial Series* (London: Chadywyck-Healey Ltd., 1990), microfiche.

[60] *Imputation of Theft: Report of the Trial of an Action Brought by Mrs. Sarah Bingham Against the Rev. John Gardiner, D.D. for a Malicious Libel, Imputing to Her That She had Stolen a One Pound Note* (London: Richard and Arthur Taylor, 1820), xv.

again.'[61] The absent-minded defense of the Bingham case protected the morals of middle-class women, but implied a not fully conscious mental state. The connotations of such a claim are different than a defense of absolute denial of the crime like Jane Leigh Perrot's: 'I . . . call that God, whom we all acknowledge and adore, to attest that I am innocent . . ..'[62]

This stress on morality created problems in the interpretation of shoplifting by middle-class women. Without the availability of the kleptomania diagnosis, there were few serviceable answers. Middle-class women did not fit the picture of the 'professional' lower class shoplifters of centuries past. These prosperous women did not need to steal, and were held in the highest moral regard. Their fall into crime must be explained by some other means. Even though they no longer faced the possibility of hanging when caught,, the shame and taint of the offense were enough to frighten any respectable lady.[63]

Part of the problem with shoplifting as a crime was that it dealt with deception and hinged on a projection of respectability. There was an inherent danger of arresting the wrong person, a person who was in reality respectable. The same month that Jane George stole her wedding finery, the police arrested what appeared to be yet another team of professional shoplifters. The dangers of not being able to separate the thief from the customer were evident in the description of the two women.

One, Elizabeth Watson, was married and 'well-dressed' while the other, Mary Elliot, was 'the wife of a highly respectable tradesman.' After buying an inexpensive item from the shop and participating in a distracting conversation with Mrs. Elliot, Watson walked out with a costly satin scarf hidden in her dress, and Elliot left the shop at the same time. Both women were apprehended and searched by a female employee in an upstairs room and both loudly declared their innocence even after the scarf dropped out of part of Watson's dress. However, one of the policemen called to the scene recognized Watson as someone who had previously shoplifted, and she was forced to own up to the crime. Watson also claimed she did not know Elliot and intimated that she merely struck up a conversation with her as a cover for her crime. Elliot, in turn, denied knowing Watson and had no stolen goods on her person. Rather than risk arresting an innocent and truly respectable woman, the police set Mrs. Elliot free.[64]

On the surface, Watson and Elliot's case seems no different than other working-class teams of shoplifting women like Clarke and Smith; however, these women were not driven by poverty to steal and they were not 'professionals.' Both were respectable, married women with comfortable incomes. The Watson case elicited this lampoon from Punch: 'At present, females 'of lady-like exterior,' with money

---

[61] Ibid., 48.

[62] Ibid., 18.

[63] See Zedner, Women, Crime, and Custody, 40-46. See also Wiener, Reconstructing the Criminal, 14-35, for an explanation of Victorian 'moralization' about crime.

[64] Times, 30 March 1844.

in their pockets, and all things comfortable at home, have shown a strange disposition to pilfer stockings, laces, scarfs, and fifty other things of the countless articles of wardrobe which the sin of Eve has brought—poor souls! for they hate dress—upon her daughters.' Describing Watson as a 'lady delinquent,' *Punch* ridiculed her response to the shoplifting charge: "I suppose there's an unfortunate moment for every one at times."[65] According to *Punch* the truly 'unfortunate moment' was England's current scourge of a 'shop-lifting mania among 'respectable' people.'[66] The forty-five year old Watson freely admitted her crime at the Old Bailey and this plea along with evidence of prior shoplifting led the Common Serjeant to sentence her to one year's imprisonment.[67] Respectable people like Watson who were neither poor nor career criminals appeared in the courts and in the press for shoplifting. These respectable female shoplifters further complicated the process of accusation for shopkeepers and efforts to label and identify the female criminal.

The lingering taint of such a criminal accusation, even if proved false, is demonstrated by a literary example from the late 1830s. In *Blackwood's Magazine* in 1838, a melodramatic short story published by Thomas De Quincey eerily prefigured many of the concerns addressed in the controversy over the trial of an actual shoplifting 'lady' that took place in 1844. In 'The Household Wreck,' the wife Agnes, out shopping alone, fends off the seedy sexual advances of a storekeeper named Barrat and is punished by an accusation of shoplifting upon leaving the store. Agnes is, of course, completely innocent, but comes to a horrible end when she dies from exhaustion after her escape from prison. It is a proper melodrama, however, and Barrat gets his just desserts when he is beaten to death by an angry mob when they discover the truth.[68]

De Quincey's 1830s tale has several elements of the shoplifting debate that took place in the 1840s after the trial of another lady, Jane Tyrwhitt. Tyrwhitt was a respectable married woman out shopping alone who claimed to be falsely accused. Rather than explain the case by a slip in her morality, Tyrwhitt, like the character Agnes, blamed the shopkeeper. Also, there is an underlying moral to De Quincey's story that is not so much about unsavory shopkeepers as about women who go into public alone. The husband in the story tells how he agonized every time his wife went out without him: 'I had a secret aversion to seeing so gentle a creature thrown even for an hour upon her own resources . . ..'[69] However, if unescorted shopping

---

[65] 'Shop-Lifting-Female Weakness,' *Punch*, 6 (April 1844), 149.

[66] *Ibid.*

[67] CCCSP, Sixth Session, 1844, p. 912.

[68] Thomas De Quincey, 'The Household Wreck,' *Blackwood's Edinburgh Magazine*, 43, 267 (January 1838): 1-32; W.J.B. Owen, 'De Quincey and Shoplifting,' *The Wordsworth Circle*, 21, no. 2 (Spring 1990): 72-76. Owen also makes a convincing argument that this melodrama was, in part, based on the 1799 Jane Leigh Perrot case in which Jane Austen's Aunt claimed to be wrongfully accused of shoplifting in Bath.

[69] De Quincey, 'Household Wreck,' 10.

ladies were an undesirable byproduct of a changing economy, they were nonetheless a growing plague in the 1840s. From the satire of 'Directions to Ladies Shopping' to the acrimonious debate surrounding the Tyrwhitt case, the increase of shopping ladies proved irksome and anxiety inducing.

The Tyrwhitt Case and the Soho Bazaar

There was no easy agreement on the question of 'respectable' women and shoplifting. In early November of 1844, a series of events took place at the Soho Bazaar that would reverberate throughout London. The unlikely cause of this affair was a small two-shilling six-pence microscope. Mrs. Jane Tyrwhitt, a respectable lady living in Berkeley Square with her own carriage and horses and connections to the aristocracy, was accused of taking it at a stall in the Bazaar. Other than Mrs. Tyrwhitt's social standing, the case reads like so many other shoplifting cases. Mrs. Tyrwhitt came by herself to a busy stall at the Bazaar and then haggled with the saleswoman, Mary Ann Lewis, over the purchase of a cheap thermometer. She apparently slipped another small article, a microscope, into her sleeve while the assistant was occupied below the counter in wrapping the thermometer. As Tyrwhitt hurriedly walked away, a watchful matron of the Bazaar, Sarah Harker, alerted the woman at the stall, and Mrs. Tyrwhitt was overtaken and asked to come to the office. According to personnel at the Bazaar, Tyrwhitt tried to quietly drop the microscope just outside the door of the office where she was to be searched.[70] In so many ways, this case echoes those of other professional and non-professional shoplifters. Tyrwhitt was well dressed, used a distracting technique, and fervently denied committing the crime. However, this woman was beyond respectable; she was positively wealthy, and appeared to have no motive for committing such a crime.

The day of the trial drew immense interest and a courtroom full of spectators. Tyrwhitt arrived at court in her private carriage, but everyone's sympathies were not with the lady who claimed she was falsely accused. She and her husband had apparently handled the entire case in a high-handed manner with her playing the 'Agnes'—the domestic angel above reproach. Apparently, her husband had said to her accuser at the Bazaar, 'Suppose she has [taken it]; is there any use in making a d__d fuss about it!'[71] Throughout the trial the Tyrwhitts appeared to be advocating different rules for different classes of people. The judge even stated in his summation that 'Character to a poor person was of far more importance than to a

---

[70] GLRO, Indictment of Jane Tyrwhitt, Middlesex Quarter Sessions of the Peace, Middlesex Sessions Papers, 19 November 1844; GLRO, Recognizance of Mary Ann Lewis, Middlesex Quarter Sessions of the Peace, Middlesex Sessions Papers, 9 November 1844. *Times*, 6 December 1844.

[71] *Ibid.* Tyrwhitt's bail had been paid be her husband Charles and two other gentleman, a Baronet, Sir Bellingham Reginald Graham and John Foster of no. 66 Jermyn Street. See GLRO Recognizance for Charles Tyrwhitt concerning trial of Jane, Middlesex Quarter Sessions of the Peace, Middlesex Sessions Papers, 9 November 1844.

person of the prisoner's station.' Her lawyer argued simply that a lady of her station would have no reason to commit such a crime.[72] Although Tyrwhitt had been caught red-handed, he contended that she had not intended to take the small microscope but may have confused it with the thermometer in her rush to leave the stall. Mrs. Tyrwhitt was found 'not guilty' but only after two and a half hours of deliberation by the jury. Appearing to swoon, Tyrwhitt managed to begin a speech before the judge interrupted her; 'I here solemnly declare that I am entirely innocent of the accusation that has been brought against me by those who have sworn falsely . . ..'[73]

Ladies Searched and 'Goods' . . . 'Recklessly Exposed'

Although one letter appeared in favor of the prosecution in the ensuing copies of the *Times*, the response of the paper's middle-class readers was overwhelmingly in favor of Tyrwhitt's innocence. Some readers were angry that the judge in the case did not consider the possibility of false arrest.[74] Other readers agreed with Tyrwhitt's lawyer that ladies of position were above such crimes. A reader identified only as 'Cavendo Tutus' told a supportive tale of how his own wife might have been wrongfully accused. According to the writer, a pair of gloves had mistakenly stuck in the deep folds of crape of her mourning dress, and when she discovered the gloves, they immediately returned them to the shop.[75] Echoing the incident of the woman taking the gold pencil case mentioned in the Bingham trial, another reader described a similar case in which he absent-mindedly took a seal from a silversmith and placed it with his in his pocket.[76] According to these *Times* letter writers, absent-mindedness seemed rampant among the wealthier classes.

Another disturbing aspect of the accusation of shoplifting for commentators, besides the specter of false arrest, was the strip searching of the accused. Although, as is demonstrated by other cases, an accused person was normally searched by an employee of the same sex, the idea of applying this practice to middle and upper class ladies was horrifying. This invasion of privacy sent shockwaves through the mind of 'W.,' a man writing to the *Times* from the Conservative Club:

> Can it be possible that my wife or daughter on going to the Soho Bazaar is liable to be stripped and searched by reason of the mere suspicion of Mrs. Harker, or some

---

[72] *Ibid.*

[73] *Ibid.* See also GLRO, Indictment of Jane Tyrwhitt, Middlesex Quarter Sessions of the Peace, Middlesex Sessions Papers,19 November 1844.

[74] Vindex to the Editor of the *Times*, 9 December 1844, *Times*, 7 December 1844; Vindex to the Editor of the *Times*, 19 December 1844, *Times*, 19 December 1844; M.A., Oxford and Cambridge Club to the Editor of the *Times*, 18 December 1844, *Times*, 20 December 1844.

[75] Cavendo Tutus to the Editor of the *Times*, 7 December 1844, *Times*, 7 December 1844.

[76] H. to the Editor of the *Times*, 11 December 1844, *Times*, 12 December 1844.

other matron or overlooker, . . . and detained all night in a filthy dungeon at the station house . . .?'[77]

W.'s tirade against this searching of middle-class women demonstrated some of the underlying tensions about shopping and the public sphere brought out by cases like Tyrwhitt's.

Fears of the invasion of privacy and the lower-class searching of a middle-class body were joined with the terror of staining a woman's reputation. A year before Tyrwhitt's case in 1843, a case of a middle-class shoplifter demonstrated the importance of reputation. In one letter to the *Times*, a reader was outraged that a Welsh lady 'of independent fortune' was permitted to wear a black veil in her trial and to be tried under an assumed name, 'Mary Rees.' The writer seemed to be calling for a more equal treatment of such offenders, or at least no special treatment.[78] This well-connected woman of 'independent means,' who had a large amount of money with her at the time of her crime, would have been the perfect candidate for kleptomania at a later date. 'Mary Rees' hid her crime behind a black veil; it would only be later that women in her position could hide behind the veil of medico-legal opinion.

'Mary Rees' was tried under this assumed name in the Westminster General Sessions May 10, 1843. Described as 'formerly a milliner,' she nonetheless had wealthy connections and her own fortune. In April, 1843, she walked into Nathaniel Hill's hosier's shop in Regent Street and stole a pair of white silk stockings worth 8 shillings. Recognizing her as a woman of some means, Hill did not want to prosecute and suggested it might be a mistake, but his shopman insisted that 'Rees' stole the goods. A search of her person proved that 'Rees' not only had the stockings, but possessed more than enough money to have purchased them legally. Rees's lawyer, emphasized her status in society claiming that 'the stockings were taken by mistake,' and referred to another case in 1842 that took place at Howell and James's large emporium. A 'titled lady' stepping into her carriage after looking at expensive jewelry was caught by a shop assistant who noticed some gold jewelry stuck to her shawl. In that case the woman claimed, like the wife of Cavendo Tutus, that the pin had stuck in the deep folds of her fashionable crepe shawl. In the case of the titled lady, Messrs. Howell and James let that explanation stand. However, despite her lawyer's tales of absent-minded ladies and impressive character witnesses including a magistrate from Cardiff, the jury debated three hours and was still unable to come to a verdict for Rees. After the judge threatened to lock up the jury for the night, the jury suddenly decided that 'Rees' was not guilty.[79]

---

[77] W., Conservative Club to the Editor of the *Times*, 10 December 1844, *Times*, 11 December 1844. See also *Times*, 6 December 1844.

[78] MARCUS, Little Queen Street Holborn to the Editor of the *Times*, 11 May 1843, *Times*, 12 May 1843.

[79] *Times*, 11 May 1843.

Without the convenient escape from the dilemma of bourgeois women's crime provided by a medico-legal explanation, those participating in the Tyrwhitt debate, like the Rees trial, turned to another explanation. Women of Tyrwhitt's status and moral training could not be guilty of such a crime; therefore, there must be some shady shopkeeper, a 'Barrat,' tricking these women with sleight of hand and false accusation. Cavendo Tutus blamed the carelessness of shopkeepers for Mrs. Tyrwhitt and other ladies' dilemmas: 'I think, that where goods are so recklessly exposed and tossed about . . . no jury ought to return any other than a verdict of 'Not Guilty'. . ..' He feared that 'our wives and daughters . . . run the almost daily risk of being brought to bar at the Old Bailey.'[80] 'W.' in his letter to the *Times*, also intimated that it was the shopkeeper and not the patron who was guilty in the Tyrwhitt and other cases. He derided the Bazaar matron's statement that "She had made many similar charges against ladies, but could not tell the number."[81] A 'J.B.' writing from Lincoln's Inn was more direct: 'It rests with the magistracy to crush this iniquitous conspiracy of the cheap shopkeepers . . ..'[82] This part of the Tyrwhitt shoplifting debate appeared to be more between middle-class husbands and the retailers who sold to their wives than between ladies and 'cheap shopkeepers.'

Shady Shopkeeper or Lady's Victim?

Most of the letters that appeared in the *Times* were written by men who claimed to be fighting for the honor of their wives and daughters. M.A. claimed no higher cause than that 'I am a married man, and my wife goes frequently to bazaars and such places.'[83] Among all these male defenders of middle-class virtue stands one letter written by a woman—the only letter writer who actually claimed to be a victim of a shopkeeper's scam. This respectable lady, W.E., was accused by shopkeepers of stealing a brooch while she purchased two cheaper articles. Like Tyrwhitt, she was alone at the time of the purchase except for the shopkeeper and assistants. The brooch was 'found' at her feet much as Tyrwhitt's microscope had been found at hers. W.E. wanted to take her accusers to court and prove her innocence, but her solicitor advised otherwise since, like Tyrwhitt, 'my only defence must be, the improbability of a lady of my character and standing in society committing such and offence.'[84] In her case a payment of thirty pounds silenced the shopkeeper.

---

[80] Cavendo Tutus to the Editor of the *Times*, 7 December 1844, *Times*, 7 December 1844.

[81] W., Conservative Club to the Editor of the *Times*, 10 December 1844, *Times*, 11 December 1844. See also *Times*, 6 December 1844.

[82] J.B., Lincoln's Inn to the Editor of the *Times*, 12 December 1844, *Times*, 13 December 1844.

[83] M.A., Oxford and Cambridge Club to the Editor of the *Times*, 18 December 1844, *Times*, 20 December 1844.

[84] W.E. to the Editor of the *Times*, 11 December 1844, *Times*, 12 December 1844.

The *Times* itself soon jumped into the 'cheap shopkeeper' conspiracy fray by siding with many of its readers. However, rather than a criticism of 'cheap shopkeepers,' the appeal of the *Times* sounds more like an ominous warning to ladies to take care in their expeditions into the public sphere:

> We believe the practice referred to by our correspondent is much more frequent than our readers would suppose . . . 'cheap shops' rely . . . upon the extortions thus made. If ladies will resort to such places they should most carefully observe that no article which they have not selected is placed with what they have purchased, and take care that they do not afford . . . an opportunity of fastening upon them a charge which against the testimony of ready swearers, it is impossible to disprove.[85]

Echoing the underlying moral of De Quincey's 1838 short story, the appeal of the *Times* sounds more like an ominous warning to ladies to take care in their expeditions into the public sphere rather than a criticism of 'cheap shopkeepers.'

In the barrage of middle-class attacks on 'cheap shopkeepers,' a single pro-shopkeeper letter appeared in the *Times* in the wake of the Tyrwhitt trial. T.W., formerly part owner of a silk warehouse, wrote in protest that middle-class women *did* steal, and gave as proof a case where the wife of a well-known physician came to the shop in her carriage. After pretending to browse, the lady was almost out the door when some shawls were missed and the lady was taken back to the shop and searched by a female assistant. The shawls were found under her dress. Her husband was called to the shop and apologized claiming that 'she must be to a certain extent insane, as she had a handsome income and establishment of her own, which placed her beyond the reach of temptation.'[86] T.W. and his fellows agreed to hush up the case and let the doctor's wife go on her way. However, this was not due to any confidence in her insanity. T.W. alluded instead to the difficulty of prosecuting well-connected people as had been demonstrated by the Tyrwhitt case. He noted how the imbalance between classes was especially shown by the preferential treatment given in the search of residences. Poor shoplifters submitted to having their lodgings searched, but no such searches occurred in the case of wealthier shoplifters. This made evidence difficult to obtain. T.W. was incensed that the shopkeepers were so vilified in the Tyrwhitt controversy and claimed that in the case of the middle-class shoplifter, the brunt was felt more often by the shop than by the patron.[87]

T.W. was not alone in his protest that shopkeepers suffered more from their shoplifting customers than the customers suffered from false accusations of shoplifting. In the 1870s the retired draper William Ablett wrote his memoirs. When Ablett started his early career in the 1820s and 30s, he was shocked to learn that many customers shoplifted: 'many of the customers who bought sewing silks,

---

[85] *Times*, 12 December 1844.

[86] T.W., Gutter Lane to the Editor of the *Times*, 12 December 1844, *Times*, 14 December 1844.

[87] *Ibid.*

and they were chiefly girls and young women, from fifteen to twenty-five years of age, were confirmed pilferers. They would lean over the little holland wrapper in which the loose skeins of black silk were kept . . . and often manage to secrete one or two.' As a dutiful employee, Ablett reported these young women to his master, and was disappointed at his master's lack of enthusiasm for prosecution; 'my master upon several occasions, . . . ordered the girls so detected never to enter the shop again, but nothing more was done to them.'[88] The line between customer and thief thinned in the nineteenth century.

If T.W. and Ablett were correct in their assumption that middle-class women did steal, why would a woman in Jane Tyrwhitt's position steal, and why would she steal such a relatively worthless object? The stall keeper herself remarked on the 'many articles upon her own stall of much higher value' which were even smaller and easier to steal.[89] Tyrwhitt's lawyer had apparently known that 'instances had occurred where persons of undoubted respectability had, under the influences of a species of insanity, been guilty of similar offences.' In 1840, the definition of 'kleptomanie' as a legal defense for a criminal act was only just beginning to be described by Dr. Marc the physician to Louis-Phillipe who based his work on Matthey and others.[90] However, that 'species of insanity' was not itself respectable yet, and Tyrwhitt's counsel did not want to expose his client to an asylum anymore than he wanted her to go to prison. For Mrs. Tyrwhitt, she preferred the label of absent-minded to insane.

The Tyrwhitt case only resulted in a heightening of the controversy, and not a solution to the problem of middle-class women and shoplifting. The idea of the extortion of the 'cheap shopkeeper' was a favorite theme in the *Times*, but was not the clear victor in the search for answers. The vague notion of a stealing 'insanity' existed, but was not the preferred answer. Biological explanations would only surface later in the century. However, the evidence of the emergence of the kleptomania diagnosis in England is clear before its official acceptance as a medical and legal doctrine. Perhaps absent-mindedness no longer sufficed as a middle-class excuse for shoplifting.[91] In February of 1845, Serjeant Adams threw a middle-class shoplifting case out of the Middlesex Sessions without a bill of indictment. Receiving criticism for the failure to prosecute Miss Osborne, the *Globe* newspaper commented that the poor woman 'is known in her neighborhood as one of mental peculiarity' and decried that the negative implications of unequal justice in English courts was unfounded.[92]

---

[88] William Ablett, 'Reminiscences of An Old Draper' *Warehousemen and Draper's Trade Journal* (London: 1 May 1872), 31.

[89] *Times*, 6 December 1844.

[90] O'Brien, 'The Kleptomania Diagnosis,' 70.

[91] As is intimated from the Howell and James 1842 case, upper-class women also shoplifted, but the insistence on protecting the names of these women has left virtually no records of their crime-other than references to a 'titled lady.'

[92] *Times*, 26-27 February 1845 and 1 March 1845.

Brain Fever and Bankruptcy: The Failure of Alternative Explanations

Some egregious cases of middle-class women shoplifts did not lend themselves to excuses of absent-minded behavior. For these cases, accusations of mental instability provided a more plausible explanation. In April of 1849, a police officer named George Wood spotted a woman lingering in the display of goods in the portico of Briant and Field's large drapery shop. He pursued her when she secreted a 65 yard roll of huckaback under her shawl and walked away. Unswayed by her explanation that she merely wanted to check the price, Wood took her to the station to be searched. In the station she ripped away part of her dress front revealing an extra large pocket containing one cashmere dress and half a dozen lace collars. Later searching her lodgings, police found a variety of stolen goods including furs, satin ribbons, kid gloves, and silks. More damning were the various disguises she possessed including wigs of various colors, shapes, and sizes.[93] On the surface, this woman, Lydia Dixon, appeared to be just like any other professional shoplifter. She had stolen from various shops, mostly linen drapers, on 20 or 30 different occasions.[94] However, Miss Dixon was or had once been solidly middle-class. Before his death, her father was a well-respected solicitor and her mother had since become 'one of the candidates for the National Benevolent Institution.' Lydia, however, seemed to make her way as a governess and at the time of her arrest claimed to be a music teacher. To protect her identity, she appeared in the Richmond police court wearing a thick, black veil in a similar manner to Mary Rees.[95] Despite her stockpile of stolen goods in not one but two residences—one in Hammersmith and the other in Richmond—Lydia Dixon found no shortage of defenders. Mr. Betts, a Hammersmith surgeon, maintained that Dixon suffered for seven weeks from a brain fever that affected her capacities. A Mr. Tapstell confirmed the surgeon's diagnosis. The magistrate committed her for trial to the Old Bailey.[96] Witnesses there testified that Dixon often 'complained of her head.' Her sentenced was deferred and she was finally given only one-month's confinement despite £45 worth of property found at her residences and a policeman eye witness to the crime.[97]

Dixon's 'brain fever' was one explanation for why a respectable woman of comfortable means would steal objects so trifling as lace collars, handkerchiefs, or a two-shilling microscope. Nineteenth century commentators puzzled over the question of the cause of precisely this type of middle-class shoplifting. One explanation might be that many of these women were not as comfortable as they

---

[93] 'Shoplifting,' *Trade Protection Record* (London) 21 April 1849; *Times*, 11 April 1849.

[94] *Times*, 23 March 1849.

[95] 'Shoplifting,' *Trade Protection Record* (London) 21 April 1849; *Times*, 11 April 1849 and 23 April 1849.

[96] 'Shoplifting,' *Trade Protection Record* (London) 21 April 1849; *Times*, 16 April 1849; *Times*, 23 April 1849.

[97] CCCSP, Seventh Session, 1849, 83-86.

appeared. Lydia Dixon and Mary Rees's employment history suggest genteel women forced by circumstance into some of the few low-paying jobs proper to their station like governess and music teacher.[98] What their independent fortunes were or who controlled them was not revealed in their trial. A fact that was never brought to light in Jane Tyrwhitt's trial, although it seems pertinent to her case, was her husband's constant bankruptcy. In October, 1828, the then Charles Tyrwhitt Jones declared bankruptcy. This gentleman and occasional horse-dealer led a life filled with financial ruin. He appeared in the Court of Bankruptcy at least five times between 1825 and 1841. He also petitioned the court of bankruptcy in 1844, the year Jane Tyrwhitt was arrested and was finally imprisoned for debt for six months in 1847 with debts totaling £2,855 Charles Tyrwhitt's income including his wife's separate income totaled £735 a year. Of this total, £335 was Mrs. Tyrwhitt's own separate income. The rest came from his son-in-law and a relative, Lady Tyrwhitt. On this income the Tyrwhitts kept three servants and a carriage and horses.[99] Keeping up the appearances of their station must have been a strain.[100] However, these very real financial strains do not enter into nineteenth-century debate of these pre-kleptomaniac middle-class female shoplifters.

The preferential treatment of middle-class and genteel shoplifters and the response of the *Times* and its readers to the Tyrwhitt, Dixon, and other cases contrasts with the treatment and perception of lower-class shoplifters. The attitude shown toward lower-class women who shoplifted was without much mercy and matter-of-fact. That these women masqueraded as middle-class only added to the reprehensibility of their crime, and their success in this deception was itself a critique of class distinctions. The deception of shoplifting and its blurring of class lines made it especially repugnant to Victorian sensibilities. If lower-class female criminals could pass as respectable middle-class wives, then the validity of respectability itself was questioned. Appearance, especially the type and manner of dress, was supposed to be an outward display of inner character. By so easily adopting a middle-class persona, shoplifters and others threatened the very social identity of the middle-class.[101]

---

[98] See Mary Poovey, *Uneven Developments: The Ideological Work of Gender in Mid-Victorian England* (Chicago: University of Chicago Press, 1988), 126-163 .

[99] *Times,* 11 October 1828; 19 December 1844; 10 May 1847.

[100] See also Brown who cites a similar case of a gentleman who was bankrupt whose wife stole to give him the money to subsist while he was hiding from creditors. Brown,' On Genteel Thieves,' 291.

[101] John Kasson argues that the dangers of such 'respectable' criminals was not so much the cost to society as the threat to middle-class identity. See John F. Kasson, *Rudeness and Civility: Manners in Nineteenth-Century Urban America* (New York: Hill and Wang, 1990), 109-110. See also Colin Campbell, *The Romantic Ethic and the Spirit of Modern Consumerism* (London: Basil Blackwell, 1987), 159-160. For a brief outline of the increasingly restrictive and ultra-feminine fashions in the first half of the century see Davidoff and Hall, *Family Fortunes,* 411-415.

The Shopkeepers' Fault: The Dangers of Shopping in the Public Sphere

Nineteenth-century commentators criticized lower-class shoplifters as deceptive, ascribing their crimes to greed or poverty; however, ignoring the pressures caused by financial strain and status competition, they could not as easily find middle-class shoplifters culpable for their crimes. The most common response to middle-class retail crime is illustrated by the Leigh Perrot case, De Quincey's short story, the Tyrwhitt case and others. Before mid-century, commentators blamed the temptation of the fraudulent shopkeeper and the dangers of the expanding consumer culture. Expanding drapery and haberdashery establishments as well as popular bazaars were the sites of some of the most famous and many less famous shoplifting cases. According to most authors, the problem only increased with the later rise of the department store. Asa Briggs notes of Lewis's 1880s Manchester store: 'In fact, the layout was not unlike that of many of the older bazaars, which have been considered . . . the prototypes of the department store.' Like the older bazaars such as Soho where Tyrwhitt stole her microscope, goods were displayed openly 'in square boxes, from which customers could help themselves.'[102] The department store mixed the dependability of a respectable drapery type emporium and the dazzling profuseness of the bazaar with the convenience of a clean, safe atmosphere, and fixed prices.[103] Prior to the late century department stores, earlier innovations like bazaars, 'cheap shops,' and emporiums created a new world of shopping for women and served as the scapegoats of the perceived rise in middle-class shoplifting.

The idea of women in the public sphere was a troublesome concept for Victorians. Lower-class women and prostitutes were expected to haunt city streets, but middle-class ladies without escorts were unthinkable. An expanding consumer culture, however, gave women an outlet in the public sphere, and the way women were warned away from participating in the new shopping culture in the middle-class debates over shoplifting is reminiscent of the criticism of 'shopping demons.' Judith Walkowitz in *City of Dreadful Delight* discusses the fears elicited by women's increasing adventures in the public world of shopping in the later part of

---

[102] Asa Briggs, *Friends of the People: The Centenary History of Lewis's* (London: B.T. Batsford Ltd., 1956), 66. This description of Lewis's contradicts Elaine Abelson's description of English department stores as being much less open than American stores. See Elaine S. Ableson, *When Ladies Go A Thieving: Middle-Class Shoplifters in the Victorian Department Store* (New York: Oxford University Press), p. 277, n. 73. See also Clive Emsley, *Crime and Society in England, 1750-1900* (New York: Longman, 1996), 155.

[103] Here I disagree with Elaine Abelson's statement: 'It was in the department store that middle-class women became shoplifters.' Abelson, *When Ladies Go A-Thieving*, 5. At least in the English case, the problem of middle-class female shoplifters predates the department store.

the century.[104] Daniel Murphy agrees that these urban myths of female danger studied by Walkowitz and others, are potent 'fears in late Victorian middle-class discourse.'[105] However, much of this fear existed as early as the 1840s Soho Bazaar case. It was based on upheavals in consumer culture and women's significant place in the growing market of nineteenth-century England. From short stories to *Times* editorials, literature writers warned them with imprisonment, shame, and death to stay at home and away from lone public ventures. The press and their husbands writing in to the *Times* begged them to remain in their proper place less they suffer the indignity of a trial or the horrors of prison. Yet ladies continued to shop, and wealthier women accused of shoplifting were excused by blaming disreputable shop owners. Unmasking middle-class women as possible criminals was not popular especially without a ready explanation based in psychology. Fears of public exposure and mixing of class lines reverberated in the debate in the first half of the century. People were incensed at the idea of lower-class shopkeepers and assistants examining accused middle-class women as well as lower-class women masquerading easily as middle-class shoppers. These earlier nineteenth century cases demonstrate that middle-class shoplifting was not exclusively linked to the rise of the *Bon Marché* in England.

The contemporary fears demonstrated by the controversy over women shoplifters in the 1830s, 40s, and 50s may make us rethink the connections between commodity culture and the crime of shoplifting. The connection between commodity culture as represented by the department store and the rise in middle-class shoplifting is weaker than turn-of-the-century psychiatrists and later historians suggest. The theories surrounding shoplifting by middle-class ladies may have been a response to the problem of upholding Victorian gender ideology in a rapidly changing society—a problem which developed long before the late Victorian era. Blaming the cheap and careless shopkeepers before mid-century, attracted attention away from the dilemma of protecting feminine ideology under the onslaught of women's growing power as purchasers in consumer culture. Shopkeepers were not just corrupting English retail; they demoralized the buyers—the woman shopper— and through fraud, trickery and tempting display even turned women into shoplifters. Concerned with more than tensions in class brought out by the idea of respectable ladies as criminals, the shoplifting debates of the thirties, forties, and fifties were also about money and control. Safeguarding the ideal of separate spheres and Victorian gender ideology, men could not directly accuse their wives of criminal acts or of taking too much liberty with the family purse, but they could lash out at the sellers who were partially responsible for their wives new economic and public liberty. The shoplifting debate provided a chance to warn women away from the *dangers* of the public realm.

---

[104] Judith R. Walkowitz, *City of Dreadful Delight: Narratives of Sexual Danger in Late Victorian London* (Chicago: University of Chicago Press, 1992), 46-50.
[105] Murphy, *Customers and Thieves*, 178.

Chapter 6

Mrs. McGregor's Sealskin Jacket: Female Frauds and the Art of Buying Without Paying

The great quality, or leading and indispensable attributes of a sharper, a cheat, a swindler, or a gambler is to possess a genteel exterior, a demeanor apparently artless, and a good address.

—*A Bow Street Officer, 1829*

Fraud and Economic Progress

Retailers did not possess a monopoly on fraud and false representations in nineteenth-century England. Like shoplifting, the practice of fraud by both lower-class and middle-class women was aided by a growing consumer culture in the nineteenth century. Fraud was also used as a way to elevate or defend one's class status. Like shoplifting, it played on nineteenth-century fears of false identities—pretending to be what one was not. Unlike shoplifters, female frauds had an added advantage in English law. Many retail frauds were not prosecutable as a criminal offense. Also married female frauds, especially middle-class ones, were protected by coverture and by the contemporary interpretation of the law of necessaries. Women of the middle-class were further protected by the medicalization of their crime as illness. This medicalization echoes the development of shoplifting 'kleptomania' and robbed women of the agency of their own rational if not legal actions in dealing with existence in an increasingly material culture.

Although the reality of female fraud in the nineteenth-century clashes with the contemporary stereotype of dashing male swindlers, this female crime was part of the preponderance of fraud that frightened nineteenth-century observers. Infesting novels, newspaper reports, and other literature, the nineteenth-century swindler was a favorite character in stories of English crime.[1] Urban areas, especially London, provided the perfect environment for the nineteenth-century fraud. Urban anonymity and the faster pace of life provided swindlers and frauds with both opportunity and protection from discovery. In 1829 'A Bow Street Officer'

---

[1] See Rebecca F. Stern, 'Historicizing Performativity: Constructing Identities in Victorian England' (Ph.D. diss., Rice University, 1997), 54-92. Stern discusses both literary and actual fraud in Victorian England and the Victorian anxieties over class identity created by these frauds.

described fraud as raging out of control in London:

> In a great metropolis, like London, where trade and commerce have arrived at such
> an astonishing height, and where, from the extensive transactions in the funds, and
> the opulence of the people, the interchange of property is so expanded, it ceases to
> be a matter of wonder that forgeries and frauds should prevail to a very great
> degree: . . . petty forgeries and frauds . . . seem to multiply and advance with the
> opulence and luxury of the country; and to branch out into innumerable shades,
> varying as the fashions of the year.[2]

The author further complained that through England's own rapid economic
progress it had outgrown its laws protecting citizens from the depredations of
fraud. If a person ordered goods, especially under his or her own name, it was
difficult for a shopkeeper to prove that person never intended to pay for the goods.
The defrauder could easily claim it was a case of bad debt and not criminal fraud.[3]
These gaps between English law and economic reality made London a fertile
criminal ground for the petty female fraud as well as the flashier usually male
swindler posing as foreign aristocracy.

Most fraud in nineteenth-century England was not the stuff of novels. The
majority of frauds committed daily were petty frauds for small amounts of money
or goods.[4] Retail fraud was closely linked to legitimate forms of consumption. A
respectable appearance along with a respectable address allowed a fraud to obtain
the credit necessary to commit her crimes. Women's access to the consumption of
goods allowed them to defraud retailers.[5] This ability to contract debt was key in
the commission of retail fraud.

---

[2] Bow Street Officer, *The Frauds of London: Displaying the Numerous and Daring Cheats and Robberies Practised Upon the Stranger and the Unwary* (No. 10, Newgate Street, London: William Cole, 1829), 3.

[3] *Ibid.*, 3 and 12. See also the case of Mary Ann Rowley, *City of London Trade Protection Circular (London)* 22 April 1848. See also Sir James Fitzjames Stephen, *A History of the English Criminal Law*, vol. 3 (London: MacMillan and Co., 1883), 124-128.

[4] Despite the significant property loss caused by these petty retail frauds, the stereotype of the fraud remained largely male during this period. Partly, this may have stemmed from men's access to larger scale white-collar crimes like bank embezzlement, but the emphasis on moral danger rather than damage to physical property in the case of female crime may also explain why Victorians outside of trade journals and societies ignored the seriousness of female retail crime. For a discussion of the moral emphasis on female crime see Lucia Zedner, *Women, Crime, and Custody in Victorian England* (Oxford: Clarendon Press, 1991), 30.

[5] See Margot Finn, 'Women, Consumption and Coverture in England, c. 1760-1860,' *The Historical Journal*, vol. 39: 3 (1996) 703-722. Finn's study refutes the pervasive view of coverture presented in such works as Mary Lyndon Shanley's *Feminism, Marriage, and the Law in Victorian England* (Princeton: Princeton University Press, 1989.

Indictments against women and men obtaining goods through fraud in England rose in the century before 1800.[6] Concern over the growth and proliferation of this fraud stretched well into the Victorian era. Crimes like fraud were especially disturbing because they were not relegated to the lower-classes. Fraud could be a middle or upper class as well as a working-class crime.[7] For the middle-class woman, fraud like shoplifting was a popular form of what one might call white-lace-collar crime in nineteenth century England.

Trade Protection Societies: Prosecuting Fraud

The constant threat of fraud did not go unanswered by English shopkeepers. As early as the 1700s, organizations to address fraud and other crimes affecting English business. One of the very oldest of these trade protection societies emerged in London in 1776. The Guardians: or Society for the Protection of Trade Against Swindlers and Sharpers consisted of tradesmen and merchants in the City of London who banded together to prosecute and expose 'those Pests of Society, called SWINDLERS and SHARPERS' who caused 'the great Loss and Ruin of many industrious Families' through fraud.[8] Although this society went through a variety of manifestations and name changes, its basic aim remained the same throughout the nineteenth century—to prosecute fraud and other retail crime whether by individuals or groups and to protect English business interests. In 1848 the society changed its name from the already shortened Society of Guardians for the Protection of Trade to the City of London Trade Protection Society. By 1848 the society claimed members all over the United Kingdom, but its main offices were still centered in the City of London and Westminster.[9]

---

[6] J.M. Beattie, *Crime and the Courts in England, 1660-1800* (Princeton University Press, 1986), 190-191.

[7] Martin Wiener, *Reconstructing the Criminal; Culture, Law and Policy in England, 1830-1914* (Cambridge University Press, 1990), 245 & 260.

[8] *The Guardians: or Society for the Protection of Trade Against Swindlers and Sharpers, Rules and Orders* (Northumberland Street, Strand, London: G. Sidney, 1816), 2. note: Society was established March 25, 1776. See also David Philips, 'Good Men to Associate and Bad Men to Conspire: Associations for the Prosecution of Felons in England 1760-1860,' in *Policing and Prosecution in Britain 1750-1850*, ed. Douglas Hay and Francis Snyder (Oxford: Clarendon Press, 1989), 113-169.

[9] PRO C114/34, Edward S. Foss, Society of Guardians for the Protection of Trade to [members] Society of Guardians for the Protection of Trade, London, January 1826; *City of London Trade Protection Circular* (London) 22 April 1848; *City of London Trade Protection Circular* (London) 29 April 1848; James Henry Dixon, *A Statement of Facts In Reference to the City of London Trade Protection Society, (13, Swithin's Lane,) and the Mode in Which it Discharges it Pecuniary Obligations* (London: Effingham Wilson, Royal Exchange, 1851).

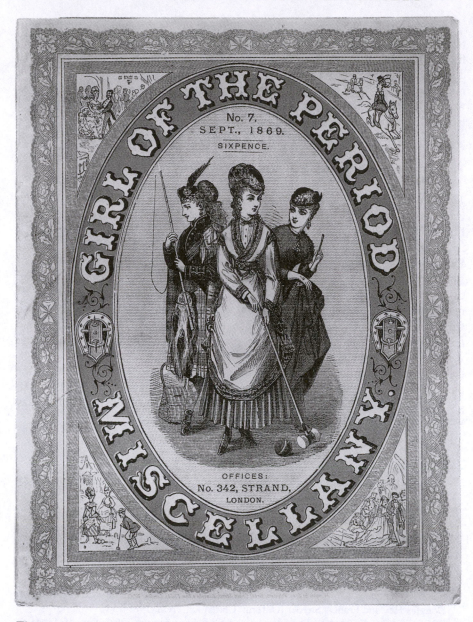

Figure 6.1 *Girl of the Period Miscellany* (cover), 1869. Bodleian Library, University of Oxford: John Johnson Collection; Fashion 14.

The activity of societies like the City of London Trade Protection Society demonstrates the serious threat posed to English business by fraud, shoplifting, and other offences throughout this period. Such protection societies remained active in England throughout the nineteenth century and some were founded by landowners to prosecute property crimes like the Highworth Association for the Prosecution of Felons and Other Thieves and the Sherborne Association for the Protection of Property.[10] However, the more urban societies centered their concerns on urban crimes like fraud, shoplifting, and especially credit fraud. The cryptically named Mutual Communication Society in Sackville Street safeguarded the interests of West End dealers in London at mid-century, and the Liverpool Society of Guardians for the Protection of Trade along with the Manchester Society of Guardians watched over trade in their respective cities.[11] In 1851 a rift between members of the administration of the City of London Trade Protection Society gave rise to yet another London society the Metropolitan Institute for the Protections of Trade.[12] Although these societies had their differences, for the most part they operated like the original London society for trade protection. The idea was to share the cost of prosecuting the increasingly burdensome retail crimes and to expose criminals to prevent them from preying on more traders.

The clearly stated aims of such societies illustrate the great fear shopkeepers felt of the frauds, forgers, and thieves who threatened their day to day business dealings. Shopkeepers might participate in the culture of fraud surrounding nineteenth-century English retail, but they were also its victims. In 1848 the City of London Trade Protection Society outlined its aims for its members:

> To caution and protect the Trading Community . . . against numerous frauds, deceptions, and impositions, to which they are daily exposed. To make all necessary enquiries for Traders, Warehousemen and others, previously to their giving credit, ... To contribute from its funds, to Members, the means of prosecuting those who may have practised any fraud or imposition, or been guilty of any Robbery, Forgery, Embezzlement, or Theft and of opposing in cases of fraudulent Bankruptcy or Insolvency; and . . . To assist members in the recovery of Debts, Rent, &c. . . ..[13]

The extent to which the trade protection societies kept these promises is difficult to judge. Perhaps the constant popularity of founding trade protections societies

---

[10] Highworth Association For the Prosecution of Felons and Other Thieves (Faringdon, Cotton, Printer, 1810), British Library; Sherborne Association for the Protection of Property, 1824, 'Police and Public Security,' Box I, John Johnson Collection, Bodleian, Oxford.

[11] *City of London Trade Protection Circular* (London) 20 May 1848.

[12] Dixon, *A Statement of Facts In Reference to the City of London Trade Protection Society*. See also a mention of the Association for the Mutual Protection of Trade and the Prosecution of Swindlers, 'Charge of Obtaining Goods by False Pretences,' *The Draper* (London) 16 February 1872.

[13] *City of London Trade Protection Circular* (London) 22 April 1848.

attests to their lack of success. Although the shared burden of prosecution definitely provided a help to its members, the trade protection societies had little hope of exposing all of the fraud taking place in nineteenth-century England.

These societies largely encouraged the prosecution of retail crime and the subsequent exposure of these criminals through monetary support to their members for prosecution. In 1816 The Guardians: or Society for the Protection of trade Against Swindlers and Sharpers in London pledged to pay its members up to fifty shillings for the prosecution of any type of robbery and up to forty shillings for the prosecution of shoplifting.[14] In 1826 the now Society of Guardians for the Protection of Trade claimed an increase in 'the fraudulent traffickers . . . exertions to rob the Public' and stated that although the main aim of the society was fraud prevention through exposure, they also spent over £237 in legal expenses for the prosecution of frauds in 1825.[15] The attempts to expose fraud included issuing a private circular with names, dates, and descriptions of offenders, and for a short time at mid-century a public newspaper named after the society.[16]

The shopkeepers and traders victimized by fraud in the nineteenth century were as varied as the offenders themselves. Haberdashers, hosiers, woollen drapers, linen drapers, and tailors joined the likes of watchmakers, bankers and warehousemen in their fight against fraud.[17] Drapers, those favored targets of the shoplifter, appear as members and fraud victims throughout the history of the London Society. In 1830, the Secretary of the Society and the person in charge of its circular was a draper named Thomas Miller.[18] Whether the criminals defrauded a draper, a watchmaker, or a butcher, the methods of fraud were similar and all resulted in pecuniary loss for tradesmen.

The records of trade protections societies, as well as police and other court cases of the period, help separate the stereotype of the dashing, extraordinary,

---

[14] *The Guardians: or Society for the Protection of Trade Against Swindlers and Sharpers, Rules and Orders* (Northumberland Street, Strand, London: G. Sidney, 1816).

[15] PRO C114/34, Edward S. Foss, Society of Guardians for the Protection of Trade to [members] Society of Guardians for the Protection of Trade (London) January 1826.

[16] *City of London Trade Protection Circular* (London) April 1848-November 1849; 'Address,' *City of London Trade Protection Society Circular* (London) 15 April 1848.

[17] PRO C114/34, Edward S. Foss and Son, Society of Guardians for the Protection of Trade to [members] Society of Guardians for the Protection of Trade, London, 15 June 1827; PRO C114/34, Edward S. Foss and Son, Society of Guardians for the Protection of Trade to [members] Society of Guardians for the Protection of Trade, London, 11 June 1825; PRO C114/34, Edward S. Foss and Son, Society of Guardians for the Protection of Trade to [members] Society of Guardians for the Protection of Trade, London, 28 January 1825. See also *City of London Trade Protection Circular* (London) 22 April 1848, 3.

[18] PRO C114/34, Thomas Miller, Draper late of Reading Berks to [members] Society for the Protection of Trade, 22 Ely Place, Holborn, London, 25 August 1830. See also PRO C114/34, Thomas Miller, Society for the Protection of Trade to [members] Society for the Protection of Trade, 22 Ely Place, Holborn, London, 26 August 1835, 5th notice 1835.

usually male, swindler of the novel from the more mundane everyday frauds that took place in England.[19] Men had no monopoly on fraud. Just as women patronized English shops as legitimate customers, they frequented them also as false customers—frauds. The retail frauds committed by women ranged from outright forgeries of banknotes to claiming the credit of legitimate customers to creating entirely false identities respectable enough for a trader to take the risk of extending credit.

Women and Criminal Fraud

False Servants

Unlike breaking a store window and dashing away with the goods, many retail frauds, involved taking on the identity of the respectable. The mock respectability required by successful frauds and shoplifters was the key to female retail crime. Often it required assuming a class identity one did not possess, or was perhaps in danger of losing. Even frauds involving servants and ex-servants were committed on the pretense that the goods were ordered by middle or higher-class customers. Women, especially the great number of working-class women employed as servants of the middle and upper classes in London, had not only access to information about their mistresses accounts but also possessed an intimate knowledge of the manners of the 'genteel.'[20] Some servants lived long enough with a family to establish a connection with their tradesmen and then used that connection to defraud the tradesmen and the family. In other situations, servants who were let go after a long service turned to fraud as a means of survival and perhaps also a revenge on the family who fired them.

Jane Mead had a shady history of employment and criminal activity when she was arrested in 1814 for falsely ordering goods at an ironmonger's for a Miss Vansittart in Downing Street. Mead had lived only two weeks with a Miss Craddock in July of that same year before she left Craddock's and started ordering goods under that lady's name. However, in Vansittart's case Mead managed to get the name and address of this respectable family without actually working there. For her various frauds Mead was sentenced to seven years of transportation at the Middlesex Sessions.[21] Mary Ann Ragan committed a similar fraud in 1853 when she used the name of her current mistress, Mary Brown, to obtain articles of food

---

[19] For a literary example of such an extraordinary swindler, see the character of Captain Wragge in Willkie Collins, *No Name* (New York: Dover Publications, 1978; reprint, New York: Harper and Brothers, 1873

[20] See Rebecca F. Stern, 'Beds, Bodices and Gravy': Female Servants, Private Property, and Perquisite Economies in Victorian Narratives of Crime (paper presented to the Southern Conference on British Studies, Memphis, Tennessee 5 Nov. 2004).

[21] *Times*, 2 December 1814; 9 January 1815.

and drink from various dealers in Westminster. By claiming to buy them for her mistress's household, Ragan managed to get fourteen pints of stout, a loaf of bread, and over two pounds weight of steaks. For her fraudulent feast, the assistant-judge sentenced her to four month's in prison with hard labor.[22] Eighteen-year old Anne Griffiths falsely ordered tea, coffee, and sugar in the name of her mistress Elizabeth Philips in 1835, and despite the evidence of several tradesmen was found not guilty. Perhaps she received this verdict because of her youth, or they may have been some doubt as to whether or not her mistress may have ordered the goods. Elizabeth Philips did not testify against her servant.[23] Although the items stolen by these discharged servants were largely food items, they were food items that normally would be economically beyond the reach of a servant maid. Beef steaks, lamb chops, tea, coffee, and sugar were not staples of a servant's diet. For a day, or sometimes a series of days, however, a servant could 'be' her mistress by enjoying the benefit of her credit and her ample food supply.

Along with these frauds by ex-servants, women and men previously employed by business owners like tailors, dressmakers, and milliners used that connection to commit frauds. They too were a sort of ex-servant pretending to be master, or at least take their master's privileges. Due to this prevalent ex-employee fraud the author of *The Frauds of London* warned tradesmen never to deliver goods only on the strength of a verbal message.[24] The case of Jane Marvin and Harriet Pregnall, women in their late teens, illustrates the ease with which this fraud was committed. In the spring of 1862 Marvin used the card of an ex-employer of Pregnall's, Taylor—a Court milliner in Cavendish Square, to obtain 31 yards of silk from Messrs. Candy a silk-warehouseman in Watling Street. As a team, Pregnall and Marvin targeted some of the most respectable and popular wholesale houses in London. Claiming to work for a dressmaker, Miss Pritchard, Pregnall took silk, cotton, and a silk umbrella among other goods from the famed Bradbury, Greatorex, and Co. of Aldermanbury.[25] Marvin obtained more goods in the name of

---

[22] GLRO MJ/SR 4889, Middlesex Quarter Sessions of the Peace, Indictment of Mary Ann Ragan, Middlesex Sessions Papers, 31 January 1853; *Times*, 2 February 1853. For a similar case to both of these please see that of Mary Fitzgerald who falsely ordered bread, pork, tea and sugar in the name of her mistress in 1845. GLRO MJ/SR 4630, Middlesex Quarter Sessions of the Peace, Indictment of Mary Fitzgerald, Middlesex Sessions Papers, 25 February 1845. See also the case of Jane Smith, a servant of John Dawson. *Times*, 27 September 1814.

[23] GLRO MJ/SR 4382, Middlesex Quarter Sessions of the Peace, Indictment of Ann Griffiths, Middlesex Sessions Papers, 14 December 1835. This indictment does not specify why Griffiths was set free, but her mistress is not included in the list of those sworn in court—this may have helped her case. See also the 1860 case of Jane Jones, an out of work servant who falsely ordered goods under the name of a Dr. Pavey in Bloomsbury. *Times*, 6 October 1860.

[24] Bow Street Officer, *The Frauds of London*, 12–13.

[25] *Times*, 1, 8 May 1862; Bradbury, Greatorex, and Company was a large, popular wholesale drapery firm. William Whiteley, founder of Whiteley's department stores,

Taylor, Pregnall's ex-employer, at Messrs. Copestake and Co. the drapers well-known for their elaborate plate-glass windows. This purchase led to their arrest because Copestake delivered the goods directly to Taylor and not into Marvin's hands. The exposure of the case brought further charges of theft against Marvin for stealing stays, stockings and other articles belonging to her ex-employer, a haberdasher on Primrose Hill who fired her in December of 1861.[26] Both pleaded guilty at the Old Bailey and at the behest of Pregnall's father the young women received sentences of only a few days.[27] Because of their own connections with clothing retail, Marvin and Pregnall's frauds exceeded those possible by such women as Mary Ann Ragan. The cost as well as the status of the goods taken was much higher, but the principle of pretending to represent another person of a wealthier class remained the same.

The case of young Pregnall and Marvin is reminiscent of an earlier case which took place in 1830 and involved two pupils educated at Elizabeth Fry's seminary at East Ham. In this case the women, Ellen Ragan and Mary Dillon, pretended to buy haberdashery goods for a Mrs. Gilson. They claimed to be acting as her servants. Dillon had worked for Mrs. Gilson, but was no longer working for her when she committed the fraud. The haberdasher, Mr. Philips arrested them and they went to Lambeth Street police court. In the end, the judge gave the women back into the custody of Fry who promised to put them in her Refuge and 'endeavour to amend them.'[28] In Mrs. Gilson's name, Fry's pupils almost managed to walk away with over three pounds worth of haberdashery goods they never could have honestly afforded. This ruse of posing as a servant and ordering goods was a common form of retail fraud among working class women. Luxury goods that a working class woman would not be able to get credit for under her own name became easily available when she posed as someone acting in the interests of a middle-class woman or man.

For the ruse to work it was not even necessary that the respectable middle-class person exist in reality. Sometimes just a name or description or reference to an address was enough to create the fictional character for whom these faux-servants ordered merchandise. In 1834 a man calling himself Thomas Cooke ordered goods from different tradespeople in London in the name of a 'Mrs. Mary Anne Winter' who never materialized.[29] In 1858, nineteen-year old Mary Johnson, described as

---

worked in this firm before opening his own shop. Alison Adburgham, *Shops and Shopping, 1800-1914: Where and in What Manner the Well-Dressed Englishwoman Bought her Clothes* (London: Barrie and Jenkins, 1960), 151.

[26] *Times*, 1, 8 May 1862. Note it is unclear whether Pregnall worked for Mr. or Mrs. Taylor because both are referred to in the case. See also a similar case where Margaret Thomas falsely ordered drapery goods for a china dealer named Phillips. 'Fraud on a Draper,' *Warehousemen and Draper's Trade Journal* (London) 1 June 1872.

[27] CCCSP, Seventh Session, 1862, p. 91. Marvin was confined for five days in Newgate and Pregnall received only two days.

[28] *Times*, 9 March 1830.

[29] PRO C114/34, Thomas Miller, Society for the Protection of Trade to [members] Society

'a smartly dressed young woman' had nine pairs of boots and shoes sent to her fictional Mistress. On the way to deliver the goods Johnson wrested away three pairs of shoes from the delivery boy before he was able to get her into custody. Johnson served six months in Wandsworth for her shoe fraud.[30] Another retail fraud, Jane Bond not only created a fictional mistress, but also used the subterfuge that the mistress disagreed with her husband about shopping expenses to get away with the goods. In August 1863, Bond went into the shop of Mrs. Grace Faultless[31] in St. Giles and ordered bonnets for the inspection of her mistress in Oxford Street. Faultless's assistant followed Bond to a tavern in that street where she claimed that her employer wanted the goods ''brought in quietly'' because she did not want her husband to know about the purchase. Asking the assistant to wait at the door for the money, Bond pretended to take the box to her mistress and made her escape. Bond was not apprehended until November of 1863 when she had committed the same type of fraud at least eight more times.[32] Bond, Johnson and others committed these crimes in the names of people who did not exist; however, the status of those fictional mistresses and not their individual or actual existence is what counted in the eyes of the tradesmen giving the goods. These frauds were also aided by the fact that having such a servant to do a family's shopping was a sign of status itself, and something that a shop owner might use to judge whether or not to extend credit. One of the more disturbing aspects of fraud was the threat its proponents posed to class by co-opting the status of employers and sometimes fictional employers.

In an 1850 fraud case, Mary Lloyd borrowed both the name and position of a Mrs. Winnall living at Leominster when she forged a request for goods in Winnall's name. The letter was addressed to a Mr. Southall draper:

> Mrs. Winnall will fell obliged If you will ples to send me Three pare of Lambs hool stockings and a verenice wintter shall ples send it dark and good hool and a dark cotton dress for a hold person, and 12 yards of Coberg Cloth a dark green or a brown and linines for 3 dresses and 3 yards of green satten ribent 8 pence per yard 3 yards of flannel 12 pence per ard and 2 yards of black cotton velvet good, and 6 yards of plum culer gose ribent for a cap ples to send it down to the Lion-ottell by a seven o clock ples send your bill and i ill send your money i dont think you can make it out ples send it as well if you can if that is eney mistake i will put it to rits.

> WensdayMorind.
> Mrs. Winnel[33]

---

for the Protection of Trade, 22 Ely Place, Holborn, London, 12 August 1834, 10th notice 1834. For another case of falsely ordering goods see PRO C114/34, Thomas Miller, Society for the Protection of Trade to [members] Society for the Protection of Trade, 22 Ely Place, Holborn, London, 20 January 1834, 1st notice.

[30] *Times*, 22 July 1858.

[31] One wonders if Mrs. Faultless was being entirely honest about her own name.

[32] *Times*, 9 November 1863.

[33] *Times*, 27 March 1850.

Perhaps if her spelling had been better she might have been able to receive those goods; however, the letter was immediately deemed a forgery and Lloyd was arrested after they delivered the goods to her at the Lion Inn. In court the stationer testified that when buying the paper, Lloyd asked him to spell the word 'cloth.'[34] Although full of miscalculations, Lloyd's attempted fraud stands as an illustrative example of the type of fraud where a working-class woman directly or indirectly claimed to represent a middle-class shopper. Through those claims she accessed goods like green satin and plum colored ribbon that she might never be able to purchase herself. This theft of status as well as goods made fraud a particularly odious crime in the eyes of contemporaries.

Some women, unlike Lloyd, were not satisfied with feigning to act in the interest of a Mrs. Winnall. These frauds used the privileges of the aristocracy to gain goods in the marketplace. In 1826 tradesmen at Kensington charged Mary Bartlett with three instances of falsely obtaining goods by pretending to be Lord Holland's housekeeper.[35] Two years later the ex-housemaid of Lady Alice Peel, sister-in-law to then Home Secretary Robert Peel, scandalized the family with her false orders for goods in Lady Alice's name. Frauds and shoplifters were often described as well-dressed or respectably dressed in trial descriptions; however, Mary Ann Bell was described as 'a good-looking woman' by the *Times*. Bell served as a maid with Peel for around nine months before she was discharged in January of 1828. The termination of her employment was probably related to her relationship with a shady character named Patrick Henry Martin who had also been convicted of fraud.[36] Using Lady Alice Peel's name, Bell procured over £70 worth of goods from one of the largest, and most fashionable retail stores of its day, the combination linen drapery, haberdashery and silk emporium of Howell and James in Regent Street. Almost saved by Lady Alice's inability or unwillingness to attend the prosecution, Howell and James were finally able to convict Bell and the judge sentenced her to seven years transportation.[37] Bell's case demonstrates that even the most well-known families were not exempt from fraud. In fact Bell used the very fame and respectability of the Peel family to make her crime a success. Her reward was much greater than a few steaks and pints of stout. Howell and James catered to London's most fashionable women and the types of items purchased there were those coveted by the growing shopping culture. Bell's case also reveals how frauds took advantage of the greed of London retailers – making over seven separate purchases before she was caught. The Bell fraud is also reminiscent of

---

[34] *Ibid.*

[35] *Times*, 14 July 1826.

[36] Martin was charged by a whisky distributor for impersonating the Hon. Spring Rice Under Secretary of State for the Home Department and asking for 'samples of whisky.' See *Times* 8 March 1828. However, this case has something of an urban legend quality to it. It is mentioned again in 1849 in the *Trade Protection Record*. See 'Gullibility of Tradesmen,' *Trade Protection Record*, London, 12 May 1849.

[37] Lady Alice was described as under an indisposition—possibly a pregnancy. *Times*, 5, 8 March 1828; 3 April 1828.

Jane Bond's 1863 shoe fraud in which Bond used the middle-class wife's desire to hide purchases from her husband as a premise for fraud. Bell claimed throughout her trial that Lady Alice had ordered her to purchase those goods at Howell and James's.

In their varied forms the frauds of working class female servants, ex-servants and false servants may seem unrelated to the pilfering middle and upper-class ladies who shoplifted or falsely ordered goods in nineteenth-century English shops. However, the crimes of these women are connected not only in the close relationship between shopping ladies and those who served them, a relationship close enough to induce traders to hand over often expensive goods, but they are also related by their common participation in creating a fraudulent identity. What separated a working-class woman fraudulently putting satin ribbons, items she could not afford, on her mistress's account from a middle-class woman shoplifting silk handkerchiefs for which she also did not possess the required ready money? The working-class woman borrowed the status of a wealthier woman to obtain goods that denoted the status of a wealthier woman. The desire of traders to gain and keep their more lucrative female customers also aided these women in their frauds. In the ultra-competitive world of English retail trade, even Grace Faultless did not balk at some bonnets slipped past a husband's notice. The women committing these frauds knew how to pique a trader's financial interest, an interest strong enough to entice a trader to participate in dishonest trade practices in order to make a sale.

Sometimes the servant scenario would be dropped, and the offender would pretend to be the master or mistress of a household. The 1829 *Frauds of London* described the operations of such frauds: 'There is another class of cheats who take genteel lodgings, dress elegantly, assume false names;—pretend to be related to persons of credit and fashion . . . purchase wearing apparel and other articles, and disappear with the booty.'[38] In the same year this description was published, Mary Johnson and Elizabeth Wilson stood accused of just such a fraud in Marlborough Street police court. In a fraud they had practiced a number of times before, Johnson, an older woman, claimed to be a lady coming into London from her country house who desired lodging. Wilson pretended to be her servant. Mr. Swaile rented out some apartments to them in his house in the West End near Bond Street. On the strength of these respectable lodgings the women procured various goods including groceries such as wine, brandy and tea from surrounding tradesmen eager to have the business of this new customer. However, Swaile suspected his new lodgers and inquiries in the neighborhood of the reputed country house confirmed his suspicions. Swaile also noticed that the women frequently came and went dressed in a bulky fashion. He discovered they had been removing their newly 'bought' goods almost as soon as tradespeople delivered them. At the police station the searcher found that each of the women had a large sack buckled underneath her clothes large enough to 'convey away a Newfoundland dog.' They used the sacks

---

[38] Bow Street Officer, *The Frauds of London*, 11-12.

to smuggle goods including wine bottles found by the police search. The plan was to live off the good graces of area tradesmen until suspicion was raised or payment asked for and then they left lodgings and all to return to their secret cache of goods.[39]

Criminal charges, however, could not be made against the women. Signing someone else's name to a check was forgery and ordering goods under someone else's name was a fraud of false pretenses under English law, but openly ordering goods in one's own name was a problem of credit and not crime. Under English law these West End tradesmen suffered from giving credit to bad risks, but could not charge the women criminally. Unless you assumed the identity of an actual person, there was no law against pretending to be of a wealthier class. The chances of ever receiving the money owed by such debtors was so negligible that the tradesmen were simply out of their goods with no chance of recompense.[40]

The only requirement to commit such frauds was to maintain an appearance plausibly respectable—something Johnson with the aid of her faux servant Wilson was able to achieve in her various frauds. Similarly, a Mrs. Garden appeared to London retailers in 1835 wearing a sable tippet, boa and muff and ordered a variety of goods sent to the house she occupied in Upper John Street.[41] Warning of her frauds in their circular, the Society for the Protection of Trade's description of Mrs. Garden's fashionable clothing is a key to understanding women's retail fraud. The boa, tippet, and muff were genuine, but the status belonging to such fashionable women was, in Mrs. Garden's case, fictional. The writer of the circular wanted his members to know that despite her fashionable trappings Garden was not the desirable customer she appeared to be. Yet these very shopkeepers promoted the consumer culture that encouraged the possession of such material goods to gain and maintain status. Knowledge of manners along with a few items of clothing was enough to transform Garden in the eyes of shopkeepers, and make her a successful fraud.[42]

---

[39] *Times*, 18 August 1829. For another case involving the immediate removal of ordered goods see the case of Mrs. Fieldhouse of Cheshire in *City of London Trade Protection Circular (private circular)*, London, 11 July 1848.

[40] *Times*, 18 August 1829. See also complaints of this legal loophole in Bow Street Officer, *The Frauds of London*, 12.

[41] PRO C114/34, Thomas Miller, Society for the Protection of Trade to [members] Society for the Protection of Trade, 22 Ely Place, Holborn, London, 19 March 1835, 2nd notice 1835. See also a similar case by a Mr. & Mrs. Tucker. PRO C114/34, Thomas Miller, Society for the Protection of Trade to [members] Society for the Protection of Trade, 22 Ely Place, London, 10 February 1835, 1st notice 1835. In the Tuckers' case, however, they did not bother to actually rent the address they gave in Kensington.

[42] See also a case of a male fraud renting a house and charging goods with no capital to back it up. See 'Charge of Defrauding Hosiers, *The Draper* (London) 6 August 1869; 'Alleged Frauds Upon Tradesmen, *The Draper* (London) 13 August 1869. See also the case of Jane Butcher defrauding a brush-maker in *Times*, 23 April 1824.

Credit and Fraud

Garden, Johnson and Wilson with their high living in the West End, and the various servants abusing the tabs of mistresses, all took advantage of credit. Without available credit, none of these women could have committed their frauds. Even those women who promised to pay when the item was delivered were taking advantage of a type of common short-term credit provided by dealers to good customers. The new shopping culture may have lauded the maxim of ready-money, but an elaborate system of credit remained alive and well. Some of the cases mentioned even took place at the emporiums built on the newer, expanded concepts of trade like Howell and James. The City of London Trade Protection Society in 1848 recognized the connection between the spread of fraud and credit: 'The Metropolis and the large provincial Towns abound with unprincipled schemers, who . . . frequently adopt the names of individuals of high standing and character; and by this trick, accompanied by a system of misrepresentation and false references, succeed in obtaining goods to a large extent on credit.'[43] The credit system benefited frauds in two ways. First of all, credit made fraud possible. If these women had to pay ready money they never would have received the goods. Secondly, under English law fraud was difficult to prove. Most frauds simply fell under the category of bad credit risks and traders could not criminally prosecute them.

Credit aided all levels of fraud from the servant drinking beer at the mistress's expense to the professional fraud pretending to be a lady of fortune to the middle-class wife shopping beyond the boundaries of her budget. Two cases in particular illustrate the ways in which credit made fraud possible. The first of these took place in the mid-1830s. Like Johnson and Wilson and other cases of such fraudulent ladies, Mary Varley was described in her trial report as being particularly 'showily attired.' Described as having a 'fashionable exterior' and being '32 years of age, dark complexion, short stature, and genteel appearance,' Varley targeted West End traders.[44] In each case her method of operation was similar. She appeared in a shop as a well-dressed middle-class woman. After perusing the goods she selected some and then made a plausible excuse to leave the store without immediately paying for them. She was particularly fond of cloth merchants. Varley duped a Mr. Newton of Messrs. Holmes and Co. of Regent Street by telling him that she wanted to take some shawls home to get the opinion of a friend before completing the purchase. When the shop sent someone to collect money the next day, Varley was nowhere to be found. Mr. Williams a silk-mercer in Regent-circus suffered a similar fate. When Williams asked the magistrates if such actions were not swindling, one of the magistrates named Dyer informed him that 'Certainly morally it is, but not legally.'

---

[43] *City of London Trade Protection Circular* (London) 22 April 1848.

[44] PRO C114/34, Thomas Miller, Society for the Protection of Trade to [members] Society for the Protection of Trade, 22 Ely Place, Holborn, London, 26 August 1835, 5th notice 1835. See also *Times*, 20 August 1835.

In the 30 or so odd cases against her all of the dealers let her take away the property willingly and could not recover by criminal action. The other magistrate, Chambers, expressed his sorrow that the traders suffered from Varley's crimes, but warned that they would only lose more money attempting to prosecute her as a fraud.[45] Because she used her real name, the shopkeepers would have to prosecute her as a case of debt, and would probably never recover their money. Varley's case is a classic example of a successful fraud who knew not only how appear genteel, but also knew the limits of the law available to her victims.

Varley's case demonstrates the close connection between fraud and credit and the ease with which some women feigned genteel status to obtain goods. Another, most likely apocryphal, case is illustrative because of its moral about female fraud and the extension of credit. The story is from a source in 1845, but supposedly took place earlier in the century. It involved one of Jane Austen's favorite retail shops, a drapery and haberdashery establishment in London known as Grafton House.[46] Grafton House was one of the first shops founded on the principle of small profit margins with the faster turnover provided by ready money. Such large volume, close to wholesale price emporia, were the hallmark of innovation in nineteenth century England and the epitome of consumer culture. According to the story, the proprietor of Grafton House, Mr. Flint served a lady customer numerous goods including silks and, knowing Flint's ready-money policy, the lady asked Flint to ride in her carriage back to her home for payment. Flint agreed, but on entering the house found himself in a private madhouse and the lady had slipped away after telling the keepers that her husband thought he was the haberdasher, Mr. Flint. The story ends happily with Flint secretly sending a message to friends who freed him from the madhouse.[47] Though the story is most likely fictional, it makes an important point about the dangers of extending even the shortest term credit to the most genteel appearing women. Credit allowed women to unleash their consumer power in dangerous ways. To encourage women to possess material goods was one thing, but without the control provided by ready-money sale, women became frauds and possessed unwarranted economic power.

Few female frauds were as dastardly as Mr. Flint's nemesis, but women's frauds took on a range of forms in the nineteenth-century. Among the genteel pretenders, like Flint's customer and Mary Varley, were frauds using a variety of methods from renting a respectable home, to giving a respectable if fictitious address, to simply putting on a good show of etiquette and fashionable display to lull suspicion. In 1848 a woman claiming to be a respectable Methodist and targeting people of that denomination plagued the tradespeople of Whittlesea and defrauded them of

---

[45] *Times*, 20 August 1835; See also *Times*, 25 September 1835.

[46] Adburgham, *Shops and Shopping*, 4. Austen's patronizing of Grafton House also shows how aware those in the countryside were of London's fashionable shops.

[47] C.B.C. Amicus, *How to Rise in Life* (London: Longman, Brown, Green, and Longmans, 1845), 44-47.

numerous goods before she disappeared.[48] In the same year the Mutual Communication Society in Sackville Street reported a Mrs. Weir who gave orders all over the West End of London with a fake Edinburgh address.[49] Women were active in shopping and active in retail frauds. This activity took place despite the legal inability of married women to contract debts in their own name. Even the ability of single women of independent incomes to pay and contract debts was suspicious. In Trollope's 1865 novel, *Can You Forgive Her?*, one character reminds another of the problem with women and finance: "The truth is, Mr. Vavasor, that bills with ladies' names on them,—ladies who are in no way connected with business,—ain't just the paper that people like."[50] Yet shopkeepers had little reticence about extending credit to these women. Again and again women were able to execute successful frauds by claiming either control over the family income or an independent income.

The Expectant 'Heiress' and the 'Wealthy' Widow

In 1847 a well-dressed woman named Mary Lee befriended the family of a florist in Upper Clapton. Lee told them among other things that she was the niece of a gentleman in Kensington who had invested £7,000 for her in the funds. She expected the money any day. Lee so convinced the Hogans of her respectability that they allowed her to move into their home rent free for six months. However, one day Lee claimed she was going out to receive her dividends from the bank, and she disappeared wearing Mrs. Hogan's silk shawl.[51] Lee practiced a popular method of fraud—that of the expectant heiress. These faux heiresses and women of imaginary independent incomes committed frauds ranging from borrowing money

---

[48] 'A Female Swindler,' *City of London Trade Protection Circular* (London) 20 May 1848.

[49] 'Weir, Mrs.,' *City of London Trade Protection Circular* (London) 16 September 1848. See also the case of Charlotte Watts in PRO C114/34, Edward S. Foss, Society of Guardians for the Protection of Trade to [members] Society of Guardians for the Protection of Trade, London, 4 November 1825, 26 Correspondence, 1825 and the case of Eliza Maria Amphlett in *City of London Trade Protection Society Circular* (London) 15 April 1848. For similar male fraud cases see PRO C114/34, Edward S. Foss, Society of Guardians for the Protection of Trade to [members] Society of Guardians for the Protection of Trade, London, 13 October 1826, 12 Correspondence, 1826; PRO C114/34, Edward S. Foss, Society of Guardians for the Protection of Trade to [members] Society of Guardians for the Protection of Trade, London, 29 September 1826, and the case of Thomas Brockelbank. See also the case of John Booth Thomas in 'Charge of Obtaining Goods by False Pretences, *The Draper* (London) 16 February 1872.

[50] Anthony Trollope, *Can You Forgive Her?*, vol. 2, (Oxford University Press, 1982) 207.

[51] *Times*, 27 January 1848. For a similar case tried in 1877 in the Middlesex sessions see the case of Jane Sears, a woman who committed frauds and obtained goods by claiming to have extensive property in Hammersmith. See *Times*, 15, 24, August; 8 September 1877.

to obtaining lodgings and, of course, gaining goods from tradespeople on credit.

One of these women was a career criminal named Mary Ann Tolfrey. Prosecuted in 1850 by the London Trade Protection Society, Tolfrey's crimes came to light in the wake of a scam where she promised to obtain government situations for people for small fees of money. However, this was only one aspect of her varied career. One London silk merchant lost over £100 worth of goods given to Tolfrey on the premise that she expected a large amount of money from a relative's will. She told the same tradesmen that the goods she bought, silk waistcoats, drawers, and stockings were for the nephew of the Duke of Norfolk. She bamboozled a linen draper in Blackfriar's road out of a similar amount of goods. Tolfrey also commissioned a seal to be made with a gentleman's coat of arms, and used letters stamped with this seal to cheat a variety of shopkeepers. For her various frauds, the judge sentenced Tolfrey to 18 months in prison.[52] Another career fraud and friend of Tolfrey's was Mary Ann Aldridge, described as 'a portly woman, handsomely attired.' Aldridge's frauds included posing as the widow of an old business partner to extort charity from an elderly gentleman.[53] Tolfrey and her friend Aldridge managed to buy silk and dress in the best fashions due to their ability to manipulate shopkeepers and others through fraud.

Another woman who feigned to be an heiress on the verge of her fortune was Mary Rowley. After her husband, George William Rowley was imprisoned for fraud, the fashionable, well-mannered Mary Rowley managed to feed, clothe, and house her family by pretending to be heir to property at Leicester, property soon to be restored after eight years of Chancery proceedings. The police prosecuting the case claimed that Rowley and her family were responsible for over 500 instances of fraud over a seven year period. Unfortunately for her victims, Rowley died on June 12, 1848, at the University College Hospital in London with her debts unpaid.[54] One of her fraud victims, a Mr. Norton, complained in her trial that English law, unlike Scottish law, allowed swindlers to claim to be merely debtors and avoid criminal prosecution.[55] English law placed the onus of fraud on the victim. If the shopkeeper was naïve enough to believe his customer and extend credit—the debts so incurred were the shopkeeper's problem.

A case that particularly illustrates the difficulties shopkeepers had in prosecuting fraud took place in 1871. Florence Cowper, a 26 year-old married woman, came to Solomon Benjamin, a tailor in Mayfair, as an acquaintance of Benjamin's longstanding friend Mrs. Graham. Benjamin lent Cowper £20 on her representation that she possessed a separate income from her husband, an income

---

[52] *Times*, 1, 6, 11, 13 June 1850.

[53] *Times*, 15, 19 August 1850.

[54] *City of London Trade Protection Circular* (London) 22 April 1848; General Information, *City of London Trade Protection Circular* (London) 19 June 1848.

[55] *City of London Trade Protection Circular* (London) 22 April 1848. See also the case of the false heiress Marianne Osborne in 1848. *City of London Trade Protection Circular* (London) 27 May 1848.

provided to her by her uncle Sir Benjamin Pyne. Cowper alleged that her uncle had been late in his last payment and she had contracted debt unknown to her husband. She claimed that she needed the immediate loan to pay that debt. Despite evidence by the prosecution that Cowper was not the niece of Pyne and possessed no separate income, but instead had come to London as a domestic servant from Scotland and was in a reformatory for fallen women in 1860, the jury found Cowper not guilty. After all, Cowper had overestimated her own respectability, but did not use a false name. Her counsel argued this was 'simply a debt transaction.' According to the verdict, the jury agreed that the transaction between Benjamin and Cowper was one of debt and not criminal fraud.[56] The tailor was unable to successfully prosecute her despite Cowper's many false assertions. His willingness to lend money to a stranger on the pretext of her contracting a debt unknown to her husband is also revealing. It suggests that such debt was commonplace. Cowper's case not only stands as a classic example of the fraudulent lady of independent means and the difficulty of shopkeepers prosecuting fraud, it also demonstrates that women, even married women, contracting debts was not seen as extraordinary.

The key to female retail fraud in the nineteenth century was the pretense of genteel status, or at least the pretense of representing someone with that status, and the fact that despite coverture, shopkeepers did extend credit to women. In her study of women, debt, and coverture in English small claims courts, Margot Finn finds similar evidence of shopkeepers' willingness to give credit to women. When a fraud successfully achieved the mimicking of status, shopkeepers assumed she had the means that went along with all the outer trappings of gentility. The case of middle class or higher female fraud, however, is more complicated. These women already possessed the prerequisite status, but did not have the funds usually associated with the genteel. Such frauds fall into various categories. Many were married or once married women who either pledged goods beyond their means or pledged the credit of a spouse unwilling to support them. Nineteenth-century women had financial power despite the laws of coverture.

Respectable Women and Fraud

Necessaries: Marriage, Separation, Credit and Fraud

Women bought, women shopped, and women contracted debts. Married women had the added advantage of the law known as the law of necessaries that was instituted in the reign of Henry VI. This law allowed wives to contract for 'necessary' goods in the name of their husbands. The law empowered women buyers in two ways. First, the definition of 'necessary' items depended on the station in life of her husband and her family. The higher the status of her husband the more expensive were the goods she could purchase. Secondly, and this is also

---

[56] 'Alleged Swindling,' *The Draper* (London) 22 September 1871.

important in relation to fraud cases, married women separated from their husbands used the law of necessaries to obtain financial support through consumption of goods.[57]

With the woman making the contract and the man liable for the debt, difficulties often arose involving married women, their husbands and debt. Due to the law of necessaries, there was often a fine distinction between retail fraud and legally contracted female debt. Even with demonstrated false pretences, shop owners had difficulty prosecuting such married women of retail fraud, and often had difficulty collecting even when prosecuted as debt cases. In 1871 a milliner in Portman Square named Phillips sued a Captain Edwards for goods provided to his wife— goods including 25 silk dresses. Although the judgement initially went in favor of the milliner, Edwards was able to get that judgement overturned and called for a new trial on the basis that the goods his wife contracted for were not necessaries but luxury items.[58] However, in another case the previous year, Miss L. Berkley, also a milliner, successfully sued Mr. R. Tyrer for over £12 worth of goods sold to his wife. Berkley had given Mrs. Tyrer the credit based on Tyrer's description of herself as a lady of property and the fact that Mrs. Tyrer always came to her shop in a pony carriage. Also the milliner claimed that Tyrer only ordered 'necessary articles.' In this case, the judge found for the plaintiff and Mr. Tyrer had to pay his wife's debt.[59] Debt cases such as Edwards' and Tyrer's demonstrate the thin line between debt and fraud. After all, Tyrer's pony carriage was borrowed from her brother and the milliner could have easily accused her of false pretences.

When marriage partners were separated the legal confusion only increased. Mr. Little, a draper and hosier in Regent Street sued an Exeter surgeon, Mr. DeNiceville, for a sum of over £30 worth of goods purchased by his wife. Over twenty years before, Mr. DeNiceville's wife brought a considerable sum of money with her into the marriage, around £5,000 along with another £800 worth of furniture. However, the DeNicevilles separated after seventeen years of marriage with Mrs. DeNiceville claiming physical abuse as the cause. After her marriage broke up, Mrs. DeNiceville went to live in London with her spinster sister. Both

---

[57] Margot Finn, 'Women, Consumption and Coverture in England, c. 1760-1860,' *The Historical Journal* vol. 39 1996, 703-722. See also Margot Finn, 'Debt and credit in Bath's court of requests, 1829-39,' *Urban History*, 21, no. 2 (October 1994): 211-36; Margot Finn, 'Fair Trade and Foul: Swindlers, Shopkeepers, and the Use and Abuse of Credit in the Nineteenth Century' (paper presented to the North American Conference on British Studies annual meeting, Washington, DC, 1995); Margot Finn, Emory University, 'Victorian Women as Consumer Debtors: Theory and Practice' (paper presented to the North American Conference on British Studies, Montreal, October 1, 1993). For the American perspective see William R. Leach, 'Transformations in a Culture of Consumption: Women and Department Stores, 1890-1925,' *The Journal of American History* 71, no. 2 (September 1984), 334.

[58] Mrs. Edwards owed a remainder of £122 on a tab that began as over £500. 'A Disputed Milliner's Bill,' *The Draper* (London) 2 June 1871.

[59] 'Doubtful Gentility,' *The Draper* (London) 4 November 1870.

women lived on money provided by their boarders along with what was left of their separate fortunes until the sister died in 1871. Three years before her sister died, Mrs. DeNiceville tried to sue her husband for divorce, but was denied because she had reconciled with him once before.[60] After her sister's death, more disputes arose about Mr. DeNiceville's refusal to provide any support to his wife and she began contracting for goods in his name. In the DeNiceville's case, the jury found in favor of the draper (and Mrs. DeNiceville) forcing the surgeon to pay for his wife's 'necessary articles.'[61] The law of necessaries provided Mrs. DeNiceville through her consumption of goods with the alimony denied to her by her husband.

In Edwards', Tyrer's, and DeNiceville's cases the wives were all empowered to contract debts seemingly denied them by coverture. This power, however, was not always beneficial to shopkeepers. Husbands like Edwards sometimes could not be forced to pay the debt. The situation became especially complicated with husbands and wives separated for long periods. One particularly poignant case in which debts contracted for 'necessaries' led to accusations of criminal fraud is that of Mary Jane Richardson. In 1865 one of the most fashionable retail warehouses in London, Hayman and Youngman of Sloane Street in Chelsea, accused Mary Jane Richardson of fraud in Westminster Police Court. In only six years Richardson was transformed from genteel wife to criminal fraud. It began with her marriage in 1859 to a gentleman of property Mr. E. Richardson of Mulberry Terrace house Lower Norwood. Mary Jane was around 35 years old when she married the already elderly Richardson who had several grown children from his first marriage. Mary Jane's own family was not very wealthy. Her brother was a struggling schoolmaster scraping a living by teaching mathematics. Almost immediately after the wedding the marriage began to fall apart and Richardson accused his wife of unseemly behavior stemming from the abuse of alcohol.[62] Mr. Richardson's suit in divorce court failed in June of 1865; however, he still refused to see his wife or to provide her with any support. He ejected her from the house. She claimed that she applied to the parish, but was rejected on the grounds that her wealthy husband should provide her with support. She soon started contracting debts all over London.[63]

Hayman and Youngman in 1869 already occupied building numbers 173, 174, 175 and 176 in Sloane street with their large drapery, haberdashery and silk mercery emporium. A respectable company, Hayman and Youngman gave their customers six months to pay their accounts before they began charging them 5 percent annual interest on what they owed.[64] In October of 1865 Mary Jane

---

[60] See Mary Lyndon Shanley, *Feminism, Marriage, and the Law in Victorian England* (Princeton University Press, 1989), 32-49; James Hammerton, *Cruelty and Companionship*, 118-133.

[61] 'Responsibility of a Husband,' *Warehousemen and Draper's Trade Journal* (London) 15 May 1872.

[62] From all the reports it seems that she was an alcoholic and this was probably the reason for the separation.

[63] *Times*, 11, 18 October; 14 November 1865.

[64] See Hayman, Pulsford & Company, 'Bill Headings,' Bill, Box 18, John Johnson

Richardson came into Hayman and Youngman and ordered over £30 worth of goods. Out of the ordered goods, Richardson requested that she be allowed to take a length of black silk and some gloves, because she wanted a dress made up as soon as possible. The rest of the goods were to be delivered to Mulberry Terrace house the next day, when she promised to pay for them. Alfred Hayman put the goods on an account in her husband's name, but when they made the delivery the next day Mr. Richardson refused to pay. On the grounds of false pretences, Hayman and Youngman took Mrs. Richardson to court for fraud, because she pretended she was still living with her husband when she contracted the debt. On the day of her case over twenty other tradesman came to complain of similar treatment. Like previous fraud cases, Richardson's method of operation was to order a large quantity of goods sent to her husband's respectable address while requesting that she be allowed to take a small quantity with her. She had been living in this way since the failure of her husband's divorce suit. Despite arguments that her behavior was perfectly legal under the law of necessaries, the judge sentenced her to prison and hard labor for eighteen months.[65]

In 1871, six years after her first trial for fraud, Mary Jane Richardson still fought for her right to support. In the interim her husband had died leaving her only £100 out of his estate worth over £10,000. She was forced to work as a housekeeper for a gentleman in Portman Square where she was arrested again on charges of fraud for contracting goods in the name of her late husband's estate. On the fifth of June 1871 Richardson walked into Chester Foulsham's artificial florist shop in Oxford Street and purchased a new bonnet from his assistant Lena Firth. Richardson left her old bonnet 'to be trimmed' and ordered the refurbished bonnet along with a quantity of flowers sent to a Mr. Richardson's in Pall Mall the next morning. Mr. Richardson was Guildford Richardson, one of the executors of her late husband's will. When the store delivered the goods, Mrs. Richardson was nowhere to be found and Guildford Richardson refused to pay. In the ensuing fraud case, Montagu Williams aided by the solicitors to the Trade Protection Association prosecuted Mrs. Richardson. Throughout the second trial Richardson claimed that she only wanted the support that was rightfully hers and intended to commit no illegal acts. The executor argued that he had no power to provide her with money other than that stipulated in the will.[66] According to the arresting officer, Richardson angrily declared on the way to the station that 'she would do so again when out of prison, and would make the public keep her, in prison or out, and she preferred a prison to a workhouse.'[67] And keep her they did. In the Middlesex Sessions Mr. Serjeant Cox sentenced her to seven more years in prison.[68]

Collection, Bodleian, Oxford.

[65] *Times*, 11, 18 October; 14 November 1865.

[66] *Times*, 9 August 1871; 'Alleged Fraud on a Milliner, *The Draper* (London) 28 July 1871; 'Obtaining a Bonnet by False Pretences, *The Draper* (London) 11 August 1871.

[67] *Times*, 9 August 1871.

[68] *Ibid.*; 'Obtaining a Bonnet by False Pretences,' *The Draper* (London) 11 August 1871.

Mary Jane Richardson possessed middle-class status because she was still legally married to a man of property; however, after the failed divorce proceedings she no longer had access to the money which preserved and promoted that status. Refusing to be denied the level of consumption appropriate to a woman of her station, she incurred debts all over London. She shopped in Sloane Street and bought silk dress fabric. Had she lived the same cloistered lifestyle as Mrs. DeNiceville the court may even have supported her rights to contract for necessaries in the name of her husband. Her case illustrates the complexities of women, coverture, debt, and fraud in English retail. Her ability to contract for goods possibly a hundred times before ever being caught demonstrates the power of women to purchase goods and to have credit—a power that Edwards, Tyrer, DeNiceville and other women used more successfully. Richardson's case also demonstrates that the line between debt and fraud could be thin. Was Mrs. Tyrer's failure to mention that she drove *her brother's* pony carriage any less false than Mrs. Richardson's failure to mention her separation from her husband? Whether these women were taken to court for debt or fraud, their cases show that in the world of English retail the inability of married women to contract debts was often ignored. Silk dresses, gloves, new bonnets—women's consumption of goods seemed almost unlimited.

Middle-class women, both married and unmarried, participated in fraud: society explained the participation of these moral exemplars in criminal practices with difficulty. In the case of Richardson and others, the fraud seemed to stem from a debt disagreement with a spouse. Yet all cases of female fraud cannot be explained as a type of consumption oriented demand for alimony. That middle-class women consumed goods on a massive scale was disconcerting enough to observers. When those women went beyond the bounds of legal consumption and became shoplifters and frauds, nineteenth century society struggled to explain their behavior in a way that would protect current gender ideals. If they were not rational criminals perhaps they were irrational 'diseased' women who had lost control of their mental faculties.

'Brain Fever' Again: Women, Insanity and Fraud

In 1849 the *Trade Protection Record* reprinted an article from the *Examiner* about retail traders and fraud. Citing a case in which an older woman pretended to be the Countess of Carlisle to extract goods from shopkeepers, the reporter commented: "It is a singular circumstance that hardly one of the persons who have been duped had the slightest suspicion of the prisoner's insanity."[69] The article further asserted that shopkeepers unable to recognize such 'insanity' as the delusion suffered by the would-be Countess were incompetent. In the same article other frauds are discussed, but all are male and none are accused of suffering a 'delusion.'[70] In this

---

[69] 'Gullibility of Tradesmen,' *Trade Protection Record*, London 12 May 1849.
[70] *Ibid.*

era in which shoplifters, especially middle-class women like Lydia Dixon and Mary Rees, were excused from their crimes by labeling them as victims of a type of insanity, female frauds who were also committing crimes of consumption were likewise denoted as insane. Insanity specifically related to middle-class female retail crime emerges in the mid-nineteenth century. Sometimes, as in the case of some shoplifters, the women themselves defended their actions as insane.

In 1859 Thomas Brandon, an Oxford Street florist, sold over £5 worth of fashionable bonnets to a Mrs. Stewart, who gave her address as the Star and Garter Hotel in Richmond. The bonnets were delivered and someone picked them up, but Mr. Brandon found out too late that there was no Mrs. Stewart staying at that hotel. Mrs. Stewart did not live in Richmond at all. She lived in Petersham, and her name was not Stewart. Her real name was Jane Tyrwhitt Jones.[71] Fifteen years after she was arrested and tried for shoplifting from the Soho Bazaar, Tyrwhitt was back in the newspapers and back in the court system for fraud. Brandon was only one of the West End retailers who accused Tyrwhitt of multiple frauds. Mr. Dod, solicitor for the Society for the Protection of Trade helped prosecute Tyrwhitt. In her final trial for obtaining goods on false pretenses in Central Criminal Court in January 1860, Brandon tried her for defrauding him of the three bonnets. A hatter from Hyde Park Corner charged Tyrwhitt with defrauding him of three ladies' hats under the assumed name of Mrs. Vernon of Close House, Windsor.[72] The last case, and the only one for which she was found guilty, was an accusation of fraud by the very fashionable and luxurious silk and shawl warehouse of Lewis and Allenby of 195 Regent Street.[73] Once again, Tyrwhitt gave her name as the 'Hon. Mrs. Stewart' and gave her current address as the Star and Garter, noting that her permanent residence was Bath. At first her defense tried to dismiss her penchant for false names as an eccentricity well understood by traders. They claimed that her trustees always paid the bills from her separate income. However, in some cases traders were not paid. Her defense then brought up the obvious explanation for Tyrwhitt's criminal behavior—she was insane.[74]

Her counsel asserted that there was only one explanation why a woman 'highly connected' with a separate income of the interest from £11,000 would commit such crimes. Dr. Green, a physician from Golden Square testified that he had known Tyrwhitt for 20 years and that she suffered from severe headaches and delirious

---

[71] *Times*, 31 January 1860.

[72] CCCSP, Fourth Session, 1860, 261-267; *Times*, 15, 22, 29 December 1859; 31 January; 1 February 1860.

[73] Alison Adburgham describes Lewis and Allenby as 'the most famous of all the silk mercers.' Only six years after they successfully convicted Tyrwhitt, Lewis and Allenby, instead of spreading into adjacent buildings, built an entirely new structure on Conduit Street for their showrooms. This firm was one of the first in London to make such a purpose-built emporium. In the 1890s this successful business was bought out by the chain of Dickins & Jones. See Adburgham, *Shops and Shopping*, 43, 105 & 240.

[74] CCCSP, Fourth Session, 1860, 261-267; *Times*, 15, 22, 29 December 1859; 31 January; 1 February 1860.

episodes. His diagnosis was simple: 'she was acting under a mania, which led her to obtain goods from tradesmen under different names.'[75] Dr. Green named this mania specifically under cross examination: 'her mania would not assume the form of paying for the goods as well as ordering them—it is merely a mania to possess, no matter whether it is paid for or not—it is called *cleptomania* . . ..'[76] Tyrwhitt went along with this defense and throughout the trial appeared to be in a sort of half-swoon and had to be supported physically by warders. The jury concluded that Tyrwhitt's actions, at least in the case of the silk merchants, constituted fraud and the judge sentenced the 45 year-old Tyrwhitt to nine months in prison but without hard labor 'on account of the delicate state of her health.'[77]

In the fifteen years since her first arrest on the criminal charge of shoplifting, the English justice system had changed enough to allow the plea of 'cleptomania' to such a criminal charge. In the face of mounting evidence, such as the letters in Tyrwhitt's handwriting produced by some of the West End tradesmen, simple denials of crime no longer sufficed for wealthier women. Slowly, the plea of 'disease' was added to that of guilt or innocence. However, the new plea was reserved almost entirely for women of the wealthier classes. A lawyer prosecuting Tyrwhitt remarked that 'the defense seemed to be based on two different interpretations of the law-one for the rich and another for the poor.'[78] He might just as well have added that there was a gender gap as well as one of class in English law.

Despite the aberration of Tyrwhitt's conviction, married or single, middle-class and wealthier women did not generally face the same risks in court as did poorer women. Another example of such a case is that of Mary Elizabeth Johnson. Although well-educated, Johnson had no connections to the aristocracy and no separate income from her father's estate. She seems to have had no income at all. The oldest of four children, her father was a rector who died in 1848 when she was in her mid-twenties. Three years later she was in court accused of defrauding tradesmen.[79]

On May 28, 1850, Johnson, a regular customer staying with a respectable family in the neighborhood of Dalston, walked into the shop of a chemist and cashed a check for £6 from the publishers of *Blackwood's Magazine*. Explaining to the chemist that the checks were for several stories she had written for the magazine, Johnson cashed similar checks in the ensuing days. Her requests were frequent and the monetary value of the checks kept increasing with each visit.

---

[75] *Times*, 30 January 1860.

[76] CCCSP, Fourth Session, 1860, p. 266.

[77] *Times*, 1 February 1860. See also CCCSP, Fourth Session, 1860, 267; *Times*, 15, 22, 29 December 1859; 31 January; 1 February 1860. See also the case of Jane Sill who also obtained millinery articles by false statements. *Times*, 15 April 1856.

[78] *Times*, 1 February 1860.

[79] CCCSP, Ninth Session, 1851, 402-404; *Times*, 19, 27 June; 14 July 1851. Once again, this case is reminiscent of the shoplifter Lydia Dixon who was left in financial straits after the death of her father, a respectable solicitor.

Finally, the chemist, Frank Senior, made inquiries regarding the checks and found that *Blackwood's* had no accounts at the bank on which the checks were drawn. When Johnson came again to his shop, Senior told her of the problem. Johnson protested that it must be some mistake on the part of the publisher and would immediately go see her cousin in Hyde Park to straighten out the matter. Senior went with her first to Cambridge Square, Hyde Park where Johnson disappeared for some time and then returned to the cab. She then told the cabman to go to Lord Villier's residence in Berkely Square. Lord Villiers was not at home so she then ordered the driver to go to the house of a solicitor at River Terrace, Islington. She told Senior after returning to the cab that the solicitor advised her to go immediately and procure the money. Senior instead had her arrested.[80]

From her initial arrest and trial, which began in Worship Street police court, to her final Criminal trial in the Old Bailey, an overwhelming transformation occurred in the image and description of Mary Johnson. The initial reports described Johnson as a well-dressed trickster who perpetrated not only the fraud on the unsuspecting chemist, but had also practiced several frauds on tradesmen in her hometown of Leamington and elsewhere. On one occasion she took £4 worth of books on credit from a Leamington bookseller and then sold those books for cash before she left town. She had practiced other frauds as far away as Birmingham where she cheated a silversmith out of over £15 worth of goods. The searchers at the police station found several false letters and documents including more fake bank notes from *Blackwood's* on her after her arrest. Johnson reportedly also asked the arresting constable if he 'thought Mr. Senior would press the charge if she paid him the money.'[81] There was ample evidence that Mary Johnson practiced criminal fraud and forgery in a variety of places where she preyed upon retailers; however, in her criminal trial her counsel argued that Johnson's actions like Tyrwhitt's were those of a diseased mind.

This calculating, rational picture of Johnson changed dramatically as her trial progressed. Before she even went to trial at the Old Bailey, Senior attempted to drop the charges against her, asserting that he was convinced that the 'prisoner had been the victim of a cruel hoax . . . and that she was under the full impression at the time she uttered the forged notes that they bore the genuine signature of the Messrs. Blackwood.'[82] In the following Old Bailey trial her counsel, Bodkin and Ballantine, depicted Johnson as a delusional young woman who had suffered a mental breakdown since her father's death. Bodkin admitted the prisoner had forged the notes, but claimed she was not in a responsible state of mind at the time. She believed that her manuscripts had been accepted by *Blackwood's*, *Fraser's*, and other popular magazines and that these magazines owed her money. Even the prosecution opened their case by stating that it was obvious that Johnson was either insane or had been tricked by some designing persons into believing she was a paid

---

[80] *Times*, 19, 27 June; 14 July 1851.
[81] *Times*, 19 June 1851. See also *Times*, 27 June 1851.
[82] *Times*, 27 June 1851.

authoress. A clergyman and a surgeon named George Babbington both testified to her 'disordered mind.' No suggestion was made that she was responsible for her own actions. The jury found her *Not Guilty* on the ground of insanity.[83]

Johnson was not an isolated case of an insanity plea for a middle-class female fraud. Three years before the Johnson case, a Miss Villiers who also went by several other names including that of a married woman, Mrs. Gillard, cheated tradesmen in and around Gloucester of over £1,000 worth of goods. One of her ruses involved posing as a widow entitled to property near Ledbury. Despite evidence of a history of false names and swindles including one involving that middle-class musical instrument—a piano forte—in Bristol, Villiers was described as insane rather than criminal. Even those champions against fraud, the City of London Trade Protections Society agreed.[84] The idea that middle-class frauds, like middle-class shoplifters, suffered from some form of insanity rather than criminal intent seemed to be spreading. In another more egregious case of fraud in 1870, the lady-like Tyrwhitt and Johnson chose to plead insanity.

Emily MacGregor's Case, 1870

Like Johnson and Villiers, Emily MacGregor possessed middle-class status, but did not possess the cash flow equal to that status.[85] In the spring of 1870, under a variety of false names, Emily MacGregor obtained goods and money in some of the finest and most popular stores in London all on false pretenses and under false names. MacGregor's case is particularly interesting because of the kinds of stores she defrauded in London. Like the bazaar in Tyrwhitt's case, many were fashionable West End traders. Almost all were emporiums on the 'new plan.' Some became England's top department stores. In her fraudulent feast of consumption, MacGregor chose stores like Marshall and Snelgrove's Oxford Street store.[86] Founded in 1837 as a small drapery shop, Marshall and Snelgrove expanded throughout the century and became one of London's first successful department stores. In 1851 the year of the Great Exhibition, the emporium opened its large warehouse on Oxford Street.[87] In 1880, ten years after Mrs. MacGregor's trial, Anthony Trollope accused Marshall and Snelgrove's of being one of the worst

---

[83] CCCSP, Ninth Session, 1851, p. 402-404; *Times*, 14 June 1851.

[84] See 'A Lady Swindler,' *City of London Trade Protection Circular* (London) 26 August 1848.

[85] Although Tyrwhitt possessed a separate income it is probable that her often bankrupt husband interfered with that income and she appeared to live beyond the means of even the separate income supplied to her.

[86] 'The Charge of Fraud Against a Lady,' *The Draper* (London) 10 June 1870; 'Extraordinary Charges of Fraud Against a Lady,' *The Draper* (London) 27 May 1870; 'The Frauds Upon London Tradesmen,' *The Draper* (London) 15 July 1870.

[87] Adburgham, *Shops and Shopping*, 45, 240-242; John William Ferry, *A History of the Department Store* (New York: Macmillan, 1960), 249; Thelma H. Benjamin, *London Shops & Shopping* (London: Herbert Joseph Limited, 1934), 160.

contributors to the decline of the small shopkeeper.[88] Two of the other stores defrauded by MacGregor, Peter Robinson's in Oxford Street and Jay's General Mourning Warehouse in Regent Street were also founded in the expanding retail era of the 1830s-1840s. Jay's was arguably the largest warehouse in London specializing in the lucrative mourning drapery trade. Between 1854 and 1860 Robinson acquired a total of six adjacent shops on Oxford Street to add to his own.[89] In these progenitors of the department store, Mrs. MacGregor committed her frauds.

MacGregor had a similar method in all of the frauds she committed in the spring of 1870. In each case, she came into one of the massive London stores and gave a false name. With a false banknote she purchased an item of dress and usually also obtained money. In one case, she purchased the item on credit with a fake address and then cashed a check under the false name. In this way, MacGregor obtained goods and cash all over London. She managed to get a sealskin jacket from Hitchcock and Company of St. Paul's Churchyard and almost got away with a gray silk dress from Jay's. A clerk at Debenham and Freebody's finally alerted the authorities when he matched her description with the handbill description of her fraud from Lewis and Allenby, the same firm that prosecuted Tyrwhitt.[90] As in the case of Mary Johnson, the prosecution possessed a large body of evidence against MacGregor. They had witnesses, mainly shop assistants from the various stores; they also had the forged checks, and when MacGregor was arrested the searcher found a list of banks with some of the names marked off. The police also had evidence she committed other frauds in Brighton. MacGregor was wearing the fraudulently gained sealskin jacket when she was arrested.[91] According to the arresting officer, MacGregor had two reactions to her arrest. The first was similar to Johnson's. She said that her solicitors would pay all of the debts if the detective could get the shops to withdraw the charges. When he persisted in the arrest, MacGregor told him that she threw the money she obtained in Brighton out of the

[88] Anthony Trollope, *London Tradesmen* (London: Elkin Mathews & Marrot Ltd, 1927), 97. 'The eleven sketches which compose this volume appeared at intervals in the Pall Mall Gazette from July 10th to September 7th, 1880.'

[89] Adburgham, *Shops and Shopping*, 42, 69, 284-285; Benjamin, *London Shops & Shopping*, 159; Ferry, *History of the Department Store*, 243-244.

[90] 'The Charge of Fraud Against a Lady,' *The Draper* (London) 10 June 1870; 'Extraordinary Charges of Fraud Against a Lady,' *The Draper* (London) 27 May 1870; 'The Frauds Upon London Tradesmen,' *The Draper* (London) 15 July 1870. See also *Times*, 23 September 1870.

[91] 'The Charge of Fraud Against a Lady,' *The Draper* (London) 10 June 1870; 'Extraordinary Charges of Fraud Against a Lady,' *The Draper* (London) 27 May 1870; 'The Frauds Upon London Tradesmen,' *The Draper* (London) 15 July 1870). See also *Times*, 23 September 1870. According to Alison Adburgham the sealskin jacket, which came into fashion around 1865 and remained there until the end of the century was an important badge of middle-class or better status. See Adburgham, *Shops and Shopping*, 210.

window while traveling and asked the policeman 'if he did not think she was mad.'[92]

MacGregor's voyage from middle-class lady to criminal fraud began when she married Major MacGregor an officer in the Indian Army. In the 1860s he showed signs of lung disease and was declared an invalid by the Medical Board. He sold his commission and invested all of his money in the Agra Bank and Bank of London. A large part of this investment was lost in the financial crash of the mid-1860s. MacGregor then turned to farming in Surrey to support his family. However, he got involved in a lawsuit with the landlord, and had to move to a farm in Sussex. In 1869, Emily MacGregor gave birth to her fourth child. At the same time the family suffered a disappointment when their shares from the Bank of London showed little profit and they owed money for stocking the farm.[93] Emily MacGregor was respectably middle-class, but her status exceeded her financial means. Although middle-class women owned silk dresses and sealskin jackets, MacGregor could not have legally purchased these items in 1870.

During her final trial in Central Criminal Court, the Silk Mercer's Protection Society vigorously prosecuted her, but her counsel adhered to the plea of insanity. The Hon. A. Thesiger defended MacGregor, connecting her supposed insanity to a mental breakdown brought on by childbearing. He claimed members of her family on both the father and mother's side had been insane. Nine months after the birth of her last child her health was so poor that the family sent her to Cheltenham 'for change of air.' Her counsel also alluded to the 'insane' act of MacGregor throwing banknotes out the window after she had obtained them.[94] Mrs. MacGregor was not criminal, he argued, she was ill—mentally incapacitated. Despite this lengthy medical testimony detailing her 'insanity,' she was found guilty, but the judge sentenced her to only six-months imprisonment, a light sentence compared to other lower-class multiple fraud offenders and considering the calculated nature of her forgeries.[95]

---

[92] 'The Charge of Fraud Against a Lady, *The Draper* (London) 10 June 1870. See also *Times*, 23 September 1870.

[93] CCCSP, Ninth Session, 1870, p. 205; 'The Charge of Fraud Against a Lady,' *The Draper* (London) 10 June 1870; 'Extraordinary Charges of Fraud Against a Lady,' *The Draper* (London) 27 May 1870; 'The Frauds Upon London Tradesmen,' *The Draper* (London) 15 July 1870. For a more complete description of the causes of the Financial Crisis which began on Black Friday, May 11, 1866 see George Robb, *White-Collar Crime in Modern England: Financial Fraud and Business Morality*, 1845-1929 (Cambridge University Press, 1992), 71-72.

[94] 'The Charge of Fraud Against a Lady,' *The Draper* (London) 10 June 1870; 'Extraordinary Charges of Fraud Against a Lady,' *The Draper* (London) 27 May 1870; 'The Frauds Upon London Tradesmen,' *The Draper* (London) 15 July 1870. Note that the *Times* description of the trial, unlike *The Draper* stressed MacGregor's mental state giving only minimal details of her actual crimes. See *Times*, 23 September 1870.

[95] See *Times*, 23 September 1870.

Emily MacGregor's case illustrates not only the ease with which women and their legal counsel adapted the *mania* argument from shoplifting cases to fit cases of middle-class fraud, it also reveals something about the state of consumer culture in England. Living in serious financial straits on her farm in Sussex, MacGregor knew exactly where to shop in London. She knew the most fashionable and popular stores. Her frauds demonstrate a particular fondness for proto-department stores like Peter Robinson's, Jay's, and Marshall and Snelgrove's. Rather than simply getting away with the cash from her forged checks, MacGregor took and wore the sealskin jacket from Hitchcock's. Denied by her husband's illness and subsequent financial problems, MacGregor finally obtained the goods that normally went with the status of the middle-class woman. Many of these middle-class frauds, Tyrwhitt, Villiers and MacGregor took objects that denoted status like piano fortes, fashionable headgear, silk dresses, and fur jackets. In this way, such female frauds fought to maintain or better their status in the same way that working-class women used fraud to obtain status through similar goods.

'One Law for the Rich . . .': Status and the Role of Insanity in Fraud

Tyrwhitt's, Johnson's, and MacGregor's trials, however, show that the legal system treated middle-class women quite differently from working women, like servants, who committed similar frauds. Few of the middle-class women were sentenced to prison and except for the case of Mary Richardson none got a sentence including hard labor. For a working-class woman, hard labor and prison or even transportation was considered appropriate punishment. A working-class woman would also be forced to stand in the dock as all defendants were supposed to in English courts. Tyrwhitt, Johnson and MacGregor were all physically supported or allowed seats during their trials. All were described as ladies and sometimes as being 'highly connected.'[96] Along with these differences in treatment was the difference in the defense available to these women. Working-class women who committed frauds were criminals; women of the middle or higher classes who committed frauds were suffering under mental delusions.

Statistically fraud does not appear to present the same threat as simple theft and shoplifting in the nineteenth century. In the 1850s only about 4 per cent of women's offences determined on indictment were for fraudulently obtaining goods, and by 1870 the number had only risen to only 4.7 per cent.[97] However, evidence from sources like trade protection societies and newspaper reports indicates that the 'dark figure' was very high indeed in female retail fraud. The women that

---

[96] See 'The Charge of Fraud Against a Lady, *The Draper* (London) 10 June 1870; 'Extraordinary Charges of Fraud Against a Lady,' *The Draper* (London) 27 May 1870; 'The Frauds Upon London Tradesmen,' *The Draper* (London) 15 July 1870; *Times*, 19, 27 June; 14 July 1851; 15, 22, 29 December 1859; 31 January; 1 February 1860.

[97] Zedner, *Women, Crime, and Custody*, 312.

shopkeepers were able to successfully prosecute for retail fraud fit into the overall trends in punishment for women in England in the nineteenth century. Working-class women, especially the repeat offenders, suffered punishment more frequently than the middle-class women who were rarely punished and when convicted usually received lighter sentences like Tyrwhitt's nine months without hard labor. Early in the century, repeat offenders from the working classes found themselves sentenced to transportation for seven years; however, in 1852 when Van Dieman's Land refused to take any more prisoners, England was forced to build more jails to house female criminals. When caught and convicted, working-class female frauds, like female shoplifters, experienced the same shift in punishment from transportation to shorter prison sentences.[98]

The relatively light punishment for female frauds and the development of the insanity defense for crimes of fraud must have been yet another frustration for English shopkeepers struggling against rampant customer fraud in a century of expansion and consumption. Already handicapped by a law that often treated fraud as a debt transaction, they were further hampered by restrictions in the law of necessaries.[99] Cases prosecuted as criminal fraud were often lost when defendants claimed they intended to pay the debt. For shopkeepers to disprove a fraud's intent to pay was difficult if not impossible.[100] When the case involved a married woman, she could declare that she contracted the debt for necessaries and had no plan to defraud the shopkeeper. The same law that allowed women to contract for goods without their husband's signature often left shopkeepers unpaid. If the woman was separated from her husband, as in the Richardson case, or the court deemed the items unnecessary as in the case of the Edwards, the retailer might never see either money or goods again. Coverture did not stop women from buying or contracting debts at retailers; however, it could be used as a way to avoid paying those debts.[101]

Like shoplifting, female fraud was a financially damaging crime. The smaller the retailer, the more serious was the effect of fraud. The hundreds of pounds owed

---

[98] For a discussion of the typical female criminals transported to Australia, very poor repeat offenders and 'professional' criminals, and the crimes they committed see L.L. Robson, *The Convict Settlers of Australia: An Enquiry into the Origin and Character of the Convicts transported to New South Wales and Van Dieman's Land 1787-1852* (Melbourne: Melbourne University Press, 1965), 80-85, and tables 4(m) to 4 (o), pages 185-186. See also for the overall trends in female punishment Zedner, *Women, Crime and Custody.*

[99] Business owners did try to reform these laws with little success. See 'Criminal Law Consolidation Bill,' *City of London Trade Protection Circular* (London) 17 June 1848.

[100] Fraud is a crime particularly concerned with intent. Where there is no intent to defraud, there is no fraud. See Stephen, *A History of the English Criminal Law*, vol. 3, 124-128.

[101] I agree with Margot Finn's assessment that ignoring the other side of coverture 'is to ignore the strategies and devices that allowed both men and women to expand promote and even enjoy the commercialization of English society in the eighteenth and nineteenth centuries.' Margot Finn, 'Women, Consumption and Coverture in England, c. 1760-1860,' *The Historical Journal* vol. 39, 1996, 722.

by Edwards to her milliner is just one example. Almost all of these frauds, barring the direct forgeries, were made possible by the extension of credit to, or to their usually female employers. Shopkeepers did not always consider payment on next day delivery as credit; however, I define credit here similar to the way in which English courts defined it. Allowing customers to leave the shop with goods without payment for them was an extension of credit no matter how short the expected time of payment. For London dealers, especially with their constantly changing clientele, the basis for the decision to give credit rested heavily on the appearance of the woman requesting it.

The irony of retail fraud in the nineteenth century was that women used the appearance of wealth and respectability including dress, manners, and speech to attain objects denoting the very status to which they pretended to belong. Urban anonymity along with extremely close competition made the appearance of respectability particularly important to London retailers. Lower-class women used fraud to raise their status or obtain goods of middle-class status ranging from luxury food items like wine and sugar to Mary Ann Bell's £70 worth of dress goods from the fashionable Howell and James. In the case of Johnson and Wilson, the faux middle-class mistress and servant, they did not restrict themselves to one particular kind of commodity, but preyed upon a variety of tradespeople. False heiresses and women pretending to have separate incomes committed similar frauds. Both married and single middle-class women used fraud to maintain a status that was slipping, or perhaps to obtain more status. Tyrwhitt was a technically wealthy woman with aristocratic connections, but her husband's long history of debt suggests financial problems.[102] Mary Johnson was, like the shoplifter Lydia Dixon, a respectable spinster, but her father's death left her with little or no financial prospects. Emily MacGregor knew where to buy the most fashionable clothing for a woman of her status, but did not have the funds to obtain those goods. In the commission of fraud, women from a range of classes were aided by the growth in English consumer culture. The thin legal line between debt and fraud and the advantage of the law of necessaries for married women helped women both to contract debts and to commit retail frauds. Women of the middle-classes were further protected by the emergence of the insanity defense in fraud cases. Although the development of this fraud 'mania' protected some women from prison, it also symbolically deprived them of the power they were exercising daily in dealing with England's increasingly commercialized culture. By transforming the women's actions from rational, if illegal, approaches to the problems of material culture to the irrational acts of weak creatures, the medicalization of their crime denied the women the power that they exercised in consumer culture.

---

[102]See Chapter 5.

Chapter 7

Solving the Problem of the Criminal Consumer: Women and Kleptomania

> SMALLEY - 'Why, man, this is felony!'
> GENERAL - 'Not at all. Kleptomania, sir—kleptomania— . . . .' [1]
> —Mark Melford, 1888

A Shifting Strategy: The Acceptance of Kleptomania

The brain fever of the shoplifting Lydia Dixon's and Jane Tyrwhitt's claim of insanity in her trial for fraud hint at the evolution of a medical concept that alleviates the responsibility of the respectable, female criminal. When Jane Perrot faced a jury in Bath in 1800, her only option was to deny her crime and blame the shopkeeper; as the number of middle-class women committing retail crimes such as shoplifting and fraud increased, the issue of representation in the nineteenth century became more complicated. Woman's role as aggressive consumer already clashed with her home-centered image, and her role in retail crime complicated class division. In trials, canting ballads, and scathing articles, critics presented an image of the retail female criminal that was greedy, fraudulent, and middle-class. Women fought against this image by denying their crimes or by participating in the creation of the developing representation of criminal women as ill rather than greedy. Beginning earlier in the century as a more general mental malady, kleptomania as a diagnosis and as a popular concept of consumer crime developed slowly. Influenced by well-publicized cases of middle-class shoplifting, especially the case of Mary Ramsbotham in 1855, kleptomania, or thieving madness, developed as a defense long before the rise of the department store. Aided by the rise of the medical professional in court, the concept of kleptomania grew along with England's consumer culture in the nineteenth century and moved with English shoppers into the realm of the great department stores by the end of the century. Women once able to represent themselves lost that ability through their own participation in the developing kleptomania defense.[2]

---

[1] Mark Melford, 'Kleptomania: A Farcical Comedy in Three Acts,' (London: 1888), 24.

[2] See Patricia O'Brien, 'The Kleptomania Diagnosis: Bourgeois Women and Theft in Late Nineteenth-Century France,' *Journal of Social History* 17 (Fall 1983): 65-67. Elaine S. Abelson, 'The Invention of Kleptomania,' *Signs*, 15, no. 1 (1989): 123-143; Elaine S. Abelson, *When Ladies Go A-Thieving: Middle-Class Shoplifters in the Victorian Department Store* (New York: Oxford University Press, 1989). However, both O'Brien

Merchants, Customers and Shoplifting in the Second Half of the Century

The shoplifting problem haunting retailers of the first half of the nineteenth century remained and worsened in the second half of that century. After 1850, trade guides continued to warn of the necessity of constant vigilance against respectable shoplifters. *A Handy Guide for the Draper and Haberdasher* cautioned in 1864: 'Another disadvantage attendant on an overcrowded place of business is that articles are frequently stolen. It is not uncharitable to say that many who visit places of business will steal what attracts their attention if they think they shall not be detected . . ..'[3] Such respectable thefts, the author further commented, often 'counter-balance' an entire day's profits.[4]

In the 1870s, as the largest drapery and haberdasher shops were in the process of becoming grand department stores, shoplifting still threatened the profits of the retailer. Customers were taking full advantage of those more open display techniques ushered in by the era of plate-glass. J.W. Hayes, a haberdasher and draper for almost thirty years, counseled merchants: 'Never use stock for blocks in window dressing, not even a packet of reels; some hands are ever ready to take anything that may be in the way for this purpose . . ..'[5] Larger stores often had shopwalkers whose job was, among other duties, to keep an eye on shoplifting customers. Mr. Jones, a character in Trollope's *The Struggles of Brown, Jones, and Robinson*, described his job: "And though I looked so sweet on them,' said he, ' I always had my eye on them. It's a grand thing to be down on a well-dressed woman as she's hiding a roll of ribbon under her cloak."[6]

The problem of the shoplifting customer complicated not only the identification of customers, but those of thieves as well. Were repeat offenders who bought *and* stole items professional criminals or ethically deprived consumers? In 1859 the Association for the Prosecution of Shoplifters prosecuted Anne Turner and Charlotte Hobbs for theft from a draper in High Holborn. Turner and Hobbs entered the shop of Messrs. Howitt and Company to look at ribbons. While Turner picked out the ribbon she wanted, her friend concealed three pieces of other ribbon under her shawl. She was spotted by an assistant and tried at the Bow Street Police Court. In court, the prosecutor for the Association complained that 'Offences of

---

and Abelson argue that the kleptomania diagnosis was a late Victorian development that emerged to explain middle-class shoplifting in *fin de siècle* department stores.

[3] *A Handy Guide for the Draper and Haberdasher* (20 Paternoster Row, London: F. Pitman, 1864), 23.

[4] *Ibid.*

[5] J. W. Hayes, *Hints on Haberdashery & Drapery* (London: Clements and Newling, 1875), 13. Note: sold at The Draper's Stationery Warehouse, 96, Wood Street, Cheapside.

[6] Trollope, *The Struggles of Brown, Jones, and Robinson: By one of the Firm* (London: Smith, Elder & Co., 1870), 43.

this description were increasing to so serious an extent that the association felt it necessary to prosecute in every case.'[7] The magistrate agreed and sent the women to trial.[8] In court and in trade literature, traders decried the rising attacks on their goods.

As respectable customers and as not so respectable thieves posing as customers, English women continually acquired the goods of drapers, haberdashers, and other shop owners without payment. Shoplifting remained an attractive vocation especially for the single female criminal. One such example of career shoplifters is the case of Sarah Johnson and Jane Wise tried at the Middlesex Sessions in June of 1864. Entering the large drapery firm of Hayman and Youngman in Sloane Street, these women, both in their later twenties, purchased numerous smaller items as a pretense for their theft of 120 yards of silk, which they hid beneath their cloaks. A shopman spotted Johnson taking the valuable silk, £18 worth, and had them arrested. With previous convictions under other aliases proved against them in court, the judge sentenced both of them to four years penal servitude.[9] Captured after a shoplifting spree in Walworth Road in 1865, another team of women, Elizabeth Cooper and Eliza Travers, managed to hide numerous articles including six gown pieces under their crinolines. A search of their lodgings revealed a large number of pawn tickets gained from other stolen items.[10] For the career shoplifter, little had changed since the earlier part of the century. Taking advantage of the anonymity of London, they posed as shoppers and turned their stolen goods into cash. Pawn tickets, evidence of other stolen merchandise, and past convictions earmarked a confirmed career criminal, but often the line between thief and customer was more blurred.

For both the career shoplifter and the shoplifting customer, drapers and other clothing retailers remained favored targets. In 1866, Sarah Reeves pleaded guilty to shoplifting in the still prestigious shop of Shoolbred's, which opened its doors in 1814.

---

[7] *Times*, 28 November 1859. The founding date of this organization is unknown, however, it appears to be similar in operation to the many other urban, trade protection societies in the nineteenth century that replaced the older associations for the protection of property in the eighteenth.

[8] *Times*, 28 November 1859. It is very likely that Turner and Hobbs were repeat offenders and probably not the middle-class shoppers they pretended to be, because they pleaded guilty and requested that the magistrate deal with their case summarily. As this *Times* article states, 'Though there was no evidence of a previous conviction, it did not at all follow that the present was their first offence. It frequently happened that old offenders, being brought to a police-court where they did not happen to be known, were dealt with summarily, whereas if they had been sent to the sessions evidence of former convictions might have been produced at trial.' *Ibid.*

[9] GLRO, MJ/SR 5194, Middlesex Quarter Sessions of the Peace. Indictment of Sarah Johnson and Jane Wise,' Middlesex Sessions Papers' 6 June 1864; *Times*, 9 June 1864; *Times*, 11 June 1864. For a similar example of a team of shoplifting women see the case of Mary Ann Kelly and Hannah Rose prosecuted in the Guildhall Police Court in 1860. *Times*, 23 May 1860.

[10] *Times*, 16 October 1865.

Reeves, a 36 year-old woman, who stole 23 silk handkerchiefs valued at £8 at Shoolbred's, had already spent a year in prison in 1859 for another shoplifting offense. As a repeat offender, the judge sentenced her to 15 months for the Shoolbred robbery.[11] Another venerable drapery firm that began in the early nineteenth century, that of Thomas Olney, prosecuted a team of shoplifting women in 1859. Annie Robinson, 30, and Jane Robinson, 18, managed to take a piece of silk valued at over £2 while the shop assistant's back was turned. When charged with the crime, Annie Robinson claimed that she had mistakenly put it in her bag instead of her pocket-handkerchief. The shopkeepers did not believe this explanation of absent-mindedness and sent the women to the police court.[12] For the female shoplifter, drapery firms remained favorite haunts in the later part of the century. Women continued to steal items like lace and ribbon which were expensive and easily purloined, and the bolder shoplifters, including some career offenders, favored the expensive silks, which could be quickly and profitably liquidated.

Sentencing Shoplifters after 1850

No longer faced with hanging or transportation for their offenses, shoplifters often saw sentences of less than a year for first offenses. In 1859, Marylebone Police Court sentenced Mary Bedwell to only three months imprisonment for stealing a jacket, scarves, and other items from a draper in Kentish-town.[13] Like Sarah Johnson and Jane Wise, the Hayman and Youngman shoplifters, Caroline Harris was also sentenced to four years imprisonment in 1860. Even she was surprised by this relatively light sentence and told the judge, 'That's only half of what I expected, so I am glad.'[14] Despite traders' complaints of being ravaged by the pilferings of shoplifters, sentencing became less harsh. In the early nineteenth century and until transportation to Australia was halted in 1852, many of the women transported were repeat offending petty thieves like shoplifters. One of the largest specific categories of theft for which women were transported was 'theft of wearing apparel.'[15] However, with only prisons available as punishment, such petty offenders faced sentences of just a few months to a few years in English prisons depending on their past offences. In the later half of the century women's imprisonment steadily declined overall in the English population despite continued

---

[11] *Times*, 16 May 1866.

[12] *Times*, 29 July 1859. Olney opened his shop in 1809.

[13] *Times*, 22 December 1859.

[14] *Times*, 11 January 1860.

[15] See L.L. Robson, *The Convict Settlers of Australia: An Enquiry into the Original and Character of the Convicts Transported to New South Wales and Van Dieman's Land 1787-1852* (Melbourne University Press, 1965), 80-81, 187. Interestingly, the 1840s witnessed the highest number of women transported for theft of wearing apparel. See *Ibid.*, 203; Lucia Zedner, *Women, Crime, and Custody in Victorian England* (Oxford: Clarendon Press, 1991), 174-177.

complaints about shoplifting by traders and the efforts of trade protections society.[16]

Although sentencing became lighter over the course of the nineteenth century, from the 1850s until the 1870s the character of shoplifting in England remained much the same. As drapery shops became emporiums and emporiums became department stores, English shoplifters followed English shoppers into the new arenas of consumption. Shoplifters still favored easily purloined but expensive items like lace and ribbons. Career shoplifters especially targeted such cashable items such as silks and ready-made clothing. Despite the continued complaints of store owners and their representatives who protested the rising incidences of casual shoplifting, most convicted shoplifters were old offenders and not light-fingered customers. Numerous well-publicized cases of respectable female shoplifting, however, required a new solution to this apparently rising tide of middle-class crime.

Shoplifters and the Early Medical Definition of Kleptomania, 1800-1850

Kleptomaniacs were criminals before they were patients. Kleptomania is therefore a disease particularly bound to the process of justice. Without doctors there would have been no kleptomania, but without female shoplifters there would have been much fewer kleptomaniacs. Before the acceptance of kleptomania, in a clear case of shoplifting which involved a respectable woman the jury had little choice but to ignore the evidence and acquit, or to incarcerate a respectable citizen—possibly a wife and mother. Very few if any respectable women suffered penalties for their crimes. In 1844 Jane Tyrwhitt walked away from her shoplifting charge with a not guilty verdict. However, the persistence of lady shoplifters made the continuation of such dismissals difficult.[17] The persistence of well-proven cases of middle and upper class female shoplifters also made the ruse of blaming the 'cheap shopkeeper' such as the early case of Jane Leigh Perrot[18] an unlikely option.

The increasing focus on female shoplifters in the nineteenth century led to the articulation of the 'kleptomania diagnosis'. The 'mad or bad' debate is an old one in criminology and insanity was linked to crime before the nineteenth century; the specific concept of 'kleptomania,' however, is a nineteenth-century development. The first to use it was a Swiss doctor, André Matthey, who in 1816 called it 'klopemanie' and described it as the impulsive 'monomaniacal' theft of an object not necessarily of great value.[19] During the same era that Matthey worked on his

---

[16] For the declining numbers of women sentenced to English prisons see Zedner, *Women, Crime, and Custody*, 213-213.

[17] See Chapter 5.

[18] See Chapter 5 and Introduction.

[19] O'Brien, 'Kleptomania Diagnosis,' 70. See also Ellis, *Studies in the Psychology of Sex*, 477-478; Miller, *Bon Marché*, 197-200.

theories, English medical doctors began to appear as expert witnesses in trials, and England entered onto the long path of medicalizing criminology. The increasing use of defense counsel at trials in the nineteenth-century especially encouraged a rising medical presence in court and the fortunes of the kleptomania diagnosis improved over the course of the century.[20]

In his 1839 *Treatise on the Medical Jurisprudence of Insanity*, Isaac Ray complained that England lagged behind other Western countries in medical jurisprudence.[21] Ray connected kleptomania, 'an irresistible propensity to steal,' to idiocy and possibly 'abnormal confrontations of the head,' and said that it often accompanied a more serious general mania. According to Ray, kleptomania might even be caused by a severe head injury. He cited the case of a French soldier injured in the Napoleonic wars.[22] For Ray kleptomania was not a particularly gendered ailment—both sexes were susceptible, but in men the causes were traumatic; whereas for women they could be part of natural physiology.[23]

Although the gendered aspect of certain designations of madness predate the modern period,[24] in the later eighteenth and nineteenth centuries, that gendered aspect increasingly focused on physiology. Doctors and alienists linked female insanity to their biology. Alexander Sutherland, Physician at St. Luke's Hospital, in 1855 detailed the cases of several women he treated whose 'hysterical' and 'puerperal' manias were caused by incidents related to childbirth.[25] As early as 1839, Ray cited a French doctor who gave a number of cases of women who, "when pregnant, were violently impelled to steal, though perfectly upright at other times."[26] There are also hints of the class element in the kleptomania diagnosis in Ray's early work. He claimed that cases of people in 'easy circumstances' who were driven by an impulse to steal was so common 'that they must have come

---

[20] Roger Smith, *Trial By Medicine: Insanity and Responsibility in Victorian Trials* (Edinburgh, Scotland: Edinburgh University Press, 1981), 8. See also Joel Eigen, *Witnessing Insanity: Madness and Mad-Doctors in the English Court* (New Haven: Yale University Press, 1995) tracing the growing importance of physicians and mad doctors in English court cases—especially murder cases. See also physician John Haslam's 1817 treatise *Medical Jurisprudence As It Relates to Insanity, According to the Law of England*.

[21] Isaac Ray, M.D., *A Treatise on the Medical Jurisprudence of Insanity* (London: G. Henderson, 1839), v-x.

[22] *Ibid.*, 171-173.

[23] *Ibid.*, 174.

[24] See Roy Porter, *A Social History of Madness: Stories of the Insane* (London: Weidenfeld and Nicolson, 1987), 103-124.

[25] Alexander John Sutherland, M.D., F.R.S. 'Pathology of Mania and Dementia,' *Medico-Chirurgical Transactions*, 38 (1855): 261-288. See also Elaine Showalter, 'Victorian Women and Insanity,' *Victorian Studies*, 23, no. 2 (winter 1980): 157-181 where she traces the development Victotrian psychiatry, and its tragic effects for the women treated.

[26] Ray, *A Treatise on the Medical Jurisprudence of Insanity* (London: G. Henderson, 1839), 174.

within the personal knowledge of every reader who has seen much of the world . . ..'[27] Despite further development mainly by French doctors, kleptomania remained largely unaccepted by those outside the medical community until the later nineteenth century, when it skyrocketed to acceptance in a blast of medico-legalization that affected other areas of criminal psychology as well. Not until the 1880s was kleptomania a well-accepted term that found its way into frequent popular usage.[28]

Although technically a genderless ailment, kleptomania became a particularly female malady as the nineteenth century progressed and was attached to other female manias like hysteria. Physiological fluctuations and maladies in women were linked to the impulse to steal. Similar to the medico-legalization of other behaviors like drunkenness, the crime of shoplifting was associated with this new disease, yet another example of women's mental and physiological weakness.[29] Kleptomania was also considered to be a 'disease' afflicting one particular class in the nineteenth century. It provided at long last a plausible explanation for why otherwise respectable women steal.[30]

By mid-century, the British medical community was already developing its own version of Lydia Dixon's diagnosis of 'brain fever.' James Duncan's *Popular Errors on the Subject of Insanity* 1853, he describes in detail a stealing or 'cleptomania;' differing from a more criminal action in 'that it is not prompted by the wants of the individual, neither is it practised with any view to the subsequent use in any way of the article that has been stolen . . ..'[31] Duncan further describes how such 'lunatic's hoard up their goods with no view to their utility. Perhaps like Dixon's stash of—

Cards of lace and fringe, rolls of silk, satin and satinets, poplins, mousselines de laine, cashmere and cottons for dresses, black satin shawls, woollen plaid, cashmere,

---

[27] *Ibid.*, 171.

[28] O'Brien, 'Kleptomania Diagnosis,' 66-72; Abelson, *Ladies Go A-Thieving*, 173-196 and Ellis, *Studies in the Psychology of Sex*, 477-482.

[29] Ellis, *Studies in the Psychology of Sex*, 486; O'Brien, 'Kleptomania Diagnosis,' 69-71; Abelson, *Ladies Go A-Thieving*, 174-183. Although William Stekel's 'cleptomania' case study in his 1924 book, *Peculiarities of Behavior*, is male, the stereotype of the cleptomaniac was still the female patient as is demonstrated by his earlier work on the 'Sexual Root of Kleptomania' published in 1911 which refers to a female patient. See also Carroll Smith-Rosenberg, 'The Hysterical Woman: Sex Roles and Role Conflict in Nineteenth-Century America.' *Disorderly Conduct: Visions of Gender in Victorian America* (New York: Oxford University Press, 1985), 197-216 for the nineteenth-century treatment of female 'hysteria' and other physiological 'manias.'

[30] Both Patricia O'Brien and Elaine Abelson note the intimate connection between class and the kleptomania diagnosis. O'Brien, 'Kleptomania Diagnosis,' 67; Abelson, *Ladies Go A-Thieving*, 174.

[31] James F. Duncan, A.M., M.D., *Popular Errors on the Subject of Insanity* (Dublin: James McGlashan, 1853), 138.

Paisley, boas, victorines, and muffs, 50 rolls of valuable ribbons, bonnets, gloves, stockings, 30 pairs of women's boots and shoes . . . .[32]

Duncan then began the familiar refrain about respectable thievery being well-known to shopkeepers who understand this 'illness' of their customers.[33] He claimed that shopkeepers often forwarded the bill for items taken by these wealthier shoplifts and that the shoplifts quietly paid for them.[34] However, Duncan did not support cleptomania as a mitigating circumstance in the commission of every case of shoplifting. He warned that only 'a careful investigation into the offender's past history and into his conduct at the time of committing the act' could delineate between simple theft and mania, and noted that many only pretended to have this mania. For him the proper place for the true cleptomaniac was the asylum and not the prison cell.[35]

A diagnosis that began as a sort of vague irresistible impulse to steal, by mid-century reached a more precise definition. This kleptomaniacal impulse did not seem to affect women or men of the working classes. The items stolen had to be unneeded, and the thief had to be in comfortable circumstances. Once gained, these items were hoarded up by the person afflicted without being sold for cash. Unlike Ray and earlier commentators on kleptomania, all of Duncan's 1853 examples were women.

Mad Doctors and the Early Gendering of Thieving Mania, 1800-1850s

Instead of building large, comfortable prisons for middle-class shoplifters, English society found an answer in developing mental science. In the nineteenth century there was a shift in the views on insanity that made it a particularly feminized malady.[36]

In the kleptomania diagnosis the feminization of madness and the problem of shoplifting women converged. Along with the many developing female manias in medical science, the use of medical diagnoses to lessen the responsibility of female criminals emerged in English courts. During the Victorian era, infanticidal women were increasingly seen as temporarily insane—puerperal maniacs.[37] Medical texts also illustrate the interplay between current medical theory and popular knowledge

---

[32] *Times*, 16 April 1849.

[33] See Ray, *A Treatise on the Medical Jurisprudence of Insanity*.

[34] Here he cites the case of an anonymous woman who always stole some of the ribbons taken to her carriage by shopkeepers for her inspection. Shopkeepers knew her tendency and always kept a close count of the items sent out to her. *Ibid.*, 138.

[35] He agreed with the judge in the 1853 case of such a maniacal lady who was sent to the asylum instead of given a prison sentence. *Ibid.*, 139.

[36] See Showalter, 'Victorian Women and Insanity,' 157-181.

[37] See Smith, *Trial By Medicine*, 143-160. See also Zedner who traces the development of 'feeble-mindedness' as a diagnosis for female criminality in the later Victorian era. Zedner, *Women, Crime, and Custody*, 264-296.

of shoplifting cases. Isaac Ray's 1839 treatise on insanity mentioned the French doctor Gall's theory of the connection between thieving mania and pregnant women.[38] In 1853, Dr. James F. Duncan published his views on kleptomania. Duncan used references to popular culture and a real case in Dublin to illustrate the difference between kleptomanical thievery—taking items without any regard to their utility or value—and the common thief who takes only what is most useful and profitable. Duncan told the story of 'the wealthy kleptomaniac.' This description of the wealthy man or woman who steals impulsively and is so well known to area businesses that they presented the person's family with a bill for the stolen goods recurs so frequently in writings on kleptomania that it takes on the qualities of an urban legend. According to the story, the family gladly pays the bill to hush up their relative's affliction. Duncan gave this urban legend as an example of a psychological case.[39] After his discussion of this story, Duncan alluded to a Dublin case in March of 1853 in the Recorder's Court where a shoplifting lady was 'sentenced' to an asylum. Duncan's work demonstrates the connection between the new mental science and the problems of consumer culture. Duncan's 1850s work specifically mentions the shoplifting lady as the type most likely to be susceptible to kleptomania.[40]

The Ramsbotham Case and the Acceptance of the Kleptomania Defense

A turning point in the cases of middle-class shoplifts in England came in early 1855. Mary Ramsbotham, the shoplifting wife of a famous and wealthy physician, inspired legal debate and even her own canting ballads. A frequent customer in the shop of Mr. John Moule, a draper at no. 54 Baker Street, Mrs. Ramsbotham came again to the shop on March 28, 1855 to buy some lining fabric. She purchased six yards of the fabric and had Mr. Moule credit it to her bill. After the purchase of the fabric, the shop assistants continued to show her gloves, handkerchiefs and other accessories. She declined the purchase of these, but when the shopman serving her went to the other end of the shop, another assistant observed her slip four handkerchiefs into her pocket. One of the shopmen, Samuel Welch, followed her to the stationer's shop next door and forced her to return with him. The police were called after a search revealed the handkerchiefs.[41] This simple case of shoplifting with a reliable witness in a respectable establishment soon initiated a wider debate over class, sanity, and the unfeeling nature of commercial capitalism.

---

[38] Ray, *A Treatise on the Medical Jurisprudence of Insanity*, 174.

[39] James F. Duncan, A.M., M.D., *Popular Errors on the Subject of Insanity* (Dublin: 1853), 138-139. For recent urban legends see Jan Harold Brunvard, *The Baby Train and Other Lusty Urban Legends* (New York: W.W. Norton and Company, 1993). Like Brunvard's urban legends this shoplifting story appears again and again usually with a wealthy lady as the protagonist, but names are never given.

[40] See Duncan, *Popular Errors on the Subject of Insanity*, f.n. page 139.

[41] *Times*, 28 March 1855, 3 April 1855, 12 April 1855.

Soon after the arrest, Moule, a draper for twenty years whose business supported at least six shop assistants, found himself the target of criticism for his accusations against Ramsbotham. Living in the fashionable Portman Square with her professional husband, Mrs. Ramsbotham was a respected lady. Like Lydia Dixon who claimed she was merely going to ask the price of her 65 yards of material, Ramsbotham at first asserted she took the handkerchiefs to ask her sister's opinion of them. However, soon she confessed not only to stealing the handkerchiefs, but to taking some frilled sleeves from Moule's earlier in the month of March. This earlier theft was the reason Moule had the shopmen watching Ramsbotham on March 28th.[42] Yet Moule received heavy criticism for not doing as she had repeatedly asked and to 'look over this, and send for Dr. Ramsbotham.'[43] During the trial her lawyer, Mr. Ballantine accused Moule of laying a trap for Mrs. Ramsbotham, and repeatedly questioned why the shopmen continued to tempt her to purchase goods after her wants had already been served— a common practice in retail.[44] After accusing Moule of un-Christian conduct, Ballantine said: 'When the affair of the sleeves took place he should have warned Dr. Ramsbotham . . .and then told him to take care of her. . . . Did he not know that many ladies had had a mania of this kind?'[45] Painted by Ballantine, Mr. Moule and his shopmen became greedy trappers of the unsuspecting female, shopkeepers whose concern for their goods outweighed their care for a delicate woman with mentally ill tendencies.

Likewise, the judges in the case, Mr. Broughton of the Marylebone police court and Mr. Serjeant Adams in the Middlesex Sessions, received censure for failing to treat the case with the proper delicacy. Broughton demanded £2,000 of bail to release Mrs. Ramsbotham from jail. Critics sent Broughton threatening letters that read: 'I have read with feelings of the greatest disgust the report in the papers. A police-court was never meant for the purpose of receiving evidence against respectable people.' The writer of this letter also stated that he was close to Lord Palmerston and would make Broughton suffer for sending Ramsbotham to trial. Similar letters were addressed to Mr. Moule. Broughton was also criticized for trying to force Ramsbotham to lift up her face-obscuring veil.[46] Broughton defended his actions by emphasizing the equal treatment promised by English law: 'that day he had sent two women for trial who were charged under nearly similar circumstances, and if he were to discharge Mrs. Ramsbotham, ought he not in common justice, to call them back from the cell and at once liberate them? . . ..'[47] Few commentators in the Times seemed to agree with Broughton's view of equal justice.

---

[42] *Times*, 28 March 1855-12 April 1855.

[43] *Times*, 28 March 1855.

[44] *Times*, 3 April 1855 and 12 April 1855.

[45] *Times*, 12 April 1855.

[46] Once again like other middle-class shoplifters. See *Times*, 3 April 1855.

[47] *Times*, 3 April 1855.

Figure 7.1 'Ladies Don't Go Thieving' (ballad), Mullins, Red Cross Street Printer. Bodleian Library, University of Oxford: John Johnson Collection; Johnson Ballads 1308. This ballad directly refers to the Ramsbotham case.

According to her lawyer and supporters, Mrs. Ramsbotham's was a case of the stealing mania. She was a woman with a delicate mind forced into a horrifying situation. The *Times'* defense of Ramsbotham in a leading article seems lifted from the pages of works on insanity like those of Duncan and Ray:

> The fact is notorious that many persons of high rank and ample means have been affected with this strange disorder. Every one who is acquainted with London society could at once furnish a dozen names of ladies who have been notorious for abstracting articles of trifling value from the shops . . . on their return from their drives their relatives took care to ascertain the nature of their paltry peculations, inquired from the coachman the houses at which he had been ordered to stop, and, as a matter of course, reimbursed the tradesmen to the full value of the pilfered goods.[48]

The writer further argued that Ramsbotham and others so afflicted are 'under the dominion of a blind impulse as the raven which pilfers a glass bead or a silver thimble . . . and hurries off with its useless trophy . . .'[49] One might argue, however, that frilled sleeves and cambric handkerchiefs were more useful to a Victorian lady than sewing implements to a raven. It appears that Ballantine had also been keeping up with his *Times*.

Ballantine also drew on medical writers for Ramsbotham's defense. His client was about 50 years of age, and he theorized that her mania had biological connections.[50] Ballantine stated the well-known fact that medical experts had connected pregnancy with 'morbid delusions' and women who committed crimes while pregnant had been declared not legally responsible for their actions. Although his client was a woman 'advanced in life,' he alluded to the fact that she was menopausal, experiencing a 'constitutional change.' In Mrs. Ramsbotham and other women this caused 'a morbid affection of the brain,' an affliction that caused her to steal. His arguments must have been somewhat convincing to the jury who after two hours could not come to agreement over Ramsbotham's case. The jury split six versus six, and the judge allowed them to be discharged without giving a verdict. Ramsbotham was sent home, not quite declared innocent, but free nonetheless.[51]

Critics of the Case: A Biased Justice System

The class bias in this newest development in the diagnosis of a stealing monomania—still not referred to by either the *Time*s or her lawyer as 'cleptomania'—did not go unnoticed by the public. The Ramsbotham case inspired two versions of a popular street ballad. The titles are 'Ladies Don't Go Thieving'

---

[48] *Times*, 6 April 1855.
[49] *Times*, 6 April 1855.
[50] *Times*, 3 April 1855; See also Ray.
[51] *Times*, 12 April 1855.

and 'Rich and Poor Law' and there are only tiny differences in the lyrics.[52] These ballads were already being circulated before the April 12th Middlesex Sessions trial.[53] Described as 'A Doctor's lady gay,' Ramsbotham's veiled countenance was compared to that of her poorer counterparts:

> If a woman very poor,
>   who never had a veil, sirs
> Only stole a skein of thread,
>   They'd send her off to jail sirs;
> Convicted they would be,
>   Because they had got no money.
> Six-months they'd have to serve—
>   Now is not that very funny?[54]

In the version of the ballad titled 'Rich and Poor Law' the last lines are replaced with 'Six-months they'd have to serve—And play amongst the oakum.'[55] Unlike the women imprisoned for stealing a skein of thread, genteel thieves like Mary Ramsbotham did not suffer legal consequences for their actions.

Another group disturbed by the Ramsbotham verdict was middle-class shopkeepers. In direct response to the debate surrounding the Ramsbotham trial, John Brown, a shopkeeper for thirty-five years, wrote an article entitled *Tait's Edinburgh Magazine* 'On Genteel Thieves.' He referred to 'that difficulty with which Mr. Moule has been lately hampered, and which he has managed so imprudently in the case of that virtuous Mrs. Ramsbotham who stole his pocket-handkerchiefs, and who wasn't and couldn't in the nature of the British Law and of a British jury, be punished for theft.'[56] Brown points out a very important reason why shopkeepers did not prosecute such respectable thieves. He did not believe in any stealing mania, but asserted that the social and financial repercussions of accusing genteel women of shoplifting were not worth the risk. He cited a case of personal experience in his early career where a young girl stole an article and he had her searched by his maid and then taken to the Bow Street station. The girl's father was a clergyman with good connections and forced Brown to withdraw the charge; 'That affair cost me fifty pounds in cash, and damaged my connection to

---

[52] A later version appears in England 1867. This version is cited by Elaine Abelson in her book on shoplifting in America and by Daniel Murphy. See Abelson, 2; See also Murphy 185 who cites this 1867 version. I want to thank Julie Anne Lambert of the John Johnson Collection, Oxford for helping me find these ballads.

[53] See *Times*, 12 April 1855.

[54] See Fig. 7.1 'Ladies Don't Go Thieving!,'[dated from ref. at 1855], 'Street Ballads,' Box 9, John Johnson Collection, Bodleian, Oxford. See also 'Rich & Poor Law,' 'Street Ballads,' Box 9, John Johnson Collection, Bodleian, Oxford.

[55] 'Rich & Poor Law,' 'Street Ballads,' John Johnson Collection.

[56] John Brown, 'On Genteel Thieves' *Tait's Edinburgh Magazine*, 26 o.s., 22 n.s. (1855): 289.

the extent of at least two hundred pounds more . . ..'[57] Later, Brown tried the method of including the stolen article in the bill along with legitimate ones with varying rates of success.[58] More successfully, he found that accusing a lady of absent-mindedness sometimes worked well. He used this method on Lady S____, the wife of a Baronet who attempted to steal an expensive article. However, most frequently he simply allowed shoplifting ladies 'to walk clear off with the plunder, to save the bother and expense of a disturbance.'[59] Brown concluded by saying that, although he often let ladies walk away free, he continued to turn in poorer thieves to the police, because he sarcastically noted, 'treadmills and hulks . . .were not made for ladies and gentlefolks, though they should happen to be thieves; that's a kind of treatment that don't suit their nerves at all, and is only meant for poor people, who have no nerves, and can't by any means be the subjects of 'morbid hallucinations' and 'constitutional changes' . . ..'[60]

Ramsbotham's Case in Medical Literature

The fourth edition of Ray's *A Treatise on the Medical Jurisprudence of Insanity* published in 1860 contained more references to women and shoplifting. Added to the text of the earlier 1839 edition are direct references to the Mary Ramsbotham case in 1855. In this 1860 edition, Ray quoted the *Times* editorial prompted by the Ramsbotham case. This editorial, which was itself a reflection of popular concepts of shoplifting mania and current medical theory, found its way into medical text: "Every one who is acquainted with London society could at once furnish a dozen names of ladies who have been notorious for abstracting articles of trifling value from the shops where they habitually dealt . . .."[61] In quoting this editorial, Ray, like Duncan, also included the now well-known story of how the families of wealthy kleptomaniacs secretly paid their bills.[62] A year after Ray published this edition, a story appeared in *The Lancet* claiming that 'it is known to those who have the best means of obtaining information, that this itch for appropriation exists . . . even amongst what is known as good society.' *The Lancet* article further suggested that shopkeepers had to appoint special staff members just to watch these customers '. . . to gently suggest that the Comtesse de l'Arceny must really restore that bracelet which accidentally got into her ladyship's muff, or to inquire whether

---

[57] *Ibid.*, 290.

[58] One woman pointed out his 'mistake' and refused to pay. Another lady sent someone to settle the account and never returned to his store. See Brown, 'On Genteel Thieves,' 289-93.

[59] *Ibid.*, 290.

[60] *Ibid.*, 292.

[61] Isaac Ray, M.D., *A Treatise on the Medical Jurisprudence of Insanity* (Boston: 1860), Fourth edition, 204-205. An article appearing two years later also uses this well-worn quote from the *Times* editorial. J. C. B. [Bucknill], 'Kleptomania,' *The Journal of Mental Science* 7, no. 42 (July 1862): 266.

[62] Ray, *A Treatise on the Medical Jurisprudence of Insanity*, Fourth edition, 204-209.

the bill shall be sent in for that bit of old lace slipped into her pocket in a fit of abstraction.'[63]

Gendering Kleptomania, 1850-1890

The evolution of kleptomania from its earlier form as a symptom of general mental illness to an irresistible impulse to steal in an otherwise law-abiding person followed the nineteenth-century medical trend of wider interpretations and degrees of madness.[64] However, the emergence of the kleptomaniac as particularly female malady relating to consumer crime developed due to the rising problem of consumer crime and in conjunction with actual cases. Even non-gendered descriptions of kleptomania contain hints that it was a condition associated with women. In an 1870s article on kleptomania, the writer gave a description of the disease where he compared sufferers to 'birds who steal bright, glittering objects of silver, gold, or polished stones; they are not appropriated for use, and they are generally secreted.'[65] This magpie-like description of the kleptomaniac seems to refer to the female perpetrator. Earlier cases from the nineteenth century also described how pregnancy was particularly associated with the disease. Pregnancy, the association between women, shopping, and a female predilection for luxury items all played a part in the development of the application of kleptomania in shoplifting cases in England.

Pregnancy and the Thieving Madness

Nineteenth-century 'Mad doctors' were concerned especially with the weaker female body as a source of madness. Dr. Alexander John Sutherland worked with female patients at St. Luke's hospital in London at mid-century. His case studies included a 22-year-old farmer's wife admitted in early 1851 with puerperal mania: 'She has been 'strange' ever since her confinement, and violent for the last three weeks.'[66] Another case of mania brought on by childbirth involved a 32-year-old clerk's wife identified as A.C. She was diagnosed as a puerperal maniac despite the

---

[63] 'Kleptomania,' *The Lancet*, II, 1994 (16 November 1861), 483. Although the legend of the wealthy shoplifter predated the Ramsbotham case, the *Times* editorial on that famous case became the template for almost all future discussions with quotes often taken verbatim from the editorial in medical texts.

[64] See Eigen, *Witnessing Insanity*, passim.

[65] 'Kleptomania,' *The Lancet*, I, 2795 (24 March 1877), 435. This animal-like fascination with shiny objects is also discussed in J.C.B. [Bucknill], 'Kleptomania,' 262-275. Mark Melford's 1888 play also compares a kleptomaniac to a magpie. Mark Melford, 'Kleptomania: A Farcical Comedy in Three Acts,' (London: 1888), 23.

[66] Puerperal mania was a madness that struck women immediatley or soon after childbirth.

fact that her youngest child was 14 months old.[67] The insanity of these women, according to him, stemmed from their female bodies—pregnancy, childbirth, and menopause.[68] Ten years after Sutherland published these case studies, Dr. W.H.O. Sankey, former Medical Superintendent of the Female Department of Hanwell Asylum, divided manias into categories like 'nymphomania,' 'hysteria,' and 'puerperal mania.' He linked 'Kleptomania,' which he described as a recently appearing variety of madness, to the early stages of more serious manias and mental diseases like 'general paralysis.'[69] According to the experts, women's biology made them more susceptible to these varieties of insanity.

The close association between pregnancy and kleptomania led to a successful acquittal in an 1851 case four years before the notorious Ramsbotham case focused attention on middle-class shoplifters. In November 1851 Esther Wyatt went to a colourman in Hoxton to request some 'blue.' A young boy assisting the colourman noticed Wyatt slipping two pieces of soap from a display into her pocket. When the boy told his employer, he sent for a policeman to arrest her. Despite begging to be set free, she was committed for trial to the Middlesex Sessions by the magistrate. Like the Ramsbotham defense, Wyatt's representatives did not specifically use the term kleptomania. Wyatt was the wife of a wealthy 'gentleman of high and indisputable respectability' and had no need to steal soap. Her representatives, including a doctor, argued that since the birth of her child in October she had suffered from hallucinations. Her representative argued that 'they should find that she was in so feeble yet so excitable state of mind, the result of extreme nervousness, . . . that she was not at the particular moment capable of controlling her actions.'[70] The judge agreed with Parry and in his summation reiterated Parry's statement that 'it was a well-known fact' that pregnant and recently pregnant women were susceptible to these impulses. The jury found Wyatt not guilty.[71]

Although finding acceptance by some medical men, judges, and juries, this thieving mania experienced by middle-class women did not always convince society at large that women suffered from this special form of mental illness. The Wyatt case elicited a letter of protest to the *Times* from a woman who experienced at least ten pregnancies without any uncontrollable impulses to shoplift. This Gloucester woman simply signed herself 'A Mother of Ten Children' and complained:

---

[67] Alexander John Sutherland, M.D., F.R.S., 'Pathology of Mania and Dementia,' *Medico-Chirurgical Transactions*, 38 (1855): 270-271.

[68] *Ibid.*, 261-288.

[69] General Paralysis was an extreme form of madness that ended in physical paralysis and death. W.H.O Sankey, MD, 'Illustrations of the Different Forms of Insanity,' *British Medical Journal* (11 February 1865), 136. Although Sankey does not designate kleptomania as a specifically female malady, by categorizing it with puerperal and 'nymphomanias' the inference is clear.

[70] *Times*, 18 December 1851.

[71] *Times*, 18 December 1851.

Sir,—As you are known to be what you profess to be—the impartial defender of all, rich and poor, you will, I feel sure, allow me, through the medium of your columns, to remind all married women of a newly discovered advantage to their estate. It appears that within a month or so before or after an event peculiarly expensive to their husbands they may make domiciliary visits to all the shops in their neighborhood for the sake of small plunder. Pieces of useful soap, cheese, small loaves, cakes, not to say articles of a more costly description, will all be 'put down' — the pockets in front, especially if deep, will do as well as muffs — to the score of their interesting situation, according to a late decision in the metropolis by medical authority, a judge learned in the law, and 12 honest jurymen.[72]

In this letter the writer criticized both the class bias in the decision, by implying that the stolen items were 'useful'—especially to a family that just had experienced a new addition—and also criticized the idea that pregnancy caused some special irrationality in women. Some medical practitioners shared the Gloucester letter writer's suspicion of this relatively new mental malady. In a discussion of a German case in which a pregnant woman was acquitted of a theft, Isaac Ray found a similar wry comment remarking that "if Eve had been in the condition of the accused, when she plucked the forbidden fruit from the tree, the curse of original sin would never have fallen on the race."[73] As Wyatt's 1851 and other cases demonstrate, early in the history of kleptomania as an illness, pregnancy was a major determining factor in its acceptance by judge and jury. In October of 1864, the *British Medical Journal* applauded a Circuit Court judge's decision to acquit a woman on the grounds of kleptomania caused by pregnancy. A married woman with no previous criminal record had stolen some baby clothes. Justice Barry acquitted her on her husband's recognizance.[74] Although no longer required to plead a thieving mania by the mid-1880s, pregnancy or womb-related illness remained influential in pleas of kleptomania in the later nineteenth century. An 1885 case in a London police court involved a shoplifting woman married to a merchant. The magistrate, Mr. D'Eyncourt, 'allowed the case to be withdrawn, remarking that had not the accused been so near her confinement he should certainly have sent the case for trial.'[75] In these cases the pregnancies and recent pregnancies convinced hesitant magistrates to accept the pleas. The kleptomania defense seemed most successful for respectable women who could prove a recent experience with pregnancy or childbirth.

---

[72] Letter to the editor, A Mother of Ten Children, Glocester [sic], December 18 1851, *Times*, 20 December 1851.

[73] Ray, *A Treatise on the Medical Jurisprudence of Insanity*, Fourth edition, 209. A later play about kleptomania in 1888 also makes comparisons between Eve and kleptomaniacs. See Melford, 'Kleptomania,' 23.

[74] 'Kleptomania,' *British Medical Journal*, II (29 October 1864), 505.

[75] 'The Kleptomania of Pregnancy,' *The Lancet*, II, 3228 (11 July 1885), 81.

The Male Kleptomaniac: Resisting the Gendering of Kleptomania

Although the groundwork had been laid by the 1850s for the later stereotype of the wealthy, female kleptomaniac and medical literature had long associated pregnancy with impulses to steal, medical science and to some extent popular culture had not yet fully accepted the notion of the kleptomaniac as typically female. In Henry Allan's 1869 *Prize Essay on Kleptomania*, a political tract masked as a medical 'prize essay,' he defamed Lord Stanley, later Lord Derby, as an unstable kleptomaniac who was unfit to hold office. From fear of libel from Lord Stanley, the publisher soon removed this book from distribution after only a few copies were sold.[76]

As Allan's essay demonstrates, the original theories of thieving mania included men as well as women. Physicians like Henry Maudsley, one of the best known Victorian mad doctors and a professor of medical jurisprudence at the University College London,[77] continued to write about and describe the males who suffered from thieving mania. This less gendered concept of kleptomania linked it more closely with serious forms of insanity. In his 1874 general text *Responsibility in Mental Disease*, Maudsley described kleptomania as a type of 'moral imbecility' connected to idiocy whose sufferers were not responsible for their actions.[78] The next year Maudsley published an article in *The Lancet* detailing how a male kleptomaniac was wrongfully incarcerated. Maudsley described the kleptomaniac: 'A person whose character has been irreproachable in all the relations of life, and whom no one would ever have suspected of an inclination to break the eight commandment, . . . appropriates what strikes his fancy at the moment, and what he has, perhaps, no use for, and, when he has got it, makes no use of . . . .'[79] The kleptomaniac in this case was Henry James Price, a once successful draper whose business failed. According to Maudsley, Price then exhibited symptoms of a mania for stealing. He took a watch from a sleeping passenger on a train. After serving

---

[76] Henry Allan, *Prize Essay on Kleptomania, with a View to Determine Whether Kleptomaniacs Should be Held Disqualified for Employment of Trust and Authority Under the Crown* (219 Regent Street, London: 1869); Letter to the Editor, D. Wilson, M.D., Brooke Street April 17, 1869, *Times*, 20 April 1869.

[77] Martin Wiener, *Reconstructing the Criminal: Culture, law, and policy in England 1830-1914* (Cambridge University Press, 1990), 168. Not only did he publish many books and articles on madness, Henry Maudsley also treated patients like Louisa Lowe the spiritualist at his private asylum for genteel women at Hanwell. See Alex Owen, *The Darkened Room: Women, Power and Spiritualism in Late Victorian England* (University of Pennsylvania Press, 1990) 183-194.

[78] Henry Maudsley, M.D, *Responsibility in Mental Disease* (London: 1874), 82, 125-126.

[79] Henry Maudlsey, 'Stealing as a Symptom of General Paralysis,' *The Lancet* 2, no. 2724 (13 November 1875):   694. See also J.C.B., [Bucknill], 'Kleptomania,' 267, for a reference to connection between kleptomania and General Paralysis. John Charles Bucknill was editor of the *Journal of Mental Science*. See Showalter, 'Victorian Women and Insanity,' 164.

two months for this offence he again stole gold watches from sleeping fellow passengers and jumped the train after the robberies. While awaiting trial in Nottingham jail, Price showed signs of madness and was transferred to the county asylum. He died there of what Maudsley diagnosed as 'general paralysis' in 1875. In this case, argued Maudsley, kleptomania was only a symptom of a much more dangerous insanity—general paralysis—that caused physical debility and then death. Maudsley criticized the English justice system for their failure to recognize and treat Price's insanity rather than incarcerate him as a criminal.[80] Maudsley's 1870s version of kleptomania illustrates how the diagnosis was still influenced by earlier theories that linked kleptomania less with consumer crime and women and allied it more with general madness. A later writer in the *Lancet* in the 1880s would bemoan the fact that the disease had become so exclusively associated with pregnancy, complaining that men also suffered from kleptomania, but that their 'sex debars them from this explanation.'[81]

Kleptomania and English Justice in the Second Half of the Century

Resistance to the Defense in Court and Medical Journals

Another case, ten years after the pregnant shoplifter, Ester Wyatt's case, prompted an anti-kleptomania commentary in the *British Medical Journal*. This 1861 Middlesex Sessions case involved two young women from respectable families, Susan Long and Hannah Murray. Long and Murray were from such respectable families that their relatives were too ashamed to appear publicly in their defense. The young women had shoplifted books on at least three occasions. Judge Bodkin toyed with the idea of trying to get their relatives to send them to the colonies, but in the end sentenced them to nine months imprisonment with hard labor.[82] The response of the *British Medical Journal* to the judge's sentence was supportive: 'Mr. Bodkin, has refused to admit the existence of a malady which has, of late, been admitted into nosology to meet the exigencies of fashionable life—we mean the thieving trick; or, as it is called 'kleptomania.' Two ladies, convicted of this 'mania,' have been very properly sentenced by him to nine months hard labour.'[83] Less than one year later, John Charles Bucknill, editor of *The Journal of Mental Science* noted in a critical article that 'in the slang of the day a burglar has become a kleptomaniac, and a prison a kleptomaniac hospital.'[84] Although medical men criticized specific cases, after the 1860s, this sort of blanket condemnation of

---

[80] Maudlsey, 'Stealing as a Symptom of General Paralysis,' 694-695.

[81] 'Kleptomania,' *The Lancet* 3274 (29 May 1886) 81.

[82] *Times*, 7 November 1861.

[83] 'Kleptomania,' *British Medical Journal*, II, (9 November 1861), 510.

[84] J.C. B., [Bucknill], 'Kleptomania,' 262.

kleptomania faded from medical journals and a more positive view of the 'disease' emerged in the later part of the century.

A Madness of the Wealthy: Lower-Class Women and Kleptomania

Soon, even old offenders from the lower classes argued that that delusions caused by their pregnancy forced them to steal. In 1866, two women, dressmakers in their later twenties, Elizabeth Hart and Ellen Sweeney, appeared in Worship Street police court for shoplifting. Entering the large shop of a draper and furnisher in High Street, Shoreditch, the women bought fabric for bed ticking, as well as some smaller items. Each time the shop assistant left them to bring back items, he noticed parcels disappearing from his counter. The assistant quietly sent for a policeman to watch the women and they were arrested after leaving the store. The women's spree was aided by the then fashionable crinoline, the hoop skirt under which they concealed various parcels: 'The packages which were wrapped in paper, were more than two feet long and five inches thick, and contained 13 pairs of leno window curtains worth £6 pounds 18 s.'[85] Sweeny asked the proprietor, Mr. Jackson, if he would let them go if she paid for the goods, but Jackson refused saying he lost £20 worth of goods in the same week to shoplifters. This case appeared to be Hart's first offense, but at the police court several past convictions for Sweeney came to light. Under other aliases she had been sentenced at Norwich in October 1862 and the Surrey Session in 1856. Despite this long history of shoplifting, Sweeney's representative, Mr. Nash, argued that since Sweeney was pregnant at the time of the crime, she 'could not reasonably be held answerable for [her] actions.'[86] This kleptomania defense did not convince the magistrate and he sent both Sweeney and Hart to face trial by jury. The use of the defense in cases like Hart and Sweeney's led to some criticism and contributed to the opposition to the defense by the public and some English magistrates and judges. For example, in 1865 Isabella Freeman, a respectable, married woman who was also a past offender, attempted to plead kleptomania-like illness in Worship Street police court for shoplifting. However, the magistrate, Mr.Cooke, refused to dismiss her case and sent her to a jury trial.[87] By 1886 a writer in The *Lancet* grumbled that 'we should be glad to see reports of kleptomania among the poorer classes, who often inherit a strong tendency to thieving . . ..'[88] Medical opinion may have helped influence the development of the defense; however, it did not dictate specifically how it was used by the courts.

---

[85] *Times*, 27 August 1866.

[86] *Times*, 27 August 1866. See also the 1865 case of Isabella Freeman who was a respectable, married woman who also had committed a previous offense. *Times*, 1 March 1865.

[87] Freeman claimed not pregnancy as the cause of her shoplifting mania but that it was prompted by the influence of chloroform a medication for a disease she currently suffered. Her defense failed to convince the magistrate. See *Times*, 1 March 1865.

[88] 'Kleptomania,' *The Lancet* 3274 (29 May 1886) 81.

Doctors vs. Judges: The Success of Kleptomania in the Courts, 1850-1890

Throughout the debate over kleptomania and its many manifestations, doctors like Henry Maudsley continued to fight for the acceptance of the condition in the English justice system.[89] In the two decades after Mary Ramsbotham's trial, medical opinion increasingly accepted the kleptomania diagnosis. An unsigned 1877 article in *The Lancet* argued for greater recognition of the disease in court: 'The test of accountability in any particular case is not self-consciousness or a 'knowledge of right and wrong,' as the lawyers crudely put it, but the existence of such a state of mind as renders the judgement incapable of controlling the will.'[90]

Only sixteen years earlier the same journal, *The Lancet*, published an article stating 'if the desire were incontrollable and the dictates of reason disregarded, articles would be taken in full sight of the owners, and not, as is always the case, craftily purloined in the belief that the theft is unobserved.'[91] Essentially, the earlier 1860s writer declared that kleptomania as it was being used in English courts was not a mental deficiency at all, but a moral deficiency on the part of greedy, privileged wealthier offenders: '[T]he criminal laws under which the poor are rigorously punished are susceptible of remarkable elasticity when the peccadilloes of the rich are brought under judgement.'[92] This description of kleptomaniacs is reminiscent of mid-century descriptions of the avaricious, calculating, middle-class female shopper.

However, by the 1870s, *The Lancet* presented a different opinion of the diagnosis, and called for greater involvement of medical men. In this short space of years law's and medicine's view of kleptomania diverged. The 1870s writer wanted this 'medical question' decided by medical men appointed by the state for just such cases.[93] Although there were no official representatives to serve this function, various physicians did appear on behalf of defendants and influenced the outcome of cases. By the 1880s, nineteenth-century medicine accepted the idea of kleptomania as a mental illness, and supported the application of the diagnosis in court. This definition was no longer dependent on a more general, irrational

---

[89] See Maudsley, *Responsibility in Mental Disease*, 82, 125-126; Maudlsey, 'Stealing as a Symptom of General Paralysis,' 694-695.

[90] 'Kleptomania,' *The Lancet*, I, 2795 (24 March 1877), 435. See also Roger Smith, *Trial by Medicine: Insanity and Responsibility in Victorian Trials* (Edinburgh University Press, 1981. See also Joel Eigen, *Witnessing Insanity: Madness and Mad-Doctors in the English Court* (New Haven: Yale University Press, 1995), 73-74 for his explanation of the rise of the 'lesion of the will' concept in which defendants acted in a rational manner, but were unable to control their own will or impulse to commit the crime.

[91] 'Kleptomania,' *The Lancet*, II, 1994 (16 November 1861), 483.

[92] *Ibid*. The writer also criticizes the use of the term 'dipsomaniac' for the wealthier 'drunkard.'

[93] 'Kleptomania,' *The Lancet*, I, 2795 (24 March 1877), 435. See also 'The Plea of Kleptomania,' *The Lancet*, II, 3026 (27 August 1881), 390 for a similar plea for a greater role for specialists in the courtroom.

madness, but could be a very specific impulse affecting an otherwise rational person.

Gaining some acceptance, especially in cases of pregnant and recently pregnant women at mid-century and rising concurrently with the use of puerperal mania as an extenuating circumstance in infanticide cases,[94] in the 1870s kleptomania continued to appear in articles by specialists. In 1874, Maudsley chastised the backwardness of English judges for their failure to recognize insanity pleas as a valid reason for acquittal.[95] In 1875 the *British Medical Journal* commended the decision of a Manchester City Sessions judge and jury who on January 9, 1875, acquitted a woman of a shoplifting charge on the grounds of insanity. This middle-class lady stole luxury items like sweets and perfume at various shops in Manchester. Her defense linked this thieving mania to an attack of puerperal mania suffered *three years* before the offense. The writer, reminiscent of Maudsley's descriptions of kleptomania in the 1870s, also alluded that, in her case, the mania was a symptom of a more serious form of insanity like general paralysis.[96] By the 1870s, actual applications of the theory in court cases overtook the non-gendered, older medical explanations and replaced them with the popular version of the kleptomaniac as middle to upper class female shoplifting objects, possibly luxury items she did not need. Although the Manchester defendant declared womb-related illness, her child was three years' old when she was arrested.

The shift in the kleptomania diagnosis from a textbook disease connected with conditions as various as head wounds, general paralysis, and pregnancy to a disease almost exclusively associated with middle-class women took place over the course of the nineteenth century. By the late Victorian era, the close association with pregnancy that worked so successfully in mid-century defenses of middle-class women would be replaced by a more general notion of kleptomania that was feminized but did not require womb-related illness. Although pregnancy still appeared as a cause in the defense of shoplifters, the class of the offender and her respectability played a more important role later in the century.[97] The popular concept of the wealthy woman who stole items she could well afford became the psychologists' definition as well. In this case, not only popular belief, but also the needs of a society experiencing female consumer crime influenced medical science.

---

[94] See Smith, *Trial By Medicine*, 143-160.

[95] Maudsley, *Responsibility in Mental Disease*, 82, 125-126.

[96] 'Kleptomania,' *British Medical Journal* (16 January 1875), 87.

[97] See O'Brien, 'Kleptomania Diagnosis,' 68 & 72-73; Miller, *Bon Marché*, 200-204; Leach, 'Women and Department Stores,' 329-34; Lisa Tiersten, 'In the Public Eye: Women Shoppers and Urban Space in Late 19th-Century Paris' (paper presented to the Interdisciplinary Nineteenth-Century Studies conference on 'The Nineteenth-Century City: Global Contexts, Local Productions, Santa Cruz, California, 7-8 April 1995), 4-5. Tiersten refers to French studies in the latter part of the century that claim wives would even turn to adultery and prostitution to pay for the numerous goods that their husbands did not know about or could not afford, see Tiersten, 5.

In 1878 the *Times* reported favorably on a French case involving a widow who shoplifted in department stores in France.—the judge sentenced the widow to six months imprisonment.[98] The *Times* article described her as a 'kleptomaniac' and disagreed with the French judges decision to sentence the lady to six months imprisonment. Like the shoplifting French widow who claimed 'that she had no need to steal, and that she had lost her senses when she did so,'[99] current medical opinion favored a concept of kleptomania stressing the irresistible impulse of the act. In the later years of the nineteenth century, the irresistibility of the kleptomaniacal impulse becomes the key marker of the disease rather than a specific physiological cause. The medical writer argued that current theory rejected that maniacal acts had to be irrational.[100] By the late seventies, English justice lagged behind English medical science in their acceptance and definition of kleptomania. In 1873, William Hammond, Surgeon General for the United States, asserted that the United States and Great Britain were the two countries most likely to acquit on the grounds of insanity.[101] In 1881, another article appeared in *The Lancet* in defense of the kleptomania diagnosis. The author said that although he understood the judges' suspicions regarding the kleptomania defense for theft: 'The power to discriminate between right and wrong exists, and the wrong is done consciously, and yet the offender is irresponsible so far as being the victim of a morbid impulse can make him so.'[102]

The Light-fingered Governess: Adelaide Bernay and the Baker Street Bazaar

In 1883, only twenty years after the *British Medical Journal* praised Judge Bodkin of the Middlesex Sessions rejecting a plea of kleptomania in the case of Susan Long and Hannah Murray, *The Lancet* lambasted Magistrate De Rutzen of the Marylebone Police Court for failing to recognize kleptomania in a shoplifting case.[103] Adelaide Bernay, a German governess, stole items from the Baker Street bazaar in late March 1883. Although fading in popularity and suffering from the competition of department stores and other large shops, commercial bazaars, like Soho, still operated in the early 1880s. Like the Soho Bazaar where Jane Tyrwhitt shoplifted in the 1840s, the Baker Street bazaar specialized in luxury items, 'fancy

---

[98] *Times*, 4 January 1878. See also the case of a husband and wife in their sixties also caught in the *Magasin du Louvre* shoplifting. In this case, *The Lancet* criticized their defense of kleptomania saying that it was highly unlikely two people would be afflicted with the same mental condition at the same time. 'Kleptomania Extraordinary,' *The Lancet*, I, 3158 (8 March 1884), 445.

[99] *Times*, 4 January 1878.

[100] 'Kleptomania and Artifice,' *The Lancet*, I, 2893 (8 February 1879), 203-204.

[101] William A Hammond (Surgeon-General), *Insanity in its Relations to Crime, etc.* (New York: 1873), 59.

[102] 'The Plea of Kleptomania,' *The Lancet*, II, 3026 (27 August 1881), 390. Similar to the earlier article 'Kleptomania,' *The Lancet*, I, 2795 (24 March 1877), 435.

[103] 'Kleptomania,' *The Lancet*, I, 3112 (21 April 1883), 698-699.

articles.' A stall attendant at the bazaar caught Bernay taking a bronze inkstand. Bernay offered to pay for the item claiming she thought that another woman had paid for it for her. Other stalls soon missed items like a letter opener, a bronze matchbox, and a leather inkstand. At the police court a physician[104] explained that Bernay suffered from kleptomania including 'hallucinations.' The magistrate, De Rutzen, ignored the medical testimony and sent her to trial saying that 'he had his own idea about kleptomania, which he need not explain.'[105] De Rutzen's comment outraged the writer for the *Lancet*, who supported the claim that the governess 'was actually under medical treatment and 'suffering from hallucinations.''[106] The writer chastised the skeptical De Rutzen for failing in his duty to have the prisoner medically evaluated before committing her to trial.[107] Possibly due to the bad publicity surrounding the case, the prosecution offered no evidence against Bernay at the Old Bailey and she was declared *Not Guilty*.[108] This case of a respectable young governess at a fashionable commercial bazaar illustrates the gap between scientific theory and court practice as well as the way in which medical theory, influenced by the long history of kleptomania and middle-class shoplifting, began to shift its focus.

Solving the Problem of the Criminal Consumer

Kleptomania, a disease which should have been equally applicable to rich and poor, male and female, was exclusively used for middle and upper-class women and in connection with cases of shoplifting. The new emphasis on kleptomania as an irresistible impulse in an otherwise rational person only seemed to widen the application to non-pregnant middle-class women, and did not give the wider application of the illness hoped for by medical practitioners. Kleptomania may have been the brainchild of medical theorists, but in practice the plea developed to fulfill the needs of the middle-class, female shoplifter. Definitions of recent pregnancies were stretched to a period of up to three years to convince judges of the biological cause of this psychological malady, but kleptomania increasingly served a narrow group. Developing in conjunction with middle-class crimes, pleas of kleptomania soon followed women shoppers and shoplifters into the small drapery shops, bazaars, and finally department stores. At the beginning of the century, a woman arrested for this crime was either a shoplifter, or an innocent victim of circumstance. By the turn of the century, she was either a shoplifter or a kleptomaniac.

---

[104]The article says 'medical man.'
[105]*Times*, 11 April 1883.
[106]'Kleptomania,' *The Lancet*, I, 3112 (21 April 1883), 698-699.
[107]*Ibid.*, 698-699.
[108]CCCSP, Seventh Session, 1883, 34.

The Reliability of the Historical Record

In the analysis of middle-class shoplifting, even court cases and psychological case studies are not reliable guides to the pervasiveness of the offense. Shoplifting by a lower-class woman was more likely to end up in a court case, as the numerous reports of such 'professional shoplifters' make clear. However, much shoplifting by women of all classes went undetected, and even when they were caught middle-class shoplifters often did not suffer official prosecution. Shop owners admit in their writing about shoplifting that they often avoided prosecution especially when it involved respectable customers. On the rare occasions when middle-class or wealthy offenders were prosecuted, the cases made headlines and caused debate in public opinion as well as medical circles. Testimony from shop owners in their trade protections societies, memoirs, and criminal cases shows that respectable shoplifting was much more widespread than the few examples of prosecuted cases like Ramsbotham's suggest. In the era of the big department store, when the watchful shop assistant was replaced by official shopwalkers and store detectives, records of shoplifting at least within a particular store were much more easily kept. The nature of the offense and the difficulty in documenting the actual number of cases helps to explain its often murky history in the nineteenth century. Even in cases where shoplifters were arrested and taken to local police courts, the records for those courts no longer exist outside of irregular and selective newspaper reports. Petty crimes like shoplifting often never made it to trials at the Middlesex Sessions or Old Bailey. Journalists tended only to report the more interesting cases.[109] Middle-class or upper-class shoplifting, however, was a mainstay of newsworthy shoplifting cases.

Class Bias

Both critics and supporters of kleptomania in the nineteenth century were aware of its glaring class as well as gender bias. From its inception, kleptomania's definition as an illness that caused one to steal without need made it particularly applicable to the wealthier classes.[110] The class bias that was evident in the medical theory became even more so in practical application. A critique of its class bias came after the 1850s along with the debates over the precise psychological characteristics of kleptomania. Memories of the protests and public opinion surrounding the 1855 Ramsbotham case were still fresh in the early 1860s. According to medical journals, the plea of kleptomania increased after this famous case. John Charles Bucknill referred to the Ramsbotham case and to the *Times* editorial on the case in

---

[109]For a discussion on the media treatment of shoplifting in England which has changed little from the nineteenth century see Daniel J. Murphy, *Customers and Thieves: an Ethnography of Shoplifting* (Brookfield, Vermont: Gower, 1986), 126-128.

[110]See chapter II; Elaine Abelson, 'The Invention of Kleptomania,' *Signs* (Autumn 1989), 131.

an 1862 article critical of the overuse of the plea in court.[111] In the 1860s, the song inspired by the Ramsbotham case, 'Ladies, Don't Go Thieving,' was still popularly sold in London and sung in music halls.[112] In 1861, a writer in *The Lancet* cautioned that 'popular belief' of the class bias in kleptomania would not disappear as long as the diagnosis was used to extenuate the crimes of respectable people as had occurred in recent cases.[113] He asked why the wealthy woman with a history of shoplifting was denoted a kleptomaniac; ' whereas when the inspector proves a dozen previous convictions against Mrs. William Sykes for shop-lifting, it is considered to show that she is an incorrigibly bad lot . . ..'[114] In 1862, John Charles Bucknill protested the use of the defense by two wealthy young women denoting their use of the defense as 'nonsense.'[115]

Class bias in the treatment of shoplifting and other consumer crime was not a new phenomenon. Earlier cases like that of Leigh Perrot and Tyrwhitt demonstrated the influence of class position in criminal cases. Class bias was not new nor was it unexpected in the justice system; however, kleptomania supposedly rested on unbiased scientific principles rather than class considerations. Throughout especially the latter half of the century the convenience of kleptomania for a particular class of offenders led to criticisms.[116] Prompted by the case of a wealthy kleptomaniac in 1896, S.A.K. Strahan criticized the diagnosis: 'The business of my life has largely been the study of diseases and disorders of the mind, but I have never met with, nor heard of, any form of insanity which only appears in a particular social grade of the populations.'[117] Yet the diagnosis flourished and grew over the century retaining and strengthening its class bias.

Kleptomania by the End of the Nineteenth Century

With a history predating mid-century, kleptomania evolved slowly over the nineteenth century in England and served to explain the phenomenon of middle-

---

[111]J.C. B., [Bucknill], 'Kleptomania,' 262-275.

[112]William Lancaster, *The Department Store: A Social History* (London: Leicester University Press), 185.

[113]He may be referring here in part to Long and Murray's case.

[114]'Kleptomania,' *The Lancet*, II, 1994 (16 November 1861),483. He is referring to Nancy, a lower-class character who appeared in Charles Dickens' *Oliver Twist*.

[115]Also possibly Long and Murrary see B., J.C. [Bucknill], 'Kleptomania,' 262-263.

[116]See 'Kleptomania,' *The Lancet*, I, 2795 (24 March 1877), 434-435. See also a letter by S.A.K. Strahan, well-known psychaiatrist, to the *Times* regarding the Ella Castle case. This wealthy American woman only received three months' imprisonment as a sentence for her West-end shoplifting and she never served the time. The Home Secretary released her. Letter to the Editor, S.A.K. Strahan Savage Club, Dec. 16, 1896, *Times*, 16 December 1896. This case is described in detail by Elaine Abelson. Abelson, *When Ladies' Go A Thieving*, 175-181.

[117]Letter to the Editor, S.A.K. Strahan Savage Club, Dec. 16, 1896, *Times*, 16 December 1896.

class shoplifting in an era of expanding consumer culture. Despite attempts to apply the concept to lower-class women who shoplifted, these women remained designated as criminals and middle-class women became associated with shoplifting as an illness or mania. In the kleptomania diagnosis changes in medical theory converged with actual court cases to produce a version of the disease almost exclusively middle class and female. The nineteenth-century feminization of madness that associated women's weak biological structures to their propensities for manias like hysteria forged stronger links between the women and the thieving mania. This process was aided by the testimony of medical representatives in court that was part of a nineteenth-century trend of professionalization and medical representation in the courtroom. Despite complaints of its class bias in sources ranging from medical journals to letters to the *Times*, the bias remained an integral part of this 'scientific' diagnosis in the nineteenth century. Most importantly, the kleptomania diagnosis provided one solution to the consumer crime of women that disempowered them and avoided the issues of money, power and status revealed by shoplifting cases. No longer speaking in their own voice by denying or affirming their guilt, court and medical representatives spoke for women denoting them as ill—weak creatures manipulated at first by their biology and later by their environment. The critique of consumer culture inherent in the earlier debates over middle-class shoplifting that blamed the fraudulent culture of retail for tempting women to crime eventually found its way into *fin de siècle* theories of kleptomania in relationship to the department store.

Conclusion

Crime, Gender and Consumer Culture in Nineteenth-Century England

Because the good old rule
Sufficeth them,—the simple plan,
That they should take who have the power,
And they should keep who can.
—Wordsworth, 1803[1]

Women are the final buyers of nine-tenths of the fruits of industry.
—Teresa Billington Greig, 1912[2]

A Length of Ribbon

In July 1885 Louisa Ryan, the 53 year-old widow of an ex-official in the Indian Government who left her a pension of £400 a year, stole ribbon from Whiteley's store. Suspecting her of attempted shoplifting earlier in the month, Alfred Strickland, a shopwalker, watched carefully when Ryan returned to the store. Buying a cheap piece of ribbon for less than two-pence, Ryan secreted a more expensive piece worth 1s. 11 1/2d. Strickland followed her into the street, and despite her protests that she had paid for the other piece of ribbon, had her arrested. However, Ryan did not claim kleptomania. She claimed that it was the store's mistake. Magistrate De Rutzen of Marylebone, the same judge criticized by *The Lancet* in the case of the German governess at the Baker Street bazaar, refused to try her case summarily and committed her for trial.[3] Perhaps Ryan was worried that as a widow, she did not have access to the claims of pregnancy-related illnesses that often made the kleptomania defense successful, or, more likely, she was using the older strategy successfully utilized by Leigh Perrot and Tyrwhitt: a lady of her position and respectable character was incapable of such a crime.

In her defense a long letter appeared in the *Times* by a Watford vicar named N. Price that reiterated earlier images of a middle-class woman wrongfully mistaken for a 'professional shoplifter.' He berated the store, the shopwalker, the police force, and the magistrate for their treatment of Ryan. Like earlier critics, the vicar remained unconvinced that shopping was a safe occupation for respectable women:

---

[1] This excerpt from 'Rob Roy's Grave' is slightly misquoted in an 1861 *Lancet* article 'Kleptomania,' *The Lancet* , II, 1994 (16 November 1861), 483.
[2] Teresa Billington Greig, *The Consumer in Revolt* (London: Stephen Swift and Company Limited, 1912), 58.
[3] *Times*, 30 July 1885.

The case at Marylebone may well make us tremble lest our mothers, wives, or daughters may not return safely from one of these *unaccompanied* expeditions, and may be prevented from communicating with their friends, with the other horrors detailed above to follow.[4]

As Price's letter demonstrates, women's public participation in the pleasures of shopping was not a settled question in the 1880s. Also both he and Ryan's defense of her innocence hearkened back to an era when class position and respectability were enough protection against such criminal charges. In spite of the clear testimony of four of Whiteley's employees, the judge at the Old Bailey found Ryan *not guilty*.[5] The kleptomania diagnosis like the older method of simple denial provided the same protection for women of the same class, but instead of allowing them to be independent agents, who vociferously denied their crimes, it transformed them into manipulated objects of an irresistible impulse.

Department Stores, Sexuality and the Blame for Thieving Mania

Shopping as a 'sport' existed well before the rise of the department store; the concentration of so much of consumer culture in one institution, however, made the problems of consumption, including middle-class shoplifting, more visible. Like bazaars and the other retail innovations of the nineteenth century, department stores met with resistance early in their history. The first true department stores in England began in the North, but the successful late century department stores of London were modeled more on French examples such as the *Bon Marché* and the *Magasin du Louvre*.[6] After apprenticing with a linen-draper, William Whiteley opened his own store in the London suburb of Bayswater in 1863. He specialized in fancy goods including ribbon.[7] Erika Rappaport maintains that Whiteley was in the forefront of those department store owners who sold the idea of shopping as a respectable source of female pleasure. Whiteley worked hard to overcome the negative image of an emporium catering to female shoppers by making his business

---

[4] *Times*, 1 August 1885. Italics mine.
[5] CCCSP, Eleventh Session, 1885, 588-590.
[6] For the influence of the French department store see Michael B. Miller, *The Bon Marché: Bourgeois Culture and the Department Store, 1869-1920* (Princeton: 1981); Rosalind H. Williams, *Dream Worlds: Mass Consumption in Late Nineteenth-Century France* (Berkeley: 1982).
[7] Erika Rappaport, 'The Halls of Temptation': Gender, Politics, and the Construction of the Department Store in Late Victorian London,' *Journal of British Studies*, 35, no. 1 (January 1996): 64. See also William Lancaster, *The Department Store: A Social History* (London: 1995) and Alison Adburgham, *Shops and Shopping: 1800-1914* (London: 1964), 150-159.

a haven of feminine respectability and safe public pleasure.[8] But even Whiteley was not immune to that plague of the retailer, consumer crime.

By the 1880s, the growing phenomenon of department stores was replacing the older era of smaller drapery and haberdashery shops.[9] As the new centers of middle-class shopping, department stores became the sites of middle-class consumer crime. Whiteley claimed that for every man caught shoplifting 300 women were detected, and most of these women were of the wealthier, middle and upper classes. In prosecuting these women, Whiteley was frustrated by the kleptomania-like claims usually associated with womb-related problems that continually saved them from punishment.[10] The elaborate displays and open atmosphere of department stores like Whiteley's were a haven for shoplifters. In 1893, the *Bon Marché* in Paris took over 600 cases to court, and no doubt many more shoplifters passed undetected.[11] The stores complained about this rising tide of crime, but soon found the finger pointed back at them when criminologists re-examined the question of shoplifting and its concurrent rise with the department store.

Charles Lasegue was the first to pinpoint the *grand magasins* as partially culpable for the rise in shoplifting. Dr. Legrand de Saulle and especially Lacassagne were inspired by his work.[12] Part of this new development in the kleptomania diagnosis was a critique of the mass consumerism prevalent in late Victorian culture, but part was also a critique of women exposed to the public sphere and 'overstimulated' beyond their means to resist.[13] Lacassagne's description of kleptomania at the turn of the century as a critique of consumer culture echoed earlier criticisms of middle-class shoplifting that blamed the open displays and aggressive selling methods of the store for female temptation into crime. However, the newest manifestation of kleptomania shifted the blame almost completely to the store and neglected the culpability of the female shopper. She was now a victim of desire, a desire purposefully created by the dreamlike atmosphere of the grand stores. This emphasis on desire also shifted the focus of kleptomania from an illness associated with biology to a malady associated with more psychological factors like sexual desire.

At the end of the century, criminal psychologists had begun to turn away from their earlier thesis that kleptomania was simply a combination of female physiology and mental weakness. The sexual undercurrent of middle-class women and shoplifting which is evident in the late 1830s and 1840s' and some later discussions

---

[8] For a full discussion of the phenomenon see Rappaport, 'The Halls of Temptation,' 58-83.
[9] See Anthony Trollope, *London Tradesmen* (London: Elkin Mathews & Marrot Ltd., 1927; Rappaport, 'The Halls of Temptation', 58-83.
[10] Lancaster, *The Department Store: A Social History*, 185.
[11] Miller, *Bon Marché*, 197.
[12] *Ibid.*, 200-206.
[13] Patricia O'Brien, 'The Kleptomania Diagnosis: Bourgeois Women and Theft in Late Nineteenth-Century France,' *Journal of Social History* 17 (Fall 1983): 73.

of middle-class shoplifting comes to the surface in later theories of kleptomania. Instead of fears of middle-class women tempted into seedy shops and attacked by evil 'Barrat's' (shopkeepers), or touched by the hands of lower-class employees, medical experts later directly connected shoplifting and middle-class women's repressed or warped sexuality. The dazzle and luxury of the massive department stores tempted women like some irresistible seducer, and women fulfilled unmet needs and desires by taking what they wanted.[14] This new definition of the kleptomania diagnosis which shifted focus from the physical to the environmental and psychological made room for those middle-class women like Louisa Ryan who had not been recently pregnant or suffered some womb-related illness.

The Role of Myth and Popular Culture in Shaping the Defense

Despite the attempts of the medical community to keep the theory of the kleptomania diagnosis separate from popular culture, the court system, and biases of gender and class, these factors remained an integral part of the diagnosis. The rise of the kleptomania diagnosis reflects not only how class and gender affected medical 'science,' but also how that science was built on very limited evidence. Most American and English authors simply reiterated the classic French examples of cases.[15] The myth of the wealthy shoplifter quickly made its way from popular culture to medicine. One of the earlier instances referring to such a wealthy shoplifter occurred in the 1844 Tyrwhitt case when T. W. of Gutter Lane told his story of the wealthy shoplifting lady in the *Times*. Later the story appeared in the work of Dr. James F. Duncan, and after the 1855 *Times* editorial on the Ramsbotham case highlighting this now well-known story, it appeared in a series of medical texts as well as popular references.[16] These stories of wealthy, female kleptomaniacs, which never gave the names of the anonymous sufferers, have an urban legend quality to them. Kleptomania was built on popular myth as much as it was influenced by court cases and actual case studies.

This stereotype of the wealthy kleptomaniac was the subject of an 1880s play. In that decade Mark Melford wrote 'Kleptomania: A Farcical Comedy in Three Acts,' in which he lampooned the concept of kleptomania and the wealthy women who supposedly suffered from the disorder. The play was first performed in London at the Strand Theatre in June of 1888. The plot involved a wealthy family whose plans to marry their daughter to a baronet are foiled by the fiancé's

---

[14] *Ibid.*, 68 & 72-73; Miller, *Bon Marché*, 200-204; Leach, 'Women and Department Stores,' 329-34; Lisa Tiersten, 'In the Public Eye: Women Shoppers and Urban Space in Late 19th-Century Paris,' 4-5.

[15] J.C. B., [Bucknill], 'Kleptomania,' *The Journal of Mental Science*, 7, no. 42 (1862): 264.

[16] See especially T.W., Gutter-lane, 12 December 1844, *Times*, 14 December 1844; Duncan, *Popular Errors on the Subject of Insanity*, 138-139; *Times*, 6 April 1855; Ray, *A Treatise on the Medical Jurisprudence of Insanity*, Fourth edition, 204-209; J.C. B., [Bucknill], 'Kleptomania,' 266.

discovery of the mother's kleptomania. After a series of comedic errors, a happy ending is achieved by marrying the daughter to a middle-class doctor. Although the family claims the mother is mentally ill, they constantly drop hints that there is a method to her particular madness:

> GENERAL. – 'Yes, yes, the mother of your betrothed. This Eve-like proclivity is the curse of my life—the evil genius my cheque-book; for whatever her ladyship attaches to herself, I have to pay for through the nose.'
>
> . . .
>
> GENERAL. 'This, to her, is a joy, a boast and a triumph and there is the secret and the fountain head of her private income.'
> SMALLEY. 'No, no! You cannot mean to tell me that her ladyship is a—a—'
>
> . . .
>
> GENERAL. 'Yes—she is a kleptomaniac!!'[17]

Throughout the play Melford reveals how the General's wife, Lady Josephine Blair, uses her 'kleptomania' as a source of 'private income.' The effect of her 'illness' is that Lady Josephine acquires whatever she desires and her husband is forced to pay for the items.[18] Melford's play demonstrates not only the popular acceptance of the term and the idea of the kleptomaniac, but he is also part of the continuing tradition of criticizing women's role in consumer culture and class bias through his satire on kleptomania. Melford's comedy and the repetition of possibly apocryphal tales as 'case studies' in medical texts reveal the influence of popular culture and media in shaping views of women's roles in consumption. The stereotype of the wealthy female kleptomaniac began long before late century psychologists and criminologists began to reshape this familiar tale by adding the element of repressed sexual desire.

Consumer Culture and Changing Retail Methods

Stressing the weakness of the women themselves, both early and mid-century versions of the legend of the wealthy woman who shoplifted avoided placing the blame on the stores that they frequented. However, it was in part the new developments in retail that made shopping outlets more susceptible to criminal consumption. The shift from the single-family, smaller shops of the 1700s to larger, multiple-employee emporiums in the nineteenth century provided the first step in the transition to department stores and mass consumer culture. Linen drapers and haberdashers introduced innovations like advertisement, ready-money sales, open-ticket pricing, and window dressing. Larger London stores initiated the trend before the nineteenth century and by the 1830s emporiums opened up in London and in

---

[17] Mark Melford, 'Kleptomania: A Farcical Comedy in Three Acts,' (London: 1888), 18.
[18] *Ibid.*

northern cities like Manchester that paved the way for the massive stores of William Whiteley and Arthur Liberty later in the century.

Similarly, charity and especially commercial shopping bazaars, which began in the 1810s and thrived well into the later Victorian era, provided the browsing, open atmosphere later associated with the *grand magasins*. These multi-vendor establishments provided a variety of goods under one roof with long counters of open displays, encouraged browsing, and were an important transitional phase in consumer culture. Bazaars sold mostly 'feminine', 'useless' goods and knick-knacks like pen-wipers—contributing, according to their critics, to a false economy. Early critics were scandalized by the intermingling of church and marketplace in the charity bazaars and by the involvement of middle- and upper-class women in the seedy business of selling. Bazaars helped to feminize the consumer experience and added entertainment and display to the humdrum business of retail sales.

The early nineteenth-century developments in methods of retailing, including bazaars and linen-drapery and haberdashery shops, created anxieties that English shopkeeping fostered a culture of fraud—an anxiety only heightened by the introduction of 'cheap shops' and discount shopping emporiums directed at the non-genteel shopper. These discount houses depended on aggressive advertising, plate-glass windows filled with garish displays, and low-priced "lead" items to entice shoppers. According to critics, these new methods crossed the borderline between good business and fraud making the 1830s, 40s, 50s, and 60s an era of dishonest retail: false bankruptcy and fire sales, fraudulent merchandise, and 'cheap shopkeepers.'

The False Retailer, Advertising and Display

Critics contended in the first half of the nineteenth century that something dreadfully wrong had overtaken a once proud nation of shopkeepers fulfilling the needs of England and the world. Women had been lured into and were supporting this consumer culture, but what had convinced them to submit to this warped system of fraudulent values? Earlier in the century it was the plague of the 'cheap shops' that refused to pay workers decent wages for their goods and undersold cheap and shoddy merchandise encouraging women to expect more and more for less money. Critics also blamed the growing emphasis on display and advertisement. The 'Magenta Houses' were responsible for the decline of English retail. Like Anthony Trollope, John Charles Bucknill lamented in his 1862 article on kleptomania:

> . . . on the whole we can find more pity for the poor woman who purloins a piece of lace, without which she thinks she will be absolutely not fit to be seen, than the smirking fellow who has caught her in his haberdashery trap by lying advertisements

that he sells for almost next to nothing the very articles she so covets in her desire to make her person agreeable and attractive.[19]

Advertising in combination with new shop methods emphasized show and display over quality and substance. Due to this rage for consumption, Bucknill asserted, women spent a large part of their leisure time 'passing from shop to emporium, from haberdashery store to magazine de mode, in discharge of that new and peculiar duty of life called 'shopping.'[20]

The mass market did not simply flash into existence in the 1880s, but was developing throughout the century.[21] It was precisely the sort of illusion created by Victorian advertising that later medico-legal men like Lacassagne claimed caused the temptation of so many bourgeois women into crime. After the department store replaced the small shopkeeper later in the century as a center of consumption, it was criticized like the Soho Bazaar and the emporia and haberdashery shops. The grand stores were accused of creating the crime of which they claimed to be a victim. Echoing the comments of outraged husbands after the Jane Tyrwhitt case and the mid-century critics of the kleptomania diagnosis, *fin de siècle* psychologists asserted that department stores should not have tempted middle-class women out of the protection of their home and family in the first place.[22] However, it was only the later response to middle-class women's crime that managed to both implicate the department stores and still deny women their agency as rational actors. Tempting an already weak creature with new desires was less unethical than direct false advertisements or planting goods in parcels.

Redefining Need: The Gender Gap in Understanding Consumer Culture

Women's expansion into consumer crime was only a corollary to their growing participation in consumer culture in nineteenth-century England. Throughout the century, the problem of middle-class female shoplifting brought, on the one hand, protests to preserve the status and ideology of what these women represented—the height of feminine respectability, and, on the other hand, a backhanded critique of consumer culture and women's participation in that culture. These debates pitted images of women as possession-mad shoppers against images of women as creatures who needed protection from the lures of the false world of English retail.

---

[19] J.C. B., [Bucknill], 'Kleptomania,' 266.

[20] *Ibid.*

[21] Lori Loeb's *Consuming Angels* traces the lush history of the Victorian advertisement and its contribution to commodity culture prior to the advent of the department store at mid-century. Lori Anne Loeb, *Consuming Angels: Advertising and Victorian Women* (New York: Oxford University Press, 1994), passim. See also Richards, *Commodity Culture*, 1-72.

[22] See O'Brien, 'The Kleptomania Diagnosis,' 72-73.

In his criticism of the overuse of the kleptomania defense by wealthy shoplifters, John Charles Bucknill, the well-known mad doctor, claimed that current consumer culture had so redefined the concept of 'need' that it encouraged otherwise wealthy women to steal:

> The struggle for existence in the middle, and even in the upper classes of our complex social system, combined with the prevailing fashion of an emulative and showy expenditure, make the sense of want felt keenly in many an English home, where no traces of vulgar poverty are discernible. The really poor steal because they want bread; the relatively poor are tempted to steal because they desire the possession of that which seems, to a mind trained in a bad school, as essential as bread itself.[23]

Consumer culture's redefinition of need destroyed older utilitarian concepts and replaced them with a world in which a yard of the most fashionable lace in the newest color was more desirable than more mundane but useful objects like utensils. And for the middle classes, lace was a much more visible testament to status than less visible domestic items. While some insisted that it was insane for a woman who could have paid for an item to steal useless articles like bronze matchboxes and silk handkerchiefs, others recognized that for the class of women stealing the items—they were quite useful indeed. In 1896, S.A.K. Strahan compared the Ella Castle shoplifting case to a case where a beadle had stolen books, 'which were much less desirable property for a beadle than fans, furs, and opera-glasses to a rich American lady.'[24] What had once been luxury and frippery was now the core of retail purchase by middle- and upper-class women.

Some contemporary critics, like Anthony Trollope, blamed the false consumer culture that stressed display over substance as the factor corrupting these women and inducing them to steal little fashionable items. However, there was a gender gap in understanding how consumer culture functioned in Victorian society. Middle-class male commentators often referred to consumption as utilitarian in an age when its meaning stretched far beyond the necessary. They were reluctant to admit the importance of a bit of lace or a bronze inkstand. These items were not only symbols but also necessities of the middle-class lifestyle. Such 'fripperies' had real significance in day-to-day life in maintaining or increasing status. Indirectly these women were stealing status. The display of such items affected not only the status of the individual woman but her family as well. Rather than being powerless puppets manipulated and mesmerized by consumer culture, or sick women, whose minds were weakened by physical maladies, middle and upper-class shoplifters stole to preserve or elevate their status in a society experiencing tremendous pressures on class and position.

---

[23] J.C. B., [Bucknill], 'Kleptomania,' 265.

[24] Letter to the Editor, S.A.K. Strahan Savage Club, Dec. 16, 1896, *Times*, 16 December 1896.

The Role of Financial Distress

Women increasingly used their powers of consumption in the nineteenth century and became the targeted consumers of goods in bazaars, emporia, and department stores. Women's growing buying power was complicated by gender ideology, which associated women with a private domestic world along with a common law technically giving property control to husbands.

In practice women contracted for debts, as numerous fraud cases illustrate, and they consumed quantities of goods wielding a considerable part of the family income; however, a financially strict or spendthrift husband might make a woman who possessed all the status of middle or a better class financially poor.[25] Jane Tyrwhitt Jones had a separate income that should have made her a wealthy woman, but her husband's constant bankruptcies threatened that financial independence, and eventually led her from shoplifting to retail fraud to acquire the goods necessary to her station in life. Emily MacGregor possessed middle-class status, but the loss of her husband's investments in a financial crash led her to a fraud spree in the most fashionable stores in London. For single bourgeois women, especially those who worked in poorly-paid positions like governess there was a similar lack of financial resources. Adelaide Bernay's shoplifting excursion to the Baker Street bazaar is a good example. On the other hand, there were women who had open access to the family purse, like the widow Louisa Bryan, who stole despite her ability to pay. All of these women used shoplifting as a means to stretch their individual or family budgets.

A Culture of Fraud and the Criminal Consumer

Ignoring the role of real financial stress and refusing to accept the necessity of status-enhancing goods in a society increasingly defined by moveable property. Critics condemned pleasure-seeking shoppers for encouraging the culture of fraud, and creating a false consumption that fed on the new retail. In satire and in the press women were depicted as shopping demons whose searches for bargains undermined their own characters and that of English trade while they exhausted and underpaid the laborers who served them. In their pursuit of fashion and finery, shoppers tossed away morality and "feminine" behavior. However, although portrayed as unethical and greedy, mid-century critics of the female shopper did

---

[25] Patricia O'Brien discusess 'wealthy' women who steal because they do not have real access to money. O'Brien, 'The Kleptomania Diagnosis,' 72-73. Elaine Abelson also discusses shoplifting as a 'budget stretching device.' Elaine S. Abelson, *When Ladies Go A-Thieving: Middle-Class Shoplifters in the Victorian Department Store* (New York: Oxford University Press, 1989), 167.

not present her as irrational. In the mid-Victorian era, women were still considered culpable for their participation in a blatantly fraudulent culture.

Like the debates over the aggressive female shopper, debates over women shoplifters reflect the changing nature of English retail. Shoplifting cases in England prior to the mid-nineteenth century reveal not only England's treatment of petty female criminals, but also how society interpreted the scourge of light-fingered ladies. Working-class women were treated as criminals, whereas, before the kleptomania defense, middle-class women like Jane Perrot in 1800 and Jane Tyrwhitt in 1844 only had the option of denying their crime or of blaming the 'cheap shopkeeper' of falsely accusing them. Before the rise of the department store, some English critics also blamed the new consumer culture for encouraging and creating the problem of middle-class shoplifting.

Like shoplifting, consumer fraud was another form of false consumption: 'buying' without paying. Women used various methods to enjoy consumer goods without purchasing them, including adopting false names, wearing goods and sending them back, and using false credit. Examining these cases illustrates not only women's shopping habits, but also their access to purchasing power and credit, and how women manipulated the English law to work in their favor. The law of necessaries gave women greater access to credit and aided women like Mary Jane Richardson who wanted to commit retail fraud. The vagueness of the law of criminal fraud also often prevented successful criminal prosecution forcing shopkeepers to prosecute fraud as debt. Requiring more advanced planning than shoplifting, crimes of fraud which did make it to trial, especially those by middle-class women, were not easily explained by mental incapacity. However, some female frauds tried to plead mental illness with varying degrees of success. The "insanity" pleas of frauds like Emily MacGregor reflect an extension of the developing representation of the middle-class, female criminal in another consumer crime—shoplifting.

Kleptomania in the Later Nineteenth Century and Today

In the 1880s and 1890s there was a perceived rise in theft by middle-class women. Psychologists like Lacassagne theorized that weak women, tempted by uncontrollable urges and driven by womb-controlled natures, began to steal in record numbers.[26] Based on older concepts of a thieving mania, the curse of

---

[26] It is unclear whether this perceived explosion in female shoplifting was a real result of a sudden rise in respectable shoplifting, or whether it was merely the result of the improved record-keeping and stricter private policing by the large department stores.

shoplifting ladies was at first explained by the medical community as a combined result of physiological problems and a weakness of the mind.[27]

Although not the first to notice this trend in modern crime, Daniel Murphy notes the operation of 'a dual standard whereby men are criminalised for their offences and women are medicalised.'[28] The significant medicalization of female crime took place in the nineteenth century. From murder to drunkenness, medical and criminal experts increasingly linked women's crimes to mental illness linked to their physiology rather than willful criminality.[29] Medicine provided a solution to the problem of the shoplifting consumer in the new marketplace, but only after years of debate which illustrate the complex economic, class, and gender dilemmas created by the woman shoplifter.

The medico-legalization of the problem of middle-class shoplifting—the invention of kleptomania—did not remain static. Around the turn of the century, psychologists and criminologists began looking more closely at the department store itself as a false and tempting paradise that drove otherwise respectable ladies to steal.[30] In its earlier phase, the diagnosis of kleptomania depended on the history and physiology of the individual afflicted, but this disease was caught up in the increasing focus on environmental causes in late nineteenth-century psychology. The department store began to shoulder some of the blame for tempting women with sumptuous displays of goods.[31] This tendency to blame consumerism itself for the rise of consumer crime remains with us today: only the strongest woman is said to be able to resist the constant temptation and manipulation of her desire. For many, including Patricia O'Brien and Elaine Abelson, the rise of the department store played a large part in creating the consumer culture that encouraged an extraordinary rise in middle-class shoplifting.[32]

The reason kleptomania became a gender and class specific disease in the nineteenth century was because it addressed one of the most perplexing problems of nineteenth-century consumerism: why did perfectly respectable women of the wealthier classes steal? The kleptomania diagnosis allowed doctors, lawyers, and judges to explain the problem in terms of mental illness linked at first to biological

---

[27] See O'Brien, 'The Kleptomania Diagnosis', 65-77, specifically for the rise of kleptomania. See also Abelson, *When Ladies Go A-Thieving*, passim and Miller, *Bon Marché*, 197-206 for discussions of this development.

[28] Daniel J. I. Murphy, *Customers and Thieves: an Ethnography of Shoplifting* (Brookfield, Vermont: Gower, 1986), 39.

[29] See Martin Wiener, *Reconstructing the Criminal: Culture, Law, and Policy in England, 1830-1914* (New York: Cambridge University Press, 1990); Lucia Zedner, *Women, Crime, and Custody in Victorian England* (Oxford: Clarendon Press, 1991).

[30] Patricia O'Brien points out this important shift toward environmental causes. O'Brien, 'Kleptomania Diagnosis,' 72.

[31] *Ibid.*, 73. See also Havelock Ellis, *Studies in the Psychology of Sex*, vol. 2.; part 2 (New York: Random House, 1936), 480.

[32] O'Brien, 'Kleptomania Diagnosis,' passim. See especially Abelson, *Ladies Go A-Thieving*, 63-90.

factors and later to psychological needs. The kleptomania diagnosis, unlike some of the debate surrounding its use, answered the question of theft by respectable women without dealing with the core of the problem—the relationship between women and money in the nineteenth-century.

That the kleptomania diagnosis evolved during the tensions of an expanding consumer culture in the nineteenth century is not surprising. In its earliest form it supposedly affected those with small mental capacity, head injury, or who showed other signs of insanity; however, for women it soon became attached to their physiology. Pregnancy was the first physiological change noted to cause it and Ramsbotham's lawyer extended this to menopause in his client's case. Eventually it was connected to all of women's life cycle changes.[33] What is surprising about the kleptomania diagnosis is that its interpretation remains little changed today:

> . . . women are more likely to suffer from kleptomania . . . Most of these women were married. . . Many of these theories have associated the disorder with anxiety, depression, and sexual disturbances. . . There is some evidence that biological factors could be involved.[34]

This excerpt is from an article in the August 1991 issue of the *American Journal of Psychiatry*. Kleptomania, an urge to steal unneeded items, still remains as a resort for the 'hysterical' modern housewife with all of the its gender and class biases, biases formed before the diagnosis itself.

Women and Consumption after the Turn of the Century

In her 1912 work, *The Consumer in Revolt*, suffragette Teresa Billington Greig argued that capitalism rests on a system in which women, particularly leisured, middle-class women, are the main consumers:

> [T]he economic system now exists, not to satisfy the needs of the consumer as a whole in the best possible way, but to reward the idleness of one body of consumers with a larger share of the fruits of labour than labour itself enjoys; it exists to support a privileged class of non-working consumers on the shoulders both of consumers and producers . . ..[35]

---

[33] See Murphy, *Shoplifting*, 185. See Abelson, *Ladies Go A-Thieving*, 7.

[34] Marcus J. Goldman, 'Kleptomaniac: Making Sense of the Nonsensical,' *American Journal of Psychiatry* 148, 8 (August 1991): 986-997.

[35] Greig, *The Consumer in Revolt*, 3. For the long history of consumers trying to work against or outside the system created by nineteenth-century economic changes please see Ellen Furlough and Carl Strikwerda, eds., *Consumers Against Capitalism?* (Rowman and Littlefield, 1999).

Greig's critique stresses the key role of the female consumer and urges women to use their buying power to change the system through forming consumer leagues. Unlike early Victorian critics of consumption, Greig saw the possibility of a positive role for the woman shopper wielding power through her pocketbook. However, Greig's dim view of modern retail culture echoed the middle-class, male commentators of the Victorian era:

> By uncounted methods of fraud, great and petty, the consumer is tricked and robbed. . . . The tricks played by every branch of the distributive trade are legion . . . they include the sham 'Sales,' for which bales of special shoddy goods are purchased and goods in stock are specially soiled and then sold at a normal price as 'Special Bargains,' the short-weights and short measures tricks, the scandalous over-pricing of fripperies and fancy goods, the substitution of one article for another and of one quality for another, the mixing of inferior goods of material with superior, ... All these and a host of other devices are employed to deceive the unwary consumer.[36]

Although Greig recognized the power women possessed as primary consumers and refused to accept the image of the female shopper as a 'magpie' collecting bright, glittering objects, she still saw consumer culture as corrupt, fraudulent, and bordering on the criminal. Ironically, this representation of modern mass retail as dazzling manipulator coupled with Victorian gender ideology was precisely what had labeled the nineteenth-century female consumer as passive economic victim.

Conclusion

Although it might be romantic to think that respectable women shoplifters and frauds were somehow 'rebelling' against the system of capitalism or even a post-capitalist consumer economy, the truth is they were largely working within it. Throughout the century, explanations for middle-class crime were complicated by a gender gap in understanding the new consumer culture. Outside of new-style retailers like William Ablett, most middle-class men had an eighteenth-century capitalist viewpoint of the purposes and methods of consumption. While male commentators bemoaned the disappearance of honest shopkeepers and bow-fronted shops, women walked and rode with pleasure to the new bazaars and emporiums. These same commentators failed to acknowledge the role, other than as frippery, that the increasing volume of consumer goods played in maintaining class boundaries. Inspired by financial distress, limited access to the family budget or simply a desire to 'win' the game of status enhancement, middle-class women both bought and stole consumer goods. Women like Louisa Ryan often stole from the very same stores where they shopped for their families. This contrasted with the methods of the professional or non-middle class thief who rarely stole from an

---

[36] *Ibid.*, 25, 39-40.

establishment more than once. The motive of the lower-class woman who shoplifted little concerned nineteenth-century society which easily labeled them as criminals simply stealing from want or a lack of moral fortitude. Public opinion and medical science were concerned much more with the motives of women of the respectable classes. Early in the century, genteel women like Jane Leigh Perrot could simply deny their crimes and blame the shopkeeper; however, as evidence of middle-class and wealthier women shoplifting continued to surface, the denial response failed to satisfy the nineteenth-century public. The earlier denial response was replaced in part by blaming the retailers themselves, especially those who adopted innovative new methods of sale like aggressive displays, ready-money and bargain advertising. The nineteenth century was a crucial transitional phase in English consumer culture from the smaller, family-run shops of the eighteenth-century to the bazaars and larger, multiple employee emporiums of mid-century and finally the *fin de siècle* department stores. In the end, blaming the stores entirely also failed, because women were so freely and willingly participating in the new consumer culture. Critics of bazaars earlier in the century and women who shopped as 'sport' in the 1840s, 50s, and 60s make this clear. After mid-century, around the time of the Mary Ramsbotham case, the debate shifts again and becomes a stand off between the doubting judges of English courts and a professionalizing group of doctors and mad doctors. The changing responses to Jane Tyrwhitt Jones' two cases illustrate this shift. After decades of battling, the doctors finally win the right to label the wealthy shoplifter—now a kleptomaniac, but the courts' use of that definition was not always to the medical community's satisfaction. When the very consumer culture based on 'fraud' and showy display that so disturbed earlier nineteenth-century critics did not disappear but reinvented itself in the department store, women, once so criticized for participating in this culture of leisured shopping and non-utilitarian consumer goods, were represented as dazzled creatures too weak to resist the displays of the *grand magasins*— susceptible to that dreaded feminine illness, kleptomania.

Bibliography

Primary Sources

Ablett, William. *Reminiscences of An Old Draper*. London: Sampson Low, Marston, Searle, and Rivington, 1876.

Allan, Henry. *Prize Essay on Kleptomania, With a View to Determine Whether Kleptomaniacs Should Be Held Disqualified for Employment of Trust and Authority Under the Crown*. 219 Regent Street, London: H. Balliere, 1869.

Amicus, C. B. C. *How to Rise in Life*. London: Longman, Brown, Green, and Longmans, 1845.

Annual Register: Or a View of the History and Politics of the Year 1844, The. London: F & J Rivington, 1845.

Anti-Corn Law League. 'Leading Article.' *National Anti-Corn-Law League Bazaar Gazette*, no. 14 (1845): 1-6.

———. 'Leading Article.' *National Anti-Corn Law League Bazaar Gazette*, no. 12(1845): 1-7.

———. 'Leading Article.' *National Anti-Corn Law League Bazaar Gazette*, no. 11 (1845): 1-7.

Austen, Jane. *Northanger Abbey*. London: Penguin Books, 1995.

B., J. C. [John Charles Bucknill]. 'Kleptomania.' *The Journal of Mental Science* 7, no. 42 (1862): 262-75.

Bazaar; or Fragments of Mind. In Prose and Verse, The. Lancaster, England: Holme & Jackson, 1831.

'Bazaar, The.' *The Gentleman's Magazine* 86 (1816): 272.

Billington Greig, Teresa. *The Consumer in Revolt*. London: Stephen Swift and Company Limited, 1912.

Blenkinsop, Adam. *A Shilling's-Worth of Advice, on Manners, Behaviour & Dress*. London: Blenkinsop, 1850.

Bow Street Officer. *The Frauds of London: Displaying the Numerous and Daring Cheats and Robberies Practised Upon the Stranger and the Unwary*. No. 10, Newgate Street, London: William Cole, 1829.

Brown, John. 'On Genteel Thieves.' *Tait's Edinburgh Magazine* 26 O.S., 22 N.S. (1855): 289-93.

Central Criminal Court Sessions Papers (1841-1885). The Whole Proceedings on the Queen's Comission of the Peace, Oyer and Terminer, and Gaol Delivery for the City of London, and Gaol Delivery for the County of Middlesex, and the Parts of the Counties of Essex, Kent, and Surrey, Within the Jurisdiction of the Central Criminal Court. Dobbs Ferry, New York: Trans-Media Publishing Co., 1981. Microfilm.

City of London Trade Protection Circular 22 April 1848-11 November 1849.

City of London Trade Protection Circular (Private Circular), 11 July 1848-3 Nov. 1848.

Collins, Mabel. 'Woman of Fashion.' *Tinsley's Magazine* 29 (1881): 137-68.

Collins, Wilkie. *Basil*. New York: Dover, 1980 [1852].

———. *No Name*. New York: Dover, 1978 [1862-63].

———. *Armadale*. New York: Dover, 1977 [1864-66].

Confessions of a Ticket-of-Leave Man. London: 1865.

Cooley, Arnold James. *The Toilet and Cosmetic Arts in Ancient and Modern Times.* 192, Piccadilly, London: Robert Hardwicke, 1866.

Dance, Charles. *The Burlington Arcade; A Burletta, In One Act.* London: Chapman & Hall, 1839.

De Quincey, Thomas. 'The Household Wreck .' *Blackwood's Edinburgh Magazine* 43, no. 217 (1838): 1-32.

Draper, The (London) 16 July 1869-27 December 1872.

Dickens, Charles. *Sketches by Boz and Other Early Papers, 1833-1839.* Ed. Michael Slater. London: J.M. Dent, 1994.

Dixon, James Henry. *A Statement of Facts In Reference to the City of London Trade Protection Society, (13, Swithin's Lane,) and the Mode in Which It Discharges It Pecuniary Obligations.* London: Effingham Wilson, Royal exchange, 1851.

Doyle, Richard and Percival Leigh. *Manners and Cvstoms of Ye Englyshe.* London: Bradbury & Evans, 1849.

Duncan, James F., A. M., M. D. *Popular Errors on the Subject of Insanity.* Dublin: James McGlashan, 1853.

Ellis, Havelock. *Studies in the Psychology of Sex.* Vol. 2. New York: Random House, 1936.

'English Thugs, The.' *Chamber's Edinburgh Journal* 23, no. 70 (1855): 273-76.

Evening Chronicle (London) 17 March 1835.

Going Out A Shopping. Dudley Street, 7 dials, London: E. Hodges, from PITT'S Wholesale Toy and Marble Warehouse, n.d. British Library.

Great Grievance of Traders and Shopkeepers, by the Notorious Practice of Stealing Their Goods Out of Their Shops and Warehoufes, by Perfons Commony Called Shoplifters; Humbly Reprefented to the Confideration of the Honourable Houfe of Commons, The. n.d. British Library.

Guardians: or Society for the Protection of Trade Against Swindlers and Sharpers, The. *Rules and Orders.* Northumberland Street, Strand, London: G. Sidney, 1816. British Library.

Haberdasher's Guide: A Complete Key to All the Intricacies of the Haberdashery Business, The. London: R.P. Moore, 1826.

Hammond, Surgeon-General William A. *Insanity in Its Relations to Crime, Etc.* New York: D. Appleton & Co., 1873.

Handy Guide for the Draper and Haberdasher, A. 20 Paternoster Row, London: F. Pitman, 1864.

Haslam, John. *Medical Jursiprudence As It Relates to Insanity, According to the Law of England.* London: 1817.

Hayes, J. W. *Hints on Haberdashery & Drapery .* London: Clements and Newling, 1875.

Hedgehog, Humphrey [John Agg]. *The London Bazzaar, or, Where to Get Cheap Things.* 19, Little Queen Street, Lincoln's Inn Fields, London: J. Duncombe, 1816.

Highworth Association For the Prosecution of Felons and Other Thieves. Faringdon: Cotton, Printer, 1810. British Library.

Hill, Frederic. *Crime: Its Amount, Causes , and Remedies.* London: John Murray, 1853.

Hindley, Charles. *The Life and Times of James Catnatch, (Late of the Seven Dials), Ballad Monger.* London: Reeves and Turner, 1878.

Holland, John. *The Bazaar; or Money and the Church.* Sheffield: Pawson and Brailsford, n.d. British Library.

Hunt, Leigh. *A Saunter Through the West End.* London: Hurst and Blackett, 1861.

Imputation of Theft: Report of the Trial of an Action Brought by Mrs. Sarah Bingham

Against the Rev. John Gardiner, D.D. for a Malicious Libel, Imputing to Her That She Had Stolen a One Pound Note. London: Richard and Arthur Taylor, 1820.

Jerrold, Douglas William. "The Linen-Draper's Assistant,' *Sketches of the English.*' *The Writings of Douglas Jerrold.* Douglas William Jerrold, 235-42. Vol. 5. London: Bradbury and Evans, 1853.

John Johnson Collection. Bodleian Library. Oxford.

'Kleptomania.' *British Medical Journal* II (1861): 510.

'Kleptomania.' *The Lancet* II, no. 1994 (1861): 483.

'Kleptomania.' *British Medical Journal* (1875): 87.

'Kleptomania.' *The Lancet* I, no. 2795 (1877): 434-35.

'Kleptomania.' *The Lancet* I, no. 3112 (1883): 698-99.

'Kleptomania.' *The Lancet*, no. 3274 (1886): 1036.

'Kleptomania and Artifice.' *The Lancet* I, no. 2893 (1879): 203-4.

'Kleptomania Extraordinary.' *The Lancet* I, no. 3158 (1884): 445.

'Kleptomania of Pregnancy, The.' *The Lancet* II, no. 3228 (1885): 81.

Knight, Charles, ed. *London*, Vol. 5. London: Charles Knight, 1843.

Ladies' Hand-Book, Being Coloured Sketches for Sale at a Bazaar, With Descriptive Lines in Verse, The. London: Privately printed, 1846. British Library.

Ladies' Pocket Magazine, The (1842).

Letters From Albion. Vol. 1. London: Gale, Curtis, and Fenner, 1814.

'London Shop-Fronts, The.' *Chamber's Journal of Popular Literature, Science and Art* (1864): 670-672.

'London Shops, Old and New.' *Chamber's Edinburgh Journal* 20 (1853): 250-253.

'Lowther Arcade, The.' *The Mirror of Literature, Amusement, and Instruction* XIX, no. 541 (1832): 210.

Mansfield, Horatio. 'The Causes of Crime in the Metropolis.' *Tait's Edinburgh Magazine* 17 N.S., no. June (1850): 329-35.

Martineau, Harriet. *Dawn Island.* Manchester: J. Gadsby, 1845.

Maudlsey, Henry, M.D. *Responsibility in Mental Disease.* London: Henry S. King & Co., 1874.

———. 'Stealing As a Symptom of General Paralysis.' *The Lancet* 2, no. 2724 (1875): 693-95.

Melford, Mark. *Kleptomania: A Farcical Comedy in Three Acts.* London: Samuel French, Ltd., 1888.

'Miss Polly Glott's Dictionary of the Future.' *Girl of the Period Miscellany*, no. 7 (1869): 240-241.

Morning Chronicle (London) 27 March 1813-10 October 1834.

'Must We Revive the Sumptuary Laws?' *The Young Englishwoman* (January 1865): 47.

Nightingale, Joseph. *The Bazaar, Its Origin, Nature, and Objects Explained, and Recommended As an Important Branch of Political Economy; In a Letter to the Rt. Hon. George Rose, M.P.* London: Davies Michael and Hudson, 1816.

'Old London Shops and Shopkeepers.' *Chamber's Edinburgh Journal* 31 (1859): 369-72.

Original Sketches and Ryhmes, Contributed by a Few Friends, for the Bazaar at Leeds. Plymouth, England: W.H. Luke, 1839. British Library.

Perkins, E. E. *Haberdashery, Hosiery, and General Drapery; Including the Manchester, Scotch, Silk, Linen, and Woollen Departments, Foreign and Domestic.* London: William Tegg, 1830.

———. *The Lady's Shopping Manual and Mercery Album; Wherein the Textures, Comparitive Strengths, Lengths, Widths, and Numbers, of Every Description of Mercery,*

Hosiery, Haberdashery, Woollen and Linen Drapery, Are Pointed Out for Domestic Economy, and Which Will Be Found of Great Advantage to the Heads of Families and Charitable Institutions for Clothing the Poor. 65, St. Paul's Churchyard, London: T. Hurst, 1834.

'Plea of Kleptomania, The.' *The Lancet* II, no. 3026 (1881): 390.

Pollard, James. 'Poultry Market.'1819. Yale Center for British Art.

———. 'The Fruitmarket (The Greengrocer).'1819. Yale Center for British Art.

———. 'The Meat Market.'1819. Yale Center for British Art.

Ray, Isaac M. D. *A Treatise on the Medical Jurisprudence of Insanity.* London: G. Henderson, 1839.

———. *A Treatise on the Medical Jurisprudence of Insanity.* Boston: Little, Brown, and Company, 1860.

Sala, George Augustus. *Twice Round the Clock: Or The Hours of the Day and Night in London.* New York: Humanities Press, 1971.

Sampson, Henry. *History of Advertising: From the Earliest Times.* London: Chatto and Windus, 1874.

Sankey, W.H.O., M.D. 'Illustrations of the Different Forms of Insanity.' *British Medical Journal* I (1865): 136-37.

Saturday Review, The (London) 26 September 1868.

Science of Dress, The. London: Groombridge and Sons, 1857.

'Shop-Lifting-Female Weakness.' *Punch* 6 (1844): 149.

'Shoppers and Shopping.' *Tait's Edinburgh Magazine* 26 N.S., no. May (1859): 291-97.

'Shopping in London.' *The Living Age* 1, no. 4 (1844): 250-254.

Smith, Eliza. *Memoir of Eliza Smith Who Was Transported for Shoplifting, Written By Herself.* Dublin: Hardy & Walker, 1839.

Stekel, William. *Peculiarities of Behavior: Wandering Mania, Dipsomania, Cleptomania, Pyromania and Allied Impulsive Acts.* New York: Boni and Liverwright, 1924.

Stevenson, Robert Louis. *The Charity Bazaar: An Allegorical Dialogue.* Edinburgh: 1866.

Stirling, Edward. *Grace Darling, or, The Wreck at Sea: a Drama in Two Acts.* London: Chapman and Hall, n.d.

Story of Old Soho, The. London: T. Pettitt & Co., 1893.

Sutherland, Alexander John M.D.F.R.S. 'Patholoy of Mania and Dementia.' *Medico-Chirurgical Transactions* 38 (1855): 261-88.

Tallis, John. *London Street Views.* London: John Tallis, 1838-1840.

Thackeray, William Makepeace. *Vanity Fair; A Novel Without a Hero.* New York: Quality Paperback Book Club, 1991.

Thackeray, William Makepeace, Albert Smith, Gilbert A'Beckett, and The Brothers Mayhew. *The Comic Almanack: An Ephemeris Containing Merry Tales, Humorous Poetry Quips and Oddities.* 2 vols. First Series. London: Chatto & Windus, 1912.

Times (London) 11 September 1811-16 December 1896.

Trade Protection Record, April 1849-30 September 1849.

Trial of Mrs. Jane Leigh Perrot at Taunton Assizes, on Saturday the 29th of March, 1800; Charged With Stealing a Card of Lace, in the Shop of Elizabeth Gregory, Haberdasher & Milliner, of the City of Bath, The. British Trial Series. London: Chadwyck-Healey, Ltd., 1990.

Trollope, Anthony. *Can You Forgive Her?* New York: Oxford University Press, 1982 [1864-65].

———. *The Struggles of Brown, Jones, and Robinson: By One of the Firm.* London: Smith, Elder & Co., 1870.

————. *London Tradesmen*. London : Elkin Mathews & Marrot Ltd., 1927 [1880].

United Kingdom. Middlesex Sessions Papers. Greater London Record Office. MJ/SR.

————. Chancery Papers. Public Record Office, London. C114/34.

Visit to The Bazaar, A. London: J. Harris, 1818.

Wakefield, Priscilla. *Reflections on the Present Condition of the Female Sex.* London: Barton, Harvey, and Darton, 1817.

Warehousemen and Draper's Trade Journal (London) 15 April 1872-13 July 1872.

Warren, Mrs. *How I Managed My House on Two Hundred Pounds a Year.* London: Houlston and Wright, 1866.

Secondary Sources

Abelson, Elaine S. 'The Invention of Kleptomania.' *Signs* 15, no. 1 (1989): 123-43.

————. *When Ladies Go A-Thieving: Middle-Class Shoplifters in the Victorian Department Store.* New York: Oxford University Press, 1989.

Adburgham, Alison. *Shops and Shopping: 1800-1914: Where and in What Manner the Well-Dressed Englishwoman Bought Her Clothes.* London: Barrie and Jenkins, 1964.

Altick, Richard. *The Shows of London.* London: Belknap Press, 1978.

————. *The Presence of the Present: Topics of the Day in the Victorian Novel.* Columbus, Ohio: State University Press, 1991.

Angeloglou, Maggie. *A History of Make-Up.* London: Studio Vista, 1970.

Barker-Benfield, G. J. *The Culture of Sensibility: Sex and Society in Eighteenth-Century Britain.* Chicago: The University of Chicago Press, 1992.

Beattie, J. M. *Crime and the Courts in England, 1660-1800.* Princeton, New Jersey: Princeton University Press, 1986.

Benjamin, Thelma H. *London Shops & Shopping.* London: Herbert Joseph Limited, 1934.

Bennett, Tony. 'The Exhibitionary Complex.' *New Formations*, no. 4 (1988): 73-102.

Berridge, Virginia. 'Popular Journalism and Working Class Attitudes, 1854-1886: A Study of Reynold's Newspaper and Lloyd's Weekly Newspaper.' Ph.D. diss., University of London, 1976.

Bowlby, Rachel. *Just Looking: Consumer Culture in Dreiser, Gissing, and Zola.* New York: Methuen, 1985.

Brewer, John and Roy Porter. *Consumption and the World of Goods.* London: Routledge, 1993.

Briggs, Asa. *A Social History of England.* London: Weidenfeld and Nicolson, 1994.

————. *Friends of the People: The Centenary History of Lewis's.* London: B.T. Batsford, 1956.

————. *Victorian Things.* London: B.T. Batsford, 1988.

Broadley, A. M. *Piccadilly 1686-1906.* London: 1906.

Brunvard, Jan Harold. *The Baby Train and Other Lusty Urban Legends.* New York: W.W. Norton and Company, 1993.

Burn, W. L. *The Age of Equipoise; A Study of the Mid-Victorian Generation.* London: George Allen & Unwin Ltd., 1964.

Camhi, Leslie. 'Stealing Femininity: Department Store Kleptomania As Sexual Disorder.' *Differences* 5, no. 2 (1993): 27-50.

Campbell, Colin. *The Romantic Ethic and the Spirit of Modern Consumerism.* London: Basil Blackwell, 1987.

Carson, Cary Ronald Hoffman and Peter J. Albert, eds. *Of Consuming Interests: The Style of*

Life in the Eighteenth Century. Charlottesville: University Press of Virginia and United States Capitol Historical Society, 1994.

Chancellor, E. Beresford. *The West End Yesterday and Today.* London: The Architectural Press, 1926.

Chesney, Kellow. *The Anti-Society: An Account of the Victorian Underworld.* Boston: Gambit, Inc., 1970.

Conley, Carolyn. *The Unwritten Law: Criminal Justice in Victorian Kent.* New York: Oxford University Press, 1991.

Cox, Nancy. The *Complete Tradesman A Study of Retailing, 1550-1820.* Aldershot: Ashgate, 2000.

Crook, G. T., ed. *The Complete Newgate Calendar.* London: Privately Printed for the Navarre Society Limited, 1926.

Dasent, Arthur. *Piccadilly in Three Centuries.* London: Macmillan and Co., Limited, 1920.

Davidoff, Leonore and Catherine Hall. *Family Fortunes; Men and Women of the English Middle Class, 1780-1850.* Chicago: University of Chicago Press, 1986.

Davis, Dorothy. *A History of Shopping.* London: Routledge & Kegan Paul Ltd., 1966.

De Grazia, Victoria and Ellen Furlough, eds. *The Sex of Things: Gender and Consumption in Historical Perspective.* Berkeley: University of California Press, 1996.

Dijkstra, Bram. *Idols of Perversity: Fanatsies of Feminine Evil in Fin-De-Siècle Culture.* New York: Oxford University Press, 1986.

Donajgrodzki, A. P. *Social Control in Nineteenth Century Britain.* London: Croom Helm, 1977.

Dyer, Gary. 'The 'Vanity Fair' of Nineteenth-Century England: Commerce, Women, and the East in the Ladies' Bazaar.' *Nineteenth-Century Literature* 46, no. 2 (1991): 196-222.

Edwards, Loren E. *Shoplifting and Shrinkage Protection for Stores.* Springfield, Illinois: Charles C. Thomas, 1958.

Eigen, Joel. *Witnessing Insanity: Madness and Mad-Doctors in the English Court.* New Haven: Yale University Press, 1995.

Elliot, Blanche B. *A History of English Advertising.* London: B.T. Batsford Limited, 1962.

Emsley, Clive. *Crime and Society in England, 1750-1900.* New York: Longman, 1996.

Feaver, William. *The Art of John Martin.* Oxford: Clarendon Press, 1975.

Feeley, Malcolm M. and Deborah L. Little. 'The Vanishing Female: The Decline of Women in the Criminal Process, 1687-1912.' *Law & Society Review* 25, no. 4 (1991): 719-57.

Ferry, John William. *A History of the Department Store.* New York: Macmillan, 1960.

Finn, Margot. 'Victorian Women As Consumer Debtors: Theory and Practice.' Paper presented to the North American Conference on British Studies Annual Meeting, Montreal, October 1993.

———. 'Debt and Credit in Bath's Court of Requests, 1829-39.' *Urban History* 21, no. 2 (1994): 211-36.

———. 'Fair Trade and Foul: Swindlers, Shopkeepers, and the Use and Abuse of Credit in the Nineteenth Century.' Paper presented to the North American Conference on British Studies Annual Meeting, Washington, DC, October 1995.

Fox, Celina, ed. *London: World City 1800-1840.* New Haven: Yale University Press, 1992.

Fraser, W. Hamish. *The Coming of the Mass Market, 1850-1914.* Hamden, Connecticut: Archon Books, 1981.

Furlough, Ellen and Carl Stirkwerds, eds. *Consumers Against Capitalism? Consumer Cooperation in Europe, North America, and Japan, 1840-1990.* Lanham, Maryland: Rowman and Littlefield, 1999.

Gatrell, V. A. C. 'Crime, Authority, and the Policeman-State.' *The Cambridge Social History of Britain.* Ed. F. M. L. Thompson. Cambridge: Cambridge University Press, 1990.

————. *The Hanging Tree: Execution and the English People, 1770-1868.* Oxford : Oxford University Press, 1994.

Goldman, Marcus J. 'Kleptomania: Making Sense of the Nonsensical.' *The American Journal of Psychiatry* 148, no. 8 (1991): 986-96.

Henriques, Ursula. *Before the Welfare State.* New York: Longman, 1979.

Hill, Georgiana. *A History of English Dress.* Vol. 2. London: Richard Bentley and Son, 1893.

Hobhouse, Hermione. *A History of Regent Street.* London: Macdonald and Jane's, 1975.

Hosgood, Christopher 'The 'Pygmies of Commerce' and the Working-Class Community: Small Shopkeepers in England, 1870-1914.' *Journal of Social History* 22, no. 3 (1989): 439-50.

————. 'A 'Brave and Daring Folk'? Shopkeepers and Trade Associational Life in Victorian and Edwardian England.' *Journal of Social History* 26, no. 2 (1992): 285-308.

Hunter, Jane H. *How Young Ladies Became Girls: The Victorian Origins of American Girlhood.* New Haven: Yale University Press, 2002.

Inwood, Steve. 'Policing London's Morals: The Metropolitan Police and Popular Culture, 1829-1850.' *London Journal* 15, no. 2 (1990): 129-46.

Jackson, Peter. *George Scharf's London: Sketches and Watercolours of a Changing City, 1820-50.* London: John Murray, 1987.

Jones, David. *Crime, Protest, Community and Police in Nineteenth-Century Britain.* London: Routledge & Kegan, 1982.

Kasson, John F. *Rudeness and Civility: Manners in Nineteenth-Century Urban America.* New York: Hill and Wang, 1990.

Lancaster, William. *The Department Store: A Social History.* London: Leciester University Press, 1995.

Leach, William R. 'Transformations in a Culture of Consumption: Women and Department Stores, 1890-1925.' *The Journal of American History* 71, no. 2 (1984): 319-42.

Lears, T. J. Jackson. *Fables of Abundance: A Cultural History of Advertising in America.* New York: Basic Books, 1994.

Lears, T. J. Jackson and Richard Wrightman Fox, eds. *The Culture of Consumption: Critical Essays in American History.* New York: Pantheon Books, 1983.

Lester, V. Markham. *Victorian Insolvency: Bankruptcy, Imprisonment for Debt, and Company Winding-Up in Nineteenth-Century England.* Oxford: Clarendon Press, 1995.

Loeb, Lori Anne. *Consuming Angels: Advertising and Victorian Women.* New York: Oxford University Press, 1994.

McKendrick, Neil, John Brewer, and J. H. Plumb. *The Birth of a Consumer Society: The Commercialization of Eighteenth-Century England.* Bloomington: Indiana University Press, 1982.

Miller, Michael B. *The Bon Marché: Bourgeois Culture and the Department Store, 1869-1920.* Princeton: Princeton University Press, 1981.

Mui, Hoh-cheung and Lorna H. *Shops and Shopkeeping in Eighteenth Century England.* Montreal: McGill-Queen's University Press, 1989.

Murphy, Daniel J. I. *Customers and Thieves: an Ethnography of Shoplifting.* Brookfield, Vermont: Gower, 1986.

Naman, Anne Aresty. *The Jew in the Victorian Novel: Some Relationships Between Prejudice and Art.* New York: AMS Press, 1980.

O'Brien, Patricia. 'The Kleptomania Diagnosis: Bourgeois Women and Theft in Late

Nineteenth-Century France.' *Journal of Social History* 17 (1983): 65-67.

Offen, Karen Erna Olafson Hellerstein and Leslie Parker Hume, eds. *Victorian Women: A Documentary Account of Women's Lives in the Nineteenth Century England, France, and the United States.* Stanford: Stanford University Press, 1981.

Ogus, Anthony. *Regulation: Legal Form and Economic Theory.* Oxford: Clarendon Press, 1994.

Owen, Alex. *The Darkened Room: Women, Power and Spiritualism in Late Victorian England.* Philadelphia: University of Pennsylvania Press, 1990.

Owen, W. J. B. 'De Quincey and Shoplifting.' *The Wordsworth Circle* 21, no. 2 (1990): 72-76.

Peck, Linda Levy. 'Luxury and War: Reconsidering Luxury Consumption in Seventeenth-Century England' [Presidential Address: The North American Conference on British Studies]. *Albion* 34,1 (Spring 2002): 1-23.

Perrot, Philippe. *Fashioning the Bourgeoisie: A History of Clothing in the Nineteenth Century.* Princeton: Princeton University Press, 1994.

Philips, David. 'Good Men to Associate and Bad Men to Conspire: Associations for the Prosecution of Felons in England.' *Policing and Prosecution in Britain 1750-1850.* Ed. Douglas Hay and Francis Snyders, 113-69. Oxford: Clarendon Press, 1989.

Poovey, Mary. *Uneven Developments: The Ideological Work of Gender in Mid-Victorian England.* Chicago: University of Chicago Press, 1988.

Porter, Roy. *London: A Social History.* London: Hamish Hamilton, 1994.

Prochaska, Frank. *Philanthropy and the Hospitals of London; The King's Fund, 1897-1990.* Oxford: Clarendon Press, 1992.

Rappaport, Erika D. "The Halls of Temptation': Gender, Politics, and the Construction of the Department Store in Late Victorian London.' *Journal of British Studies* 35, no. 1 (1996): 58-83.

_____. *Shopping For Pleasure: Women in the Making of London's West End.* Princeton, New Jersey: Princeton University Press, 2001.

Richards, Thomas. *The Commodity Culture of Victorian England: Advertising and Spectacle, 1851-1914.* Stanford: Stanford University Press, 1990.

Robb, George. *White-Collar Crime in Modern England; Financial Fraud and Business Morality, 1845-1929.* Cambridge: Cambridge University Press, 1992.

Roughead, William. 'The Siren and the Sorceress; or, Beautiful Forever.' *Rascals Revived.* London: Cassell and Company Ltd., 1940.

Sachs, Albie and Joan Hoff Wilson. *Sexism and the Law; A Study of Male Beliefs and Legal Bias in Britain and the United States.* New York: The Free Press, 1979.

Schor, Hilary M. 'Urban Things: The Mystery of the Commodity in Victorian Literature.' *Interdisciplinary Nineteenth-Century Studies Conference* University of California, Santa Cruz: 1995.

Shanley, Mary Lyndon. *Feminism, Marriage, and the Law in Victorian England.* Princeton: Princeton University, 1989.

Shaw, Donald. *London in the Sixties.* London: Everett & Co., 1908.

Showalter, Elaine. 'Victorian Women and Insanity.' *Victorian Studies* 23, no. 2 (1980): 157-81.

Smith, Roger. *Trial By Medicine: Insanity and Responsibility in Victorian Trials.* Edinburgh, Scotland: Edinburgh University Press, 1981.

Smith-Rosenberg, Caroll. 'The Hysterical Woman: Sex Roles and Role Conflict in Nineteenth-Century America.' *Disorderly Conduct: Visions of Gender in Victorian America.* New York: Oxford University Press, 1985.

Stern, Rebecca F. 'Historicizing Performativity: Constructing Identities in Victorian England.' Ph.D. diss., Rice University, 1996.

———. 'Beds, Bodices and Gravy': Female Servants, Private Property, and Perquisite Economies in Victorian Narratives of Crime. Paper presented to the Southern Conference on British Studies, Memphis, Tennessee, 5 Nov. 2004.

Tebutt, Melanie. *Making Ends Meet: Pawnbroking and Working-Class Credit.* London: Methuen, 1984.

Tiersten, Lisa. 'In the Public Eye: Women Shoppers and Urban Space in Late 19th-Century Paris.' Paper presented to the Interdisciplinary Nineteenth-Century Studies Conference on The Nineteenth-Century City: Global Contexts, Local Productions, Santa Cruz, California, 1995.

Tonkovich, Nicole. 'Foreign Markets in Domestic Locations: Frances Trollops's Cincinnati Bazaar, 1828-1830 .' Paper presented to the Interdisciplinary Nineteenth-Century Studies Conference, Yale Center for British Art, 1996.

Turner, E. S. *The Shocking History of Advertising!* London: Michael Joseph, 1953.

Vicinus, Martha, ed. *Suffer and Be Still: Women in the Victorian Age.* Bloomington: Indiana University Press, 1973.

Walkowitz, Judith R. *City of Dreadful Delight; Narratives of Sexual Danger in Late-Victorian London.* Chicago: University of Chicago Press, 1992.

Walvin, James. *Victorian Values.* Athens, Georgia: University of Georgia Press, 1988.

Whigham, Frank. *Ambition and Privilege: The Social Tropes of Elizabethan Courtesy Theory.* Los Angeles: University of California Press, 1984.

Wicke, Jennifer. *Advertising Fictions.* New York: Columbia University Press, 1988.

Wiener, Martin J. *English Culture and the Decline of the Industrial Spirit, 1850-1908.* New York: Cambridge University Press, 1981.

———. *Reconstructing the Criminal: Culture, Law, and Policy in England 1830-1914.* New York: Cambridge University Press, 1990.

Williams, Amy. 'Illegitimate Male and Female Trading in Eighteenth Century: a Case Study of Devon and Somerset 1735-1785. Paper presented to the Second Exeter International Gender History Conference: Women, Trade & Business, University of Exeter, 1996.

Williams, Rosalind H. *Dream Worlds: Mass Consumption in Late Nineteenth-Century France.* Berkeley: University of California Press, 1982.

Zedner, Lucia. *Women, Crime, and Custody in Victorian England.* Oxford: Clarendon Press, 1991.

Index